P9-ASH-925

FOURTH EDITION

TELEVISION FIELD PRODUCTION AND REPORTING

FRED SHOOK

Colorado State University, Fort Collins

PEARSON

Boston ■ New York ■ San Francisco
Mexico City ■ Montreal ■ Toronto ■ London ■ Madrid ■ Munich ■ Paris
Hong Kong ■ Singapore ■ Tokyo ■ Cape Town ■ Sydney

Series Editor: *Molly Taylor*
Series Editorial Assistant: *Michael Kish*
Marketing Manager: *Mandee Eckersley*
Production Administrator: *Michael Granger*
Editorial-Production Service: *Omegatype Typography, Inc.*
Composition and Prepress Buyer: *Linda Cox*
Manufacturing Buyer: *JoAnne Sweeney*
Cover Administrator: *Joel Gendron*
Electronic Composition: *Omegatype Typography, Inc.*

For related titles and support materials, visit our online catalog at www.ablongman.com.

Copyright © 2005, 2000 Pearson Education, Inc.

All rights reserved. No part of the material protected by this copyright notice may be reproduced or utilized in any form or by any means, electronic or mechanical, including photocopying, recording, or by any information storage and retrieval system, without written permission from the copyright owner.

To obtain permission(s) to use material from this work, please submit a written request to Allyn and Bacon, Permissions Department, 75 Arlington Street, Boston, MA 02116 or fax your request to 617-848-7320.

Between the time Website information is gathered and then published, it is not unusual for some sites to have closed. Also, the transcription of URLs can result in typographical errors. The publisher would appreciate notification where these errors occur so that they may be corrected in subsequent editions.

Library of Congress Cataloging-in-Publication Data

Shook, Frederick.
 Television field production and reporting / Frederick Shook. — 4th ed.
  p. cm.
 ISBN 0-205-41846-5
  1. Television broadcasting of news. 2. Television—Production and direction. I. Title.
 PN4784.T4S53 2005
 070.4'3—dc22

2004044492

Printed in the United States of America

10 9 8 7 6 5 4 3 2   09 08 07 06 05

Credits appear on page 376, which constitutes an extension of the copyright page.

*The National Press Photographers Association recommends
this book for both beginning students in the field of news photography
and for advanced educational training. Professionals who have been in
the business for years will find the pages to be a wonderful refresher course
and the thoughtful reader will see that this book not only teaches, but
makes us think . . . no matter what our level of expertise.*

—NPPA

CONTENTS

CHAPTER TWO

The Visual Grammar of Motion Picture Photography   27

CHAPTER THREE

Video Editing: The Invisible Art   55

CHAPTER FOUR
Field Techniques of Shooting Television News   76

CHAPTER FIVE

The Magic of Light and Lighting   98

CHAPTER SIX
The Sound Track   122

CHAPTER SEVEN

The Broadcast Interview: Shooting
the Quotation Marks 150

CHAPTER EIGHT

Television Script Formats   167
by Luan Akin

CHAPTER NINE
Writing the Package   178

CHAPTER TEN
How to Improve Your Storytelling Ability   191

CHAPTER ELEVEN
The Role of Talent Performance in Field Reporting   209

CHAPTER TWELVE

Live Shots and Remotes   231
by Luan Akin

CHAPTER THIRTEEN

The Assignment Editor and Producer: Architects of the Newscast   253

CHAPTER FOURTEEN
Sports Photography and Reporting   274
by Bob Burke and Marcia Neville

CHAPTER FIFTEEN
Law and the Broadcast Journalist   292

CHAPTER SIXTEEN

Journalistic Ethics   314

PREFACE

For all its supposed similarity, television news remains an entity distinct from other, more traditional forms of journalism, sometimes as vaguely understood as on the day it was created.

In part, this is because television news is a journalistic anachronism. Today, as always, the profession remains a journalistic hybrid of filmmaking, journalism, theater, and radio—all rolled into one. It communicates at its best when it involves the emotions. It routinely communicates nonverbally. It uses color, sound, and motion to create meaning. It borrows from music, art, literature, and most of the other fine arts. Surely, the critics have maintained, this cannot be what journalism is about. And the critics would be right, were it not for other journalists who have discovered the distinction of television news by employing those hybrid qualities of television to great effect.

What these journalists have proven beyond further debate is that television news is unsurpassed in its ability to capture a moment, complete with a sense of time and place, and transmit that experience to viewers. Television news thus also excels at showing people to people. As not only eyewitnesses, but as participants in absentia, television viewers are granted an unprecedented ability to gain insights into the larger meaning of news events and the issues they address. Although not every news story reaches such lofty heights, the potential exists.

The reporters and photojournalists who realize this potential employ reporting concepts that are demonstrably more suitable for television than are the techniques of print reporting in which stories are built primarily around words. Among their peers these journalists have come to be called *visual storytellers*, a term that describes journalists who link words, pictures, and sounds to create news reports that communicate a sense of experience to their audience.

From the small markets to the networks, these individuals have demonstrated that visual storytellers are to television news what narrative essayists are to print journalism. Their work creates a reference for a larger fraternity of television journalists whose calling is to help define who we are as a society, where we have been, and where we are headed, and who seek to accomplish this mission in ways that will attract and hold news audiences. This book is an effort to share their message, and to examine all the known reporting tools that visual storytellers will employ in the new millenium.

For that reason, this fourth edition of *Television Field Production and Reporting* features extensive updates, virtually all new photographs, and two new chapters: Chapter 13, "The Assignment Editor and Producer," and Chapter 14, "Sports Photography and Reporting."

ACKNOWLEDGMENTS

As in all such acknowledgments, a complete roster of contributors is impossible, but the following individuals and institutions deserve recognition for their contributions to this undertaking:

The National Press Photographers Association (NPPA) for its sponsorship of the annual Television News-Video Workshop at the University of Oklahoma. This workshop is internationally recognized for its achievements in illuminating the art of effective visual storytelling through use of television, its arts, and its peripheral crafts. From the distinguished faculty who give this workshop its direction have originated many of the concepts that appear in this book.

No individual has influenced this book more profoundly than NBC News senior correspondent Bob Dotson, a close friend whose reporting has long been a hallmark on the *Today* show and the *NBC Nightly News*. Throughout his career Bob Dotson has told his stories through people whose accomplishments and memories reflect a living history of the land. His reports mirror our lives and our heritage and help us better understand ourselves through the stories of "ordinary" people engaged in extraordinary pursuits. Chapter 1 of this book, "Telling the Visual Story," reflects a close study of Dotson's work and reporting philosophies and is a product of interviews and correspondence conducted with him for more than a decade.

Grateful recognition also is extended to Ernie Leyba, the Denver photojournalist whose pictures illustrate this book; to KUSA-TV: Roger Ogden, president and general manager; Patti Dennis, news director, who provided access to staff and facilities for many of the photographs that illustrate this book; Eric Kehe, director of photography, and photojournalist Manny Sotello; to KCNC-TV: news director Angie Kucharski, chief photographer Bob Burke, sports reporter Marcia Neville, and helicopter reporter Luan Akin; and to all KUSA and KCNC staff and private citizens who appear in photographs throughout the book.

Other important contributors include the reviewers: Dale Cressman, Brigham Young University; Richard Lenoce, Middlesex Community College; and Carey Martin, Barry University.

To these individuals and to those whose contributions are recognized elsewhere in this book, the author extends most grateful appreciation.

ABOUT THE AUTHOR

Fred Shook's professional experience encompasses television reporting, production, writing, photojournalism, and video editing. He has taught and worked nationally and internationally as a television producer, consultant, writer, director, and editor for commercial television, corporations, and government agencies. Shook is a member of the faculty of the annual National Press Photographer's Association Advanced Team Storytelling Workshop. He has written *Television News Writing: Captivating an Audience*, *Television Field Production and Reporting*, *The Process of Electronic News Gathering*, and is coauthor of the *Broadcast News Process* and the forthcoming *Newswriting for Television and Interactive New Media* by Allyn & Bacon.

INTRODUCTION

Books need writers who understand the magic of words. Television—and television news—need writers who understand the much larger magic of words, images, and sound that work to stir the soul and the imagination in ways words alone seldom match.

Writing for television is an encompassing and evolving discipline, in which sets of instructions are written for translation into visual images and a sound track that can communicate complex, often abstract, ideas to viewers.

Although this is a book about television news reporting, photography, and editing, it is essentially a book about exploring the additional pleasures that are available to us as writers. Much of this writing is nonverbal, because scenes have meaning and are infused with new meanings when placed in relationship to other shots. Most of all, it is a book about visual storytelling, using television's full complement of storytelling instruments: the camera, microphone, video editing console, and computer terminal.

TELEVISION IS A LANGUAGE

Television is a language apart from the words that help guide its content. Television uses words, but its primary content lies in the visual images that unfold on one of the most powerful communication tools ever devised: the television screen. Since its infancy, television has distinguished itself as a medium that works best when it communicates visually. In a word-oriented society television has its detractors, chiefly those who fail to understand the television screen's ability to impart ideas and to make those ideas stick in people's minds.

The detractor's observations have become cliches: "If you printed the average script for a television news show, you couldn't fill half the front page of the *New York Times*," or "In television, all your time is spent setting the stage to look at pictures, not getting to content," or "If you eliminated the visual side of the average thirty-minute television newscast, you'd have about the same content as the average five-minute radio newscast delivers." Such comments imply that visual imagery is somehow an invalid form of communication.

Words are essential guides, but they are not the medium's essence. Today those who use the medium to best advantage know that in television, words serve only as guides for the pictures and sound that make up television's content. Television scripts are blueprints for what will be on the screen and come through the speaker. Just as

1

blueprints are distinctly different from the buildings whose construction they guide, so is television news different from the words that serve as its blueprints.

Much of the confusion about the nature of television communication lies in the medium's complexity. Television can record and communicate sound, just as radio does. Television can also display the printed word on the screen, just as newspapers do. It can broadcast still photographs, the stock market index, and editorial cartoons. But none of these things is what television does best. What television can do that no other medium except motion pictures can accomplish is to communicate with pictures that move. Television's primary strength is the television screen, and through that screen its ability to help viewers vicariously experience—and hence understand—current and historical events.

The entry-level television reporter whose background is in print journalism will naturally fall back on the ways of a more familiar medium, using words as the primary communication tool. The radio journalist who enters television can be counted on to use words and sound. The television journalist who doesn't understand how the medium works to best advantage will be inherently tempted to write a script and read the words into a microphone. Even the pictures this journalist chooses to communicate the story may be of him- or herself standing in front of a camera and reading the script. At best, the pictures will be treated as visual chewing gum or what some journalists call "eyewash" or "wallpaper video"—something for the folks at home to watch while they listen to all those words. The greatest tragedy of all occurs when the habits of these print, radio, and aspiring television journalists persist long enough to become entrenched "as the way it's done in television." In a word-oriented society, we are somehow compelled to verbalize our experiences—even those experiences to which we are eyewitnesses. The noted photographer Minor White once complained,

> People in our culture talk photographs rather than experience them visually. Whatever is being looked at, photographs or anything else, the input is visual while the tagging is verbal. So for most of us words, words, words, overwhelm and warp any significance appropriate and becoming to visual perception. Some students even claim, that unless they name it—until they name it—the thing seen has no meaning!

What, then, are the components of the language that is television? The first of these components is the visual image. Without the image, television would be radio. Implicit in the notion of visual imagery as it relates to television are the interrelationships of motion and time, and their allied moods. Television is much like music. Its meaning is established when it plays out through time according to predetermined rhythms and moods. Television is not meant to survive as a still photograph, or even as a series of unrelated scenes in which message, context, and meaning speak for themselves. Just as a single note in music has virtually no meaning, so a single television scene is virtually mute. Only when the scene is placed next to others, and the complete work is absorbed, does it assume larger meaning.

A second component of television language is sound, which in its own way can be as eloquent as visual imagery. A shot of tall buildings accompanied by the sound track of a Central Park carriage tells us we are in New York City. Words are unnecessary to set either the mood or the location. Add romantic music and the mood is established even more precisely—again, without words. Add sounds of an angry crowd and the effect is equally as dramatic. Sounds—from the bustle of Christmas shoppers to the eerie silence of the bombed-gutted streets in Belfast—are part of the language of television.

A third component of television language is the videotape editing process. In print, the writer structures ideas and gives them their relationship to one another. In television, the same job falls to the videotape editor. Almost a century ago the Russian filmmaker Pudovkin defined motion picture editing as the "compulsory and deliberate guidance of the thoughts and associations of the spectator." Although Pudovkin described film editing, he might have applied the same definition to almost any creative endeavor. Most certainly, he could have used it to describe the job of the television storyteller.

Writing, the fourth component of the language of television, is itself a deliberate attempt to guide an audience's thoughts and associations. The goal is to create and to reveal an atmosphere of understanding. Words are essential to describe what the camera missed, or is unable to communicate. Words clarify, emphasize, provide tone and mood, but even with these great abilities words alone are powerless to create television news that communicates with strength and impact. Only when all the writing instruments of television are incorporated by the television storyteller—the visual essayist—can the medium realize its potential.

The time has arrived for television news people to define their reporting responsibilities as much greater than those embodied in the traditional definitions of reporter, or photographer, or producer, or videotape editor. In television news, everyone is a writer. The reporter does not simply gather facts and write words at a keyboard, nor does the photographer merely take pictures, or the editor simply join scenes. In television news, the roles of the reporter, photographer, and editor are equally important. Theirs is a partnership of storytelling skills and talents which contribute equally in reaching out to touch television viewers.

Only when the reporter, photographer, and editor understand the interrelationship of their respective skills, and only when they work to understand each other and to think like one another, can the great potential of television news be realized. If this book can serve in some way to help stimulate such understanding, it will have accomplished its purpose.

Although this book speaks frequently to the requirements of field production and reporting for television news, it will also serve as a valuable reference for corporate videographers and producers alike. Virtually all the principles contained in the book are universally applicable to the process of visual storytelling and communication, irrespective of discipline.

CHAPTER ONE

TELLING THE VISUAL STORY

Today, news stories can be more compelling and more meaningful to their audiences than at any time in journalism's history. Two reporting instruments, the television camera and the microphone, make this possible. Journalists can use the microphone to capture the sounds of news events and of people in the news. Most important, television journalists can use the camera to show people as they enact their own stories. The camera and microphone can put viewers at the scene of news events and help viewers feel as if they have experienced something of those events (Figure 1.1). Visual storytelling is thus among the most experiential forms of news communication, and in experienced hands it can be one of the most compelling forms of the storytelling art.

FIGURE 1.1 Photography that captures tactile impressions of the news environment can help heighten the viewer's sense of vicarious experience.

VISUAL STORIES BEGIN WITH A CLEAR FOCUS

Visual stories take form the same way any other story originates, with a summary statement that identifies the story to be told. This summary statement of the story is sometimes called the **focus** or focus statement. Some stations use the term *story commitment*. Regardless of the word, the process is as simple as summing up the story in your mind before you start to shoot. Defining the story focus forces the television journalist to not just identify the story, but to identify what is most important and interesting about that story. It embodies the centuries-old concepts of theme, story line, premise, and the reporter's point of view.

The focus is a simple, vivid, declarative sentence expressing the heart, the soul, of the story as it will be on air.[1] Until you know the story yourself, it will be difficult to tell it to anyone else. "If you can't express your idea for a story on a 3 × 5 card, in one sentence, you don't understand the story," says television journalist Shellie Karabell.[2]

Sometimes reporters and photojournalists say, "My focus—or commitment—is to show the demonstration . . ." or whatever story they happen to be covering, but defining the story's focus goes beyond merely showing the subject. The story itself remains unidentified until it can be stated as a complete sentence: "The economics of farming affect all Americans." Focus statements help define the essence of the story. Until you know what the story is, you can't tell it to anyone else. Simple as the idea sounds, it is often overlooked.

THE VISUAL STORYTELLER DEFINED

A telling distinction separates photographers and **photojournalists.** "Anyone with a camera is a photographer," says Larry Hatteberg, a KAKE-TV journalist, who has been telling award-winning stories with his camera for most of his career. "My mother is a photographer; my grandmother is a photographer," says Hatteberg, "but no one is a photojournalist until they learn how to tell the visual story."[3] Hatteberg's definition of the photojournalist extends to all members of the television reporting team. "In television news the story is a group effort," says Hatteberg, "and everyone's contribution is coequal."[4] Still, some television photographers have never tried to tell a visual story, and not all television reporters have learned to think of themselves as visual storytellers, even though their final product is the news report built around—and on—images.

To achieve excellence in visual storytelling, reporters must sublimate their presence in stories told narratively. "Telling" the audience is lecturing. "Showing" the audience is teaching. "Letting the audience experience the moment" is visual storytelling. Wise reporters know they are never the story or even the "star" of the story. They work instead to step back and produce other people's reality. They work to sell the people in their story and then let the people themselves sell the story.

At first, this approach may feel foreign, even awkward, to reporters whose job is, after all, to report the news. Reporters know better than anyone that their name is on the final result of their labors. When a story shines, they receive a great deal of the credit. If it fails, they receive almost all the blame. Reporters may also associate their number of on-camera appearances with fame and fortune, and at personality-driven shops this may be true, although rare. The number of times a reporter appears on camera will never matter if viewers don't remember the story or understand why the story is important.

"If people remember your stories, they'll more likely remember your name," says NBC News senior correspondent Bob Dotson.[5] And therein lies the reality that modern television journalists must confront if they are to excel—and survive—in their profession (Figure 1.2 shows a photojournalist at work).

WRITE THE PICTURES FIRST

The strongest television news stories result when reporters remember to *write the pictures first*. This advice requires that reporters think first about the left side of the script (the video instructions) before they think about the words that will be in the report. In the field, look first for pictures that will tell your story. Search for sounds (and sound bites) that will add impact, emotion, and meaning to your reporting. Use words to interpret and explain what the pictures can't say (see Figure 1.3).

FIGURE 1.2   The photojournalist is a visual storyteller, separate and distinct from photographers who think of their job as merely to take pictures.

FIGURE 1.3   In television news, words serve as
blueprints to help guide the pictures and sounds that
make up television's content.

Often reporters don't even use the pictures they bring home to really show viewers what happened. They use the pictures to illustrate their scripts, which are first written, then later "wallpapered" with available video. Slide shows, not compelling video,
are the result.

SHOOT SEQUENCES

The human eye fragments the world in front of it by taking in thousands of glimpses—
in close-up, medium shot, and long shot—of first this thing and then that thing. Further impressions of reality are gained from sounds taken in through the ear. The mind
makes constant choices from the sights and sounds that are available, then uses some of
those fragments to reconstruct, within the mind's eye, an understanding of the larger
world. In effect, we are film directors: We construct mini-movies in our mind's eye.
The process is similar to reporting the news story: As journalists we understand (and
visually manage) the larger world by first fragmenting it into its component parts, then
reconstructing it from the fragments.

In television news, the same processes must be followed when shooting and
editing video if viewers are to have a sense of experience from news reports. Sequential pictures with action that matches from one shot to another replicate how viewers would break down the action if they were at the scene. In real life we routinely

and unconsciously construct **sequences:** As we walk up to a telephone booth, we notice the directory is missing. We dig in our pocket or purse for a handful of change, counting the number of quarters we produce. We look at the push buttons as we dial our friend's telephone number. We turn, lean against the wall of the phone booth, and watch people walk by. We notice their faces, their shoes, how they walk, and what they carry. We watch buses and cars as they go past. We notice license plates, the drivers, styles of vehicles, even the soot coming from exhausts. If we were to isolate each of these separate views our eyes took in, we would have a sequence made up of **long shots (LS), medium shots (MS),** and **close-ups (CU):**

> View of telephone booth (LS)
> Look around for directory (MS)
> Look at handful of change (MS or CU)
> Push buttons (CU)
> Watch people (LS, MS, and possibly CU)
> Buses and cars drive past (LS, MS, and possibly CU)

If we photographed these same shots with a camera, instead of with our eyes, we would have produced a sequence that could be edited together for the screen, much as we experienced it with our own eyes. Sequences consequently help to create a heightened sense of realism.

Because sequential video is difficult to achieve when pictures are forced to fit a prewritten script, it becomes imperative that reporters learn to think in sequences and commit themselves to "write the pictures first." And although television cannot yet transmit the smells and tactile impressions of the physical world, good writing can at least allude to those qualities from the news environment and further heighten the viewer's sense of vicarious experience.

PROVE THE STORY'S FOCUS VISUALLY

Once the story has been assigned and researched and the story's focus identified, the reporter and photographer can proceed to prove the focus visually. Perhaps your assignment is to report about a new school district policy that requires teachers who suspect child abuse to notify police within twenty-four hours.

If you state your focus as "School officials have adopted a get-tough policy toward child abusers," you have charted a very specific course in the way you'll cover this story. If your focus is "Abused children have a new friend in the public schools," then the story may concentrate more on the teacher's role in helping protect children and veer away from officials who talk tough about putting child abusers where they belong.

If your subject is a routine warehouse fire, you may identify the focus by the statement "This is a big fire." Your visual proof will then follow naturally. If your focus is "Firefighting is long days of boredom, followed by moments of sheer terror," then your visual proof will change accordingly. If, in the same story, your focus had been "This fire offered a study of the firefighter's ability to endure searing heat and freezing cold," your visual emphasis would have been still different.

Imagine the pictures and main points that would result if your story focus involved the high sugar content, and potential health dangers, of your community's top-selling soft drink. Now imagine how the pictures and main points of your story would change if your story focus were to address that soft drink's emerging popularity as a status symbol in developing countries. Clearly, your focus statement drives not only the story you tell, but the pictures you bring back from the field.

THE FOCUS MAY CHANGE

Sometimes, through prior research, you can adequately identify the story's essence and state its focus before you enter the field. At other times the real story can't be nailed down until after you arrive at the scene. You may discover, contrary to the assignment editor's best educated conjecture, "This is not a big fire." Or you may determine "Tighter security could have prevented this fire," or you may watch even the most valid focus change before your eyes as the story develops (a firefighter becomes trapped inside the warehouse and rescue efforts fail).

The essential responsibility is to be ready to change your focus if the story changes or was improperly identified at the start. Any story suffers when a reporter or photojournalist tries to impose a preconceived focus on it, and the damage will be instantly apparent to the audience. Just as obviously, any story suffers when a focus is absent.

LOOK FOR A STORY FOCUS
IN SPOT-NEWS EVENTS

There is a story in every event you cover, even when you are under a tight deadline and the story is not under your control. Assume that you have just received word of a fire in the central downtown area. You jump in the van and within minutes arrive at the scene. At this point, you may not know what's going on, whether anyone is hurt, or even what caused the fire. You spend lots of time shooting the smoke going up, the walls falling down, and perhaps you capture a moment or two of drama as fire victims are rescued. But you commit an unpardonable professional error if you return home without having asked yourself, regardless of whether you are the photographer or the reporter, "What is the story?"

IDENTIFYING THE LARGER SPOT-NEWS STORY

Whenever you cover **spot news,** the first rule is to shoot what presents itself, what must be shot before it's lost forever, and what must be shot to protect your job, then to step back and ask yourself, "What's the real story here?" You may want to ask that question of the fire officials or the tenants or the business owner or whoever is available. Once you've identified the larger story, you can begin to shoot again. This time, perhaps phase two of the story becomes your main focus. This attitude assumes that the photographer considers himself or herself to be a member of the reporting team. It also assumes that the reporter has learned to think as a photojournalist.

TELL YOUR STORY THROUGH PEOPLE

Try to tell your stories through strong central characters engaged in compelling action that is visual or picturesque. So often, reporters try to tell the story themselves, using authority figures—the mayor, the fire chief, the sociology professor—to explain what ordinary people enact every day in far more compelling ways. The sociologist can tell you that suburban neighbors live in isolation, relatively anonymous to one another, but so can one of the neighbors. Simply ask her if she knows her next-door neighbor's name. When she scrunches up her shoulders, hesitates, then says sheepishly, "I don't," her information is just as valid and far more visually interesting and memorable. Why do we need the mayor to tell us the earthquake scene is a frightening mess when residents of the area can take us into their homes and describe the damage themselves? Sometimes you will need authority figures in your stories, but strive to include everyday people as well. Such people can help sell your story, so your job is to "sell" them by bringing them to life on your viewers' screens.

Storytellers are far less compelling when they tell audiences the story after it takes place, rather than couch it as a story unfolding in the present moment.[6] Strong central characters let viewers live someone else's life for a moment, and experience the story as it unfolds. Viewers become more powerfully engaged and may feel as if they're living in the story environment itself.

STRONG NATURAL SOUND
HELPS TELL THE STORY

Night after night television viewers sit and watch a half hour of news, then can't remember what they saw because they have been told what happened—not allowed to experience something of the event themselves. "The television reporter's contract with the audience lasts for about fifteen to twenty seconds," says Bill Taylor, CEO of Nu-Future.TV. "Every fifteen or twenty seconds, the reporter must renew that contract, or risk losing the audience."[7] The use of strong natural sound gives the reporter a way to renew the contract: Nothing beats it to help heighten a story's sense of realism. The sharp, crisp sounds of news events give us a sense of being there and of having experienced the moment (Figure 1.4).

FIGURE 1.4   In television news, sound is a primary form of communication. The microphone is thus a form of "writing" instrument that can be used to heighten the story's sense of realism.

BUILD IN SURPRISES

When you report, try to build surprises into your stories to help sustain viewer involvement. A surprise is any device that helps viewers feel something about the story, helps lure uninterested viewers to the screen, or connects them more directly with the story's subject or main character. John DeTarsio, National Photographer of the Year, San Diego, launches a fire rescue story with natural sound of the rescuer's words, "Gimme air! I need air!" John Goheen, three times named National Photographer of the Year, Denver, lets audiences peer into the bottom of a small bucket as the rancher holding the bucket says, "I call this my rain gauge. I reckon it rained an inch and a quarter or so." Inevitably, audiences chuckle to themselves as they are permitted a peek into the rain gauge. Surprises can be compelling visuals, unusual or unexpected sound, short sound bites, or poetic script, such as Bruce Morton wrote for a piece on atomic radiation: "Once upon a time on a Pacific Island, the sun exploded."[8] Always, surprises are little moments of drama, regardless of their form, that help renew the contract with viewers and lure them back to the screen.

KEEP SOUND BITES SHORT

Short bites can be used effectively to help prove the story you are showing. They are less effective when they are used as substitutes for your own reporting. An effective approach is to think of the sound bite as an exclamation point, both to help enhance the visuals and to punctuate story content. Especially in television, sound bites work best when they're kept short (five to fifteen seconds) and when they are not used as an essential part of the main story. Sound bites should enhance the story, but they should never take over to the point where their absence would destroy the story.

ADDRESS THE LARGER ISSUE

Most people will watch a story that tells them "Vacations are fun," but they may wonder subconsciously, "So what?" if that's all you tell them. Few viewers will forget your story if you address the larger issue: "The typical family vacation creates more stress than it relieves." Even routine traffic accident stories can address larger issues if you look beyond the event and search instead for the meaning of the event. An easy way to check whether you have addressed the larger issue is to ask the "So what?" question: Immediately after you have stated the story's focus to yourself, challenge the commitment with the question "So what?" If you believe the audience also will say "So what?" when your story airs, look for a new focus before you begin to report. Often, it's as simple as challenging your original focus statement by asking, "What's most interesting or important about that?" Some reporters always try to "focus their focus," sometimes asking the magic question, "What's most interesting or important about that?" repeatedly until their focus gels and they're confident they have the strongest story line possible.

MAKE THE REPORT MEMORABLE

The strongest stories are memorable. Viewers relate best to stories that touch their emotions, so it's important to tell a story in such a way that your audience will be able to feel something about the story and its subjects. If feeling is present, the story has a better chance to connect with the audience.

NEWS PACKAGES ARE FACTUAL "MINI-MOVIES"

Television news stories can be thought of as miniature movies with a beginning, middle, and ending. Just as any other visual story, they tell the viewer where the story is headed, deliver the main points and prove them visually, and build to a strong visual close. In some ways they are similar to television commercials, which have a beginning (to establish a problem or a need), a middle (to introduce the product and show it in use), and an ending (to resolve the problem). Typically, the thirty-second television commercial delivers its messages with strong, often unforgettable, visual proof. Effective commercials further integrate strong sound, memorable writing, and creative editing to enhance the message. The same principles are true of the best television and Hollywood films—and of the strongest television news stories.

THE LEAD

The beginning of any **package** is the lead, and like all story leads it should instantly telegraph the story to come. Ideally, the lead is visual. If the story subject is a stranded rock climber, the package will better serve viewers if it begins with a shot of the stranded climber, not of bikers pedaling down a nearby highway. If the subject is the hardships of poverty, there probably is a more meaningful visual than an establishing shot of the county courthouse in which the welfare office is housed.

PROVIDE VISUAL PROOF FOR ALL MAIN POINTS

Throughout the package, one of the television journalist's greatest obligations is to tell the visual story and to prove its main points visually. The main body of the story, the middle, cannot be constructed until the journalist has identified the story's main points.

"So often journalists find themselves with a notebook full of facts and a half hour of interviews, and they still may not have the story firmly in mind," says NBC News senior correspondent Bob Dotson. "The trick is to realize that all those facts are your research, not your story. Then you can sit down and ask yourself, 'All right, what are the three or four main points I've learned today about this story?' Once you've identified those main points, you can then find ways to prove them visually."[9]

Perhaps a main point in your report about child abuse is that some 300 elementary students are abused each year in your community. Through voice-over narration you can tell your audience that figure, but the audience may soon forget what you said. No member of the audience can so easily walk away from that number if you communicate it visually.

A simple standup can accomplish the objective: A reporter in an empty school gymnasium points out the rows of bleachers those abused children would fill each year, then cuts to an extreme long shot to show that about every five years enough children are abused in just this one community to fill the entire gymnasium.

With sufficient thought and hard work, almost any main point in any story can be proven visually. The alternative, which will never amount to good television, is to write and narrate the main points verbally and illustrate them with generic video.

Even abstractions like inflation can be brought to life through pictures, in ways that will stick in the viewer's mind. Say you've been given a half hour to shoot a story on inflation and have been told to determine the story's treatment. "The typical approach is to crank up the graphics machine and make some charts with arrows that point up or down," says NBC senior correspondent Bob Dotson. "But if you can think through a way to report the story with visuals your report will have far greater meaning for your audience."[10]

On assignment to show inflation's effects, Dotson entered a Fort Worth meat market and with the camera running gave the butcher a ten-dollar bill and asked how much stew meat that ten dollars would have purchased a decade earlier. The butcher displayed a hefty chunk of beef. "Now," Dotson asked, "show me how much beef that same ten dollars would buy five years ago." The butcher grabbed his cleaver and chopped the once generous purchase approximately in half. "Now show me how much sirloin I could buy today with the same ten dollars," Dotson prompted.[11] The butcher again apportioned the meat in half and handed Dotson the remaining tidbit. Reporters who saw the story remembered it several years later during interviews with the author.

As another example, perhaps a main point in a story is that new restaurant openings suggest that eating out is becoming a more popular pastime. Perhaps a main point in yet another story is that trucks that exceed state load limits are damaging interstate highways in your region. In either case your creativity and imagination can provide an effective way to prove those main points visually. In the first instance you might simply show the number of new entries in the telephone company's restaurant listings. In your story about road damage, your visual proof must be equally graphic. An interview with an expert who only tells you what happens to roads when trucks exceed their legal carrying capacity won't effectively prove your main point. Neither will voice-over narration, illustrated with trucks traveling down the interstate. What may work to make the message memorable is something like a close-up of hot pavement in the summertime, bending and stretching in slow motion as truck tires hammer their way through the potholes.

THE CLOSE

The story's close, the ending, should be so strong that nothing else can top it. Ideally, the moment you first arrive on scene, you will begin to look for a closing shot. You can then build the rest of your story toward the close when you write it because you already know how the story will end.[12]

The closing shot of a story on poverty might be of a woman on Social Security as she sits at her kitchen table one night, before her a pile of monthly expenses she must somehow cover with her meager income. The story of a national figure who has just died might build to a closing shot of file video of that person, waving a final good-bye to a crowd of admirers.

At all costs, avoid the lazy way out by ending your story on a sound bite or standup. Such stories simply stop, rather than building to a powerful, obvious, and definitive ending. Stories demand satisfying endings. Sound bites that end abruptly rarely satisfy. Reporters standing on camera reciting their names before the story truly ends almost certainly never satisfy.

BE HARD ON YOURSELF AS A WRITER

The most inviting newspapers and magazines contain "white space," and the most inviting broadcast scripts contain frequent pauses in narration (audio **white space**) to let a moment or two of natural sound play out or to allow a compelling moment of video to make its point. Unnecessary words destroy the impact of otherwise memorable moments. Yet, as former NBC news executive Reuven Frank once put it, "Almost nobody writes silence anymore." Wall-to-wall narration is powerless to draw viewers into a story with the same effect that even a few seconds of strong sound and picture can accomplish. "White space only happens, though, if the writer remembers to stop writing once in a while," says author Paul Paolicelli.[13]

The moment of drama that plays without narration may be something as simple as five seconds of video and **nat sound** as a passenger jet with damaged landing gear approaches for a landing. Perhaps the drama is that final moment in a pro golf tournament as the front-runner sinks a complicated putt for the grand prize—no words, just that pregnant moment as the ball makes its way across the green and finally plops into the cup.

"When the pictures are telling the story, we should be able to get an idea of what the story is about, even [without narration]," says Butch Montoya, a former news director at KUSA-TV, Denver.[14] WFAA photographer Tom Loveless and reporter Scott Pelley (now with CBS News) vividly demonstrated that concept in a report entitled "Boater's Rescue." The report, which earned an NPPA First Place Spot News Award, shows the rescue of two persons who had been pitched from their open boat into a storm-tossed lake. Time and again two volunteers on the bow of a tossing rescue boat reach into the water for the survivors—a twenty-year-old man and a nine-year-old boy. Finally, after eight hours in the water, the two survivors are pulled into the boat, brought to shore, and given artificial resuscitation. The story runs two minutes, twenty-seven seconds. It features forty-seven seconds of narration, a nine-second sound bite with an eyewitness, and segments totaling eighty-nine seconds that consist exclusively of pictures and natural sounds of the rescue, with no voice over. Two of the most compelling segments play for more than thirty seconds each with only pictures and sound telling the story.

Photojournalist Ed Fillmer also believes that even without sound, pictures should tell the story. Fillmer proves his conviction even in his coverage of routine news conferences when, for example, local church officials announce plans to build a new parochial school and address reasons the school is needed. The story is obvious without sound because of the visual sequences of architectural plans, priests and nuns in classrooms, a shot of the local public school superintendent, and other visual evidence of an overcrowded school.

In television, the reporter's larger commitment must be to clarity, and to attract and hold the audience's attention. Fresh, conversational writing and delivery and powerful storytelling visuals help to achieve these goals, as does a commitment to eliminate the unnecessary in every report. Audiences who fail to see much difference between competing newscasts and anchors these days will appreciate your originality and your memorable stories.

WRITE FROM THE VISUALS

Some journalists might contend that the audience is at fault for not remembering or understanding the stories on last night's newscast. But it's more probable that the blame lies with reporters whose stories flow over and around their audiences and fade quickly from memory because there was no drama, no compelling story, and few devices to engage the viewer's attention.

Even when words are essential to help tell the story, writers frequently put up with too much laziness and uncritical thinking from themselves. It is difficult to be harsh with oneself, but every television writer can eliminate information the viewer already knows or that the visuals communicate more eloquently. A more workable approach is to *write from the visuals*. In a story on homeless Americans, for example, the pictures might show a man in tattered clothes as he walks down the sidewalk with a liquor bottle in a brown paper bag. If you write *from* the visuals, whose message is "Whiskey numbs loneliness," your voice over might say something like "Joe carries his best friend in a brown paper bag." The opposite approach is to write the script first, then find visuals that support the script. But this approach tends to damage visual and story impact. Words can more easily be written to the visuals than preshot visuals can be edited from the narrative script.

THE EDIT CONSOLE IS A REWRITE MACHINE

The video editing console is a writing instrument, just as surely as the word processor or newsroom computer console are writing instruments. And those who control the consoles are writers, just as surely as those who sit at computers (Figure 1.5).

In a world that considers words on paper to be the only form of writing, such ideas might at first appear to be heresy. But the edit console, just as the word processor, is where television journalists put one idea in relation to another, where quotations from news sources take form as sound bites and are positioned to help give the news story its clarity. The edit console is also where nat sound is positioned and emphasized within the story, to help strengthen story meaning. And the edit console is where voice over is tightened and sometimes "rewritten" after it has been transformed from words on paper to words in air to words on tape. In its most classical sense, **editing** is an essential part of the storytelling art, for it is the *process* through which scenes and sounds are selected, arranged, and timed in order to impose certain rhythms, meanings, and moods on the final result.[15]

FIGURE 1.5   The video editing console can be thought of as a "rewrite" machine where the editor structures ideas and gives them their relationship to one another.

Editing, in the words of the Russian filmmaker Pudovkin, is the "conscious and deliberate guidance of spectator thoughts and associations." If we adopt Pudovkin's view, editing becomes a life force in the process of visual communication, no longer misconstrued as the simple joining of scenes or as eliminating "the bad parts" so that only good material remains.

REPORTORIAL EDITING

The process by which the reporter oversees all elements of the news story is called **reportorial editing.** Reportorial editing occurs in the mind's eye before any scenes are shot, before any interviews are conducted in the field, or before any words are written on paper or recorded on tape. Reportorial editing is the process of previsualizing the story, including the pictures, the sounds, the words, and even the visual and audio transitions that will be needed to move the final edited story forward with logical structure and continuity. In essence, reportorial editing is the field search for the building blocks of visual communication, the equivalent of a mind's-eye **storyboard** that begins to take shape even before you arrive on location.

The concept of reportorial editing must be applied even to spot news, because otherwise you may return from the field without the building blocks that will be necessary to reconstruct the story. Without a focus, you may not be able to identify the story until you sit down at the keyboard and the edit console. And at that point, your story can only be what you brought back—not necessarily what it was, or could have been.

In the partnership among reporter, photographer, and editor, reportorial editing is the common thread that links all disciplines. There is no "partnership," no "team effort," until all members of the crew begin to see the story in their mind's eye along common lines.

Normally, such harmony of vision is impossible until all members of the reporting team, including the editor, begin to share their ideas, their visions, their perceptions of the story. Such communication is rare, and without some effort on everyone's

JOHN DETARSIO, PHOTOJOURNALIST

John DeTarsio (see Figure 1.6) is a network freelance photojournalist and former director of photojournalism at KNSD-TV, San Diego. He has consulted for the Danish Broadcasting Network, CBC Canada, and the Armed Forces Network in Europe, Asia, and Central America. He conducts seminars and workshops at stations across the country.

John is a faculty member of the National Press Photographers Association (NPPA) annual workshop and has been guest faculty at the Poynter Institute's Leadership in Photojournalism workshop for chief photographers. He was regional chair of the NPPA and has served on the National Association of Television Arts and Sciences (NATAS) board of governors.

His awards include: NPPA National Photographer of the Year, NPPA Regional Photographer of the Year, six national NPPA awards, and

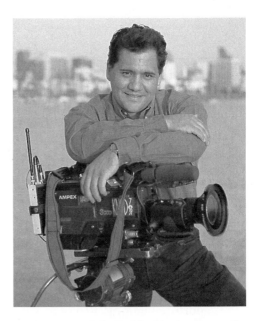

FIGURE 1.6   John DeTarsio, photojournalist, San Diego.

thirty NATAS Emmys. He is the only photographer ever to receive the Southwestern Area Emmy for Journalistic Enterprise. In addition to sixteen San Diego Press Club Awards and five Golden Mic Awards, he has received more than thirty-five regional NPPA Awards.

part it cannot happen. But without communication, the reporting team, like all partnerships, can never realize its full potential.

Perhaps the best approach is this: Talk out your ideas and negotiate them with one another. Talk to the assignment editor. And the minute you get in the car with the photographer or reporter, start talking again. Ask yourself and one another, "What is the story we're about to cover, and what do we want out of it?" In the following section, freelance network photojournalist John DeTarsio explains his approach to this process.

A BLUEPRINT FOR SHOOTING SPOT NEWS

John DeTarsio

Often, reporting spot news doesn't leave much time for shooting, reporting, and editing a story. Under severe pressure, we sometimes have to put three two-minute packages on the air, and no less than three live shots on the air, sometimes in just a few hours. We can do it, though, if we keep our story focus tight, tell that single story of what we encounter, and nothing more.

The Most Compelling Element in Spot News.   My commitment in shooting and reporting spot news is to transmit the experience of being at whatever situation I cover. That's usually the most compelling thing anyway, so thank goodness I stumbled onto this format early in my career.

Capture a Sense of What It Is Like to Be There.   The best spot news is experiential. It almost lets viewers touch and feel (and hear and smell) the news directly. The transmitting of an experience, the kind we would experience if we were eyewitness viewers, will always work in television stories until the end of time.

It may be the snap of flames, the anger in voices, the smell of smoke, the sounds as people walk through broken glass, or it may be an environment engulfed in silence. Our job is always to capture this total experience, not just photograph the flames or whatever, shoot a few interviews and a standup, and call it quits.

Shoot Sequences.   From the second my reporter and I arrive at a scene, we click right into automatic. The wireless microphone goes onto the reporter, and I monitor her in my earpiece as I start shooting pictures. My first reaction is to shoot an opening shot and a closing shot, then a wide shot, medium, and tight shot, then an action shot and a reaction shot. These things automatically go through my head.

My instinct is to record six or seven good, solid shots of the main action, then a wide shot, medium shot, and tight shot. Then three or four super tight shots of the main action that fills my screen, and sounds and silences from the natural environment. Then a standup within or near the main action if possible. If the action is swirling around us, the reporter gets two takes and no more.

Shoot Action–Reaction.   Reaction shots make the story memorable. Spot news action usually doesn't last long, so I record action shots first, over a span of maybe four or five minutes. After that, I turn my back to the action, because that's where the story lies. Whether it's a fire, a car accident, a riot, or any kind of spot-news situation—be it a death scene, murder scene, or whatever—that's simply and only the action. The *reaction* is where the story is—where the emotion is. So I spend the minimal amount of time shooting action—shooting the actual fire, shooting the actual murder scene, shooting the actual cars crashed—then my back goes to the action, and the rest of my time is spent on the reaction, because that's where you find all the memorable stuff. Once I cover the reaction, then I feel comfortable.

Record Sound Bites That Tell the Story.   I monitor the reporter on my earpiece, so not only can I tell what she's doing while I'm taking my pictures, but when she has an interview lined up she can just go stand next to the person and I can pick up the sound. If I'm on my tripod, I just swing around and shoot it from across the street in a situation like that.

Shoot the Closing Shot and Closing Sound.   I'm always looking for the closing shot whenever I shoot a story. I try to find it early, so I know what shots I'll need to build the story to that great closing shot. Sometimes I find it almost immediately after I arrive at a scene, other times I have to keep an eye out until it's time to leave. But I never go home without a closing shot, even if it's just someone walking, driving, flying, or ice skating into the sunset. Once I have the closing shot and some strong, closing sound, I breathe much easier.

A Blueprint for Shooting Feature Stories

Reporting and producing a feature story means using a different set of storytelling elements. It involves a different way of thinking and approaching things. One story in particular comes to mind. I called it "The Club," the story of a hockey club for the over-thirties that meets late on Monday nights. I wanted to do this story because I heard about a seventy-two-year-old man who still plays hockey with guys between thirty and forty years of age.

Look for a Beginning and Ending.   In every story I'm always looking for a beginning and an end. This story was all shot at a single location, what we call a "one-shoot location." As a springboard, I originally thought about opening the story with the guys getting dressed or going onto the ice.

   I also needed a closing shot and closing sound, almost always the hardest part of a story to find. Most stories can be ended with a traditional close—"the riding-into-the-sunset shot." I always record that shot as soon as possible, but then hope for something more original and thought-provoking. But at least I record that traditional ending 95 percent of the time. At least I know I have an end, and then hopefully along the way I can come up with something better.

Sound Is the Other Half of the Close.   Trying to wrap up a feature story in a single sentence so often turns out to sound real hokey. To avoid that, I like to end on sound in a lot of my feature stories, whether it's natural sound or from a sound bite. In a piece on a wood carver, for example, I would try to combine sound where the guy is walking out the door, and you hear him say, "Well, I've been doing this all my life, and I figure I'll be doing it till the day I die." That's basically how this hockey story ended. One of the players had finished this hour on the ice, and as he was leaving he said, "I don't know when I'll stop. When it stops being fun, probably." And that's how the story ends.

It's the combination of the shot and the sound that really pulls the end together. I needed conclusive sound to go along with that shot. I also needed a strong story focus or commitment. In this case, the focus to my story was Les Krengin, seventy-two-year-old hockey player, who still loves to play hockey and plays with the young pups. I now had my story; I had my character; I had my focus; and I had an idea for my beginning and ending shot.

I also knew what my middle would be—Les playing hockey, and sound from Les. But when all you have is one focus, a beginning, and an end, then a lot of times you're talking about a one-note song. You end up telling everything right away, and there's nowhere left for the story to go. So I'm always looking for whatever I can find that may raise an eyebrow or reveal additional layers of the story. It's almost like peeling an onion as you go down through the story's different layers. That way the viewer can learn and discover new things along the way.

Build the Story in Your Mind's Eye as You Go.   On my way to the story at 10 p.m. on Monday night, an idea came to me that changed my open. Here it was, late at night, and these knuckleheads were going off to play hockey. The thought came to mind, "My gosh, most people are settling in for the night, forgetting about the stresses of the day or getting ready for bed, and just starting off the week, but then pow, pow, pow, for some it's time to play." With that idea, I pulled over and started taking pictures of porch lights and fronts of homes, and a traffic light changing from green to red on a street with barely any traffic, and that's how I set up the story. So there is the story's first layer.

When I arrived at the hockey club, I discovered not only seventy-two-year-old Les Krengin but another man by the name of Chuck Cross, who was sixty-seven years old. So I thought, "Wow, another layer to the story." Chuck would be my next layer. So pow, pow, pow—for some it's time to play, and then we start to see people taking the ice and beginning to play, and of course, they have their helmets on; you can't see faces or tell who's who; and I say, "Chuck Cross has led this group for years." Natural sound. "And years." Natural sound. "And"—natural sound—"years." And then you see Chuck pull off his helmet. At that point in the shot he turns to me, because I had said, "Chuck, when you take off your helmet, just tell me how old you are and what your name is, or the other way around." And so he pulls off his helmet and says, "Chuck Cross, sixty-seven years old." So there I had another layer.

We then follow Chuck for fifteen to twenty seconds, and you see him out on the ice. After a couple of natural sound breaks he says, "It's best not to find a rocking chair." My next line is something to the effect, "After all, he's just a pup next to—" and then Les Krengin looks at the camera, and he says, "Les Krengin, seventy-two." So there was the story's next layer. By this time we're fifty seconds into the story, and we're just meeting Les, but we've been going along on a ride. The story unfolds and unfolds and unfolds. And then, a man who looks like he's pushing forty tells me that when he was in little kid hockey years and years ago, Les was his coach. Now, here he is playing hockey with him, a real neat thing, so here is yet another layer of the story I found along the way. You can see why these layers are very important, and why I'm always looking for things that surprise me while I'm out there.

Feature Interviews.   Then there are the interviews. Usually a feature story will be centered around a character. Even if my story is on a certain thing, I'll find a character behind the thing, and then with that character I'll do two different types of interviews. One type, which comes at the very end, will be a sit-down, relaxed kind of interview. Sometimes I'll have the camera on and sometimes not, and I'll ask all kinds of deep questions to get to the philosophical stuff, the personal things, and some good kind of thoughts like that.

The other kind of interview occurs while I'm shooting. All during the shoot I interact with my character, but at the beginning of shoots I try not to invade their space. I shoot from a little distance and collect most of my sound on the wireless microphone. As the story progresses, I move in closer and I move in closer and I move in closer. I don't pay much attention to the camera, but just try to keep a real loose atmosphere. I like to look around the camera and make little asides and comments to the subject about what's going on. By doing this, my strategy is to get off-the-cuff statements from people who aren't thinking about the camera and think they're just talking to me.

All the natural, candid moments occur during these off-the-cuff statements. You can see by watching TV that they're talking to me in natural, candid asides, not giving me staged answers or anything like that. This is where genuine, real TV starts to happen—where you can get lost in the story and really get the feel of the person. That's really some of the most important stuff to me.

Shoot Rock-Steady Shots.   As far as actual picture-taking, I believe in solid, rock-steady shots. Whenever our eyes look at an object, it does not shake. Our eyes have stabilizers. Whenever I'm on a tripod, I also want to stabilize the action. I frame the shot, lock down the camera, and make certain the shot is perfectly steady.

Sometimes shakiness is justified if it's a one-time shot and you don't have time to use a tripod. But most news stories are not like that. Often you can miss parts of it and it's not the end of the world. You have plenty of other times to get the story, so I believe in being in control of the shoot, not letting the shoot get control of you, and understanding that you're not going to collect every piece of everything in the brief time you're there. I prefer a few high-quality shots rather than tapes and tapes worth of low-quality shots.

This style of shooting really pays off in the edit bay. If there's a bunch of high-quality shots, almost everything can be used. And if the photographer is in control of the shoot and not panicking, there won't be a lot of slop in between shots. When the photographer or editor gets into the edit bay, they don't have to wait for shots to steady up or see if they last long enough, because they're all lasting for ten seconds, which is another rule.

Ideally, I want shots to last at least ten seconds, so there's plenty of usable footage in the middle. This gives the camera time to settle down if there's a little shaking in the beginning and toward the end, and still leaves plenty of usable video. You can be confident about having "enough meat in the middle," especially when deadlines are tight and all you can do is just lay down long-running shots with everything already there.

Use Handheld Shots in Close Situations.   Handheld shots are most useful in very close situations when you're right up next to your subject, with the lens on a very wide shot. It's almost like you're dancing with the subject and the movement is all with the feet. It's all tracking, side to side, front to back, zooming and panning with the feet and not with the fingers on the zoom control, and the shoulders pivoting around, and always with the camera on a wide shot and always used up close. It's a person walking down the hall and me walking with him—never standing and panning as the person goes by, but walking along in a tracking motion.

Déjà Vu All Over Again

It's January, the start of a new year, and I'm in bed, and I feel just a little bit of rumbling in the bed early in the morning. By the time I realize it was an earthquake, just so very faint and feeling so very far away, it is over and I go back to sleep. About an hour later frantic relatives call from Ohio and say, "We just wanted to know if you were alive, if your house survived the earthquake. We've been trying to call you; all the lines have been busy; thank God, everything's okay!" I turn on the TV, and all I see is live reports from Los Angeles, 100 miles to the north. Again that same feeling of wanting to hide under the bed consumes me. Instead, again, I take out the same bag I took to the Los Angeles riots and start packing it with clothes. I call the station. Irv Kass, the news director, says, "Just head straight up to Los Angeles." The only difference was that this time I would not be working with a reporter. I would be filing reports on my own, originating live shots on my own, and being a complete one-man band. Already I was beginning to feel the same buzz you feel whenever a big story is happening, and beginning to think of subject; story; focus; beginnings; middles and endings; action and reaction; sequences; strong characters; little sounds; storytelling bites; and moving in close. It was time to tell another story, and I was on my way.

SUMMARY

In television news, there are only two ways to tell stories. One is with pictures. The other is with sound. Photojournalists, who may be both photographers and reporters, use the television field camera and microphone as writing and reporting instruments to tell compelling visual stories. In television news, the written word, while crucial to the storytelling process, seldom stands alone but is part of a complex package of information made up of images, colors, actions, sounds, and silence.

The most effective visual stories typically communicate a sense of experience to viewers by incorporating matched-action sequences and natural sounds. Something happening can be seen to happen. When the camera is closely involved in the action, the process somewhat duplicates how eyewitness observers and participants would experience the event.

Crucial to the visual story is a story focus, the journalist's equivalent of the scriptwriter's story line or premise. In news, the focus statement is a declarative sentence that summarizes the story to be told and helps give it focus. Each story also requires a beginning, middle, and ending. Often the strongest stories are told through people engaged in visual and interesting activities. In most stories, it also is desirable to build white space or pauses in the voice-over narration to allow compelling pictures and sounds to involve the viewer more directly in the story.

Besides the camera, microphone, and computer console, another essential tool of photojournalists is the edit console. Here, ideas are put in relationship to one another, story pace is adjusted and refined, and the story's emotional outlines are given their emphasis.

DISCUSSION

1. What qualities separate the photographer from the photojournalist?

2. In what sense are the camera and microphone "writing and reporting instruments"?

3. Why can the edit console fairly be called a "rewrite" machine?

4. How does the nature of a television news report differ from a newspaper story?

5. What is the role of the written word in television news?

6. To what extent should television news stories be anchored around the word? Around the picture?

7. What is the important role of picture sequences in television communication?

8. Why is sequential video usually more engaging and compelling than illustrative video?

9. What is the story commitment or focus statement, and what are the procedures for determining it from one story to the next?

10. Why can most television reports benefit from a focus statement?

11. Explain the value of learning to write from the visuals.

12. What is the role of natural sound in television news reports?

13. Why are short sound bites often preferable to lengthy bites?

14. What techniques can the photojournalist use to help make news stories more memorable?

15. What purpose lies behind the need to "address the larger issue" in news stories?

16. In a television news story, what is meant by the term "visual proof"?

EXERCISES

1. Using only natural sounds and visual imagery, photograph or script a sequence or two that captures the moment and communicates a sense of experience about the subject.

You might choose to capture the mood on a ski slope at opening time, the feeling of test-driving a used car, or of planting and watering a tree or flower. At all times, keep the camera involved in the action. The key is to help viewers feel as if they have participated in the event and experienced something of the story's environment.

2. Critically study the field reports in a television newscast for the presence of sequences and matched action. Note how many stories contain sequences and how many rely primarily on illustrated scripts (illustrative rather than sequential video).

3. Study television stories and commercials for the "visual proof" of their main points. How frequently are the main points proven verbally when they might have been made far more memorable with strong visuals?

4. View several television news stories and define the story focus for each. If the story's focus seems vague and uncertain, supply a story focus that would have given the story a clear meaning.

5. Turn your back to the television set during a newscast and listen for examples of the effective use of natural sound and sound bites in news stories and commercials. Pay attention to how often the sound or voice-over narration entices you to look at the screen.

6. Analyze sound bites and compare the impact of short, five- to ten-second bites with interviews of thirty seconds or more.

7. Study news stories and commercials for examples of "surprises" or moments of drama that reengage the viewer and make the story more memorable. If the stories you watch lack such moments, consider what elements could have been added to make the story more interesting and memorable.

8. Study a newscast and its commercials with the sound off to determine how "intelligent" or literate the visuals are. As a photojournalist, how might you have improved the level of visual literacy in the stories you viewed?

9. Watch a newscast and determine how many stories address "larger issues" as the term was discussed in this chapter.

N O T E S

1. Fred Shook and Don Berrigan. "Glossary: Television Field Production and Reporting," Atelier Sur le Récit Visuel, Service National de la Formation et du Développement, Bureau de Montréal, Société Radio Canada, Montréal, Canada, 1991.

2. Comments made by Shellie Karabell to participants in the NPPA Advanced Team Storytelling Workshop, Lexington, KY, 22 April 2003.

3. Larry Hatteberg, "People Oriented Photojournalism," a presentation at the NPPA TV News-Video Workshop, Norman, OK, 17 March 1998.

4. Ibid.

5. Conversation with the author, 13 March 1994.

6. Jack M. Bickham, *Scene and Structure* (Cincinnati: Writer's Digest Books, 1993), 2.

7. Conversation with the author, Aiken, SC, 1 February 2003.

8. Cited by Ed Bliss in his address, "Newswriting," to the 42nd Annual Radio-Television News Directors Conference, Orlando, FL, 3 September 1987.

9. Quoted from e-mail correspondence with the author, 14 September 1998.

10. Ibid.

11. Bob Dotson, "Reporters Are More Than Mic Stands: The Write Way to Combine Pictures, Sounds & Words," a presentation at the NPPA TV News-Video Workshop, Norman, OK, 15 March 1994.

12. Frederick Shook and Dan Lattimore, *The Broadcast News Process*, 6th ed. (Denver: Morton Publishing Co., 2001), 107.

13. Comments to WDSU-TV reporting staff, New Orleans, 22 May 1985.

14. Quotes from "National Press Photographer's 1983 Best Photography Awards" videotape presentation. This and similar tapes are available from National Press Photographer's Association, P. O. Box 1146, Durham, NC 27702.

15. Karel Reisz and Gavin Millar, *The Technique of Film Editing* (New York: Hastings House Publishers, 1968), 168–170.

CHAPTER TWO

THE VISUAL GRAMMAR OF MOTION PICTURE PHOTOGRAPHY

In television journalism, the primary goal of visual communication is to expand the viewer's consciousness. The photojournalist seeks to reconstruct events in such a manner that viewers develop a sense of having observed and experienced the moment.

Throughout the reporting process, the emphasis is on reconstruction of events from raw material shot in the field rather than on the re-creation of events. And in television, just as in theatrical filmmaking, photographic reconstruction works best when it embodies a sense of continuity or consecutiveness to help heighten the viewer's sense of experience.

To accomplish such feats consequently requires an understanding of the **visual grammar** that enables the field journalist to break simple action into its complex parts for later reconstruction at the editing bench. In television, neither the photographer nor the reporter can excel without an ability to previsualize and properly manage this reconstruction process. Moreover, reporters who must shoot their own footage, especially those in smaller markets and individuals newly hired following graduation, will find such proficiencies a requirement for survival.

THE SHOT

In motion picture photography the basic unit of expression is the **shot,** or the single, continuous take of material that is recorded each time the camera is turned on until it is turned off. Each shot made in the field is raw material for the editing console and can only assume larger meaning in relation to the shots that come before and after it.

Depending on action and content, the "average" shot is recorded in the field for some eight to ten seconds and occasionally longer. The guiding rule maintains that it is easier to shorten a shot at the editing bench than to lengthen it. Of even greater importance when deciding how long to make a shot is a commitment to remember the editor's needs: When recording in the field, hold the shot long enough for the action to conclude, or to portray subject matter adequately within the shot, and remember to give the editor adequate length in every shot.

The Sequence

Shots are the building blocks from which the editor builds a reconstruction, or representative composite, of the event. A number of shots, related to each other to convey a single message, are combined to form the sequence (Figure 2.1). Action flows across the edits from one shot to another to create the illusion that viewers are watching a continuous, uninterrupted event. Sequences help a viewer feel he or she has experienced an event because they reconstruct the event much as eyewitness observers would experience it.

Surprisingly, some photographers have never shot a sequence, and others cannot identify a sequence with any reasonable certainty—the consequence of scripts that are first written then illustrated, sentence by sentence and paragraph by paragraph, with random, nonconsecutive bits of video.

FIGURE 2.1   The sequence is a succession of related images that shows an event as it unfolds. The process duplicates how an observer in real life might take in the event. In an edited motion sequence, action continues smoothly from one shot to the next with no disruption in continuity.

BASIC SHOTS

In essence the photographer has only three shots with which to build sequences: the long shot (LS), the medium shot (MS), and the close-up (CU) (Figure 2.2). All other shots, including the medium close-up (MCU), extreme close-up (ECU), and extreme long shot (ELS), are variations of these three.

The **long shot,** or wide shot, provides a full view of the subject. Accordingly, the long shot may show a full view of an individual from head to toe or perhaps be a view

FIGURE 2.2   The three basic shots in motion picture photography are the long shot (top left), medium shot, and close-up. All other shot compositions are variations of these three shots.

of an entire mountain valley. Whatever the subject, the distinguishing feature of the long shot is its ability to show an entire view of the subject.

The **medium shot** brings subject matter closer to the viewer and begins to isolate it from the overall environment. While a long shot might show us an entire federal courthouse building, the medium shot might show only the main entrance. Whereas a long shot of an individual might show the person from the feet up, a medium shot would show the individual from the waist up. The medium shot can be used to place the viewer's general attention where the photographer or editor wants it, without the jolting effect that might result from cutting directly from a long shot to an extreme close-up.

The **close-up** isolates the subject entirely from its surrounding environment. It shows a person from about the shirt pocket up and may show nothing more of a building than the doorway or a sign that identifies it.

Because of its relatively small screen size, at least in comparison with motion picture theater screens, television has been called a close-up medium. Close-ups can help the viewer achieve a greater sense of intimacy and vicarious involvement with the subject. This leads to the suggestion that if you want close, intimate shots, you must move the camera physically close to the action. In other words, if you wish to involve your audience in the action, you must involve your camera.

HOW SHOTS WORK TOGETHER

The long shot, medium shot, and close-up function together in sequences in a manner roughly equivalent to how the eye works. Whenever we first encounter a situation we normally make a visual overview to acclimate ourselves to the surroundings. When we first walk into an airport, we see the crowds of passengers and long rows of ticket counters. This overview is somewhat equivalent to making a long shot with our eyes.

Once we have taken in the full view and oriented ourselves, we begin to inspect the environment more closely, perhaps searching, through medium and close views, for an overhead TV monitor that displays flight departure information. For detailed visual inspection, we may walk closer to the monitor for very close-up views.

Even without moving physically closer it is sometimes possible to create the photographic equivalent of a medium or close-up shot in our mind's eye through our ability to isolate an object of interest within the environment and concentrate primarily on that object with our full attention.

The basic shot designations of long shot, medium shot, and close-up identify shots according to their image size and composition. Other shot designations derive their names from particular camera movements or how shots are used within the storytelling process.

CAMERA MOVEMENT

The main job of the motion picture camera is to record action, not to create it. While the photographer can animate otherwise static shots with pans, zooms, and tilts, the goal is to record actual motion whenever possible rather than to infuse the scene with artificial camera movement. Nevertheless, pans and tilts have their place, provided they are used with discretion.

In the **pan,** the camera is swiveled on a tripod to show an overall scene, or the handheld camera is moved in similar fashion to "show all the scene" in a single shot. The pan is an artificial device that tends to call attention to itself. Although our head can swivel, our eyes never pan, just as they never zoom. They only take individual shots. To confirm this observation, try to pan a view with your own eyes: Notice how your eyes cut from one part of the scene to the next as you move your head. Even when we view a pan shot on the screen, the eye darts from one "shot" to the next within the pan as it isolates various views and builds a composite image. When you do pan with the camera, hold the shot steady for at least three seconds before you begin to pan, and again hold the shot steady for another three seconds after you end the pan. Editors love this technique because less awkwardness results on home screens if the beginning of the shot is held momentarily on static footage before the pan begins. Shooting a few seconds of footage before and after the pan also provides the editor with static footage that can be used separately if necessary as static shots.

If the camera swivels on a tripod or other fixed support to follow action, such as to follow a bicycle race, the result is a **moving** (or follow) **shot.** The moving shot is sometimes called a "pan with a purpose," but because the photographer's motivation here is to follow action rather than show a static object in panorama, the moving shot is technically not a pan.

A variation of the pan and moving shots is found in the **combination shot.** The camera follows the action until a new moving subject enters frame, then picks up the new subject and follows it. The camera, for example, might follow a jet plane as it taxis; when a second plane appears in frame, taxiing in the opposite direction, the camera then follows the second plane. The combination shot produces a relatively long "take," which the editor on tight deadline can substitute for two or three shorter shots that otherwise would have to be edited together separately.

The **tilt shot** is the vertical equivalent of a pan: The camera tilts up; the camera tilts down. The tilt is commonly used to show an entire object that would be too tall to be photographed in a single shot or to reveal some new aspect of the subject. Perhaps the object is to photograph the unveiling of an artist's mural that covers the entire wall of a hotel lobby three stories tall, or to tilt up from a close shot of clapping hands to the square-dance caller's face. The tilt shot also is useful to keep subjects in frame, such as when football fans stand to cheer a touchdown or in order to follow a firefighter's ascent up an extension ladder.

■ ■ ■ ■ ■ ▬▬▬▬▬▬▬▬▬▬▬▬▬▬▬▬▬▬▬▬▬▬▬▬▬▬▬▬▬▬▬▬

RULES FOR PANNING

The rules that govern the pan are intended to help keep the viewer's attention on the subject matter rather than on the techniques of artificial camera movement.

Avoid panning altogether unless the pan is motivated by action within the scene.

Shoot static footage before and after the pan to give the editor a range of cutting points.

(continued)

RULES FOR PANNING   Continued

Always have something on the screen as you pan. Compose the shot so that as one object leaves the screen, a new object comes into view.

Adjust the speed of the pan to the subject matter in order to make camera movement less obvious.

Let each object you pan remain on the screen long enough for viewers to have a clear view of it.

Feather the start and stop of the pan, so that camera movement begins and ends smoothly and imperceptibly.

Alternatives to panning include building an overall composite of the entire environment to be shown, in long shot/medium shot/close-up, just as the eye builds its own composite of reality.

In the **tracking shot** the camera actually moves through space to keep moving subjects in frame. No longer does the camera merely swivel to follow bicycle racers as it would in the pan. In the tracking shot the camera is mounted on some means of conveyance and physically moved through space to keep the bicycle riders in frame. For a tracking shot of a pedestrian walking down a sidewalk, the camera would be mounted in a car or other conveyance to keep pace with the subject.

In the **trucking shot,** the camera itself moves past fixed objects. A trucking shot would result if, for example, a camera were mounted atop a cargo van and driven down a neighborhood street past Victorian homes or if the camera were mounted in the seat of a wheelchair and moved past a row of students in a classroom.

In the **dolly shot,** the camera moves either toward the subject or away from it: The camera is said to dolly in (toward an object) or dolly out (away from the object). To achieve smooth movement, the camera tripod is attached to a dolly, a simple frame or platform mounted on wheels. Anything from a professional dolly to a wheelchair or snow sled can be used for dolly shots, provided the device glides smoothly without bumping or jerking the camera. In some shops, the dolly shot may be called a *tracking shot.*

Camera movement inevitably introduces the possibility of unwanted shakiness on the screen, especially when shooting scenes from vehicles and aircraft. Increasingly, professional and amateur photographers alike rely on the **gyro-lens** to electronically steady otherwise shaky images. Special circuitry constantly monitors the image being photographed, electronically counteracting unexpected shifts and shakiness in the image from one moment to the next. Even handheld, walking shots can look smooth and fluid. If the camera is moved or shaken violently, however, the image may take a moment or two to stabilize. The lens takes its name from the gyroscope that allows planes and ships to maintain a steady course despite the contrary effects of wind, water, and gravity.

Changes in Camera Perspective

On occasion the **zoom shot** may serve as a passable substitute for the dolly shot, provided the zoom is introduced coincidentally with subject movement. If a child on a bicycle turns onto a country lane and pedals toward camera, for example, the camera can be zoomed back to keep the child in frame in an effect similar to the dolly's. A substitute shot is possible in a reporter standup if the camera zooms back to preserve proper composition as the reporter walks toward camera.

Notice that no change in perspective is possible unless the camera itself moves through space. Because the camera remains in one physical location in the zoom shot, there can be no change in perspective. For this reason, if you wish to take a close shot of an object, move the camera physically close to the subject. While you can keep the camera at a distance and zoom in for what appears to be a close-up, the lack of true closeness to the subject is immediately apparent (Figure 2.3).

The **aerial shot** is achieved by placing the camera in an airplane or helicopter. It is unequaled in providing overall, bird's-eye views of traffic, floods, fires, terrain, and related subject matter. Because the camera physically moves through space, the aerial shot also can be used to produce both tracking and trucking shots.

SHOTS THAT HELP TELL THE STORY

The long shot is commonly used as an **establishing shot** because of its easy ability to introduce viewers to the story's locale or to the story itself. Among professional photojournalists and editors the practice is to avoid establishing shots of walls, which tell viewers almost nothing about the story to come, and to concentrate instead on shots, whatever their composition, that help to engage the viewer instantly and communicate the story to come.

While an establishing shot can be a wide shot, it can also be a close shot, for example, of a foot tapping to the music at a blue grass festival. A jury foreman reading a verdict may be a more effective "establisher" than a long shot of the federal courthouse building with a sign in front.

FIGURE 2.3   Note the change in perspective between the left close-up, taken from a distance with the zoom lens set on a long focal length, and the close-up on the right, taken by moving the camera physically close to the subject. The subject in the right photo almost looks three-dimensional by comparison.

From time to time within a scene, the **reestablishing shot** is useful to introduce new action or subject matter or to reestablish a sense of the setting in which action is occurring. In a typical example, we might first see the activities of a motorist looking under the hood of a car at the engine, followed by a reestablishing shot of the overall scene in which a patrol officer pulls up to offer assistance. In another example, we might see a close shot of a little girl blowing a party horn, followed by a reestablishing shot to show her mother as she enters frame with a birthday cake and walks toward her daughter.

The **insert shot** provides the audience with close-up, essential detail about some part of the main action. If, in one shot, we see a woman slip something into her purse, the insert shot shows us the object in close-up detail.

The **point of view (POV) shot** shows the view as seen through the subject's eyes (Figure 2.4). If a ship captain looks out to sea in one shot, the point of view shot shows us the view as seen through his eyes. The camera effectively substitutes for the captain's own eyes.

In this context, the camera can be used either from the perspective of the involved participant in the action or from that of the uninvolved observer. Whenever the camera represents the participant's point of view, the style is referred to as **subjective camera:** Action is portrayed as the subject would see it. If the action is portrayed as an observer on the sidelines would see it, then the style is referred to as **objective camera.**

Action and reaction are critical components in the visual storytelling process. An action occurs, followed by a reaction. A woman looks down and smiles at an object offscreen. In the next shot, the **reaction shot,** a baby coos and smiles in response. A waitress accidentally drops a tray of dishes on her return to the restaurant kitchen. In the

FIGURE 2.4   The point of view shot depicts a view as an individual observer would see it.

FIGURE 2.5   Action–reaction is a useful device to heighten viewer interest in a story. Left, drum beats make the air reverberate (the action) to the delight of onlookers (the reaction). The shot of the onlookers could also serve as a cutaway shot.

reaction shot, diners pause in their conversation at the sound of the breaking glass and then applaud as the waitress takes a bow. Yet again, a baseball player knocks a home run. In the reaction shot, the team's coach jumps for joy. Reaction shots tell us how people feel about what happened (Figure 2.5). The face and the eyes mirror the soul and the depth of feeling. Therefore, if you show action in your photography, look for the reaction as well. "The reaction is where most things happen," writes filmmaker and author Edward Dmytryk. "Reaction is transition, change, movement—and movement is life."[1]

INCORPORATE ACTION IN EVERY SCENE

The great strength of film and television is movement. Children smile. Flags flutter and ripple in the breeze. Rabbits scutter casually through the grass. Rockets climb into the sunrise. The alternative to movement is still life and static subject matter, the stuff of every slide show. For this reason walls and signs make poor establishing shots in television.

In television news, the goal must be to incorporate movement into every scene. If you have decided to shoot an establishing shot of the courthouse, photograph people as they walk up to it in an establishing shot, rather than photograph the static side of the courthouse building. If the subject is a sheer rock cliff, follow an eagle's flight with the cliffs in the background. If the assignment is to photograph a lifeless fence, show it as it moves in the wind or as a bird takes flight from a corner post.

The **reverse-angle shot** (Figure 2.6) is commonly used to introduce new action or to advance the action within a scene. Assume a scene in which a barber has just finished cutting a patron's hair. The patron pays the barber and exits frame. The barber

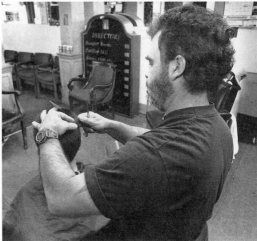

FIGURE 2.6 A reverse-angle shot is accomplished by shooting an establishing shot of a subject (left), then shooting a second shot from behind the subject in the opposite direction along the same axis line.

yells "Next!" and a second patron enters frame with his back to the camera. The reverse-angle shot can then be used to give viewers a frontal view of the new patron as he approaches camera. To accomplish the reverse-angle shot, the camera simply shoots back along the axis line as originally established in the first shot.

LOCATION SHOOTING

Much of a photojournalist's life seems to be spent making **interior shots** inside buildings. Interior shots routinely confront the photographer with decisions to make about lighting, filters, power sources, electrical equipment, heat, and the distractions of lights and shadows.

Just as obviously, **exterior shots** taken out of doors involve still other considerations. These include the weather, heat, cold, angle of sun, time of day, as well as the total illumination and color temperatures that are available.

ONE SHOTS TO CROWD SHOTS

Other shot designations are defined according to the number of people who appear in the shot. Into this category fall the one shot, two shot, three shot, group shot, and crowd shot. In the group shot, anywhere from five to a dozen people or more, it is possible for viewers to identify individual faces. In the crowd shot, it is difficult to differentiate among individuals.

MASTER SHOT WITH CUT-INS

Over the years in traditional theatrical filmmaking, directors have commonly relied on the **master shot,** in which a single camera records a continuous take of the entire scene from one location and at one focal length lens setting (Figure 2.7). After the main action is recorded in one take, the action is then repeated (or the crew waits for the action to reoccur), in order to photograph **pickup** or **cut-in shots.** Typical cut-in shots include the close-up or insert shot, reaction shot, and point of view shot, as well as new camera angles to emphasize particular elements of the action.

MULTIPLE-CAMERA PHOTOGRAPHY

A variation on the master shot with cut-ins occurs in the television studio or at outdoor sporting events whenever multiple cameras are used to record different facets of the action as it unfolds. Video signals from the various cameras are fed simultaneously to a central switcher in the control room or field production van and displayed on a bank of video monitors. At the central switcher a director looks at the monitors and decides when to punch up a particular shot "on air" or to record it for later broadcast. Because the various cameras view the same action from multiple angles and compositions, it is relatively simple to cut from one camera view to the next as the action progresses. From one shot to the next, the action is perfectly matched.

FIGURE 2.7   A master shot (left) is used to record an uninterrupted take of the entire action. The photographer then asks for the action to be repeated, or waits for it to repeat, and photographs insert or pickup shots to emphasize detail and improve story pace.

HOW TO SHOOT MATCHED ACTION
WITH ONE CAMERA

Even when photographing with a single camera, the photographer can produce shots that can be edited together in **matched action** (Figure 2.8), provided that the photographer shoots **overlapping action** in the field. Using one camera, the photographer must move it from one location to the next, corresponding to the locations of the various cameras as they would have been placed in a multiple-camera setup. Either the action is repeated or the photographer waits for the action to repeat itself in order to capture the developing action from each of the various angles. Done correctly, the result can be virtually indistinguishable from the action recorded in a master shot with cut-ins or through multiple-camera photography.

FIGURE 2.8   When an action is edited so that it continues smoothly and without interruption from one shot to the next, the result is matched action.

OVERLAPPING ACTION

Overlapping action means simply that action taking place in one shot occurs identically in at least one other shot (Figure 2.9). In other words, an identical action must be present in at least two shots. If a fly fisherman throws a line into the river in an idyllic backlit shot, a close shot might show the fishing fly as it lands on the water's surface. Because the line can be seen to land on the water's surface in both the long shot and the close shot, the action in the two is said to be overlapping. The editor can produce matched action between the two shots by cutting out of the long shot at a point in the action identical to the continuation of the action in the close shot.

PHOTOGRAPHING ACTION UNDER THE PHOTOGRAPHER'S CONTROL

Overlapping action can be photographed in one of two ways. If action is under the photographer's control, the subject can be asked to repeat a particular action, and inanimate objects (such as computer disk drives and copy machines) can be made to repeat action while matched-action sequences are photographed. In the previous example,

FIGURE 2.9   Many activities in life, including those in most news events, are repetitive. Photographers who are sensitive to repetitive action can record shots of overlapping action in the field and use such shots to create matched action at the editing console.

the photographer could ask the fisherman to throw the line into the water in a long shot, then ask him to throw the line a second time within a designated area in order to obtain the close shot. Just as simply, a subject can be asked to mail a letter in a long shot, then remail it while the photographer takes a close shot of the person's hand placing the letter in the mailbox.

Obviously, the rules of staging apply in such situations. Guidelines at some local stations and at the network level prohibit staging in any form. These organizations hold that staging imposes the journalist's influence too directly on the story and might convert the story into an event that would not have occurred in the journalist's absence. Other station policies hold that it's generally acceptable to ask subjects to repeat action those subjects would have performed on their own whether or not the camera was present.

PHOTOGRAPHING ACTION NOT UNDER THE PHOTOGRAPHER'S CONTROL

Even if the action is outside the photographer's control, or if station policy prohibits staging, overlapping action is still possible provided that the photographer either anticipates the moment or waits for the action to repeat itself. With a single camera, documentary filmmaker Frederick Wiseman once created a perfect matched-action sequence of worshipers singing a Christmas hymn during religious services at a hospital. The music continued uninterrupted through a succession of long shot/medium shot/close shot sequences, in which the action was always perfectly matched. To create this feat Wiseman simply allowed the camera to run uninterrupted as the hymn was sung in its entirety at the 9 a.m. service, then rephotographed the 11 a.m. congregation singing the same hymn with particular attention on medium and close insert shots.

MATCHED-ACTION SEQUENCES CAN BE SHOT IN SPOT NEWS

Even in spot news, the action often is repetitive regardless of whether it is of firefighters battling an apartment house fire or a police officer directing cars away from a flooded intersection. Even events that happen only once can be shot sequentially if the photographer anticipates the action. If a defendant is led into court, for example, the photographer can find out in advance where the hearing room is located, think in terms of distance, and determine the amount of time the subject will take to walk from point A to point B. The photographer might decide to hold the defendant in frame during a continuous shot, **snap zooming** to the defendant's feet or to the grim face of the accompanying marshal, or the photographer might determine to shoot the action in such a way that the defendant will enter and leave frame a certain number of times. Snap zooming is a technique in which the photographer snaps the zoom lever, instantly zooming in or out for a new shot of an action. At the editing bench the editor eliminates the few frames of video in which the snap zoom appears and edits together the action as though it had been shot simultaneously with two cameras, one set for a medium or long shot, the other set for a close shot.

The result of such planning in the field is overlapping action, the raw material that will enable the editor to cut together matched action. When the action cannot be edited together seamlessly, or when it must be abridged, the editor will look to the photographer to shoot cutaways, inserts, reverse-angle shots, and reestablishing shots.

Jump Cuts

Jump cuts in finished video occur when action jumps unnaturally forward or backward in time or when an object jumps unnaturally into a new position on the screen. If in one shot the speaker at an outdoor rally has on a hat but in the next shot an instant later has lost her hat, a jump cut has occurred. Technically, a jump cut is an action that could not occur in real life. The action "jumps"; for example, a woman at the beach is seen wearing sunglasses in the first shot but no glasses in the shot immediately following or a computer screen displays text in an establishing shot, followed by a medium shot of the same screen that is now blank (Figure 2.10).

The Cutaway

The most commonly used device to eliminate jump cuts and to condense time is the **cutaway,** a shot of some part of the peripheral action that diverts the viewer's eye for a moment so that when the eye returns to the main action, the "jump" will be less obvious. In the case of the woman at the beach who wears glasses in the first shot, a shot of the setting sun and perhaps a second cutaway of a sandpiper hopping along the beach could be inserted just before shot 2 of the same woman now seen without glasses. Viewers can be expected to assume that while they watched the sunset and sandpiper, the woman had time to remove her glasses. In the story of a chess match, the cutaway could be a shot of the clock used to measure the time allowed each player to contemplate the next move. At a press conference, the most hackneyed cutaway shows a bank of television news cameras recording the event or a close shot of a reporter taking

FIGURE 2.10 A jump cut occurs when an object changes position or appearance on the screen instantly and unnaturally from one shot to the next.

notes. Besides the use of cutaways, such optical effects as **dissolves** and **wipes** can be used to eliminate the jump cut.

The Motivated Cutaway

The typical cutaway is simply a device the photographer shoots to help the editor eliminate a jump cut and/or to condense the action (as when editing together two short cuts from a lengthy speech). Even more ideal is the cutaway that contributes desirable or essential new information to the scene. Such a shot is distinguished by its ability to contribute new information, hence the term **motivated cutaway.** Instead of the gratuitous shot of television cameras at the press conference, a motivated cutaway might show the proud faces of the speaker's relatives as she announces her candidacy for office. Whatever the setting, the essential contribution of the motivated cutaway is to help drive the story forward and help sustain story development by providing new information.

The Transition or Reveal Shot

The typical news package, just as the typical theatrical film, is a series of sequences or scenes linked one to another. The linkage between scenes can be accomplished with a straight cut (cutting straight from one scene to another), an optical effect (dissolve, flip wipe, etc.), or a **transition shot,** also called a **reveal shot.** Transition shots give the editor a way to pivot from one sequence to the next, a way to link separate scenes. Transition shots can be used to disorient the viewer momentarily, as in this example from film editor Michael Kahn, who describes a scene in which a group of people are sitting around the table, followed by a scene in which the same people are in line waiting to go to a movie.

> Normally you'd cut to the marquee to show a geographic reference, but in this case you cut to a close-up of the counter and hands exchanging money for tickets, or even a close-up of somebody's face. You [the viewer] don't know where you are, but you know you're somewhere different. Then you cut back to the master (shot) of all of us in line waiting to enter the movie. You go right to a close-up and then cut back to reveal the new scene.[2]

In another example, a close-up shot of a ship's whistle could be used to move the story from a fish market along the wharf to shots of canning operations aboard a fishing ship.

Similarly, in a video package about diseases in ponderosa pine and elm trees, the transition shot might be used to move the story from a mountain setting to an urban area. In this example we first see a logger with chain saw cutting down a ponderosa pine in a forest setting. Next we see the transition shot, a close-up ostensibly of the same chain saw the logger used in the previous shot, followed by a cut to a long shot of an elm falling in an urban setting.

The field equivalent of an optical wipe occurs in the film *Absence of Malice.* During a tracking shot in a newsroom the camera moves past a white pillar that fills the screen. The pillar creates the illusion of a screen "wipe" from screen left to right. In the midst of this wipe, while the pillar is still full screen, a cut is made to a tracking shot that reveals Paul Newman striding into the newsroom. The result is a natural wipe without the need for studio effects.

In order to photograph such transitions in the field, the photographer must already be thinking like an editor as he or she shoots. "Create a mental bank account of what you have shot and what you need to shoot," advises TV documentary producer Mary McCormick Busse.[3]

SCREEN DIRECTION

In real life, subjects move in predictable directions. Yet on many versions of the nightly news, subjects can be seen to swap directions on the television screen as though they were Ping-Pong balls. The rule of thumb regarding screen direction is to keep the subject moving in one consistent direction—either screen right or screen left. Otherwise, viewers are left confused and consciously or subconsciously frustrated.

The underlying cause of illogical changes in screen direction begins in the field, when photographers unwittingly "cross the axis line" to produce shots in which a subject first faces one direction on the screen, then in the next shot is shown to face the opposite direction. To envision the phenomenon, ask two people to face one another while you photograph them. In the camera viewfinder, the person on your left (subject A) will face screen right and the person on your right (subject B) will face screen left. Now, go to the opposite side of the two individuals, again viewing the shot through the camera viewfinder. This time subject A will face screen left; subject B will face screen right. The result is called a **false reverse.**

How to Avoid the False Reverse

The only way to avoid the false reverse is to avoid crossing the **axis line** (Figure 2.11). When the first or primary shot is made of a subject in the field, an axis line is established. One form of axis line is an imaginary straight line projected from the tip of the camera lens through the center of the subject and beyond. Some photographers use the term *vector line*, a similar concept used to describe the compass direction along which planes and ships move. Still other photographers simply call the axis line "the line." After the first or primary shot is taken, the photographer must commit to shoot on one side of the line or the other, but not both. If shots are taken on both sides of the line, the result will inevitably be a false reverse in the action.

Another form of axis line occurs when the action plays out parallel to the camera, for example, at a football game. The photographer can shoot on one side of the line or the other, but never on both sides of the line (Figure 2.12).

Conflicts in screen direction can be eliminated in the field if the photographer simply remembers to keep the subject facing the same direction in the viewfinder at all times. If a freight train is moving screen left in the first shot, the train must continue to move screen left in all the other shots. The problem is more difficult to correct at the edit bench, but the editor can at least soften the harsh effects of action that instantly reverses on itself.

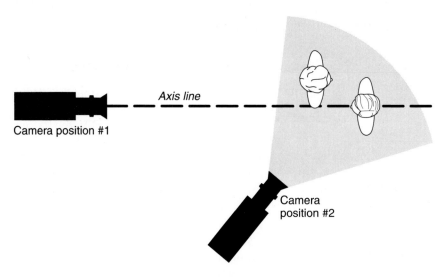

FIGURE 2.11 Eliminate false reverses in the subject's screen direction by remembering to establish an axis line, then consciously shooting only on one side of that line, not both.

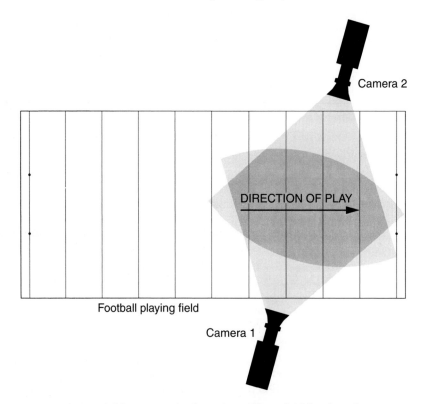

FIGURE 2.12 A false reverse in the action will result if the shots from camera positions on both sides of an axis line are spliced back to back. Shots made from camera 1 will produce action that progresses from screen left to screen right. Shots from camera 2 will produce action that moves screen right to screen left.

How to Eliminate the False Reverse at the Edit Bench

The most obvious solution to a false reverse is the cutaway. A shot of the football player running screen right can be followed by a shot of the crowd or a referee, preferably looking somewhat toward the camera rather than obviously right or left, followed by a cut to the player running screen left. Another device to neutralize the false reverse is a **head-on shot** of the action coming straight toward camera or a **negative-action shot** of the subject moving away from camera. Yet another device is to continue photographing the shot as the camera moves across the axis line, taking the audience with it. If such a shot is unavailable, an optical effect such as a dissolve or wipe can be used.

VARY CAMERA ANGLES

Variations in camera angle give the photographer a way to enhance visual interest from one shot to the next and are essential to help maintain viewer interest. Viewers will soon feel a monotonous sameness in the photography if every shot is taken from a flat, straight-on angle, with the camera at the same unvarying height from the ground. In every shot, then, work the camera to find angles that are exactly right, even if you must climb a tree or lie on the ground. "But if you see audience members tilting their heads to see your picture, it's a pretty good indication your angle didn't work," says Dick Hoff, Eastman Kodak representative.[4]

"When you're shooting down the railroad tracks, don't just stand and shoot. Put the camera down low, on the rail. That way you build in some foreground interest and a more dramatic angle," says WCVB photojournalist John Premack. "Or when you're shooting down a supermarket aisle, move over against one side of the aisle, close to the shelf, and note the increase in visual impact."[5]

Photograph People at Eye Level

The rule of thumb is to photograph people at eye level, and to show both eyes. When you photograph children, lower the camera so that it looks straight into their eyes. Similarly, photograph adults straight on, not looking up or down at them with the camera unless, of course, you want to achieve a particular psychological impact (Figure 2.13).

ANGLES PROVIDE PSYCHOLOGICAL IMPACT

For less static video, vary camera height so the camera is not the same distance from the ground in all shots. Variations in camera angle also help you enhance visual interest from one shot to the next. Just as important, camera angle gives the photographer a way to influence the viewer's psychological response to subjects. **High-angle shots,** taken with the camera high and looking down at the subject, tend to diminish the subject. Viewers may even feel a sense of superiority when they view high-angle shots. The effect is similar to the relationship that occurs when one person stands and talks to a person who remains sitting. The person who stands maintains a psychological dominance.

FIGURE 2.13   The angle of the camera, whether high or low, affects how viewers perceive the subject. In the picture on the left, emphasis is on the top of the subject's head because the camera was allowed to remain high and look down at the subject. A more desirable composition (right) is to photograph the subject at eye level.

Such is the situation when the supervisor stands but the employee is told to sit, or in an adult—child relationship in which the adult dominates simply by virtue of his or her greater height.

Low-angle shots, taken with the camera low to the ground and looking up at the subject, make the subject more dominant and may even destroy the viewer's sense of control or superiority. Low-angle shots of an earth mover on a highway project can make the machine seem overwhelmingly powerful and destructive, whereas a high-angle shot taken from atop a nearby hill can make the same earth mover pale to insignificance against the enormity of the surrounding terrain.

Be on guard to avoid unnecessarily flat, straight-on angles. Such angles sometimes work, but sometimes do not. Most often, they produce a sense of monotony.

CONTRAST AND COMPARISON

Visual sameness is the equivalent of dullness. In most areas of life, including visual communication, we seek variation. Just as a meal made up of four bowls of potatoes and gravy lacks interest, so does a story with four back-to-back shots of the elderly at a nursing home. Do show us the faces of the elderly, but show us also the unwrinkled youth and vitality of the children who come to visit or photographs of the elderly when they were young. If your story is about the desert, try occasionally to show viewers something cool and green or perhaps simply the drops of water that slide down a bottle of beer as moisture condenses in the heat. In all stories, contrast and comparison is a powerful device to help give your subject additional screen presence.

COMPOSITION

Photography is another way of seeing, and in television news it is a way of seeing on behalf of others. **Composition,** or the placement and emphasis of visual elements on the screen, lets the photographer control what viewers see and helps clarify the messages to be communicated. In motion picture photography, composition may be less noticeable to viewers because no shot stands by itself or communicates an entire story as it does so often in still photography. In motion picture photography, only when all the shots have played out is the story complete.

Rules of Composition

Balance, harmony, depth, scale, and perspective are virtues to be preserved in all photography, and the rules of composition that have served artists over the centuries remain valid for the photojournalist. Opportunities to improve mastery in the classic techniques of artistic composition are abundantly available for photographers through books, classes, and seminars. This section therefore addresses primarily those approaches to composition that are of most immediate consequence in enhancing the photography of television news stories.

Television Is a Horizontal Format. Everything on television happens either within a 4 × 3 horizontal format, or in the case of **high definition television (HDTV),** in a 16 × 9 horizontal format (Figure 2.14). The screen most of us grew up watching is four parts wide, three parts high, while the HDTV screen is 5.33 parts wide, three parts high, a fact of life that even aficionados of the vertical format must live with. In television photography, there is no possibility of turning the camera sideways to record a

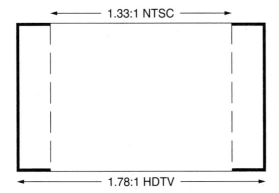

FIGURE 2.14 HDTV, which has a width-to-height ratio of 1.78:1, extends the width of the normal NTSC television screen, which has a width-to-height ratio of 1.33:1.

vertical shot, unless, of course, the photographer is willing to place the TV set on end in order to view the result. While the horizontal-only format may require some adjustment, for most photographers it is not necessarily limiting because the entire horizontal field needn't be used all the time.

The Rule of Thirds

The **rule of thirds** offers a way to improve the composition of individual scenes (Figure 2.15), especially when composing for the 4 × 3 format. Mentally divide the viewfinder into thirds both horizontally and vertically. Place subjects or interest-catching features in the scenes at one of the points where the lines intersect.

A water-skier moving screen left to screen right, for example, might be placed on the imaginary line identified by numbers 1 and 2. This composition gives the skier room to move into the frame. A man petting a dog might be placed at intersection 2 with the dog at intersection 3. A speaker addressing a large crowd might be placed at intersection 1 with the crowd filling the remainder of the screen.

Using the same approach you can place horizon lines either on the line identified by numbers 1 and 2, and thereby emphasize the foreground, or on the line identified by numbers 3 and 4, and thereby emphasize the sky or background. In all cases the composition will be less static and more interesting than if action is consistently parked in dead center of the frame.

Show Viewers What You Want Them to See.   One of the most freeing rules of composition is to show viewers only what you want them to see. Although the mind concentrates on what it wants to see and filters out the rest, the camera records everything before it, so show the camera only what you want viewers to see. "Study the viewfinder just as if you are at home watching the scene on television," advises KCNC photojournalist Gary Croshaw, "and never let anything on the screen take you by surprise."[6]

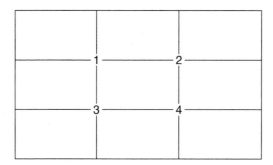

FIGURE 2.15   The camera viewfinder, divided into imaginary lines, permits composition of scenes according to the rule of thirds.

On Every Shot, Think before You Shoot. Ask yourself, as you peer into the viewfinder, "Is this important?" "Is this relevant?" If the answer is yes, push the button.

Elevate the Ordinary. "Don't turn on the camera unless what you see in the viewfinder makes you say 'wow,' or otherwise impresses you with its impact," advises photojournalist John Premack.[7] Premack's advice helps explain the ability of some photographers to make the mundane seem extraordinary and memorable. In the hands of the skilled photographer, an ordinary hen's egg or ballpoint pen can be rendered as an object of great beauty. Regardless of the subject matter, creative vision coupled with the skilled use of light, shape, form, and tone make possible unexpectedly forceful renderings of even mundane objects.

Screen Space. In shots with action, screen space and visual balance change constantly as subjects move about in the frame. To maintain a visual treatment that is relatively transparent and unnoticeable to home viewers, some vigilance is necessary to help maintain acceptable composition.

- Make good use of the entire screen when composing a shot. Fill the screen with important subject matter.
- Avoid tilted horizon lines. Use the leveling bubble on the tripod or line up the camera viewfinder with a horizontal line to be certain the camera is level.
- Avoid cutting the screen exactly in half with the horizon line.
- Remember that movement or bright lights in background pull the viewer's eye away from the subject. Eliminate these distractions from the frame whenever possible.
- If the background is distracting, move the subject or the camera if possible; otherwise, throw the background out of focus by changing the focal length and focus point of your lens or by reducing light so you can shoot at a wider aperture and thereby reduce depth of field.
- Avoid placing the speaker's face dead center in the frame when shooting sound bites. Place the speaker's eyes above the center of the frame and provide "looking room" within the frame. Also leave room at the bottom of the shot for superimpositions of the speaker's name.
- When doing over-the-shoulder shots, avoid filling the frame with the back of the person's head.
- Composition can be unconsciously disturbing if the subject appears to be moving or looking out of frame instead of into frame. As a rule of thumb, action moving frame right should be positioned in the left third of the frame, or at least slightly to the left of center, and vice versa. This leaves space for the subject to move into.
- Avoid big gaps of space between people, such as in interview settings. If wide spaces exist, either recompose the shot by physically moving the camera or, if ethically warranted, by repositioning the subjects themselves. Normally, people can position themselves closer together on screen than would be customary in real life.

- Photograph individuals in full facial shots that show both eyes, rather than in profile shots that show one eye and one ear. In real life we normally see eyes in pairs but are only subconsciously aware of ears. Side profile shots incorrectly emphasize the ear.
- Create the illusion of depth in your photography by including foreground interest in the shot and by photographing shots that contain two or more planes of focus for the subject to pass in front of and behind.
- Maintain crisp focus on your subject.

Composing for HDTV[8]

Composing for any format, TV, theatrical, or Cinemascope, has always been subjective. Composing for HDTV is no different. However, there are some aesthetic and practical points to consider:

- Paint to fill your canvas. This is most problematic. With so much more room on the left and right edges, you'll want to place people and interesting backround edge-to-edge in your frame. Unfortunately, we find ourselves in the same position that theatrical producers have found themselves in for years: With so many people watching on conventional 1.33:1 screens—do you compose for the wide screen and let them suffer the impairment of losing the edges? Or do you compose for the predominant 1.33:1 format and rob consumers who bought wide-screen TVs of the wide-screen capabilities they paid for? Until a majority of households have the new 1.78:1 TVs, many news producers will opt for protecting the older 1.33:1 aspect ratio.
- On the practical side, bear in mind that if a 30 mm lens approximates a normal field of view for conventional U.S. television sets, then a 55 mm lens will more closely approximate the normal field of view for those watching on HDTV. If you're seeing too much of the background around the edges, tighten up!
- Use care in interview situations where the interviewer is off-screen. With such a wide frame to work with, the interviewee may appear to be looking off into space if the eyeline is too far left or right of the center of the frame. Place the interviewer almost directly behind the camera to help avoid this disturbing appearance.

■ ■ ■ ■ ■ ▬▬▬▬▬▬▬▬▬▬▬▬▬▬▬▬▬▬▬▬▬▬▬▬▬▬▬▬▬▬▬▬▬▬▬

HIGH DEFINITION TELEVISION

NTSC VS. HDTV

Powerful visual storytelling demands realism. The more lifelike the on-screen portrayal, the more viewers feel as if they're experiencing the story environment or event. For a moment, they can inhabit another place, another time, have a new experience, even feel as if they're living someone else's life.

Imagine, then, the gift of images so lifelike you can almost reach through the screen and dip water from a lagoon, or feel the rough texture of an alligator sunning itself on the river bank, or perhaps visit a tornado-ravaged neighborhood to experience nature's fury first hand.

NTSC Gives Way to HDTV

High definition television (HDTV) makes such realism possible. Since the first regular television broadcasts in the United States, viewers could watch only a medium-resolution image of 525 lines, the National Television System Committee (NTSC) standard that employs the familiar 4 × 3 (1.33:1) aspect ratio.

Today the world has begun to abandon such old-style analog technology in favor of digital video, moving ever closer to lifelike images comprised of from 740 to 1,080 horizontal lines of video, based on how networks, local stations, and cable companies transmit their images, as well as the viewer's choice of converters, tuners, computers, video projectors, and television screens. Moreover, HDTV abandons the old 4 × 3 format in favor of wide-screen images, using a 16 × 9 (1.78:1) aspect ratio similar to motion picture theater screens. At its best, HDTV provides picture resolution up to three times sharper than NTSC video, along with six channels of audio.

Forces of Change

The NTSC analog waveband gobbles electromagnetic spectrum in fearsome amounts. HDTV, a more efficient digital technology, leaves the analog spectrum available for the telecommunications industry, which wants it for high-tech, higher bandwidth mobile video phones and related technology. As NTSC transmissions gradually end, the electromagnetic spectrum they once occupied can be reassigned and resold.

Transition

Congress originally set a 2006 deadline for broadcasters to move from NTSC to HDTV. Commercial HDTV broadcasts began in the top U.S. markets in November 1998 (New York, Los Angeles, Chicago, Philadelphia, Atlanta, Boston, Detroit, Dallas-Ft. Worth, San Francisco, and Washington, DC).

From the beginning, though, those affected wanted more time to implement the new standard. The switchover, they said, would financially impact manufacturers and broadcasters, consumers, electronic component manufacturers, retailers, and video producers. The Federal Communications Commission (FCC) later ruled the 2006 transition date could be extended under certain conditions. The most important exception occurs when fewer than 85 percent of viewers in a given area can receive and display digital broadcasts. The ruling says they must have either an HDTV tuner that receives broadcast digital signals, or a set-top box that converts the digital broadcast for viewing on analog television sets. The 85 percent requirement thus is a better indicator of when the switch will occur in any given market.[9]

The Implications

Rarely does the human species adopt a lesser standard once exposed to something better, whether the advance be in art, technology, or design. Wide-screen news, in stereo, is on its way to a set near you. In some markets, it's already a reality. More realistic images are the most obvious reward. "Seeing any politically charged location in High Definition is a completely different experience than traditional TV," said HDNet Chairman Mark Cuban. "In traditional TV, they try to give a little flavor, mainly through verbal description. With High Definition, the camera can do what it excels in. A burned-out truck or a mortar shell on the ground—you see it. Someone in pain, you see it. HDTV coverage sets a new standard for immersing the audience in pictures and stories that increasingly convey to viewers the raw, visceral experience of the conflict."[10] And the transmission of experience, what it was like to be there, results in another payoff. Through HDTV, viewers can become more involved in meaningful stories than ever before in the history of television.

Allow for TV Cutoff.   Whenever you compose a shot in the camera viewfinder, allow for **TV cutoff.** Often, home screens will clip off the edges of the transmitted image. In close-ups, if composition is too tight, home screens may even clip off the top of a person's head. To avoid TV cutoff problems, some camera viewfinders are manufactured to show less of the image than is being recorded. If the viewfinder does show the entire picture being recorded, then compose shots that are slightly looser than normal.

Trust Your Instincts.   The world's libraries are filled with advice for developing artists and photographers on how to become more artistically sensitive and proficient. No one must wait to be taught these things, of course. Often the best approach is to move ahead, experimenting with new approaches, adopting what works for you and discarding what doesn't. Rather than doubt yourself too often throughout this process, learn to trust your instincts. And learn to listen to yourself before you listen to any other critic. No one knows more about your ability than you do.

SUMMARY

Visual grammar comprises the rules that govern the visual reconstruction of events, including both the raw material shot and recorded in the field and the process of editing the material for broadcast. In television, the basic unit of expression is the shot. A matched-action sequence of long, medium, and close shots can be linked to convey a message.

Shots are further defined according to camera movement and function. Shots that incorporate camera movement include the pan, tilt, dolly, tracking, trucking, and aerial shots. Shots classified according to their function include the establishing shot, insert, point of view, reaction, reverse-angle, and master shots.

Matched-action sequences can be created at the edit console only if the photographer has shot overlapping action in the field. In other words, identical action must be present in at least two shots. If overlapping action cannot be photographed, or if action must be compressed, then unnatural jumps in the action—jump cuts—can be avoided through the use of cutaways or optical effects.

Transition shots allow the editor to create transitions from one time, location, or subject to the next within a story. Angles and composition further impact the treatment of subject matter and how viewers will react to the subject.

Always, the goal is to create a visual reconstruction of events so compelling and involving that viewers are unaware of technique.

DISCUSSION

1. Explain the meaning of the term "visual grammar."

2. List the three basic shots in motion picture photography and describe their functions.

3. Explain how the three basic shots can be joined to achieve a sense of continuity or consecutiveness in a scene.

4. What considerations help determine when a shot or the image size of a subject should be changed in a visual story?

5. Explain why it is important in film and television to have action in virtually every scene.

6. List and define the various shot categories, describing each shot according to its function. Be certain to differentiate between the pan and the moving shots.

7. Describe when an insert shot might also serve as a reaction shot.

8. Can a reaction shot ever serve simultaneously as a point of view shot? If your answer is yes, provide an example. If your answer is no, explain why not.

9. Provide an example of a master shot and list six possible related pickup or cut-in shots.

10. Explain the essential distinction between matched action and overlapping action.

11. Explain how jump cuts can be eliminated (a) when shooting a scene and (b) when editing a scene.

12. Describe the functions of the transition or reveal shot, and give an example as part of your discussion.

13. How can the photographer avoid the false reverse (a) when shooting action and (b) at the edit bench?

14. Define the psychological impact of variations in camera angle as a function of camera height in relation to the subject.

15. What unique considerations of composition affect television photography?

E X E R C I S E S

1. Shoot a simple sequence of a subject that is under your control, using a long shot, medium shot, and close-up.

2. Shoot the same sequence, but this time purposefully cross the axis line so that you create a false reverse in the action.

3. Purposefully photograph two shots that would result in a jump cut if edited together and a related cutaway. First, edit together the two shots to produce a jump cut, then edit them so that they are separated by the cutaway. View and analyze the result.

4. Make two shots of an action plus a generic cutaway that can be used to divert the audience's attention from the main subject. Now shoot a motivated cutaway that also diverts the audience's attention but contributes useful new information to your story.

5. Pan a static subject, then introduce a moving subject, such as a person who walks in front of your subject, and follow the moving subject with the camera as a way to motivate the pan. Compare the result.

6. Shoot a master shot with at least six related pickup or cut-in shots.

7. Shoot a sequence in which the subject progresses through space, this time allowing the action to move into-frame, out-of-frame.

8. Shoot a matched-action sequence that contains an insert shot. Be certain each shot has overlapping action so that action can be matched at the editing bench.

9. Shoot a matched-action sequence that contains action-reaction shots.

10. Shoot a matched-action sequence that contains a point of view shot.

11. Find a subject that is not under your control and shoot a matched-action sequence. Remember to anticipate the action rather than to react to it.

12. Shoot a story in which you can move from one time, location, or subject to the next. Shoot at least three transition or reveal shots that can be used to move the story to the next time or location.

13. Experiment with camera angle on a subject and note the variations in psychological impact that result.

14. Practice picture composition based on the rule of thirds. Experiment with subject placement within the scene by mentally dividing the viewfinder into thirds both horizontally and vertically and placing subjects at the points where the lines intersect.

15. Learn to critically inspect all elements within the viewfinder. Practice consciously composing scenes so that you show viewers only what you want them to see.

16. Practice composing a shot with two people in an interview situation until the shot is pleasing and well balanced and good enough to be used on television.

17. Find a routine subject and photograph it in a new way. As an example, you might show a knife from a Halloween pumpkin's point of view or a fast-food restaurant from a transient's point of view.

NOTES

1. Edward Dmytryk, *On Film Editing* (Stoneham, MA: Focal Press, 1984), 65.

2. "Michael Kahn: Film Editor at the Top," *Moving Image*, 1 (September/October 1981), 46–47.

3. Mary McCormick Busse, "The Beginning, Middle and End: Continuity," *The TV Storyteller* (Durham, NC: National Press Photographers Association, 1985), 4.

4. Dick Hoff, "Composition," a presentation at the NPPA TV News-Video Workshop, Norman, OK, 17 March 1986.

5. John Premack, comments to critique group, NPPA TV News-Video Workshop, Norman, OK, 11 April 1984.

6. Comments to journalism class, Colorado State University, Fort Collins, 11 April 1995.

7. John Premack, "Avoiding Mistakes," a presentation at the NPPA TV News-Video Workshop, Norman, OK, 14 March 1994.

8. Written by Kirk Bloom, Los Angeles, CA, September 1998.

9. A. Stillwell, FCC, from a private interview, 26 March 2002, cited in "HDTV Implementation: Why 2006 Is Unrealistic," by Natalie Chin, Jennifer Lee, Chris Pietila, William Shappell. A Capstone paper submitted as partial fulfillment of the requirements for the degree of Masters in Interdisciplinary Telecommunications at the University of Colorado, Boulder, 9 May 2002.

10. Debra Kaufman, "HDNet Turns To Hard News," www.digitaltelevision.com/2002/June/feature2.shtml (Accessed 27 May 2003).

CHAPTER THREE

VIDEO EDITING
The Invisible Art

Few viewers ever watch newscasts for the editing, and just as certainly the editor's name on a film rarely sells tickets at the movie theatre. Because true art conceals art, the best editing is invisible. People see the footage, but not how beautifully put together it is.[1] Those who have never edited may think of editing as a mere joining of scenes, or as an "elimination of the bad parts," but before you adopt a point of view about editing and its contribution to the storytelling process, listen for a moment to perspectives from two working professionals. Their characterizations of editing are universally venerable, formed in the knowledge that unless you understand editing you can't communicate in a visual medium; you can't preplan the story in your mind; you can't shoot raw footage that tells a story. "Through editing, interest is held. A story is told," says John Premack, chief photographer at WCVB-TV.[2]

Glenn Farr, who received an Academy Award for his editing of the motion picture *The Right Stuff*, also speaks of the editor's critical role in the storytelling process. "The editing of any story is the final element of an important process," says Farr. "Photographers and reporters need to understand this importance as much as editors need to know what good photography and writing can do to help shape the idea being communicated."[3]

TOWARD A PHILOSOPHY OF EDITING

Editing is so important to the visual storytelling process because it duplicates the manner in which the *mind* sees. We all "edit" reality with our eyes and with our minds. The composite understanding of the imagery we store in our mind's eye becomes our reality and contributes to our definitions of experience. The art of editing lies therefore in creating both illusion and new realities, new relationships, and in stimulating and sometimes controlling emotional responses (Figure 3.1).

EVERYONE IN TELEVISION NEWS IS AN EDITOR

If the goal of television news is to tell a story that captures a moment and communicates a sense of experience, then everyone—reporter, photographer, writer, narrator—is an editor. This is so because only through editing can one emphasize, reveal, pace,

FIGURE 3.1   The picture and sound editing process allows journalists to emphasize, reveal, pace, and structure the various elements that make up a television news story.

structure, guide, tantalize, juxtapose, select, ignore, and enhance the story and the storytelling process.

THE NATURE OF EDITING

Editing, then, begins not at the final stage of the storytelling process but rather at the beginning. Editing, in its simplest definition, is selection, arrangement, timing, and presentation.[4] The shots and sounds, their timing and arrangement, and their framing and composition, should become part of everyone's thinking the moment a story is identified.

The photographer's choice of shots and composition is one form of editorial *selection*. Only through selection is emphasis possible. The order in which the shots appear is a form of *editorial arrangement*. Shot length is a form of editorial timing, a way to control dramatic tension through quick cutting or a more relaxed mood that lets the eye wander across the screen until the heart and the mind are satiated. Even the photographer's and reporter's preplanning for matched action and for transitions in subject matter and through time and space will determine whether *presentation* is harsh and noticeable or smooth and seamless.

Ultimately, only when reporting, writing, photography, and editing are invisible to the audience can a story communicate a sense of experience and realism. And only when everybody's an editor can such goals be realized.

THE CUT

In television, every scene has a relation to at least two other scenes—the scene before it and the scene that follows it. For the most part, these scenes are tied to one another by the cut, a deceptively simple joining of one scene to the other. The well-made cut is deceptive because it is virtually transparent.

In effect the cut is a handoff, a way of transferring attention from one image to another. In similar fashion, whenever we observe happenings in the real world, the mind directs the eye's attention from one image to another. We glance here, we glance there. The camera becomes the audience's eyes, free to move through time and space from one point of view to another.

Transferring that principle to the television screen, the editor can create tremendous viewer participation. Because the editor can cut from any image to any other, and can direct the eye's attention to any detail or happening, the viewer can be given absolute freedom of movement and virtually unlimited variations in perspective. From bird's-eye view to intimate close-up, the audience is allowed to inhabit a limitless world of heightened realism and expanded emotion. Suddenly, viewers are free to see events from different angles in rapid sequence, an ability completely outside the range of human experience.

EVERY CUT NEEDS A REASON

Because cuts direct the eye's attention and transfer attention from one image to the next, it follows that they must be made purposefully. This is why you would not cut two medium shots of the same subject back-to-back or two close-ups or two long shots back-to-back. If you wish to change shots, do it for a reason, and do it obviously.

CHOOSING EDIT POINTS

The point at which one shot is surrendered and a new shot begins is called the **edit point.** Every shot that contains action has an ideal moment when it should begin and another ideal moment when it should end. If you will "listen" to the action and observe it closely, the action itself will suggest where the cuts should be made. Suppose that we have two shots: (1) a college student approaching a mailbox and depositing a letter, and (2) a close-up shot of the mailbox in which the student's hand enters frame and we see that the letter being stuffed into the slot is addressed to "Navy Recruiter."

The scene could be edited in as many ways as there are editors, yet there is only one ideal edit point. For the sake of discussion, consider cutting from scene 1 at that point where the audience would most likely want to see a closer shot of the letter.

You could cut out of shot 1 just as the student approaches the mailbox and her body language indicates that she is about to post the letter (letting her arm motion determine the edit point), then cut to the close shot in which we see action that has already begun in scene 1 continue smoothly and conclude in scene 2.

You also could cut the action out-of-frame/into-frame. In this approach the student would exit scene 1, followed by a cut to scene 2 (close shot of the mailbox), and the shot would hold momentarily until the student's hand came into frame. This technique is perhaps less desirable because there would be little motivation to cut from the shot of a student walking down the sidewalk to a static shot of the mailbox. In effect, the editor would be saying, "Here's a shot of a student about to mail a letter. Now let's cut to a shot of the mailbox and wait for her to catch up with us."

THERE CAN BE NO MATCHED ACTION WITHOUT OVERLAPPING ACTION

When editing shots from a single-camera setup, it is possible for the editor to produce **matched action** on the screen only if the photographer in the field has shot **overlapping action.** Overlapping action means simply that an identical action must be present in at least two shots. If, for example, in a long shot a swimmer dives into a swimming pool and presently surfaces near the pool's edge, a close shot might show the same swimmer surfacing after the dive. Because the swimmer can be seen to surface in both the long shot and the close shot, the action in the two is said to be overlapping. The editor can produce matched action between the two shots by cutting out of the long shot at a point in the action that is identical to the continuation of the action in the close shot.

EDITING ACTION THAT WAS UNDER THE PHOTOGRAPHER'S CONTROL

Overlapping action can be photographed in one of two ways. If action is under the photographer's control, the subject can be asked to repeat a particular action, and inanimate objects (such as oscillating fans and automatic water sprinklers) can be made to repeat action while matched-action sequences are photographed. In the example above, a photographer could ask the swimmer to dive into the pool in a long shot, then ask the swimmer to dive a second time and surface within a designated area for the close shot. Just as simply, a subject can be asked to sign her first name on a credit card receipt in a long shot, then sign her last name while the photographer takes a close shot of the woman's hand writing her signature.

CUTTING ON ACTION OR AT REST

Whether the action is a fistfight or a horse race, if the edits or cuts (or shot changes) occur while the action progresses, the technique is called **cutting on action.** If the edits occur at a moment in which the action on the screen has stopped, the technique is called **cutting at rest.** Cuts might be made with the action "at rest," for example, in a three-shot sequence of a woman being served coffee at a resort hotel. In the first shot the waiter would enter frame and place coffee before the woman. The coffee cup is at rest. In the next shot, the camera might cut to a close shot of the same coffee cup (still at rest), then to a shot of the woman's face as she looks at the cup.

Even a fistfight can be cut at rest if the cuts are made at that moment when the fighter's arm is fully extended during a punch or when a scene change is made from a shot of a fighter who takes a hard blow to the face and collapses, to a shot of the fighter lying unconscious on the floor.

The decision whether to cut on action or at rest lies with the editor. Generally, action scenes should be cut on action if the editor wishes to sustain pace and provide fluid story development and continuity. If the subject matter should be treated more deliberately and at a slower pace, cutting at rest may be appropriate. Here, the axiom that "performance follows content" holds true. Let content dictate the proper treatment.

Regardless of the choice you make, the action must be edited so that it flows smoothly and effortlessly across the cuts without the editor's work calling attention to itself. The editing will be strongest if it is as seamless and transparent as when we look at an event with our own eyes, unaware even of the process by which we are observing it. For this reason, avoid cutting out of a moving pan, tilt, or zoom to the middle of another zoom, pan, or other shot that contains artificial camera movement. If you must edit such shots together, consider linking them by a dissolve, fade-in or fade-out, or similar optical effect to soften the edit.

INTO-FRAME/OUT-OF-FRAME ACTION

In cutting matched action, most editors try not to let a continuing action "fall out of the splice" at shot changes. In other words, they cut from an outgoing scene while the subject is still visible in frame, then cut to the incoming scene at a point where the subject has obviously entered frame. If the action disappears from view at splice lines, pace will drop and viewers may wonder why the subject momentarily disappeared. Exceptions occur frequently, however. Photographers may be forced to maintain continuity when shooting uncontrolled action by shooting into-frame/out-of-frame action. In such cases they begin to shoot before the subject enters frame and continue to shoot after the subject has exited frame. Once the subject has left frame, the editor can cut to virtually any new scene without a jump. Cutting into-frame/out-of-frame action also is useful to create a transition from one time or locale to the next or even to move a subject through time or space, because the editor can cut from an empty frame to anything else.

JUMP CUTS *2 def similar shots*

Jump cuts in action occur when action jumps unnaturally forward or backward in time. If at one instant the speaker at an outdoor rally is seen to be shielded by an umbrella, but in the next shot an instant later the umbrella is nowhere to be seen, a jump cut has occurred. Technically, a jump cut is an action that could not occur in real life. The action "jumps," as, for example, a woman who has a red dress in shot 1, yellow dress in shot 2; or a dog with a collar around its neck in shot 1, but no collar around its neck in shot 2.

POP CUTS

Be vigilant not to confuse the jump cut with the **pop cut.** They're different animals. Pop cuts occur whenever you edit together two or more shots that were photographed along the same axis line, even if the action is perfectly matched. Maybe the photographer first photographed a long shot, then zoomed in for a medium shot, and then a close-up.

If the camera remained on the same axis line, shooting down the same straight line toward the subject, then a pop cut will occur. The photographer could physically move the camera closer to the subject for each successive shot, but if the camera remains on the same axis line, a pop cut results.

The solution is to "shoot and move" while taking shots in the field. For each new shot, move the camera so as to establish a *new* axis line. When you shoot and move, matched-action edits together more naturally. The result is smooth, seamless, distraction-free matched action.

THE CUTAWAY

The most commonly used device to eliminate jump cuts is the **cutaway,** a shot of some part of the peripheral action that diverts the viewer's eye for a moment so that when the eye returns to the main action, the jump will be less obvious. In the case of the speaker with the umbrella, a cutaway shot of people in the crowd could be inserted just prior to the shot of the speaker with no umbrella. In the case of the dog with a collar around its neck in shot 1, a cutaway of a fire hydrant or of a smiling child at the park could be inserted just before shot 2 of the same dog with no collar around its neck. Besides the use of cutaways, such optical effects as dissolves and wipes can be used to eliminate the jump cut.

DEVICES TO COMPRESS TIME
AND ADVANCE THE ACTION

Cutaways also allow the editor to condense time. In fact, any shot that momentarily diverts audience attention lets the editor cut back to the main action at a moment further ahead in time than could be the case in real life. The **insert shot** is an example. Unlike the cutaway, which diverts audience attention from the main subject, the insert provides the audience with close-up, essential detail about some part of the main action. At a press conference that continues in real time for nearly a half hour, for example, a politician announces he will end his candidacy for office. In the edited report, we see the politician announce his decision (the statement is edited from a point early in the news conference), followed by a close-up insert shot of the candidate. In the insert shot a reporter asks, off camera, whether the candidate wishes to comment on published reports that he has been unfaithful to his wife, and the candidate replies "No comment."

The insert is followed by a final shot in which the candidate turns and leaves the press conference. With the help of an insert shot, a half-hour press conference has been depicted in just three shots totaling thirty seconds or less.

Two other shots, the reaction shot and the point of view shot, can be used in similar fashion. In the **reaction shot,** the subject reacts to something that has just happened in the previous shot: In a medium shot a doctor gives a child a flu vaccination; the reaction shot shows the child's stoic response to the pain.

In the **point of view** shot, the subject sees or reacts to something off screen, and we see the thing from the subject's point of view. For example, shot 1 shows a woman sitting in an airport waiting lounge as she looks down at her wristwatch; shot 2 provides a close-up of the wristwatch from the woman's point of view. From that point, the editor can advance the action by cutting to another shot of the woman taken some minutes later and thereby condense time. Note that in this example, the point of view shot also functions as an insert shot.

ADVANCE THE ACTION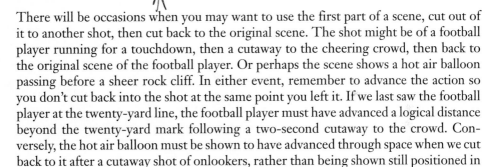

There will be occasions when you may want to use the first part of a scene, cut out of it to another shot, then cut back to the original scene. The shot might be of a football player running for a touchdown, then a cutaway to the cheering crowd, then back to the original scene of the football player. Or perhaps the scene shows a hot air balloon passing before a sheer rock cliff. In either event, remember to advance the action so you don't cut back into the shot at the same point you left it. If we last saw the football player at the twenty-yard line, the football player must have advanced a logical distance beyond the twenty-yard mark following a two-second cutaway to the crowd. Conversely, the hot air balloon must be shown to have advanced through space when we cut back to it after a cutaway shot of onlookers, rather than being shown still positioned in front of the same reference point against the rock cliff.

The best rule of thumb in such cases is to advance the action the same amount of time as the cutaway remains on screen. If the cutaway is left on screen for two seconds, an equal length of footage should be eliminated from the primary scene before the action is resumed (Figure 3.2). Occasionally, it is possible to go beyond this rule of thumb by advancing the action a logical distance. In other words, you can advance the action further than it might have gone in real life, provided the progression of the object through time and space appears natural and logical.

PARALLEL CUTTING

If neither overlapping action nor appropriate cutaways or other shots are available in the raw field tape, at least the illusion of matched action can sometimes be accomplished through **parallel cutting,** or intercutting between separate but developing actions.

FIGURE 3.2   Proper pacing and screen logic result when the editor cuts shots to reflect a logical progression in the action. In this example, the editor has used the first part of a shot (top left), cut to a shot of the woman (top right), then cut back to the original scene at a point about two seconds beyond where audiences last saw the action (bottom).

Parallel cutting was routinely employed in early westerns as the screen cut back and forth between an out-of-control stage coach and bandits in hot pursuit.

Today, the technique can be just as effectively used in television news in situations where overlapping action is difficult or impossible to photograph, for example, a hostage situation in which little matched-action footage is available. In this case, footage that may be little more than a series of "grab shots" (shots taken on the run as action unfolds before the camera) can be intercut to first show police officers surrounding the building where hostages are held, to shots of efforts to evacuate nearby citizens from the neighborhood. This back-and-forth cutting as the action progresses can help impose a continuity otherwise unavailable.

SHOT ORDER IMPACTS THE ILLUSION OF CONTINUITY

Even acceptably edited matched action sometimes just looks wrong, even when a close, frame-by-frame inspection of the edit shows the action to be perfectly matched. In this case the rule is "If it doesn't look right, it isn't right." If the eye just doesn't accept the match, you have a problem.

One solution is to follow the advice of Seattle photojournalist Phil Sturholm. "If you have a problem matching your action perfectly, edit the action from a close-up to a long shot rather than a long shot to a close-up," says Sturholm. "The long shot has so many things coming at you it's hard to see if something doesn't match exactly."[5]

CONTENT DICTATES PACE

Broadcast journalists are often heard to say that, in television news, pace is everything. The truism means simply that audiences will lose interest if story development is too plodding, dull, boring, or predictable. While there are few guidelines about what constitutes acceptable pace, most video editors and virtually all members of the audience instinctively know it when they see it. Simply put, a story's pace either feels right, or it doesn't.

The key to good pacing is to recognize that content dictates pace. Slow does not necessarily mean dull. Fast does not necessarily mean interesting. Good editors listen to their feelings and let the story suggest its own pace. Depending on the photographer's commitment and the story's point of view, a motorcycle hill-climbing event may be told better either in a series of slow-motion shots that play out on the screen over long seconds or in a flurry of action, colors, and sounds that hit the screen with the staccato beat of machine-gun fire. Only visual content and story commitment can determine which treatment will be more effective.

CUTTING TO CONDENSE TIME

One of the natural consequences of editing is to convert real time to **filmic time.** In television news, the happenings of real life are commonly mirrored in one-and-a-half-to two-minute packages, although those same events actually may have occurred over hours, days, or sometimes even months or years.

Two overriding considerations influence the length of news packages. First, after time is subtracted from the average half-hour television newscast for commercials, sports, and weather, only about sixteen minutes remain for news. Because the average newscast has twenty to twenty-five stories, packages and reader copy must be kept short if story count is to remain acceptable. Second, one of the great virtues of visual communication is its ability to compress time. Such a simple event as a police officer leaving the patrol car, entering an apartment building, walking upstairs, and entering an apartment can be accomplished in two or three shots: officer leaves car and walks out of frame, officer enters frame at top of stairs and exits frame, officer walks into frame and enters apartment. An action that required up to a full minute in real life is accomplished in as little as ten seconds of filmic time.

SHOT LENGTH

Most of the individual shots in a typical television news story average four to seven seconds, yet if an editor were to conform to this average, story pace would go out the window. Of more use are the following guidelines:

- Cut at the point of viewer anticipation or just before that moment the mind says, "Let's see what it is . . . "
- Hold the shot long enough for the viewer's eye to absorb the shot's message or pertinent detail or for the action to conclude sufficiently.

- Wait for artificial camera movement (pans, zooms, tilts, etc.) to end unless the two shots are linked by a dissolve, fade-in or fade-out, or similar optical effect to soften the edit.
- Wait for dialogue to end, although dialogue can carry over to another scene.
- Match shot length to the story's overall mood and pace.

If in doubt about shot length and the overall pace of your editing, remember that few shots must be shown in their entirety. The cardinal rule is to let viewers complete some action in their mind, so as to supply some of their own knowledge and experience and thereby to participate more directly in the action. Above all, remember not to let the pace drop. Keep the audience engaged in your story.

COMPOSITION AFFECTS PACE

Shot length is but one element of pacing. Equally important is the composition of the various shots in a story as the framing switches from long shot to medium shot and close-up.

In the past, because of its small screen size, television has been considered a close-up medium. Today, as screen size increases, the size of images on the screen can be varied more dramatically. Image size allows the editor to place emphasis on subject matter more precisely and allows greater control of the "distance" to be created between audience and subject.

From one shot to the next, however, the speed of an action on the screen can be altered by such factors as focal length, distance from subject, and the relative lens perspective. If the action is unfolding at one speed in the first shot, then at a different speed in the next shot, the editor has a problem. "Even if it's right, but it doesn't look right, then it's wrong," says photojournalist Darrell Barton.[6]

REVEAL MEANING THROUGH COMPOSITION

Composition influences not only visual and dramatic impact, but the amount of information that can be delivered. Consider the story that hinges on the make of a gun used to murder a holdup victim. A medium shot of the gun may be insufficient to show an important trademark crucial to the jury's deliberation. A close-up of the gun may be necessary, held on the screen for several seconds so that the viewer's eye may discover and study the all-important trademark.

Conversely, a close-up of a single rose might deliver its entire meaning in a couple of seconds, while a long shot of tulip beds in Holland may require triple that screen time to deliver its message. Clearly, both the editor's intent and the story's content will dictate individual shot length and the story's final pace. After all, the editor's responsibility is to reflect not only the story's information, but its feeling and atmosphere as well.[7]

SCREEN DIRECTION

In real life, subjects move in predictable directions, so the rule of thumb regarding screen direction is to keep the subject moving in one consistent direction—either screen right or screen left. Otherwise, viewers are left confused and consciously or subconsciously frustrated (Figure 3.3).

Conflicts in screen direction can be eliminated in the field if the photographer simply remembers to keep the subject facing the same direction in the viewfinder at all times. If a subject moves screen left in the first shot, then it must continue to move screen left in all the other shots. Otherwise, the result is a **false reverse** (Figure 3.4).

EDITING TO ELIMINATE THE FALSE REVERSE

At the edit bench the most obvious solution to a false reverse is the cutaway. A shot of a passenger jet taxiing screen right can be followed by a shot of an air traffic control

FIGURE 3.3   In real life, most subjects move in predictable directions, hence the need for consistent screen direction of subjects in motion picture photography and editing.

FIGURE 3.4   If a subject suddenly and illogically swaps directions on screen, the result is called a false reverse.

tower, followed by a cut to the plane now taxiing screen left. Another device to neutralize the false reverse is a **head-on shot** of the action coming straight toward camera or a **negative-action shot** of the subject moving away from camera. Yet another device is to continue photographing the shot as the camera moves across the axis line, taking the audience with it. If such a shot is unavailable, an **optical effect** such as a dissolve or wipe also can be employed.

THE TRANSITION OR REVEAL SHOT

The typical news package, even the typical theatrical film, is a series of sequences, linked one to another. The linking device can be a straight cut (cutting straight from one scene to another), an optical effect (dissolve, flip wipe, etc.), or a **transition shot.** Transition shots give the editor a way to pivot from one sequence to the next, a way to link separate scenes.

Transition shots are often used to momentarily disorient the viewer. In a video package about a glass blower, for example, the transition shot might be used to move the story from the artist's studio to a retail shop. In this example we first see the artist twirling molten glass into a vase. Next we see the transition shot, a close-up ostensibly of the vase being turned (as if the close-up were a continuation from the previous shot), followed by a cut to a long shot of a customer holding the vase in her hands as she examines it in the retail shop.

A classic illustration of a transition forward in time occurs in the classic film *Little Big Man*. A young Cherokee played by Dustin Hoffman rides down to a mountain stream on horseback, dismounts, kneels by the stream, and scoops water to his face. The screen cuts to a close shot in which Hoffman's hand covers his face. When Hoffman lowers his hand to reveal his face, we see it is the same person, but now eighty years old.

Occasionally it is useful for television journalists to study such techniques of transition, even those in theatrical motion pictures, to more effectively apply the principles to television news. Applying the principle illustrated in *Little Big Man*, a photographer-editor might use the simple device of a bath towel as a visual "wipe." First we might see a track star pick up a towel to wipe her face in the field just after a successful run, followed by a cut to a close shot of the towel full screen as the star wipes her brow and lowers the towel to reveal her face, followed by a matched cut as the star lowers the towel in a medium or long shot of the star now talking with her coach in the locker room.

In another example, a photographer and editor in communication with one another might accomplish the following sequence: A weightlifter looks down off-screen at something, followed by a shot of the barbell to be lifted, followed by a cut back to the weightlifter looking down as before. Now the camera pulls back to reveal the weightlifter speaking to an interviewer.

Such sequences can be edited with relative ease if the photographer remembers to keep three shots in mind while shooting in the field: *the shot just taken, the shot being taken, the shot that will be taken next.* If a shot has been made while the player wiped her face with a towel, the photographer can then wait for the player to wipe her face again, this time with the camera set for a close-up shot. Later, in the locker room, the photographer can again anticipate the moment when the player may wipe her face and photograph that action as well.

Even if the photographer has failed to create transition shots consciously, transition opportunities may still be possible during editing, as in the story of a black swan that sticks its head beneath the water. In a closer shot, in which camera angle and action are exactly matched with the previous shot, a white swan pulls its head from the water.

Such opportunities do not always present themselves, but they occur frequently enough that photographers are advised to be alert. If photographers consistently ignore opportunities to create meaningful raw material for the editor, perhaps it's time to reestablish communication. Always, the goal of such efforts is to preserve visual continuity while inviting and reengaging viewer participation.

SOUND AS A TRANSITIONAL DEVICE

Another transitional device is the use of what is known variously as the *sound overlap, sound bridge,* or *incoming sound.* The technique allows incoming sound to be heard for a moment or two before the accompanying shot appears on-screen. Normally, the incoming sound begins over the last second or two of the outgoing shot, although it can be introduced even earlier.

Consider how this technique would work in connection with the shot of a cruise ship lying idle at dockside, then a close shot of a ship's whistle followed by shots of passengers coming aboard the ship. Sound could be laid in so that viewers would hear the incoming sound of the ship's whistle over the last two seconds of the shot showing the ship lying idle. At the conclusion of the lying-idle shot, the ship whistle would appear on screen with its accompanying sound continuing.

In addition to its utility as a transition device, the sound bridge provides for a moment or so of white space or breathing room in voice-over narrative and helps to lend a feeling of realism to the package.

COLD CUTS

The sound bridge also helps the editor to eliminate tiresome successions of **cold cuts.** Cold cuts occur when a shot ends and its accompanying sound ends, only to be replaced at the splice line by a new picture with new sound. To avoid cold cuts, let outgoing or incoming sound carry over the splice line or make edits *on* words or other sounds. Avoid edits at the end of a sentence of voice over, and strive to avoid edits during a pause or at the conclusion of other sound. If the phenomenon is difficult to imagine, watch any television newscast and notice how often the shots in the news package end coincidentally with the end of sentences in the voice over.

FLASH CUTS

Some stories on television, including those in television newscasts, go better with music. Television, with its relatively smaller screen and with audiences that have been taught to thrive on pace, is uniquely suited to a style of editing called **flash cutting** or **rapid montage cutting.**

In this technique, brief fragments of shots are cut to exact rhythm against a musical beat or sound. The visual information comes quickly, but not so fast that it fails to leave an impression or message, whether on a twenty-five-inch TV or a forty-foot theatre screen.

CUTTING TO LEAVE SPACE
FOR AUDIENCE REACTION

Wall-to-wall narration has become a hallmark in news packages at news operations around the country. In part, the phenomenon occurs because conscientious reporters hope to communicate as much information as possible in the little time available. But no communication is complete until there is understanding. Viewers need time to assimilate information. When news is fired at viewers as if from a scattergun, the news does not lodge in their minds: It simply washes over them and fades quickly from memory.

For that reason, all packages need white space or breathing room, occasional moments in which pictures and sound play while the viewer takes a momentary respite from the narration. If, in a shot, a plane with crippled landing gear is just about to touch down on the runway, the editor owes his or her audience a moment or two of silence during the landing, even if a sentence or two of the reporter's voice over must be eliminated from the package.

Packages are not built on words alone. Because the most effective packages stop talking occasionally to let viewers participate in on-screen action and absorb the meaning of voice-over narration, the editor has an obligation to provide occasional moments of picture and natural sound. Some negotiation with the reporter may be necessary, especially if five seconds of voice over must be eliminated from the script to provide some breathing room in the package, but if viewers need that little moment they should have it.

THE BURDEN OF "RAMBO VIDEO"

Photographers are sometimes heard to say, "That so-and-so editor used my worst stuff yesterday and made me look bad." Most oversights involve no malice on the editor's part but are a consequence of the unrelenting deadlines the editor faces. Too often, the editor must simply "edit off the top" of the field cassette if air time is to be made.

Elsewhere it has been suggested that photojournalists should photograph only what they want on air. In fact, photographers who avoid indiscriminate shooting can endear themselves to TV news editors who inevitably have too little time and too many packages to edit. Editors love photographers who anticipate the action, who preplan what they'll shoot, and who wait for action to occur and are ready to shoot when it does occur. Short tapes, after all, are easier and quicker to edit. And if the video contains no meaningless shots, soft focus shots, or shaky footage, then the photographer has become at least a silent partner in the editing process.

In truth, too many photographers around the country turn in "run and gun" **Rambo video**—they shoot everything that moves with little regard to story line or subject matter. Once again, if the problem is ever to be solved, editors and photographers are advised to communicate more openly with one another. If, as a photographer, you would like to see certain shots aired or avoided in a story, tell the reporter or editor. If you can't talk face to face, at least write a note to the editor. If, as reporter or editor, you see your photographer shooting far too much Rambo video, tell the photographer your concerns.

CRASH EDITING

The reality of television news makes it a business of deadlines. Even editors deeply committed to storytelling, artistry, and precision of craft must sometimes sacrifice excellence to the tyranny of news deadlines. "Crash editing" becomes the norm as the editor butts together scenes, fast-forwarding from one acceptable scene that presents itself to the next, striving to get something—anything—put together just to meet deadline. Anyone who watches such an editor frantically at work, or who assumes that such practices epitomize the nature of editing, might be forgiven for believing that editing is but a mere "assemblage of scenes."

Editors under tight deadline, or who must constantly wade through piles of cassettes filled with Rambo video, can follow a system advocated by photojournalist Greg O'Malia. "If you're working against the clock, first lay down your voice over and bites," says O'Malia. "Then go back and fill the holes, where only narration exists, with continuous scenes. Then, if time still remains, you can go back and fine-tune your editing."[8]

DISSOLVES AND OTHER OPTICAL EFFECTS

The most common way to connect two shots is with a straight cut. Straight cuts work so well because they imply relatedness as one scene cuts to the next. Often a simple straight cut may be adequate to move viewers along even from one unrelated scene to the next, but at other times the editor may want to use such optical effects as fades, wipes, dissolves, or more elaborate digital video effects to indicate that scenes, although significantly different, are related.

In general, the **dissolve** indicates a change in time, location, or subject matter. One scene melts into another. In other words, one scene optically fades to black on top of another scene that optically fades from black to full exposure. The longer the dissolve, the more obvious is the separation. Common dissolve lengths are from two-thirds of a second to two and a half seconds or more. Occasionally, editors use dissolves to more artistically connect scenes or eliminate jump cuts within a real-time sequence, but the result may be confusing to audiences who have been conditioned to understand that dissolves mean a change in time, location, or subject matter.

Wipes and flip wipes, whether horizontal or vertical, are used to indicate a more noticeable separation between scenes. Wipes help indicate to the viewer that a new subject, idea, or location is being introduced.

Fades, including the fade-in and fade-out, are among the most obvious transitions. The scene fades to black, or sometimes to white, or fades from black to full exposure. The fade is seldom used in news packages, although it is commonly found in public affairs and documentary programming and is used at some stations just before commercial breaks.

Because no rule book exists to tell editors how or when to use optical effects, editors can profit from the axiom that true art conceals art: The best optical effects may be those that go unnoticed because they are used so logically. Remember, also, the beauty of the straight cut, which is the most transparent optical effect of all.

Ultimately, the key to good editing is to make all your work go unnoticed. If your technique is invisible, if continuity is present, and if your pace is smooth and flawless, then you will have helped viewers achieve that incomparable feeling of "being there."

NONLINEAR VIDEO EDITING

Eighteenth-century authors were known to write sentences in large print, cut the words apart, and hang them individually on a clothesline. This produced something of a word processor, allowing the writer to move words around within the sentence until it sounded best. Nonlinear video editing allows a similar freedom, in that images and sounds can be moved about, shortened, and even lengthened independently of one another, something like a word processor with pictures. Anytime an element is added or deleted, the system automatically reconfigures everything before and after the change so as to maintain synchronization.

The process requires only a computer with a prodigious memory and a software editing system such as **Avid**®, Media 100®, or Adobe Premiere®, along with a series of high-capacity computer storage disks. Raw sound and video can be input from videotape, camera video disk, DVD, optical disk, microwave signal fed from videotape, or directly from the field camera. Images and sound are first stored and edited within the computer memory. The final edit, complete with visual effects and even graphics, then is recorded to videotape, broadcast live on air, or stored on a computer hard drive.

Nonlinear editing has roots in double-system film editing, a process in which film scenes and multiple sound tracks are manipulated independently of one another, in full synchronization. Using physical splices in film scenes and magnetic audio tracks, the film editor cuts separate reels of natural sound, narration, and dialogue, along with two or more reels of images and music to allow for crossfades, dissolves, and other special effects. Thus, the double-system or nonlinear film editor can easily substitute one image for another, or move a scene, a natural sound, or a section of narration track anywhere at will (Figure 3.5).

Nonlinear editing is steadily replacing linear video editing, a more restrictive form of **editing** which appeared in the 1970s with the introduction of portable field cameras and videotape recorders, a system known within the television news profession as **electronic news gathering** (ENG) and elsewhere as **electronic field production** (EFP). The basic linear edit system includes a videotape playback unit, a controller, and a videotape recorder. Images are recorded, one after another, on videotape. The process involves only the re-recording of electrical signals, never any physical splices in the tape itself.

Typically, the editor first records voice-over audio by feeding prerecorded bits of sound, in order, from the video playback machine to the videotape recorder. Frequently, the editor first records narration, sound bites and standups (with accompanying video), and natural sound on audio tracks 1 and 2, then rewinds the tape and lays in remaining video, scene by scene, to match the sound track. No change in total length is possible without re-editing everything following the change. If you wish to substitute a short scene for a long one in the finished edit, or lengthen a scene, or change the narration in a particular section, you normally must re-edit all video and/or sound from that point forward.

With the advent of nonlinear video editing, happy days are here again.

SUMMARY

Editing is important to the visual storytelling process because of the ways in which it duplicates how the mind works. Shots, or fragments of reality, are combined to form a composite understanding of the original experience or event. Everyone involved in the reporting process is an editor and uses editing to emphasize, pace, structure, and reveal the story.

The most fundamental editing technique is the cut, the joining of one scene to another. Deceptively simple as a creative device, the cut creates new meaning. A shot

FIGURE 3.5 Nonlinear editing allows images and sounds to be moved about, shortened, and even lengthened independently of one another, something like a word processor with pictures.

of a child crawling on the ground, intercut with a shot of a snake crawling toward camera, creates meaning that was not present in either shot by itself. If the two shots are reversed, their meaning is again altered and new meaning created. Editing also allows the journalist to expand or condense time. The essence of an event that occurred over hours or days in real life can be reconstructed on the screen in only a minute or so. Similarly, events that happened during the span of a few seconds can be depicted for far longer times on the screen by repeating the action through shots from multiple cameras and slow-motion photography.

Pace, a critical component in all visual communication, is affected not only by shot length but by composition, cutting points, and the content itself. Normally, in scenes with action, pace is more natural if scenes are cut on action, or in other words, while the action progresses.

Various shots can be used to emphasize and reveal action and control pace. Among them are the insert shot, reaction shot, and point of view shot. Common editorial devices to eliminate unnatural jumps in action, or jump cuts, include the cutaway and insert shots. Like the photographer, the editor also is responsible for helping preserve screen direction. Generally, pictorial continuity is best served when subjects move logically in one direction on screen, rather than randomly swap directions from shot to shot.

Editing also encompasses sound, which can be used as a transition device to move from one shot to another, as in the use of incoming sound a second or so before its accompanying scene is shown. Sound also helps provide perspective in a scene and helps to heighten the viewer's sense of realism. Optical effects such as fades, wipes, and dissolves offer further means of visual punctuation.

Competency in television reporting and photography relies on more than a passing acquaintance with editing. Editing is not simply the final process in the art of visual reconstruction: It guides the reporting process from start to finish.

DISCUSSION

1. Why are the best editing techniques often invisible to home audiences?

2. Describe how editing can be used to help enhance the visual storytelling process.

3. Explain why an understanding of picture editing is important to all members of the reporting team.

4. Describe the role of the cut in video editing.

5. Explain the meaning of the phrase "pace is everything" as it applies to television news.

6. Explain what is meant by the term "filmic time" and provide an original example.

7. Describe the considerations that influence the length of individual shots in an edited television news story.

8. Distinguish between the terms "cutting on action" and "cutting at rest."

9. What considerations guide determination of the edit point in beginning and ending a given shot?

10. Define parallel cutting and provide an original example of the concept.

11. Explain how sound can be used as a transition from one time, subject, or location in a story to the next.

12. Explain the difference between cold cuts and flash cuts.

13. Describe typical uses of the most common optical effects.

EXERCISES

1. Arrange three video shots, each with separate but related subject matter, and consider them to be shots A, B, and C. If you lack access to a video editing console, use still photographs and place them side by side.

   An example of three shots might be: A—a mobile home in perfect condition on a well-manicured lot; B—a woman removes the lid from an empty quart jar and holds the jar in the direction of something off-screen; C—a mobile home that has been overturned by high wind. Notice how the linkage of shots A and B produces new meaning that neither shot by itself contained. Notice further the new meaning created when shots B and C are linked. Now, if the visual result will make sense, relink your three shots in the following orders and compare the outcome: A-C-B; C-A-B; B-A-C.

2. Analyze television news stories, commercials, and theatrical films to determine what factors motivate the cut or edit that transfers the viewer's attention from one shot to the next. Note to what extent the content influences the pace of the editing.

3. Find an event that occurs over the course of several minutes or hours in real life, then photograph and edit a reconstruction of the event into a one-minute presentation. Reedit the one-minute version into a thirty-second reconstruction, and finally into a twenty-second reconstruction.

4. Ask a video editor, preferably a willing acquaintance, to determine the proper screen length for a long shot and a close shot of identical action. Compare the running time of the two shots.

5. Edit footage of an action, first on action, then at rest. Play and critique the result.

6. Edit together two versions of out-of-frame/into-frame action from the same footage. In the first version, take care to avoid letting the action "fall out of the splice." In other words, surrender an outgoing shot while the subject is still visible at the edge of frame, and pick up the incoming shot with the subject already in frame.

   In the second version, recut the action so the subject disappears entirely from frame in the outgoing shot and does not reappear for several moments after the incoming shot has begun. Compare and evaluate the two approaches.

7. Edit together precisely matched action from raw field shots that contain overlapping action. View and discuss the raw and edited footage with the photographer.

8. Using footage from separate events, cut together an example of parallel cutting.

9. Insert a cutaway in the middle of a shot in which the action continues to progress, such as an athlete running down a playing field. Pick up the action after the cutaway precisely where it ended in the outgoing shot just before the cutaway. Now recut the scene, this time eliminating from the action scene following the cutaway a length of footage equivalent to the length of the cutaway. Compare and discuss the result.

10. Edit together two scenes that result in a false reverse in the action. Use any other appropriate shot available to you to soften the impact of the false reverse.

11. Use sound or a video shot of your choice as a transitional device from one sequence in a story to the next.

12. Edit together two examples of the cold cut, followed by examples in which you have eliminated the cold cuts you originally created.

13. Practice editing flash cuts. Cut footage of your choice to the beat of music of your choice.

14. Study examples of the effective use of optical effects as they are used in television and film.

15. Practice editing voice-over narration against video pictures, leaving white space with natural sound in the track as appropriate.

16. Explain the roots of nonlinear editing from the perspectives of the contemporary writer or reporter and the double-system film editor.

17. Explain the differences between linear and nonlinear editing. Describe both processes as part of your explanation.

NOTES

1. "An Interview with Cheri Hunter," *Editing* (Eagle Eye Film Company, 4019 Tujunga Avenue, Studio City, CA 91604) (July 1986), 1, 2.

2. Telephone conversation with author, 12 August 1985.

3. Matt Williams, "Academy Winner Extols Editing," *Rangefinder* (Utah State University, Spring 1985), 40.

4. Karel Reisz and Gavin Miller, *The Technique of Film Editing* (New York: Hastings House, 1968), 46–48.

5. Phil Sturholm, "Creative Photojournalists—They Are the Future," a presentation at the NPPA TV News-Video Workshop, Norman, OK, 20 March 1986.

6. Comments to journalism students at the University of Oklahoma, 5 November 2003.

7. Reisz and Miller, 142.

8. Conversation with author, Fort Collins, CO, 23 July 2002.

CHAPTER FOUR

FIELD TECHNIQUES OF SHOOTING TELEVISION NEWS

Photojournalists who endeavor to refine their work often discover that relatively small changes in photographic technique can translate into substantial improvements on the screen. As the photographer brings one element after another under control in the photographic process, a substantive and individual style begins to emerge. The process is an affirmation that professional development never ends and that no detail is too unimportant to master.

USE A TRIPOD WHENEVER POSSIBLE

Even the simple use of a tripod can help distinguish the work of one photographer over another, yet an inspection of television news stories yields the inescapable conclusion that not all photographers use tripods. Especially at smaller market stations, cameras tend to be handheld and the scenes unacceptably shaky, and among some photographers in large markets the problem persists.

Handheld shots are faster and easier to make, but too often they are the result of photographers taking the easy way out. While spot news and other fast-moving events are best photographed with a handheld camera, most other stories can be routinely shot from the tripod (Figure 4.1). If no tripod is available at the station where you work, or if the tripod assigned to you is wobbly or inadequate and repair or replacement appears unlikely, consider buying your own tripod. The improvement in your work will be obvious.

THE HANDHELD CAMERA

With only minor accommodations in technique, most photographers can master the handheld camera. For maximum steadiness, use the tripod whenever possible; otherwise, convert the body into a tripod. Find a wall, a telephone pole, a tree, or whatever else is handy and push the camera up against this object. Indoors, if a straight-backed chair is handy, sit backwards on the chair and use the chair back as a camera support. Further support the camera with a sandbag, pillow, or cushion. For steadier shots, you

FIGURE 4.1 The steadiest shots are created when the camera is mounted on a tripod.

can also kneel, a technique that provides good perspective on many shots. When kneeling, sit on your heels and rest elbows on your knees, or even set the camera on an equipment case. You can also place the camera on the ground or floor, straddle it with your knees, and use a wallet or similar object as a wedge to position the camera properly.

Rather than kneel or crouch to obtain correct camera height, you can hold the camera at waist level (cradle it in your arms) or at arm's length. Most viewfinders can be swiveled to virtually any angle the photographer might need to compose the shot conveniently.

Balance Camera

When handholding, balance the camera's weight on your shoulder. On most cameras the shoulder pad can be positioned so the camera balances naturally. In this manner you have only to balance the camera gently, rather than to support its full weight with your arms (Figure 4.2 shows correct stance).

Stance

A wide stance gives the body more support. Stand with feet about shoulder-width apart, and stand so that the body is straight, with the pelvis tucked forward and elbows close to the body. The stance photographers describe as "posterior out, elbows flying in the breeze," is unacceptable. It produces wavering shots.

FIGURE 4.2   Proper stance is vital if the photojournalist is to produce steady shots with the handheld camera. Balance the camera until it rests comfortably on the shoulder and use the left hand to make focus adjustments. Note that the steadying right arm remains close to the chest.

Shoot on Wide Focal Length

The steadiest handheld shots are produced with the camera lens set on a wide-angle focal length. Most photographers find that steady handheld shots are almost impossible to shoot with the lens set on telephoto.

Control Breathing

As you prepare to shoot, relax. Breathe in, let half the air out, then hold your breath like a target shooter. If the shot is long, breathe in shallow breaths.

Preplan Body Movement

Preplan your body movement for pan shots or whenever you follow action with the handheld camera—to follow a plane taking off, for example, or to follow a person moving past the camera. Position your feet in the direction the shot will end, then swing your body back around to capture the approaching action. As you shoot, your body will "uncoil" much like a spring. Otherwise, your body will bind up as you "coil up."

Walk in Lockstep

Another trick to minimize the shakiness of handheld shots is to photograph only objects that move. Subject movement renders camera movement less obvious. For smoothest action whenever you follow a subject in a walking shot, stay in lockstep with the person you're photographing. When the person steps on the right foot, you also should be stepping on your right foot. If you are walking backward, reverse this procedure.

Avoid Unplanned Camera Movement

When you zoom, take care to avoid bumping the camera as you reach for the zoom button or lever, and be especially careful to avoid hard starts and stops at the stop limits of the zoom range. Such techniques instantly call attention to themselves. And when shooting spot news, take your hand off the camera's start-stop button so that if you're frightened or startled, you don't accidentally shut off the camera. Finally, for video that captures more of the action, and for greater personal safety, try shooting with both eyes open so you know what's going on around you.

HOW TO USE THE ZOOM LENS

The most legitimate zoom shots have a purpose other than simply to lend artificial camera movement to the scene. Ideally, the zoom is made to reveal something new within a scene, to "discover" new meaning, so to speak, or to keep a subject in proper composition within the frame as it moves toward camera.

Because nothing marks the amateur photographer more indelibly than unnecessary zooms and pans, practice self-control whenever you are tempted to make these shots.

When you do zoom, do so sparingly and with a reason. As you begin your career in television news, regardless of whether you will be a photographer, reporter, producer, or editor, consider adopting a philosophy that limits the number of zooms and pans you will allow in any given news story. Some professionals recommend allowing oneself approximately one zoom per year—if absolutely necessary.

Avoid Calling Attention to the Zoom

Normally, the best zoom shots glide so smoothly and slowly that viewers are hardly aware of them. One trick is to introduce the zoom simultaneously as subject movement begins, as when a jet at the end of the runway begins to gather speed for takeoff.

Another device to help make the zoom shot less noticeable is to use only a portion of the zoom range, rather than zooming through the lens's entire focal length range from wide angle to telephoto. A sensitivity to composition will suggest the appropriate zoom range for a particular subject.

Adjust Speed and Duration of Zoom
to Story Mood and Pace

Remember also to control the speed, length, and duration of the zoom so that it will match the overall pace and mood of the larger sequence in which it is to appear. Sometimes fast, "snap" zooms are most appropriate. At other times, a slow, lazy zoom will work best. Zoom shots that are always made at the same speed, and are predictably long and artificially slow, will inevitably damage the story's pace.

When you zoom, remember to hold the beginning of your shot steady for about three seconds, then zoom, and again hold the shot steady for another three seconds before you stop the camera. If you decide not to use the zoom when you edit, you will have at least three seconds of usable footage from the beginning and end of the original shot in the form of static shots. Also attempt to "feather" the beginning and end of your zoom shots: Accelerate slowly to predetermined zoom speed, then gradually deaccelerate the zoom as you come to the end of the shot. This avoids the hard stops and starts that occur when zooms begin and end instantly.

Recompose the Shot as You Zoom

As you zoom, remember to tilt the camera up or down as necessary to keep such factors as head room in acceptable composition. Beginners often start a zoom shot with the subject centered close-up in the frame, then zoom back to a longer shot without tilting down the camera to keep head room above the subject in acceptable proportions. The result is a long shot of the subject in dead center of frame, with most of the top half of the frame wasted on empty space.

Remember, also, the good advice of professional photographers: "When you zoom, don't 'play the trombone.'" Don't zoom in, then back out, during the same shot.

STORYTELLING AND PLANNING

It is possible for the photographer to shoot everything that moves and still not have a story. Photographers who have learned to think as reporters produce not just a succession of pretty pictures, but pictures that tell stories. Identify the story. Research the subject. Decide what you want your audience to learn. Know the story so you can tell it effectively to others with your camera. Ask yourself as you shoot, "What offers visual proof of the subject, of my point of view, my story focus?"

Remember also to give every story you shoot a beginning, a middle, and an ending. Stories without an ending are the visual equivalent of unsigned letters.[1]

ESTABLISH COMMUNICATION IN THE FIELD

Once you have identified the story in your own mind, talk over your ideas with other members of the reporting team. Make contributions as appropriate to the story and how it is to be covered and edited. Only if you establish communication with other members of the reporting team can you know what they are thinking and reach final agreement on the story to be told (Figure 4.3).

Communication with the subjects in your story is just as vital. The contributions of subjects who trust the reporting team, and who feel safe enough to share something of their inner selves, can elevate the story from the routine to the exceptional.

THINK BEFORE YOU SHOOT

To further separate your work from the competition, exercise imagination every time you shoot. Try to make your photography communicate not only what you see and ex-

FIGURE 4.3   In television news, reporting is a collaborative effort among all members of the news team. Ongoing communication between the reporter and photographer is essential on every assignment.

perience in the field, but what other observers may have missed. Show the event, but also give viewers a reason to want to watch the story, and look for ways to help viewers feel as if they have participated in it.

SHOOT SEQUENCES

A proven method to heighten the viewer's sense of involvement in the story is to shoot matched-action sequences. Through sequences, photojournalists can reconstruct an event much as first-person observers would see the action. To shoot sequences, learn to recognize action that repeats itself and break "simple" action into its complex parts. If the assignment is to show a child boarding a school bus, show the child's face, a close-up of her scuffed tennis shoes, the sapphire-chip ring on her ringer, her fingers tightly curled around her lunch box handle, her point of view of the approaching bus, the driver's smiling face, the cars stopped behind the bus, her father waving good-bye, the bus door closing, and the bus resuming its journey. During editing, the shots can be used in any given selection and order to emphasize particular aspects of the message.

SHOOT AND MOVE

After every shot you make in the field, try to physically move the camera to a new location and angle. A series of shots composed with the zoom lens and photographed with the camera on the same axis line results in edits that yield a distinct visual jump—an effect sometimes referred to as the *pop cut*. Pop cuts are most apparent when the zoom lens is used to shoot a long shot of a subject (say a person) from a distance, followed immediately by a close-up without having moved the camera off the original axis line (Figure 4.4).

To avoid the pop cut, simply remember to shoot and move. When you first photograph the subject, establish an imaginary axis line projecting from the lens through the center of the subject. Shoot the subject, then physically move the camera to a new setup position for each new shot. To avoid arbitrary false reverses, in which the action appears to reverse from one cut to the next, remember to shoot all shots from the same side of the original axis line.

ANTICIPATE ACTION

If you can study the action before you shoot and learn to anticipate what happens next, your photography will have originality. "You have to learn to anticipate in which direction someone's going to walk before they take a step," says Chuck Richardson, photojournalist.[2] If you find yourself shooting behind the action, try to preplan your shots. Wait for the action to occur and be ready to shoot when it does occur. "Don't let

FIGURE 4.4   A distinct visual jump called the "pop cut" results if the camera is allowed to remain on the same axis line from one shot to the next. To avoid the problem, remember to shoot and move. In other words, physically move the camera to a new location and angle after every shot you make.

yourself get behind the story," advises freelance photographer Bob Brandon. "Otherwise you will always be shooting aftermath."[3]

SHOOTING ACTION OUTSIDE THE PHOTOGRAPHER'S CONTROL

Action that occurs only once and that is outside your control can still be shot sequentially if you anticipate it. Even in spot news, sequences happen all around you. Perhaps in the aftermath of a tornado, firefighters search for survivors beneath the rubble of fallen buildings as a cold rain falls. Elsewhere gas utility workers look for the shut-off valves on gas mains. An elderly woman is discovered alive beneath the rubble of her home. In the absence of stretchers, firefighters carry the injured piggy-back to waiting ambulances. Perhaps you can shoot a sequence if you know in advance where the firefighter will carry the elderly woman who has just been found. As you plan the sequence, think in terms of distance. You can then estimate the amount of time required for the firefighter to walk from where you'll begin to shoot to where you'll finish shooting.

SHOOT INTO-FRAME/OUT-OF-FRAME ACTION

You also can decide in advance whether to hold the firefighter in frame during a continuous shot as he or she carries the woman, or how many times you will allow the firefighter to enter and leave frame. In fact, one of the easiest ways to maintain continuity when shooting uncontrolled action is to shoot lots of into-frame/out-of-frame action. Begin to shoot before your subjects enter frame and continue to shoot after they have exited. Once the subject has left frame, an editor can cut to virtually any new scene without a jump.

SHOOT ONLY THE SHOTS YOU NEED

Most photographers have had the experience of seeing a bad shot make air. Usually the editor is blamed: "The shot was out of focus/too shaky/too fuzzy/too green. *Why* did you put *that* shot on the air?" and so on into the night. In turn, the editor usually blames deadlines that prevented a more critical review of the footage prior to broadcast. Rest assured that if a shot with poor focus or an unsteady zoom resides in your video, it will somehow make its way onto the screen.

The answer to such problems is to be found in the wisdom of professionals. "If you don't want it aired, don't shoot it," says Atlanta editor Butch Townley.[4] This means that when you focus the camera, focus it before you pull the trigger to begin recording. Sometimes, things will happen so fast you may have to roll while you're focusing the lens, but in general try to work out all your shots, including zooms and pans, and rehearse them before you turn on the camera.

AVOID INDISCRIMINATE SHOOTING

Until the mid-1970s, television news photographers commonly shot news stories on rolls of film with projection times of either three or eleven minutes. If a one-minute story was edited from a three-minute roll of film, the **shooting ratio** was approximately 1:3, meaning that one minute of film was aired for each three minutes of raw stock shot in the field. Given such tight shooting ratios, photographers were of necessity more selective about the field shots they took.

With the introduction of twenty- to sixty-minute field cassettes, hard drives, and memory sticks, many photographers overshoot their subjects. They simply shoot until the video is full, sometimes shooting twenty minutes of video or more for a simple thirty-second spot. This practice of shooting "editing fodder" unnecessarily wears down field batteries and forces editors under tight deadlines to handle unnecessary volumes of footage. As every editor will attest, less footage is easier and quicker to edit.

Even if every shot on the cassette is award-winning material, the editor faced with a ten-minute deadline may still have to cut the spot from the first two minutes of raw video anyway. If you discover that your best footage often is near the end of the shoot, strive to become more selective and avoid shooting the camera randomly. The goal is to assess the story visually in your mind before you shoot each scene and to have a purpose for every shot you take, a process made easier if you have first identified the story to be told with your camera.

HAVE A REASON FOR EVERY SHOT

Occasionally photographers return home after shooting everything that moved in the field, but still have no story. Generally the fault can be traced to a lack of story focus or to a breakdown in communication between the reporter and photographer. If no story has been defined, or if the photographer is unsure of the reporter's ideas, the tendency is to protect oneself by shooting everything that presents itself in the field, then try to create a story out of all the random footage back at the editing bench. The truth, of course, is that a story can never transcend the footage brought back from the field. If the footage is random and vague, similar ailments will afflict the edited story.

EDIT IN THE CAMERA

Many of the best photographers are also experienced editors. Their experience at the edit console allows them to previsualize or edit a scene in their mind before they even shoot it. This ability allows the photographer to **edit in the camera,** shooting sequences and overlapping action in generally the same order in which they later will be aired. The technique can save valuable editing time on stories that are being covered very close to air time. The technique can even help to ensure that a story will be edited as the photographer wants it to be aired.

When you edit in the camera, it is important to concentrate on three shots at a time: the shot you're taking, the shot you just took, and the shot you will take next. With this approach, you will intuitively shoot more sequences and can more naturally maintain continuity in the action from one shot to the next.

If you retake a shot without altering composition, take steps to avoid the inadvertent airing of identical takes by placing your hand to the lens to blank out the screen, or by recording a few frames of color bars between your identical takes. When you are editing against deadlines, or whenever someone else edits your footage, these visual separations will help prevent jump cuts from making air.

Just as important, when you want particular footage to be aired, especially when the editor is on deadline, submit your footage for editing or digitizing with the video already cued to the best footage.

SHOOT TO ELIMINATE THE FALSE REVERSE

As you edit in the camera you can eliminate false reverses in the subject's screen direction by remembering to establish an axis line, then consciously shooting only on one side of that line. If the axis line is a confusing concept, just remember to keep action moving in the same direction in the viewfinder from one shot to the next. If the train is moving screen right, keep it moving screen right in every shot.

To soften abrupt reverses in action, buffer with a shot of the action as it approaches the camera head-on, provide a cutaway to divert audience attention from the abrupt reversal in action, "take the audience with you" by running the camera in a shot as you cross the line, or soften the reverse with a dissolve or other optical effect.

INVOLVE THE CAMERA IN THE ACTION

Audiences come to television for a sense of involvement and first-person experience, so try to move in close to your subjects and involve the camera in the action as intimately as possible. When you involve the camera in the action, you involve the audience. Go for detail and try to include full facial close-ups of people in the news, in views that approximate how we see people in real life during our everyday, one-on-one encounters. Otherwise, the audience may feel cheated.

Full facial shots derive much of their impact by virtue of their emphasis on eyes. Close-up, detailed shots of eyes help reveal to the audience what the subject is thinking and feeling, so try to show both of the subject's eyes, rather than a profile shot that shows one ear and one eye (Figure 4.5).

In this context, telephoto shots seldom count for actually moving the camera close to the subject. Shots made on long focal length settings magnify the subject but tend to produce an artificial and unappealing sense of perspective. Telephoto shots rarely involve the audience as intimately as the camera that is truly close to the subject.

FIGURE 4.5   Full facial composition in which both of the subject's eyes can be seen is preferable to the often observed shot that shows only one of the person's eyes and an ear.

HOW TO GIVE TAPE THE RICH LOOK OF FILM

Photographers who made the switch from film to videotape sometimes talk wistfully of the soft, subtle expressions and richness of color that could be captured on film. That look is again possible, thanks to digital cameras with settings that produce the look of film. If your camera or computer plug-in lacks this feature, you still can achieve film-like effects by following the lead of former NBC staff cameraman Henry Kokojan.

With experience that encompasses more than forty years in military photography, television commercials, feature films, and television news, Kokojan has found ways to manipulate the electronic camera to more nearly produce the look of film. The following methods are basic to his technique.

1. Because of variations in performance from one brand of camera to the next, different cameras produce differing images. The photographer should select a camera that produces the most pleasing image.
2. Engineers may or may not adjust camera circuitry to factory specifications. Sometimes, they can be asked to "tweak" color circuitry to make colors a little richer.
3. For rich-looking colors in early morning and late afternoon, Kokojan recommends that the camera be white-balanced by pointing it at a white card illuminated by a 3200° Kelvin incandescent (tungsten) light with no filter or a clear filter behind the lens. Once the camera is white-balanced, the #85 (amber) filter is clicked into position before the scene is shot.
4. For warmer pictures at other times, Kokojan recommends that the camera be white-balanced normally, but in the shade instead of in sunlight.

5. If available light is strong enough, no matter what the location, use it instead of artificial lights.
6. To give black-and-white photographs the appearance of age, create sepia (yellowish-brown) tones by first white-balancing the camera on a pale blue card.

WORKING WITH PEOPLE

Because news is about things that happen to people or otherwise affect their lives, an emphasis on people can help give virtually all television news stories larger meaning. Without people in your stories, your reporting will tend toward institutional treatment, which many viewers may find dull and uninviting. Often, when you tell your stories through people, you can use their presence to help illuminate the larger meaning of events.

Working with strangers in the field is less intimidating than it might at first appear to be. Most strangers will be willing to cooperate, provided you approach them with an attitude of courtesy and respect. Most people are flattered to learn they'll be on television.

To alleviate nervousness or concerns people may have about their "performance," you can suggest that they go about their work and routines just as though you weren't present. Within a few minutes, in the majority of cases, the initial trauma of being on television will have faded from mind.

Confidence in yourself and your ability helps you avoid being intimidated by your gear or by onlookers or even by the subject of your story. If you do feel inhibited or intimidated, remember that self-confidence develops as a product of experience. In a short time you should feel entirely at ease telling the stories of other people. Note, however, that not all stories are worth intruding on the privacy of others, especially if your presence would add unnecessary emotional distress in the situation.

AVOID DISTRACTING THE SUBJECT

Because the camera and other hardware of television act as barriers to reality, try to avoid drawing attention to yourself or any of your equipment whenever you work with people. Set up sound and lighting equipment with as few distractions as possible, preferably before your subject arrives, and try to make yourself "fade into the wallpaper."

If people are worried about how they'll look or how they should behave in front of the camera, they won't give you their best heat or white light. **Heat** is present when sound bites are spontaneous and believable and when they embody moments of emotional and intellectual intensity. **White light** occurs whenever the subject is natural, unaffected, and emotionally transparent while on camera. When white light occurs, viewers know they are experiencing something of the real person in a real environment.

As a way to further preserve an atmosphere of spontaneity, consider not showing the microphone in frame. The microphone intimidates many people and acts as an additional barrier between you and the subject. Furthermore, mike flags (station logos affixed to handheld microphones) tend to pull the viewer's eye away from the person and the person's emotion. With the exception of satellite trucks, mikes are the only piece of reporting equipment journalists routinely continue to photograph. Unless station policy dictates otherwise, consider substituting a wired lavaliere or wireless mike instead (Figure 4.6).

Staging versus Motivating

When working with people, the photographer has at least three options to consider when photographing their activity. The first is to photograph people as they go about their affairs. This technique results in perhaps the most honest and natural depictions of the subject. A second approach is to ask the subject to perform a particular activity on camera. If the wood carver has decided not to work on the day you show up, you may have to ask him to carve anyway so you can shoot the video you need and get on to your next story assignment. Most photographers consider this practice to be ethically acceptable, on the grounds that the subject only performs as he or she normally would in the photographer's absence. A third alternative, unacceptable at virtually all

FIGURE 4.6   The handheld or "stick" mike (left) can draw attention to itself and unnecessarily act as a barrier between the audience and reporter. The miniature lavaliere microphone is far less intrusive (right).

news operations, is to **stage** the action and ask people to do what they don't normally do or direct them to engage in activities that are obviously out of character.

The far more preferable alternative to staging is to motivate people to do what they normally do. The process can be as simple as making an observation: "I'll bet you can still outrun your grandkids." If the photojournalist's luck holds, Grandpa may reply, "It's a fact. Here, let me show you."

THE ONE-PERSON BAND

If you were to watch a one-armed man hang wallpaper while he played a piccolo, you'd have an idea of the demands placed on reporters who are asked to perform as one-person bands at TV stations all across the country. The reporter in the **one-person band** researches and produces the story; lights, photographs, and reports the event; conducts the interviews; shoots his or her own standups; writes the copy; edits the tape; and sometimes introduces and presents the story on air.

Notice that not only must reporters who labor alone simultaneously photograph and conduct the interviews for their stories, they must even photograph themselves in standups before the camera. With only a little practice in the field, both techniques are easily mastered.

How to Shoot and Conduct Interviews Simultaneously

Interviews are most easily conducted if the person to be interviewed remains busy at a familiar task. This allows the reporter-photographer to carry on a discussion with the person, sometimes without even formally asking questions, and without the need to "interrupt reality" by placing the person in a staged interview setting. People usually are less self-conscious in this setting, so interviews can be more spontaneous.

Holding the camera during the interview seems to result in greater spontaneity than if the photojournalist mounts the camera on a tripod and concentrates most of his or her attention on the viewfinder. Preferably, the photojournalist can hold the camera while asking questions or making observations from "off camera." The shotgun mike supplied on most field cameras usually is sufficient to pick up remarks from both the interviewer and interviewee. Because the camera mike is close enough to pick up the reporter's "I see's" and "Uh-huhs," the reporter can indicate an interest and understanding of the interviewee's comments with an occasional and barely audible "Mmmm."[5]

The reporter can work the camera quite close to the interviewee, provided the individuals have established rapport with one another. To help keep the subject from looking straight into the camera lens as they photograph the interview, some reporters hold their left index finger to their left ear. Most subjects will obediently attach to this visual reference point during shooting, rather than to the camera lens, especially if they have been told in advance of the interview what to expect. The reporter's other hand, of course, is used to balance the shoulder-mounted camera and turn it on and off.

How to Photograph Your Own Standup

If you are shooting yourself in a static, nonmoving standup, simply place a light stand in front of the camera to mark the spot where you will stand. The top of the stand can extend to within a couple of inches of your height. Tape a business card or other small object to the stand at the same height as your eyes. Use this card or other object to help focus the lens and to establish correct framing and headroom. Clip a lapel mike to your clothing, set sound levels, roll video, and step in front of the camera to deliver your standup. Your body will block out the light stand you used as a reference point during the setup. If you must use a handheld mike, hang it on the mike stand before you roll the videotape. When you step in front of the camera, simply grasp the mike, turn so that your body is centered in front of the light stand, and deliver your standup to the camera.

If you are doing a walking standup, frame the shot so that you leave room to move into and out of frame. Again, you can use the light stand to help you establish proper framing and headroom height. Set up the light stand where you want the right side of the scene to be framed, then move the stand and use it to help find where the left side of the frame ends in the viewfinder. You can mark both right and left limits of where you will enter and exit frame with a couple of rocks or with some gaffer's tape or any other suitable object. Now, with the lens set on the desired composition, roll the camera, walk into frame, and "root" yourself, meaning that you set your body so that you don't begin to sway as you address the camera. When you are finished talking, give yourself an edit point before you exit frame or else exit frame naturally as you finish talking.

SHOOTING IN COLD WEATHER

When shooting in cold weather the cardinal rule is to keep batteries, camera, and recording media dry and covered and to keep them as warm as possible. Especially try to avoid storing tapes or batteries in the car during cold weather. When you move the camera inside from the cold, give it adequate time to warm slowly to room temperature (Figure 4.7).

Humidity and condensation can occur not only on the camera lens but inside the video recorder itself as the equipment is moved from a very cold environment to a warm, relatively moist room condition. Most recorders have a special sensor that shuts down the recorder when moisture levels climb too high. The machine is rendered inoperable until the moisture has evaporated or until the record heads are field stripped and dried.

Cassettes allowed to become overly cold can tear and break during taping, and if they are exposed suddenly to a warm environment moisture may condense inside the cassette. Clogged video heads soon follow.

When you must be in the cold, try to install batteries in the camera or recorder at the last possible moment, then try to spend as little time making your shots as necessary. Try to keep batteries and video cassettes as warm as possible, preferably under your winter coat next to your body. When the shots are made, remove the batteries

FIGURE 4.7　Plummeting temperatures take their toll on field equipment, batteries, and news employees.

from your equipment and if possible return to a warm car and let warm air from the car's heater or defroster blow across them. If you must shoot outdoors in extremely cold weather for prolonged periods, consider covering the camera housing with a padded cover to which you can tape portable hand warmers of the type used by hunters. Some camera covers are constructed or can be made to order with pockets specially built to accommodate such hand warmers.

SHOOTING IN BAD WEATHER

Professional-quality electronic news gathering (ENG) cameras and videotape record heads have been designed to operate in all manner of weather extremes, yet because they are electronic, certain precautions are necessary. Field experience shows that during heavy rain or snowfall, the best solution seems to be a kind of fairly loose "raincoat" that allows excess moisture to escape before it can damage the camera lens or condense inside the video recorder. This so-called raincoat is nothing more than a loose cape that can be purchased or constructed from waterproof materials to fit the machinery at hand.

(continued)

SHOOTING IN BAD WEATHER   Continued

One caution is to avoid sealing the videotape recorder tightly inside a waterproof container. If the bag sweats, excess moisture can build up inside the machine; at that point special sensors will prevent further operation until the moisture has evaporated.

SAFETY FIRST

When you cover spot news you learn to recognize when it is best not to cross the line. If you are to expose yourself to danger while covering the news, the event must be terribly worthwhile. Possibly no event is worth risking death or serious injury. Train yourself to be aware and learn to recognize that the brick wall in front of you may collapse at any moment or that you are in the middle of the S.W.A.T. team's line of fire or that noxious fumes and smoke are creeping your way. "Be careful when you cover the news, or you'll be part of the news," advises KCNC's Marcia Neville.[6]

While you can be physically hurt while covering the news, it is just as possible to be emotionally hurt. Perhaps a man's wife has just died or a family has lost its home in a fire, or perhaps a three-year-old girl in a story you cover suffers from terminal cancer. No law says journalists must be the tough, silent type. The important thing is to admit your feelings and to discharge them appropriately. "If it bothers you, talk it out with someone," says Bob Burke, chief photographer at KCNC.[7]

Distancing

Also of potential concern when you cover the news is a phenomenon called **distancing.** As you watch the action unfold in the camera viewfinder, a feeling develops that you're watching the event on TV. The event may seem remote, even unreal, and at such moments you may almost feel that nothing can hurt you. Dozens of photographers have looked up to find parade floats and football players almost upon them, all because of the erroneous sense of distance that resulted from the false perspectives of wide-angle and telephoto lens settings.

Safety in Numbers

At such times, the extra set of eyes provided by the reporter can offer the photographer an important margin of safety. While the photojournalist's attention is focused in the viewfinder, the reporter can be alert to action that develops outside the viewfinder frame. The reporter can also perform the valuable function of protecting the photojournalist in dangerous crowd situations, making paths through crowds as the photojournalist tapes the action, or acting as driver while the photographer makes shots on the move.

Plan to Make Plenty of Mistakes

Many of the problems photographers encounter the first few times in the field have happened to every photographer. In fact, with only slight exaggeration, some photographers suggest that you really can't be a professional until you've committed every mistake there is to commit, at least twice. Mistakes, after all, are how we learn. The following list of areas in which the most common mistakes occur forms a starting point; you may wish to add additional notes based on your own field experiences.

Shakiness. Tripod all shots until you learn to hold the camera rock steady. If you don't have a tripod, support the camera and your body by leaning or resting against stationary objects, and remember never to hold the camera when the lens is set on telephoto.

Color Balance. Set the camera's white balance to achieve an absence of color at white. Adjust white balance each time the light source changes. Some cameras have a memory chip that allows you to preset indoor/outdoor white balance values. Thus, if you're following a suspect from fluorescent light inside a courthouse hall to bright sunlight outside, you can hit the white balance switch as you move outside and be assured of proper white balance.

Wrong Filter. Determine that the proper camera filter is in place under each source of light—sunlight, fluorescent, artificial, mercury-vapor, athletic playing fields, and so on.

Record Color Bars. Remember to record color bars for ten to fifteen seconds at the start of each tape or disk. Color bars provide a reference of the field camera's color output, contrast, and video signal strength. Color bars also provide space at the start of videotape for edit prerolling. Without space for the edit preroll, the beginning of the first scene on tape cannot be edited.

Exposure Problems. Guard against under- and overexposure and hot spots in the frame. Use the automatic camera meter to set exposure, but then shoot on manual iris, in order to avoid the exposure "bloom" that results from moving objects when the lens is set on auto iris.

Focus Problems. Establish crisp focus; avoid zooming in to unintentional soft focus or zooming out to soft focus.

Contrast Problems. Avoid high-contrast backlit scenes that occur when the main light is behind the subject you are shooting. Use front fill light if necessary. Some examples of backlit scenes: shooting the person's face against the back-ground of a bright sky; shooting the subject against a light-colored background; shooting a subject in front of a window (close the curtains behind your subject).

Composition Problems. Compose each shot carefully. Avoid distracting backgrounds. Adhere to the rule of thirds to avoid placing subjects in the dead center of frame. Leave room at the bottom of the shot for superimpositions of the speaker's name. Avoid tilted horizon lines.

Too Much Panning and Zooming.   Practice self-control when you zoom and pan. Hold the beginning of your shot steady for about three seconds, then zoom or pan, and again hold the shot steady for another three seconds before you stop the camera.

Sound Problems.   Monitor sound quality in the field through earphones. If you hear high-quality sound while you are recording, you know the sound will be usable for broadcast.

Wind Noise.   Protect against wind noise when recording sound in the field. Use the foam rubber windscreen furnished with the microphone, or wrap a dark-colored cloth neatly around the microphone. When fashioning a homemade windscreen, avoid white because it may "bloom," or appear to be overexposed, on home screens.

Anticipate the Action.   Unless the recorder is in "pause," allow three seconds for videotape recorder start-up when you begin to record a scene. Some videotape recorders require time to wrap around the tape drum and reach full speed before they lock onto a stable picture. If the tape is not already threaded and you fail to anticipate your subject's movements, you may miss the important beginning of an action.

Spot-Check Tapes and Digitally Acquired Images in Field.   Preview the video you have shot in the field before you return home. Most systems feature instant playback through the camera viewfinder. The playback lets you spot troubles that have developed during shooting before you return to the station, while reshooting may still be possible.

Label All Video.   Immediately label each cassette, hard drive, or memory stick with subject matter and date. Unlabeled video will drive you and the editor to distraction.

Dead Batteries.   Number field batteries and use them in sequence so you know which ones are still full. When working some distance from the news car or helicopter, take extra recording media and one extra battery, fully charged.

Protect Field Equipment.   Field equipment is extremely sensitive and the quality of pictures and sound depends on careful handling. Regularly clean and check all equipment, including front lens elements. See that no one bangs, jars, or drops equipment. Protect cords and cables against rough treatment. Fragile electrical connections may short-circuit or come loose, resulting in loss of power, picture, and/or sound. Neatly re-coil all cords and cables and return them to their proper cases. Replace the lens cap on the camera. Don't leave the lens cap in the field by accident.

On Returning to the Station

- *Charge batteries.* Immediately recharge all batteries that have been depleted in the field.

- *Be considerate of the next crew.* Be certain to leave a blank recording medium with each camera so the next crew doesn't go into the field unprepared.
- *Store equipment properly.* Store equipment in its assigned place on returning from the field.
- *Report damage.* Report any damage or malfunctions immediately.

SUMMARY

Attention to small details in photographic technique can markedly differentiate the work of one photographer from the next. Often, the most professional techniques are transparent to home viewers. A hallmark of professional photographers is their ability to hold the camera rock steady. Use of a tripod or appropriate stance and breathing techniques are necessary to produce a steady image. Professionals always have a reason to pan and zoom: Leave excessive panning and zooming to amateur photographers.

Beyond mastery of technique, skills in storytelling and planning are essential requisites for the professional photojournalist. Discrimination in the order and choice of shots made in the field helps preserve story focus, reduces the amount of unnecessary footage and time wasted in the field, and speeds the editing process.

Television is a medium of close-ups, textures, and details, so the viewer's greatest sense of involvement and first-person experience naturally results when the camera is involved in the action. Equally important is the need to focus more on people than on institutions during the reporting process. The photographer also must learn to work comfortably with people in order to portray them naturally and with spontaneity, and to work safely and prudently whatever the environment. Ultimately, success depends on mastery of creative and technical principles through unflagging attention to detail.

DISCUSSION

1. List the advantages and disadvantages of using a tripod when shooting television news.

2. What are the most important techniques that can be used to steady the handheld camera?

3. Explain the primary considerations that govern panning and zooming.

4. Why is it important to establish interactive communication in the field between the photographer and reporter?

5. What techniques can be used to avoid the pop cut?

6. Define the term *editing in the camera*, and discuss situations in which the technique can be useful.

7. Why is it important to involve the camera in the action?

8. What approaches can you use when working with people to make your stories more natural and interesting?

9. What is the difference between staging action and motivating it?

10. Explain the steps involved in shooting your own standup in the field.

11. Explain how to simultaneously shoot and conduct an interview in the field.

12. What precautions must the photographer observe when shooting in a cold environment?

13. Discuss the elements of safety you should observe whenever you cover news events.

EXERCISES

1. Continue to practice holding the camera until you can hold it rock steady. Adjust the camera until it is balanced on your shoulder; observe proper breathing technique and stance. Shoot a shot while standing up; shoot the same shot while leaning against a support. Rest the camera against the back of a chair or other support while you shoot. Compare handheld shots taken with the lens set on wide-angle and telephoto focal length settings.

2. Practice panning and zooming a subject at differing speeds. Then photograph the same subject without panning or zooming. Compare the result.

3. Create a pop cut for analysis: First shoot a long shot of a subject under your control, then physically move the camera toward the subject along the same axis line as you shoot medium and close shots. Now, move the camera back to its original position. Again shoot a long shot of the subject, but remember to move the camera off the original axis line as you shoot and move to photograph the medium and close shots. Edit the scenes together and compare the results.

4. Shoot a simple sequence in which you edit action in the camera. Shoot only those scenes you want on the air, in the order you want them to appear, with action as closely matched as possible. Show the result without editing any of the scenes.

5. Shoot fairly close shots of action from a distant location with the lens on a telephoto setting. Now, involve the camera in the action by physically moving it close to the action to record shots. Compare the screen results.

6. Working with a friend or willing stranger, try to motivate an action that would be familiar to your subject without letting the subject know your intent, such as the observation made to a spelling bee champion, "I'll bet you can even spell chrysanthemum." Now, stage the action, perhaps telling your subject, "Okay, why don't you sit here, and I'll tell you a word to spell. Ready?" Compare the degree of spontaneity that results from each approach.

7. Practice photographing yourself in a field standup, using the suggestions offered in this chapter.

8. With the help of a friend who can act as your interview source, practice holding the camera while you interview your friend.

9. Ask a couple of friends if you can follow them around with the camera. Practice photographing moments of heat and white light.

10. Using the guidelines on pages 86–87, "How to Give Tape the Rich Look of Film," practice white-balancing the camera on different color sources as a way to make colors in your scenes more rich and pleasing.

NOTES

1. Comments to journalism students at the University of Oklahoma, Norman, OK, 5 November 2002.

2. Nelson Wadsworth, "Richardson Talks about 'Distancing,'" *Rangefinder* (Utah State University) (Summer 1985), 54.

3. Comments in a critique session at the NPPA TV News-Video Workshop, Norman, OK, 20 May 2003.

4. Butch Townley, "Videotape Editing: The Basics," a presentation at the NPPA TV News-Video Workshop, Norman, OK, 14 March 1994.

5. Larry Hatteberg, "Working with People," a presentation at the NPPA Television News-Video Workshop, Norman, OK, 16 March 1992.

6. Comments made to journalism students at Colorado State University, Fort Collins, 23 April 1998.

7. Ibid.

CHAPTER FIVE

THE MAGIC OF LIGHT AND LIGHTING

Until the advent of photography, we could neither see nor hear the past. The photons that streamed toward our forebears from objects and events did not linger, but vanished at once.[1] Today television journalists enable viewers to be direct observers of the past. And in television the past is recalled not simply from memory, or through words, but from a tangible record the original photons created when they glanced off the actual subjects of our stories and were captured on video. Through videotape and digital recordings, the past can be captured, condensed, and reviewed at will. This is the magic embodied in the word **photography,** which is taken from Greek root words meaning "writing with light."

As the artist's palette in this electronic medium, light is thus far more important to the work of the television journalist than merely as a source of illumination to provide an exposure. Light does illuminate, but when properly controlled it also lends texture, emphasis, and emotion. In television news, light is form. Light is mood. Light is meaning. The most "natural" light is natural light. The best lighting is invisible. In fact, the strongest and most honest television stories often contain little or no lighting. "Camera folks run from 9 or 12 or 18 dB gain, preferring a roomful of lights to the more honest look of natural light. I'm always amazed," says Ray Farkas, network freelance producer and photojournalist. "As a journalist, I'm usually one or two or three lights more honest than you are."[2]

PHOTOGRAPHY IS THE ART OF CONTROLLING LIGHT

In many ways, photography is the art of capturing and controlling light. Until the advent of electronic cameras, the photographer was forced to manipulate light, its intensity and color, to suit the whimsy of film stock. But today, with electronic cameras, the photographer can adjust electronic circuitry to adapt to the existing conditions of light and color.

Color Temperature

The **color temperature** of lighting sources is measured according to a scale of degrees Kelvin (°K), which indicates the proportion of red to blue light radiated by the light source. Daylight is a combination of all the light rays in the visible spectrum, but daylight contains a higher proportion of blue than some other sources. Tungsten halogen lights, commonly used in television lighting, also contain all the light rays of the visible spectrum, but with a higher proportion of red hues than daylight produces.

Television field cameras are set up to reproduce colors accurately only under light sources with a color temperature of 3200°K. If light entering the lens is anything other than 3200°K, the scenes will be either too green or blue (at color temperatures above 3200°K) or too red or orange (at temperatures below 3200°K). This means that outdoors, without compensating filters, the camera will "see" sunlight as overly blue.

An understanding of color temperatures is important for photojournalists because the camera must be adjusted for proper white balance in order to reproduce pure white and accurate colors under each of the various light sources. *White balance* is defined as the absence of color at white.

The laws of physics that influence color temperature are different from our psychological and physical reactions to color and temperature. Human experience leads us to associate the color blue with cool or cold objects and the color red with warm or hot objects. In the case of color temperature, just the opposite is true (Figure 5.1). As the

Color Temperature Scale

	DEGREES KELVIN	TYPE OF LIGHT SOURCE
Reddish hues	1700–1800°K	Match flame
	1850–1930°K	Candle flame
	2000–3000°K	Sun at sunrise or sunset
	2500–2900°K	Household tungsten bulbs
	3000°K	Tungsten lamp 500W-1k
	3200–3500°K	Quartz lights
	3200–7500°K	Florescent lights
	3275°K	Tungsten lamp 2k
	3380°K	Tungsten lamp 5k, 10k
Bluish hues	5000–5400°K	Sun: direct at noon
	5500–6500°K	Sun (sun + sky)
	5500–6500°K	Sun: through clouds/haze
	6000–7500°K	Sky: overcast
	6500°K	RGB Monitor
	7000–8000°K	Outdoor shade areas
	8000–10,000°K	Sky: partly cloudy

FIGURE 5.1 The color temperature of various light sources is measured in degrees Kelvin (°K) as an indication of the proportion of red to blue light radiated by the light source. As light sources change, the television camera's white balance must be adjusted to produce an absence of color at white under these varying hues of color.

Source: "Kelvin Color Temperatures," http://www.3drender.com/glossary/colortemp.htm, downloaded May 28, 2003. Based on information by Jeremy Birn, *Digital Lighting & Rendering*, Indianapolis: New Riders Publishing, 2000.

color temperature increases, the light becomes progressively more bluish. As color temperature decreases, the light becomes progressively more reddish. Thus, with color temperatures, blue is "hot"; red is "cool."

Tungsten Halogen Light Sources

The artificial light source most often used in television news is the tungsten halogen bulb. Small, lightweight, and portable, tungsten halogen lights produce brilliant illumination at a relatively constant color temperature of 3000°K to 3200°K (see Figure 5.1). The color temperature can be held constant because the bulb is filled with an inert gas, either iodine, fluorine, bromine, astatine, chlorine, or some other substance, that prevents the glowing tungsten filament from discoloring the inside of the bulb as it burns. Because of the inert gas, tungsten halogen bulbs have the capacity to "renew" themselves. In an atmosphere in which virtually no combustion is possible, particles that evaporate from the filament eventually are redeposited back onto the filament.

Filters

The television photojournalist relies on three basic filter applications to control light and color temperature. These applications encompass filters used on cameras, artificial lights, and windows.

> *camera-mounted filters:* filters that are mounted on the front of the camera lens or just behind the lens inside the camera
>
> *light-mounted filters:* gel or optical glass filters that are positioned directly on the light head in a mount or clamp-type holder
>
> *window-mounted filters:* filters mounted directly on windows and normally used to change the color temperature of sunlight entering a room to 3200°K

In each case the goal is to correct the color temperature or to change the quantity of light entering the camera so a different aperture can be used to control depth of field. No filter is required on the camera when a light source has an intrinsic color temperature of 3200°K. Under all other color temperatures, some form of filter is required.

Camera-Mounted Filters

The most commonly used camera-mounted filters are the amber (#85), fluorescent (FLB or FLD), and neutral density (ND) filters. On some cameras these filters are built into a filter wheel that can be clicked into proper position behind the lens according to a reference chart printed on the side of the camera body. With other cameras the filters must be attached directly to the front of the camera lens.

#85 B Filter.   The amber-colored #85 filter converts sunlight in the vicinity of 5400°K to 3200°K. Average daytime sunlight, which otherwise would appear overly blue to the camera, is reduced to the same color temperature as the artificial light from tungsten bulbs so that normal color results. An amber filter must be used anytime the light source, regardless of whether it is natural sunlight or artificial fill light, is 5400°K, or reasonably close to that figure.

Practically speaking, in average daylight conditions, the #85 filter can be used anytime from a couple of hours after sunrise to within a couple of hours before sunset. It is best, however, to use no filter or a clear filter within one hour after sunrise or one hour before sunset. At these times of day, color temperature is already between 3200°K and 3500°K, a range that closely parallels the camera's preset preference for color temperature.

Fluorescent (FL) Filters. Two designations of camera-mounted fluorescent filters can be used to accommodate fluorescent light that otherwise would be reproduced with an undesirable greenish-blue cast. The first of these is the FLB filter, used under fluorescent bulbs that produce color temperatures in the range of 4500°K. The second is the FLD filter, used under "daylight" fluorescent bulbs that produce color temperatures in the range of fine to cloudy daylight, or 6500°K. Once again, FL filters produce the appearance of a color temperature around 3200°K.

Neutral Density (ND) Filters. A third type of camera-mounted filter, the ND filter, reduces the amount of light entering the camera but otherwise has no effect on either color temperature or the colors of objects within scenes. The primary function of this dark, smoke-colored filter is to cut exposure—either to help reduce depth of field by permitting use of a wider lens aperture (resulting in less emphasis on the background and greater emphasis on the subject), or to reduce exposure under very bright light sources to acceptable limits.

Light-Mounted Filters

The *dichroic filter* is most commonly used on lights. This filter, made of gel or optical glass, has a pronounced bluish hue. It boosts the color temperature of quartz-halogen lights (3200°K) to the approximate color temperature of sunlight (5400°K). The filter is used to achieve balanced color temperatures when sunlight and artificial light are mixed. Artificial **fill lights** outfitted with dichroic filters are commonly used outdoors, with the sun used as the **key light,** and indoors regardless of whether sunlight entering through a window is used as the key or the fill light.

Window-Mounted Filters

Semiflexible panels and flexible sheets of #85 amber filters are frequently used on exterior windows to convert sunlight to 3200°K. The sheets also can be taped to car windows, thereby allowing the use of 3200°K fill lights inside the car—for example, to photograph an interview with a police officer as she patrols a neighborhood. These filters also can be taped over house and office windows to convert the sunlight entering a room to 3200°K. It is then possible to supplement the sunlight with artificial lights with a color temperature of 3200°K. If sunlight at 5400°K is allowed to enter the interior of a car or room, then artificial fill light must be pumped up to 5400°K by means of a dichroic filter mounted on the light head. This alternative is less desirable because more lights and higher wattage bulbs may be required to overcome the exposure-reducing effects of the dichroic filter.

Filter Factors

All filters, even clear glass, filter out some light. With clear filters the light loss is virtually unnoticeable, but with other filters the light loss can be significant enough to result in underexposure. The amount of loss for a given filter is expressed as the **filter factor** (see Table 5.1).

TABLE 5.1   Filter Factors and Their Light Loss Equivalents

FILTER FACTOR	LIGHT LOSS (IN F/STOPS)
1	0
1.5	.66
2	1
3	1.5
4	2
6	2.5
8	3
10	3.33
12	3.5
16	4

■ ■ ■ ■ ■ ■

TRY YOUR HAND WITH FILTERS AND LIGHTING

The following situations are provided as a means for you to check your understanding of how various light sources and camera filters can be used in combination.

Situation 1: Outdoors, under normal sunlight, set up an artificial fill light and balance its color temperature to sunlight.

Situation 2: You're shooting an indoor scene in front of a window. Across the street, in sunlight, is other important action that can be seen through the window. What combination of lights and filters can be used to achieve balanced color temperatures?

Situation 3: You're shooting an interview inside a moving car. You've placed a #85 gel filter on the driver's window to convert sunlight to 3200°K and have decided to use a quartz fill light with a color temperature of 3200°K. Which filter do you use on the camera?

DISCUSSION

In situation 1, the sun, with a color temperature of around 5400°K, serves as the key light while the fill light produces a color temperature of 3200°K. A dichroic filter must be mounted on the light head to boost the artificial light to the color temperature of sunlight. In addition, a #85 amber filter must be placed on the camera lens.

In situation 2, two solutions are possible. If sunlight is the dominant light source inside the room, the camera should be outfitted with a #85 amber filter. To match the color temperature of sunlight, all quartz fill lights should be outfitted with dichroic filters.

If, in situation 2, artificial quartz lights provide the dominant light (3200°K), then no filter should be used on the camera lens. Sunlight entering the room should further be converted to 3200°K by use of #85 filter sheets placed on the window.

In situation 3, simply shoot the scene as is, with no filter of any kind on the camera lens.

Each factor of 2 cuts the original amount of light in half, an amount equal to one f/stop decrease in the amount of light entering the lens. Thus, if a scene were being photographed at f/16, a new exposure of f/11 would be necessary if the scene were to be rephotographed using a filter with a filter factor of 2. Cameras with automatic exposure circuitry compensate automatically for this light loss, but an understanding of filter factors is still important to the professional photographer.

The ND filter, for example, allows the photographer to achieve normal exposure in extremely bright light conditions. ND filters also allow the photographer to shoot at wider lens apertures in any given lighting environment than would otherwise be possible. Wider apertures, in turn, result in reduced or shallow depth of field.

ND filters are supplied in a variety of densities. The ND 0.3 has a factor of 2, the ND 0.6 has a factor of 4, the ND 0.9 has a factor of 8, and the ND 1.0 has a factor of 10. Using the ND 0.6 with a filter factor of 4, for example, would cut exposure by two stops, allowing the photographer to open the lens aperture two stops (i.e., from f/11 to f/5.6, or from f/8 to f/4).

Filters Used in Combination

Note that each filter factor of 2 results in the equivalent of one f/stop of light loss. To determine the light loss that occurs when filters are used in combination, it is necessary to *multiply* the filter factors. Because some picture quality is lost when two filters are used together, manufacturers commonly combine dyes with the characteristics of two filters into the physical properties of one filter.

One of the most common filters of this type is the 85N6 filter, which combines the color conversion characteristics of the #85 amber filter (with a filter factor of 1.5) and the light-reducing properties of the ND 0.6 filter (filter factor of 4). Thus, the combined filter factor of the 85N6 filter is 6:

$$
\begin{array}{rl}
1.5 & = \text{filter factor of \#85 filter} \\
\times\ \underline{4} & = \text{filter factor of ND 0.6 filter} \\
6 & = \text{combined filter factor}
\end{array}
$$

To better understand the logarithmic progression of filter factors, note that while a factor of 4 results in two stops of light loss, a filter factor of 8 results in three stops of light loss rather than four stops, as demonstrated in the following equation.

$2 \times 2 \times 2 = 8$ (filter factor)

$(1)(1)(1) = 3$ (stops of light loss)

As another example, the light loss that results from a filter factor of 16 is equivalent to four stops, not eight:

$2 \times 2 \times 2 \times 2 = 16$ (filter factor)

$(1)(1)(1)(1) = 4$ (stops of light loss)

MIXING LIGHT SOURCES

Poor color reproduction can result when light sources are mixed. Indoors, the photographer should strive to avoid mixing fluorescent light (greenish hue) with daylight (bluish hue) or tungsten lights (reddish hue). Outdoors, an inadvertent mix of sunlight and tungsten light also produces undesirable results. Any of the light sources used alone—fluorescent, daylight, or tungsten—are acceptable, but they should never be mixed unless they can be balanced with filters.

Check for the presence of various light sources as one of the first steps after you arrive on location. If daylight in the room is strong enough, it may be used to the exclusion of any other light source. If different light sources are present, perhaps you can turn off all fluorescent lights in the room, close curtains in the room to block unwanted sunlight, and light the scene only with tungsten lights. If the fluorescent lights can't be turned off, use them if they provide sufficient illumination. Otherwise, you will have to overpower them with artificial lights or perhaps a combination of sunlight and artificial light color-balanced to the temperature of sunlight.

BASIC LIGHTING PATTERNS

Most lighting patterns in news photography borrow from nature's design. The most frequent pattern is one dominant light source (the sun or an artificial light) combined with a secondary light source. The dominant source produces direct light rays that throw strong highlights and distinct shadows in an effect called **specular light.** The goal is to make the light look as though it originates from one source, even when three lights are being used, and to light in such a way that subjects have dimension, not flatness.

The secondary light source, whether artificial or from the sun's rays that reflect off objects in the environment, is soft and diffused. Secondary light yields no hard shadows and no distinct highlights because it has been broken up and randomly scattered as it reflects off the multitude of objects and surfaces within an environment.

THE ROLE OF ARTIFICIAL LIGHT

For most photographers the sun remains a favorite light source. But for all its charm, sunlight is never reliable or under a photographer's control, and it seldom is available in sufficient quantity when the shooting moves indoors. In such conditions artificial light gives the photographer control over illumination, and when properly controlled, can be used to recreate the natural look of available sunlight. Proper light control also gives the illusion of depth in scenes and makes possible the creation of textures and interesting highlights and shadows.

KEY LIGHT

For natural-looking news scenes that replicate the look and feel of available light, almost all artificial lighting setups have one dominant light source called the **key light.** This light represents the function of the sun and provides the distinctive highlights and shadows in the scene.

The key light usually is placed higher than the subject to be photographed and to one side of the camera, somewhere between 30° and 45° over from the camera axis and high enough so that the light can be aimed down 45° or steeper at the subject, in a pattern called *high side lighting.* The key light is placed properly when it throws a triangle of light on the shadow side of the subject's face (Figure 5.2).

Outdoors the photographer can achieve the same effect using the sun as the key light. In this approach the subject is moved until the triangle appears on the shadow side of the face.

Variations to the high side light pattern include the *side light,* sometimes called **hatchet light** because it splits the subject in half, and *side-rear lighting,* in which the key light is placed to the side and somewhat behind the subject.

Another variation is *top lighting,* with the key light almost directly above the subject. This technique throws deep shadows beneath the eyes, nose, and chin. A variation of top lighting is called **butterfly light** (Figure 5.3). The light remains high but is slightly in front of the subject so that no harsh shadows appear in the eyes or under lips. This lighting pattern takes its name from the butterfly-shaped shadow that appears beneath the subject's nose and can be an excellent choice of patterns when only one light is to be used. Butterfly lighting is also called *glamour lighting* because it is commonly used with models, actors, and actresses.

CONTRAST CONTROL

Video is less sensitive to detail than the human eye and in dark shadow areas it may lose detail altogether. Such loss of detail may be fine for effect if the photographer wants stark, dramatic pictures, but is less acceptable when the pictures must meet high quality standards for broadcast. To open up detail in shadow areas, the photographer can use a **fill light** (the secondary light source) set to produce illumination about half as intense as the key light (Figure 5.4). The same fill effect can be achieved outdoors with a

FIGURE 5.2   High side lighting occurs when the key light is placed high and to one side of the camera in front of the subject. Note the triangle of light on the shadow side of the subject's face.

reflector or with a battery-powered light equipped with a dichroic filter that raises the color temperature of tungsten lights to that of sunlight.

For soft fill outdoors, use a white reflector with a matte surface, or for hard fill light, an aluminum foil reflector. White walls and other objects also can be used outdoors if they reflect light of the same approximate color temperature as the key light source.

THE INVERSE-SQUARE LAW OF LIGHT

The fill light is located approximately mirror opposite the key light and adjusted so that it illuminates the subject at about half the intensity of the key light. To arrive at this intensity, the photographer can use the **inverse-square law of light.** This law states that at twice the distance from a subject, artificial lights provide only one-fourth their original level of illumination (Figure 5.5).

Stated another way, if you have two identical lights, one twice as far from your subject as the other, the farther light will provide only one-fourth the illumination of the closer light. This would provide a key-to-fill contrast ratio of about 4:1. In other

FIGURE 5.3   Butterfly or glamour lighting occurs when the light is positioned high but slightly in front of the subject. Note the modeling in the subject's face created by shadows beneath the eyebrows, nose, lips, and chin.

FIGURE 5.4   A key light is used to illuminate the right side of the subject's face (left). In the picture on the right, a fill light has been added to open up detail in harsh shadow areas on the subject's face.

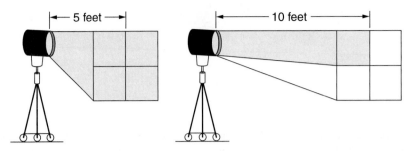

FIGURE 5.5   The inverse-square law of light can be visualized by looking at the above diagrams. When distance doubles, the intensity of light is only one-fourth the original level.

words, the key light is four times brighter than the fill light. For television lighting the normal contrast ratio should be approximately 3:1 for best color and contrast control. To achieve this, the fill light should be placed about one and a half times the distance of the key from the subject. In this way the key light will be about three times stronger than the fill light for a contrast ratio of approximately 3:1.

LIGHTING RATIOS

Lighting ratios are expressions of the difference between the most brightly illuminated areas of a subject and the areas of least exposure. Calculations are based on the difference in intensities between the key and fill lights. In the following table, a 1:1 ratio indicates that key and fill light intensities are identical: There is no difference in illumination on either side of the subject's face. A 4:1 ratio indicates that light on the key side of the face is four times brighter than on the fill side. In the case of the 4:1 ratio, exposure is determined by the key light. If the key light were to be turned off but the fill light left on, the subject would be two stops underexposed.

DIFFERENCE OF INTENSITY BETWEEN KEY LIGHT/FILL LIGHT (IN F/STOPS)	LIGHTING RATIO (KEY-TO-FILL)
0	1:1
2/3	1.5:1
1	2:1
1.5	3:1
2	4:1
2.5	6:1
3	8:1
3.33	10:1
4	16:1
5	32:1

Assume, for example, that the key light is six feet from the subject to be photographed. To maintain proper contrast control for videotape, the fill light in this case should be placed about nine feet from the subject.

BACKLIGHT

To the key and fill lights, the photographer can add a **backlight** (also called the *accent* or *separation light*). This light is placed opposite the key and shines down on the subject from behind to give the subject's hair added texture and sheen and to separate the subject more obviously from the background. A fourth light, the *background light*, can be used to illuminate the background and to provide even more separation of the subject from its background.

BROADLIGHTING AND SHORT LIGHTING

When the key light shines on the side of the face closest to the camera, the effect is called **broadlighting.** Generally, broadlight is the preferred lighting pattern for interviews and news conferences. In **short lighting** the fill light shines on the side of the face toward the camera. The technique is used more widely in portrait photography than in news photography, but it can be used as warranted in news to achieve a different mood and feeling.

FLAT LIGHTING

When the photographer must shoot fast-moving action, there often is not time to properly light the scene. For this reason most electronic news gathering (ENG) cameras can be operated with a single battery-operated quartz light that mounts directly to the camera. This approach frees the photographer's hands to make camera and lens adjustments, but it results in a pattern called **flat lighting,** which produces uninteresting pictures with little sense of depth or modeling.

A better solution, whenever possible, is to use the single light high and to one side of the camera. In this position the light yields satisfactory modeling on the subject's face by providing shadows that give depth and interest to the face. One common mistake that occurs with the single light is the harsh shadows that sometimes result on the background behind the subject. At least three remedies are possible: Hold the light so that shadows fall outside the viewfinder frame, move the subject farther away from the background, or compose a closer shot in such a way that no shadows are visible within the viewfinder.

LIGHT DIFFUSION

In all lighting patterns, softer, more natural light can be produced with some kind of diffusion material over the lights. A few of the diffusion materials available include spun glass, heat resistant plastic, metal window screen, and metallic mesh. Diffusion materials reduce glare and harshness in the scene by breaking up direct light rays and radiating them in random directions. Diffused light also is less noticeable to persons who otherwise would be uncomfortable and self-conscious under the harsh glare of direct television lights.

BOUNCE LIGHTING

Bounce light is another way to produce soft, natural lighting. Bounce lights can be reflected (bounced) off a ceiling, wall, or some other reflective surface. Bounce light is diffused and less harsh than direct lighting, but care should be taken to avoid unwanted color temperatures when bouncing the light off colored surfaces.

EYE REFLECTIONS

In real life and in natural portraiture, each eye normally contains only one highlight. When lights are improperly placed, however, the subject's eyes frequently contain two highlights (catchlights), which make it obvious that the subject is being "lit." The problem is compounded when eyeglass lenses and frames produce still other distracting highlights. While dual highlights and unwanted reflections cannot always be eliminated, they can often be minimized. The most common solution is to move the camera or to change the projection angle of the lights, or to use some form of indirect lighting that may solve the problem altogether.

UMBRELLA LIGHTING

Photojournalists seem to spend much of their working life shooting indoor interviews. All too often these interviews are illuminated by one light source on the camera, a technique that results in hot, flat lighting and distracting reflections off eyeglass lenses and frames. Interview subjects sit in the hot, harsh glare of the lights and wish they were somewhere else. The scene is illuminated, but it cannot be said to be naturally lighted. At other stations photographers may use no more than two light heads mounted on stands, with 1,000 or more watts of light falling directly on the interviewee. The lighting is uncomfortably harsh and obvious.

Umbrella lighting offers a quick, inexpensive way to improve such lighting dramatically. In fact, the umbrella reflector is an excellent way to convert a single light into a viable light source. With an umbrella reflector, the light head is pointed *away* from the subject. The light is then reflected back to the subject via a metallic-colored, heat resistant umbrella attached to the light stand or head (Figure 5.6). In a sit-down interview, the light can be placed over the reporter's head or where the reporter would be if present.

Light from this single source wraps naturally around the subject. Shadows are soft and naturally smooth, and in close-up shots only a single highlight or catchlight

FIGURE 5.6   Use of an umbrella reflector can result in
dramatic improvement in lighting quality.

is obvious in each of the subject's eyes. The light from umbrella reflectors is so pleasing that it is virtually unnoticeable to home audiences. Interview subjects are noticeably more at ease under this soft, indirect lighting, and they are more comfortable because of the cooler temperatures that result from the indirect light. Umbrella reflectors are available at most camera and photo supply stores for under fifty dollars, a relatively small investment considering the dramatically improved lighting guaranteed to result.

EXPOSURE

At their most basic, scenes are either correctly exposed, too light from overexposure, or too dark from underexposure. Proper exposure results in a rich cross section of pleasing colors and details.

In the case of cameras with automatic exposure control, electronic circuitry behind the lens "sees" only what the lens shows it. If the main subject shows up against a dark background, the scene may be overexposed as the camera struggles to properly expose the predominantly dark area in the background. The same subject in front of a white background might be underexposed because the camera would be fooled by the light background.

The solution in both cases is to move in closer with the camera or zoom lens to eliminate the background and let the camera meter see only the primary subject. Once exposure is properly adjusted, the exposure control can be clicked from automatic to its manual position. The exposure will remain until the control is readjusted or switched back to the automatic mode, so the shot can now be recomposed and recorded.

ESSENTIAL LIGHTING EQUIPMENT

Surprisingly little equipment is necessary to produce professionally lit scenes in the field. The following list of essentials is recommended by John Premack, chief photographer at WCVB-TV, Boston:[3]

- two focusing quartz lights such as the Lowel Omni (see www.lowel.com/) with stands, barndoors, dichroic filters, 650- and 300-watt lamps, and extra-small Chimera soft boxes (see www.chimeralighting.com). An alternative to the Chimera, which requires a mounting ring that interferes with the placement of other accessories such as barndoors and dichroic filters, is Lowel's RIFA 44, a small, folding softlight complete with bulb, socket, and stand-mounting bracket
- one focusing mini light (such as the Lowel Pro) with stand, 2-leaf barndoor, and diffusion filter
- one folding fabric reflector to provide fill light from the primary light source, indoors or out

The quartz light heads should include at least one head that can be mounted directly to the camera body for fast-breaking news events. Especially useful are the small reflector lamps that mount on the camera body and can be powered by the camera battery. Round out the list with spare light bulbs, two-inch-wide silver cloth gaffer's tape to hang lights and to tape cords to the floor to keep people from tripping, and plenty of extension cords. Also desirable is a package of mixed gels, a portable, 12-volt battery-operated light and battery pack for covering big spot-news stories at night, as well as scrims and other diffusion materials.

LIGHTING IN SUNLIGHT

Bright sunlight produces distinct highlights and black shadow areas with little or no detail. The problem can be especially acute when subjects are silhouetted against the sky. In these situations, fill light will be required—either from an artificial quartz light outfitted with a dichroic filter or from fill light supplied by a portable reflector or similar source.

Some of the most pleasing lighting patterns occur when the subject is lit with indirect sunlight. If the sun is behind the subject, the backlight on the person's hair and shoulders may be used to especially flattering effect, with quartz light or reflector fill light used to enhance illumination on the subject's face (Figure 5.7). If the sunlight is especially bright and straight overhead, a 1,000-watt quartz light with dichroic filter may be required to balance illumination levels to the same intensity of sunlight. Another pleasing form of indirect sunlight is **open shade,** in which the subject is photographed in shade, well away from direct sunlight, but with nothing above the subject to obstruct secondary light from the sky itself.

Strong sunlight also can overpower artificial light being used to photograph subjects indoors, converting the subjects to silhouette. The problem is most evident when subjects are photographed in front of open windows. In such situations try to close the curtains behind the person to be interviewed. If there are no curtains or they cannot be closed, try to reposition the subject in front of a more neutral background. Failing that, you may have to boost illumination on the subject's face to the same intensity as the sunlight behind the subject.

FIGURE 5.7 A portable reflector is used to kick fill light into the shadow side of the subject's face.

HOW TO LIGHT A NEWS CONFERENCE

Most news conferences can be nicely lit with a three-light setup. Set up a key light and fill light and add a backlight to help separate the subject from the background. If your lights will be more than seven or eight feet from the subject, use at least 650-watt bulbs.

If time or equipment are at a premium, two lights will do an adequate job. Eliminate the fill light and cheat the backlight by putting it on flood and opening the barndoor a little more. If you have only one light available, use it to bounce light onto the subject or to create a butterfly lighting pattern. The single light also can be used high and to one side of the camera, ideally with a scrim to help diffuse the light and make it softer, or the light can be moved back toward the side of the speaker's face.

If you must work with only one or two lights, make a commitment to shoot at the lowest level of illumination that produces acceptable skin tones. If you find it impossible to achieve light levels of f/8 on the subject and f/8 on the background, consider settling for an illumination level of f/2.8 on the background. If the skin color of the main subject is accurate and if illumination of the main subject is acceptable, little harm will result if exposure levels and color temperature of the background are allowed to stray. Once again, it is important that existing lights be turned off or that your own lights be converted with filters to match the color temperature of the existing light source.

As you adjust the lights, you can solicit either your soundperson, your reporter, or a volunteer to serve as a stand-in. If it's obvious the speaker will throw unwanted shadows against the background, try to move the podium away from the background or reposition the lights and/or camera to eliminate unwanted shadows from the frame.

As you position your lights, set a chair or other object by each light so the stands won't be inadvertently bumped or knocked down. It also is advisable to tape extension cords securely to the floor so passersby don't trip and break their legs or send your light stands crashing to the floor.

SETTING UP LIGHTS IN COOPERATION WITH OTHER CREWS

While news conference lighting is not art, inept lighting calls attention to itself and inevitably distracts viewers' attention from the speaker and what is being said. For that reason, be alert for the damaging influence of other crews who arrive and set up their own lights without regard for the lighting patterns and levels of illumination you've already established. Gentle negotiation to establish acceptable lighting patterns will work to everyone's benefit.

If you must work within the confines of **pack journalism,** arrive early enough to stake your claim to an ideal camera position and proceed with determination to hold your ground. Newspaper and radio reporters may swirl around you and complain that you're blocking the view, but their requirements are different from yours and they're virtually certain not to understand your needs.

LIGHTING ETIQUETTE

Regardless of the situation you are lighting, remember to practice lighting etiquette. If the subject can walk into a room that has already been lit, so much the better. Most people will adapt quickly to the lights and soon forget about them. Otherwise, when you first plug in the lights, try to tilt them down to the floor, then swing up the light heads gently so as not to blind your subjects suddenly. Another approach is to use your hand to block the light when it is first switched on, then slowly lower your hand from the light head to permit gradual, full illumination of your subject.

LIGHTING SPOT NEWS AT NIGHT

No matter whether you're photographing a nighttime political rally outdoors or covering spot news at night, the most logical place for the light is on the camera. Spot-news photography demands that the photojournalist move quickly to keep up with the action, which means that light stands are generally out of the question. Further, the camera-mounted light may be the only illumination available when the camera is diverted from the main action to shoot cutaways.

Especially at night, it's important not to use any more light than you need (Figure 5.8). This means the camera-mounted light is an excellent choice for night photography because of its relatively low level of intensity. If light levels on the main subject are too high, the background at night will be pitch black. "The more light you put on your subject at night, the greater discrepancy there is between your subject and the dark background at night," says photojournalist John Premack. "You're trying in effect for balanced light, even at night, so shoot with the aperture wide open if the image looks clean and acceptably exposed."[4]

PHOTOGRAPHING SUBJECTS WITH DARK SKIN

Whenever you light subjects who have dark skin, look for backgrounds that are slightly darker than the subject. Another practice is to keep as much light as possible off the background, in order to keep contrast ratios to acceptable levels. If the background is too light or too brightly lit, essential detail may be lost in the subject's face, or the subject may even be reproduced in silhouette. Keep light levels as low as comfortable, and if possible, err slightly on the side of overexposure rather than underexposure.

FIGURE 5.8 At night, try to use relatively low levels of illumination. The higher the intensity of light used to illuminate a subject at night, the less visible the background will be.

LARGE-SCALE LIGHTING

Occasions may occur when you have to photograph uncommonly large areas, such as hotel ballrooms, auditoriums, show rooms, and supermarkets. In such cases, the rule of thumb is to work with the light you have and to supplement existing light rather than bring in an entirely new light source. If the predominant light source is fluorescent light, for example, consider adding your own portable fluorescent fixtures to provide additional fill or accent light. Color temperature should remain relatively constant if the light bulbs are all the same type. Otherwise, you may need to use a correcting gel filter.

If sufficient illumination is unavailable or if extremely deep areas are to be lit, enough lights will be needed to light foreground, middle ground, and background adequately. If the area is very large, high wattage lights of 1,000 watts or more may be necessary. If an examination of the viewfinder shows that certain areas within the scene are too bright, the photographer can use **barndoors** (Figure 5.9), or **flags** (opaque panels that block light from certain areas), or **cookies** (flags with regular or irregular cutouts that form patterns of light and shadow on the background) and nets to enrich or subdue particular areas within the scene, a practice that Ross Lowell, of Lowell Light Manufacturing, has called *painting with shadows*.

FIGURE 5.9   A portable light with "barndoors" that can be moved to control light falling on the subject and background.

CAUTIONS

Lights are extremely bright and hot, and they pull lots of electricity when plugged into wall outlets. The obvious precautions apply when using artificial lights:

- Never touch quartz bulbs. Serious burns can result, and bulbs can be damaged from the natural oils on fingers.
- Allow bulbs to cool before packing them away or setting on objects (including carpeting, camera cases, and vinyl-topped tables).
- Serious retinal damage can occur if bright lights are used closer than three feet to human or animal subjects.
- Avoid shining bright lights directly into the lenses of older cameras. Cameras with pickup tubes can be permanently damaged.
- Avoid plugging more than three lights into an electrical circuit. Excessively high-voltage drains can cause overheated cords or tripped circuits.
- Avoid 1,000-watt bulbs whenever possible, because they tend to blow fuses.
- Use only extension cords that are large enough to handle the job. Cords that are too small cause voltage drops and can overheat to the point of causing fires. Voltage drops also alter the color temperature of artificial lights.
- Never discharge batteries completely or overcharge them.

TOO HOT TO HANDLE

Imagine going to someone's home to cover a story, and burning down their house. It can happen if you overload the home's electrical circuits. Plug in too many lights, overburden an old fuse box, add one too many extension cords, and you could send an entire family's way of life up in smoke. Imagine the misery you might cause were you to overload the circuits in an apartment building, or a horse barn, or an airport hangar.

Basic savvy can help you avoid such tragedies. Building codes require 20-amp circuits in most U.S. structures built since the mid-1980s. Before that the standard was 15 amps. Remember that your equipment rarely is the only electrical appliance on a circuit. If you exceed those loads by plugging in too many lights, stand by to call the fire department. What to do?

Just remember the rough formula for converting watts to amps: divide by 100. If you're using a 1,000-watt light, divide by 100. This tells you the light draws 10 amps. You are good to go. If you were to use three 1,000-watt bulbs, however, that would be 3,000 divided by 100, or 30 amps. Run for your life.

The consequences might not be life-threatening. You could just blow fuses or trip the circuit breakers. But you could start a fire. Even your extension cords could break into flames. Why risk the danger? Remember to divide the number of watts by 100. It's the smart way to operate.

In the final analysis, lighting creates mood. Mere illumination destroys it. Within every shot, light is the most visually important element—the raw material for every television journalist, the essential substance of every television story. As documentary historian William Bluem observed, "A photographer who cannot light is not a photographer. A reporter who underestimates the importance of light is a fool."[5] Happily, in today's environment, light is a commodity more easily controlled than ever before in the history of photojournalism.

SUMMARY

One of the photojournalist's most important writing tools is light. A primary characteristic of light is its color temperature, an expression of the proportion of red to blue light that the light source radiates. Under each varying light source the camera must be white-balanced to produce an absence of color at white. Avoid mixing light from sources with different color temperatures.

In television news, the artificial light source most commonly used is the quartz bulb, which produces a color temperature of 3200°K. Under light of any other temperature, filters must be used. Camera-mounted filters are used to correct the color temperature of sunlight, to filter out the excessive greenish-blue hues of fluorescent light, or to reduce the quantity of light entering the camera so a different aperture can be used to control depth of field. Light-mounted dichroic filters are used to boost the color temperature of quartz light to the approximate color temperature of average daylight. Semiflexible sheets of filter gel also can be mounted on windows to convert sunlight to 3200°K. All filters reduce light to some extent; the amount of loss is expressed by the filter factor. Each factor of 2 cuts the original amount of light by one-half.

Basic lighting patterns involve use of a key or dominant light and a fill or secondary light. The key light normally is positioned 30° to 45° over from the camera axis and high enough so the light can be aimed down 45° or steeper at the subject. Variations include side light, side-rear light, and top light, with further refinements available, such as butterfly or glamour lighting.

The intensity of illumination between key and fill lights helps determine contrast ratios within the scene. Generally, the key light is set one and a half to two stops brighter than the fill light. Often, diffused light is softer and more pleasing to the eye. Sunlight is naturally diffused on overcast or foggy days or when subjects are in open shade. Diffusion of artificial light also can be achieved through bounce light or umbrella lighting or with any of various diffusion materials.

While most lighting assignments can be accomplished with a key, fill, and backlight, large-scale interiors and night lighting present special challenges. In the final analysis, light creates mood and meaning. Mere illumination destroys it.

DISCUSSION

1. Discuss the extent to which light is the true medium of television journalism.

2. What is color temperature and how does it affect the television picture?

3. List the filters most commonly used in television news photography (camera-, light-, and window-mounted) and describe their uses.

4. Explain filter factors and how they are used to determine the light-reducing properties of filters.

5. Explain what happens when light sources with different color temperatures are mixed. How can the photographer avoid the problem?

6. Describe the differing roles of the key light and the fill light.

7. Describe the basic lighting patterns commonly used in television news photography.

8. How are key-to-fill lighting ratios (lighting contrast ratios) determined?

9. Explain the difference between broad lighting and short lighting.

10. How can light rays be diffused or otherwise controlled to create softer, more pleasing lighting patterns?

11. What minimum lighting equipment should the photojournalist have available for field assignments?

12. What special considerations are necessary when using supplementary artificial lights outdoors under bright sunlight? Why are artificial lights sometimes necessary under such conditions?

13. Explain how to light a news conference.

14. What considerations should you keep in mind when lighting subjects outdoors at night? When lighting large-scale subjects such as warehouses and supermarkets?

15. What safety precautions should you observe when you work with lights?

EXERCISES

1. Color-balance the camera for 3200°K light, then without altering color-balance, photograph scenes illuminated by a normal 60-watt household bulb, under sunlight at noon, and one hour before sunset. Compare the results.

2. With the #85 filter in place and the camera properly white-balanced, shoot a scene under sunlight at noon with and without the #85 filter. Repeat the exercise indoors under artificial quartz light with the camera properly white-balanced for a light source of 3200°K. Slate or otherwise identify each scene.

3. Shoot a scene indoors under artificial quartz light with no #85 filter on the camera. Again shoot the scene, but this time with a dichroic filter on the artificial quartz light.

4. Shoot a daytime scene of a driver from inside a car using a battery-operated, 3200°K artificial fill light and no filter on the camera. Shoot the scene again with the same light and camera setup, but this time with a #85 gel filter taped to the window that is visible behind the driver.

5. Shoot a subject indoors silhouetted against the sunlight or other backlight coming through a window behind the subject. Set up an artificial fill light with dichroic filter to balance exposure on the subject's face against the light in the background.

6. Set up a key light on a subject. Properly position the key light so that a triangle of light appears on the shadow side of the subject's face. Now, set up a fill light of equal intensity, but position the fill light approximately twice as far from your subject as the key light. In this configuration, what is the approximate key-to-fill ratio?

7. Reposition the fill light in example 6 so that your key-to-fill light is approximately 3:1.

   A good way to accomplish this feat is to set the key light first and take an exposure reading with an exposure meter or by letting the camera circuitry determine proper exposure. Note the f/stop setting that would be required for proper exposure when using the key light by itself.

   At this point, turn off the key light. Adjust the intensity of illumination from the fill light by moving the light stand forward or backward until the exposure reading on your subject's face is one and a half stops less intense than the key light reading.

   In other words, if proper exposure for the key light alone is f/8, position the fill light so that proper exposure for the fill light alone would be halfway between f/4 and f/5.6, or one and a half stops less intense (thus the need to open the aperture to a larger setting). The fill light is always farther from the subject than the key light, provided that both lights are of equal intensity.

   Finally, turn on both lights and shoot the scene. Remember to stop down so that you shoot the scene at f/8, the proper exposure value for the brightest light.

8. Using a single light, first shoot a scene using a flat, front-on lighting pattern, then move the light to create high side lighting, and finally, butterfly or glamour lighting on the subject.

9. Outdoors, under bright sunlight, use a reflector fill or artificial quartz light with dichroic filter to provide fill light on the shadow side of the subject's face.

10. Photograph a subject using broad lighting and short lighting and compare the result.

11. Light a scene to create first a low-contrast image, then a high-contrast image.

12. Practice diffusing artificial light with a diffusion screen or other material, bouncing light from the ceiling, and using a heatproof lighting umbrella.

13. Inspect the shots you have made of people during practice lighting sessions for the presence of single highlights in each eye. If two highlights appear, relight the subjects properly and again photograph them.

14. Light a person outdoors at night, first using brilliant illumination, then consciously subduing the illumination to the lowest intensity possible. Compare the results.

15. Attend a news conference or other media event and observe lighting techniques and practices. View the scene that night on television.

NOTES

1. Isaac Asimov, "The Third Sense," *American Way* (28 May 1985), 15–16.
2. Notes from talks by Ray Farkas shared in a letter to the author dated 23 September 1993.
3. John Premack, in correspondence with the author, 8 June 2003.
4. John Premack, "Lighting—Making It Work for You," a presentation at the NPPA TV News-Video Workshop, Norman, OK, 19 March 1986.
5. A. William Bluem, *Documentary in American Television* (New York: Hastings House, 1965), 274.

CHAPTER SIX

THE SOUND TRACK

Today viewers and news operations alike acknowledge the importance of sound in television news. Viewers spend millions of dollars on stereo television receivers, and television news operations demand of their field crews the full, clean sound that heightens realism in virtually all news reports, regardless of their content. And when used to its ultimate purpose, sound, like words and pictures, is another of the symbols that journalists can use to communicate meaning and to enhance the impact and intrinsic drama of their reports. After all, there are only two ways to communicate in television news: One is with pictures; the other is with sound.

For all the bandwidth we dedicate to imagery, both in our airspace and in our minds, the stubborn fact remains: Sound carries much of the meaning of our stories. We are thinking creatures; one thing that separates us from animals, and science from art, fact from feeling, is our ability to distill our perceptions into words and to reconstruct an experience from the shorthand of speech.

When a passenger jet crashed into the wooded hills outside of Pittsburgh, the pictures of the aftermath could only frame the words: "The plane was on an approach to the airport when the aircraft apparently banked sharply to the left and dove 6,000 feet, in twenty-three seconds, to the earth."[1] Without the words, we see a trash dump in the woods—with them, we see a tragedy. And when the flight recorder was recovered, the Federal Aviation Agency decided not to release the audio contained thereon in order to "spare the passengers' loved ones" the sounds of human suffering.[2] Such is the power of audio.

NED HALL, AUDIO-RECORDING ENGINEER

The late Ned Hall traveled the world as an audio-recording engineer for NBC, ABC, CBS, PBS, Fox, Disney, HBO, and MTV for such programs as *48 Hours, 60 Minutes, Prime Time Live,* and *Today.* Ned espoused author Diane Ackerman's philosophy that the world would not be nearly so interesting if it were silent. He brought home a rich fabric of sounds from the Arctic Circle to the Cape of Good Hope to the Gulf of Mannar. His work included music videos for artists from Neil Young to the Royal Philharmonic Orchestra. In the dark, windowless world of postproduction, he sweetened shows like PBS's

Creation of the Universe and the syndicated series *The Story of Rock and Roll.* In his own post-production facility, he generated several Random House Audio Books and composed music for NBC News videos and for documentaries for the Discovery channel. Friends and colleagues knew Ned as an artist who sculpted audio, revered it, and shared his love of life's sounds with all of us. Ned rewrote and contributed much new information for this chapter before his death. You will recognize his humor in the following pages, and his wisdom. We have dedicated this chapter to Ned's memory and to those who will follow in his footsteps in the pursuit of storytelling audio, wherever that pursuit may take them.

The most spectacular images of an exploding oil refinery cannot answer some very important questions: Where is the refinery? When did this explosion occur—last weekend? last year? fifteen minutes ago? Was anyone hurt or killed? How many? Who is in jeopardy right now? Is the neighborhood being evacuated? The most revealing shots of the fire chief's face as he arrives at the scene will tell you no more than the tone of his voice as he dispatches the firefighters.

Recording sound, like recording images, is fishing, casting about for the best story elements you can coax from the undergrowth of the world. You can catch a trophy fish on a bent pin and a string, but chance favors the angler armed with experience, patience, and the necessary tackle.

HOW MICROPHONES WORK

The magic of recorded sound begins with the microphone. Sound is vibrating air, and microphones convert those vibrations into electrical energy. *Ceramic* and *crystal* microphones generate an electrical signal when their diaphragms, vibrating in sympathy with the sound waves in the air, act upon a piezo-electric element. These microphones, because of their limited frequency response and relative insensitivity (read: lousy sound), are largely a thing of the past in professional applications.

The diaphragm of a **dynamic microphone** moves a coil of wire in the field of a magnet, rather like a dynamic speaker, in reverse. Dynamic microphones commonly are used in news reporting and in stage and music applications. Dynamic mikes produce high-fidelity sound at reasonable cost and are among the most rugged units of all.

Ribbon microphones operate in a fashion similar to dynamic microphones, but use a thin ribbon of metal foil inside a magnetic field for a diaphragm. Ribbon microphones can be "warm" sounding, flattering to the male voice, and thus are commonly encountered in announce booths and radio studios.

A *condenser* microphone's diaphragm acts as one of the two plates of a capacitor in an electronic circuit. When the diaphragm vibrates, the capacitor changes value in the circuit. This type of mike requires power, supplied by the mixer/preamplifier or a separate power supply and sent through the mike cable, or by a battery in the mike itself.

Condenser mikes can be the most sensitive of microphones and are used in a variety of music and voice applications.

DIRECTIONAL PATTERNS

The simplest microphone, suspended in open space, can "hear" sound equally well from any direction. You might imagine the directional pattern of that mike as a sphere. Microphones can be designed to favor specific areas in a sphere, allowing you to point the mike at the sound you want to record while lessening to some degree the pickup of sounds you don't want. Unfortunately, this is not like a camera lens that sees only where you point it. A camera can take a picture of a clear mountain stream without revealing that the idyllic brook runs six feet from the highway. A microphone will report faithfully the traffic density on that highway, complete with a truck count, no matter what the directional pattern of your mike may be.

The directional characteristics of mikes are more pronounced as the frequency of the sound increases. Low-frequency sounds will "leak" into any mike regardless of its type or orientation, and sound reflects off objects in thousands of unpredictable ways.

Light may be stopped with an upraised hand or a dropped eyelid; sound can only be stopped with mass or distance.

Omnidirectional

A mike with an **omnidirectional** pattern picks up sound equally from all directions. The majority of handheld and lavaliere microphones are omnidirectional. However, an "omni" mike mounted on a person's chest becomes hemispherical in pattern—the mass of the body blocks sound coming from behind the subject.

Unidirectional

A mike with a **unidirectional** pattern tends to reject sound from the rear and sides. Unidirectional mikes are good for news conferences and meetings because of their ability to minimize audience noise and feedback. They come in these basic flavors, each more directional than the last:

> cardioid (sound is picked up to the front and sides of the mike)
> hypercardioid
> short shotgun
> long shotgun

Bidirectional (Figure Eight)

Sound is picked up in front and back but not to the sides of the **bidirectional** microphone. The user must correctly position the microphone to record desired sound while rejecting unwanted sounds.

ON CHOOSING A MIKE

At first consideration, given the incredibly cluttered soundscape in which we live and work, one might be tempted to grab a **shotgun mike** and be done with it. And, in fact, many soundpeople seem to settle on a short shotgun mike as the one first pulled from their kit and mounted on the end of their boompole. Indeed, if you are fishing for sound bites in an unknown sound environment, that's a good choice. However, there are other points to ponder.

A key point to bear in mind when placing a mike: When you halve the distance between a mike and a sound source, you increase the level by three **decibels** (dB). One reason lavaliere mikes, though omnidirectional, seem to reject so much extraneous sound, is that they are positioned so close to the source of the sound. The closer you can get your microphone to the sound, the less unwanted sounds will intrude.

IMPEDANCE

Microphones also are designated according to their **impedance,** a characteristic related to, but not to be confused with, electrical resistance. The **ohm** is the measure for both. Low-impedance microphones (generally in the range of 50 to 250 ohms) are standard for field sound recording and include most dynamic mikes. These mikes can be used with any practical length of microphone cable. Consequently, it is possible for reporters to work several hundred feet from the video recorder or live transmission facilities without noticeable loss in sound quality. High-impedance microphones (in the range of 1,000 ohms and higher) are limited to cable lengths of twenty feet or less. Generally, modern high-quality mikes are low impedance.

FREQUENCY RESPONSE

The human ear is said to be capable of hearing frequencies ranging from 20 **hertz** (Hz) to 20 **kilohertz** (kHz). There is considerable but conflicting evidence that we can sense overtones much higher and that an American adult can't hear beans above 15 kHz. Be that as it may, a microphone company that boasts of a mike with a frequency response from 20 hertz to 20 kilohertz is suggesting that their mike can "hear" any sound your ear can. Microphones with the same published frequency response can sound very different, though, so make your selections based on what you hear in your headphones.

MICROPHONES FOR THE BROADCAST JOURNALIST

At a minimum, reporter's crews should carry an omnidirectional hand mike, a unidirectional mike for stand use (to exclude audience noise at news conferences and meetings), a shotgun mike, at least one miniature lavaliere mike, and at least one wireless transmitter-receiver system. Some stations provide their crews with far less than this basic complement, although wireless transmitters and inconspicuous lavaliere mikes lead to more spontaneous interviews and even to more compelling demonstration standups. Almost always, progress depends on performing at a higher level of excellence than your competitors. If the station refuses to provide you with the tools you need in this endeavor, you should consider buying those tools yourself.

The Handheld Microphone

Both directional and omnidirectional hand mikes are the workhorses of the newsroom. You can tape them onto tree branches to record the passing sounds of the parade, position them at the edge of the gym floor to record the squeak of basketball players' shoes, or tape them to the speaker's stand at a news conference. Rugged, reliable, and affordable, dynamic handheld microphones are indispensible tools for the broadcast journalist. The standard electronic news gathering (ENG) mike is usually an omni because it is rather like a hand grenade: You don't point it so much as heave it in the general direction of whatever is making the noise. They are often chosen for their bullet-proof construction and for how they look wearing a **mike flag,** that little box imprinted with the station logo that pops into view so frequently (Figure 6.1).

FIGURE 6.1   The handheld microphone is an indispensable field reporting tool. Such microphones can intimidate some news subjects, however, and they can draw unwarranted attention, especially when they are outfitted with a mike flag that carries the station's logo.

Often, however, the handheld mike is used with such little thought that it intrudes on news content. Journalists continually thrust handheld mikes into people's faces and further compound their intrusiveness with mike flags. The effect is intimidation, which will silence a wise man but will incite a silly one to greet his mother. This curious phenomenon has never been explained, but you will experience it time and again.

Given the level of today's technology, there is no longer a need for viewers to see the microphone. Its presence serves merely to remind viewers that the story is being reported, thereby reducing the viewer's level of involvement in the story. Occasionally, station management requires the station logo to appear on the hand mike and encourages the presence of the mike on screen. But, gradually, managers are beginning to search for more effective ways to promote the station's presence in the field. Someday, in an ideal news world, mike flags will be just a curious footnote in the history of broadcast journalism.

Lavaliere Microphone

During interviews, reporter standups, and similar applications, the use of a **lavaliere microphone** often is more appropriate than using a handheld mike. These small microphones clip to the speaker's clothing or can be taped directly to the speaker's chest and are easily hidden from camera view (Figure 6.2). Lavaliere mikes are designed to be used close to the speaker's chest cavity, never handheld, and their output may become less vibrant and more tinny the farther they are used from the sound source.

Shotgun Microphone

Other microphones are used in situations where you can't move close enough to the speaker. News conferences are an example. Here, you may have to use the so-called **shotgun microphone,** which picks up sound from a relatively narrow area in front of the microphone. This mike derives its name from its resemblance to a miniature shotgun barrel (Figure 6.3). The shotgun mike has a pickup pattern vaguely similar to the angle of view of a telephoto lens and allows usable quality sound to be recorded from quite a distance in a perfectly quiet environment. Because the shotgun mike is highly directional, you must "show" it precisely what you want it to hear. If your aim is poor, you may pick up the sound of a taxiing jet and miss the speaker's most important comment at a news conference. To help keep the microphone accurately pointed at the sound source, you must listen carefully with headphones.

THE WIRELESS TRANSMITTER-RECEIVER

Useful in many situations and crucial in some is a miniature radio transmitter and receiver set, commonly referred to as a *wireless*. Used most often in conjunction with a small lavaliere mike connected by a short, thin cable to a small transmitter worn inside a pocket or hooked to a belt, the wireless can be invisible or no more obtrusive than a pager. Transmitters can also be used with a handheld mike or with a mike placed inconspicuously in a likely spot (often referred to as a "plant" mike), or, with a special cable, to public address (PA) systems or hi-fi's.

FIGURE 6.2   Small lavaliere microphones can be clipped to the speaker's clothing or can be hidden entirely from view by taping them to the speaker's chest or inner clothing.

Wireless transmitters provide speakers with great mobility and give reporters the freedom to move about during standups and interviews. Using two wireless systems, the reporter and interviewee can walk and talk during interviews without the restriction of microphone cables and without the annoyance of microphones intruding on the interview process (Figure 6.4). The transmitted sound is picked up by a matching receiver(s), which in turn feeds directly into the video recorder or the mixer or into live broadcast transmission facilities.

Range

In a perfect world, a wireless transmitter would have infinite range. In reality, its working range often seems to be about two feet less than you need! Several factors limit wireless range. One is the relatively small power output of the transmitter, measured in

FIGURE 6.3   The shotgun microphone is highly directional. It has a pickup pattern somewhat similar to the angle of view of a telephoto lens. The microphone seen here is equipped with an acoustic foam windscreen.

FIGURE 6.4   The wireless transmitter-receiver system allows reporters and news subjects to move about freely without the restriction of microphone cables.

fractions of a watt, and, like all radio transmitters, regulated by the Federal Communications Commission (FCC). Another is the possible presence of interference.

Watch Out for Interference

Although wireless transmitters are relatively expensive, they cannot deliver the sound quality of a regular hardwired mike. For one reason, a wireless introduces special signal processing circuits into the signal path in the interest of delivering a clean, usable signal. The transmitter has an audio circuit called a compresser that "squeezes" the signal into a very narrow dynamic range, a term relating to variations in intensity. The receiver contains an expander that then restores the signal. While these components function as intended, they limit the frequency response and the dynamic range that could be preserved by a simple microphone cable. Another reason sound quality is poorer is because the transmitted signal is susceptible to any outside electrical interference that may be present, whether it's electrical ignition noise from poorly maintained cars in the area, the periodic snap-snap of an electric cattle fence in the country, the unwanted intrusion of radio frequencies (RF) from a radio or TV station in the vicinity, or from another crew across the street using the same frequencies you are. Further, the physical mike cord wire that feeds into the wireless transmitter can act as a radio antenna and serve to convert the field recorder into an AM or FM radio receiver, which can pick up perfectly clear reception of broadcast programs. Some units also are susceptible to occasional interference from shortwave broadcasts, walkie-talkies, and microwave transmissions.

Dropouts and interference also can occur when the signal from the main transmitter arrives at the receiver just as a secondary signal reflected from a wall or other nearby reflecting surface reaches the receiving antenna, so monitor your sound and move the receiver if necessary. Occasionally, even fluorescent or neon lights produce interference. If you can, turn off the lights. Otherwise, if you suspect the lights as a source of interference, reorient the receiver or move it to a different location. Murphy's Law postulates that the interference will be intermittent and will occur in direct proportion to the status of the person being recorded. Often the problem will exist on one frequency and not another, making a spare wireless a lifesaver.

Interference often increases as the distance between the transmitter and the receiver increases. As the signal becomes weaker, the receiver is less capable of discriminating between the desired signal and a spurious one. In general, it is best to keep that distance as short as possible. Remember that you are broadcasting a radio signal, and that you will occasionally "take a hit" and hear a pop, zizz, whistle, crackle, tick, ding, hash, or clang. En garde!

Frequency

The frequencies available for wireless use are assigned by the FCC. Although these units output very little power, the FCC requires that radio transmitters be licensed in the frequencies made available for wireless use. Certain areas of VHF band (from about 169 to 216 mHz) were home for these devices until some spots in the UHF band (470 to 890 mHz) were more recently made available, and this higher frequency, coupled with the relatively (for now) uncrowded condition of these wavelengths, makes for some desirable improvements in wireless performance. Back when wirelesses were mostly in the VHF band, a buyer who planned to use his units in locations all around the United States was urged to buy them in the 169 to 172 mHz range. These "traveling frequencies" are safe from interference from VHF television stations. But be aware that when dozens of news crews are working at the same location, many of them will be using those traveling frequencies.

Antenna Placement

In the past, wireless transmitters were always equipped with a short wire tail that served either as an antenna or as a ground plane. The distinction is a hazy one to anyone but a radio frequency (RF) engineer, and the ideal antenna configuration for a body-mounted transmitter was hotly debated in some circles for a time. A seldom-heard corollary to Murphy's Law states that the worst possible location for a radio antenna is intimately adjacent to a large, moist leather bag filled with conductive fluid, and any RF engineer worthy of his or her pocket protector will gladly go on at length about the terrible things that happen to signal strength under such conditions. The fact is that you will mount the transmitter where you can and use it unless it sounds bad. The most popular modern VHF wirelesses have dispensed with the tail and use a combination of the case of the transmitter and the mike cable to achieve a usable range similar to the older designs. UHF units still sport a very short antenna.

Whenever you use a wireless transmitter, placement is important. When the antenna, or the mike cable that serves as an antenna, is poorly positioned, some wireless units tend to cut off or "clip" certain frequencies, making voices sound thin and artificial. Try to keep the wire straight and, ideally, keep the antenna on the front of the person, facing the camera, so signals don't have to pass through the speaker's body on their way to the receiver. To help reduce dropouts, keep the antenna away from metal (is your subject playing with car keys and change in his pocket?) and, if your transmitter has both antenna and mike cable, keep them as separate as possible. To further reduce interference, place the receiving antenna as high as possible, preferably atop the camera or on the shoulder strap of the mixer, or even, in desperation, on a pole placed high enough so that it is above the subject. If you are in a nightmare situation and your wireless will only work for a few feet, tape the receiver to the end of a pole and "boom" the antenna, keeping it just outside the picture frame.

USING MULTIPLE WIRELESS MIKES

Wireless microphone setups have been in use for many years but, since the mid-1980s, have been put into more and more complex setups. Before the one-piece camcorder came into common use, camera people were connected to their sound operators with a thick video cable. The sound operator carried the video recorder as well as the various accoutrements that soundpersons invariably accumulate. As more ambitious production

(continued)

USING MULTIPLE WIRELESS MIKES   Continued

was attempted in the field, the soundkit grew to include a four-channel mixer and two or three channels of wireless as well as a boom mike. Then, when camcorders became common, sound operators added two wireless transmitters to their mixers, sending their two-channel mix to two receivers affixed to the camcorder.

This "cutting of the cord" gave video the freedom that film crews have had since recorders like the Nagra IV allowed them to discard the sync cable that had camera and sound recorder joined until the end of the 1960s. Relegated to fireside fable are tales of "clotheslining," when the cameraperson and the sound operator race off in opposite directions (most entertaining when working in front of a large audience, say, at a football game) or on documentary shoots when the camera squeezes onto an elevator with the subject but the soundperson doesn't . . . quite . . . make . . . it.

It is important to note the difference between a wireless link between mixer and camera and a true "double system" of audio recorder rolling in sync but separate from the picture recorder. A double system puts control of the sound recorder in the hands of the soundperson; this allows audio to be recorded even when the camera is not rolling. Small pieces of incidental audio, or "wild track," can add greatly to a finished piece; **nat sound** needn't be merely street noise recorded while the camera shoots an exterior shot of a building. A double system also gives the soundperson the opportunity to roll on dialogue that the camera operator might not be aware of; in casual, less structured environments you may be documenting a conversation rather than shooting a formal interview. Sometimes your subject will say the most telling things just as the camera stops rolling (see Murphy's Law).

In a double system, the soundperson's headphones can monitor the sound as it is being recorded; in a wireless link, any interference that occurs between the mixer output and the camcorder can only be heard at the camera, by the camera operator. This risk must be regularly evaluated (check playback often!) to help determine the best method to employ. Most crews using a wireless link are ready at a moment's notice to abandon the wirelesses and revert to an audio "snake" that, in addition to sending two channels of audio to the camera, will as well return the mixed audio from the camera's earphone jack back to the soundperson. In fact, it is best to "hardwire" in this manner for any situation that does not require mobility. If you are riding around in the back of a police car, wireless links will prevent the "clothesline" phenomenon; if you are doing a sit-down interview of the Dalai Lama by the Pope, hardwire.

Wireless mikes also can quickly eat up batteries, so remember to carry plenty of spare batteries into the field. The crackle and static you hear in your earphone may be simply the sounds of a battery growing weaker. Some photojournalists use fresh batteries on every assignment on the proven theory that batteries are less expensive than failed productions.

THE MIXER

As a photojournalist, you may find yourself working by yourself or with a reporter. Often in this situation the mike mounted on the camera and one wireless velcroed to your battery pack may be all you need to capture the audio required to tell your stories. Sometimes, though, the way you cover a story may demand more complex setups. When the assignment calls for interviews by a reporter with one, two, or three or more people, multiple microphones in different locations can dramatically enhance the pictures you take. These assignments may take the form of a discussion between two or more people walking down the street, a question-and-answer session after a speech (including a telephone call-in), a conversation, or even situations where one shot pans from a summit conference to an angry protest just outside the window.

Whenever you have more potential audio sources than you have channels, the mixer becomes an essential tool. The need for a soundperson, who can devote all attention to whomever is speaking, to whomever might speak next, or where the best place to stand to record the sounds of a passing marching band might be, also becomes apparent. It is the job of the soundperson to choose microphones expertly and decide where and how to place them, and to see that good quality sound is being recorded at the appropriate level.

The microphone mixer is the tool used to choose the appropriate audio sources, to control the levels of those sources, to assign and mix those sources to an appropriate channel on the recorder, and to monitor those sources via headphones. A good mixer can provide power for condenser mikes and can accept both mike- and line-level signals of various strengths as well as output signals at mike or line level for more than one recorder. It can insert high-pass filters on individual channels separately, and it can generate the tones used to record a reference level to tape.

ESSENTIAL POINTS FOR AUDIO

How to Dress News Subjects with the Miniature Mike

Concealing the microphone is almost an art form in itself. When the microphone is out of sight, the reporting process itself is less intrusive. In fact, if you are not careful, it may be inadvertent. A completely concealed microphone can create ethical questions, so if you find yourself concealing a microphone for the purpose of recording someone without his or her knowledge, be sure you have some good ethical reasons.

There are many approaches to mounting a mike on a person. Often, unobtrusive mounting might prevail over invisible mounting, because seeing a lav in a news interview is more common than seeing one on a character in a movie. In a film, reminding viewers that the scene before them is contrived is a sin. In a TV news interview, it is merely a distraction, and it is up to you and your employer to determine whether it is an acceptable one. When a reporter is speaking to the camera there is no point in pretending that he or she is not on television. But when you are following a subject through the paces of a "typical day" (typical except for, of course, the two people bristling with video gear tagging along behind), it is best to see no mike at all. In any case, a black lav clipped to the middle of a white shirt with the cable dragging off to one side is unacceptable unless you are trying to create the impression that the interview was shot by amateurs.

■ ■ ■ ■ ■ ▬▬▬▬▬▬▬▬▬▬▬▬▬▬▬▬▬▬▬▬▬▬▬▬▬▬▬

NED HALL ON MICROPHONE PLACEMENT

In ENG work the handheld or "stick" mike is often, but not always, an omnidirectional, dynamic mike. This is usually a good choice for a correspondent or presenter honoring the Hand Grenade Principle. If the hand that is holding the mike is waving the mike around, as during an impromptu interview, the background noise can change drastically. For example:

Your reporter is interviewing a farmer standing out in his field (for being outstanding in his field, one supposes). The field is bordered on one side by a busy freeway. On the opposite side of the field is the farmer's son idly gunning the engine on his rusted all-terrain vehicle (ATV). Behind you is a barn, containing six newborn calves, lowing for suck. Directly next to the farmer is his shiny Behemoth MkIII tractor, which shakes the ground slightly as it idles. What to do?

Well, first, ask the farmer to shut off his beautiful Behemoth. Then, send the producer over to talk Sonnyboy into turning off the ATV, preferably after he has driven it a long way away. This leaves you with the barn and the freeway to deal with. If the reporter has a directional mike in her hand and she is facing the freeway, then when she points it away from her, the freeway's roar will be much louder under the farmer's comments than under her questions. If you can reorient the pair so that the mike is always pointed away from the freeway, you will have largely farm sounds under your whole interview. This is desirable, as the background noises will then reinforce the location as seen by the camera. If the mike is omnidirectional, the background noise won't change so drastically, but just how annoying the freeway noise is depends on how far you are from the road.

The only way to ameliorate this is to move further from the road and closer to the barn. The omni will pick up a more consistent background, but it also must be much closer to the mouths of the speakers to achieve an acceptable difference between the volume of the speech and the volume of the lowing calves. If you could get that omni mike very close to the desired sound source, you would minimize the volume of most of the background sound, but that big object in the picture would be quite distracting.

Enter the lavaliere. Usually omnidirectional (because the omni is less susceptible to handling noise and is more forgiving of head turns and other sound source anomalies), the lav will usually achieve the most isolation from background noise of any miking technique. Remember, if that farm is located four miles from the closest road, then a cardioid condenser mike held over the heads of your subjects may yield the most pleasing, open, and natural sound, complete with crickets cricking, grasshoppers whirring softly through the moist grass, the cows softly lowing in the barn, the breeze rustling the rushes down by the creek, the old windmill cranking and banging in the next pasture, the bedsheets the farmer's wife hung on the line billowing and snapping, the flies buzzing on the compost heap back by the truck garden, the phone ringing in the next farmhouse over. . . . A good quality, sturdy, and quiet mixer that will accommodate as many channels of input as you foresee needing is an essential part of your kit.

A mike clipped to a tie or to a collar will have much less chance of being rubbed and scraped by other clothing than will a mike you have attempted to hide completely. Some degree of "clothes rustle" may be present no matter what miking technique you employ; a nylon windbreaker can play havoc even with a boom mike. Your headphones will tell you whether you have an intolerable problem or not.

Different lavs conceal more effectively than others; you will find a favorite that mounts the way you like, sounds good, and seems to yield the cleanest track. There are some general methods that apply to any mike you choose: Lavs usually sound good mounted at about sternum height; a mike mounted too high on the neck may sound muffled, with the subject's chin blocking some sound; a mike mounted too low may sound thin and distant. (If your goal is to pick up both sides of a conversation with only one mike, a low position might be better, because both subjects' mouths may then be about the same distance from the mike. Be willing to experiment.)

If necessary, tape the mike firmly to the shirt or body to keep it from producing extraneous noise when the person moves, and tape in an isolation loop to keep the mike cord free of stress. Gaffer's tape, folded into two "sticky-side-out" triangles and sandwiching the mike, makes a flat, sticky package that can easily be concealed in a shirt or blouse opening or under a lapel or a tie.

If you clip the mike to a coat lapel, choose the side where the speaker is most likely to be looking during the interview (body right or left). Sound quality will diminish if the microphone is attached to the person's left coat lapel but he or she looks mostly to the right.

If the speaker wears a low-cut blouse or sweater, fasten the microphone right under the lapel or neck band with a safety pin or a small piece of gaffer's tape. Keep the mike cable out of sight, preferably beneath the person's clothing. Women can be directed to an area where they will have privacy and asked to drop the mike plug down the front of their dress or blouse. The cable need not necessarily run down the subject's front. It might be easier to tape it at the shoulder or under a collar and let it trail down the person's back. If the speaker is wearing a tie, you might conceal the mike cord by running it through the tag on the back of the tie.

If the person wears casual clothing, a jogging outfit for example, or will be active, use safety pins and tape to hold the microphone and cable in place. If the safety pins show through the clothing, bend them to conform to the clothing and the person's body and cover them with gaffer's tape.

Place the transmitter wherever it is least obvious—in the person's pocket, for example, or in the back of a bra. Sometimes the transmitter can be taped to the small of a person's back or even inside the person's thigh. Tuck all cables and wires neatly out of sight (and don't tangle the mike wire with the antenna).

Work quickly, but remember that Murphy states that if you wire someone with the thought that he or she will never be seen on camera from the waist down or from the back, the cameraperson will go for a wide shot or the reporter will ask the subject to stand up and retrieve the photo album from the bookcase behind him or her. Remember that you are invading your subject's personal space when you mount a mike. How you handle the process can make the person more nervous or less nervous. It's your choice.

Tips for Good Sound

Achieving good quality sound is a matter of learning to listen for sound and to differentiate between what is acceptable and what is not. "Good sound is the absence of bad sound; bad sound is sound that is distorted," writes Murray R. Allen, president of

Universal Recording Corporation in Chicago. "Distortion is any signal that unintentionally sounds different on output as against input."[3] Listen to sound recordings for hiss, buzz, boomy sound, low volume, and distortion. If you hear any of these elements, take steps to eliminate the unwanted sounds.

Experiment with Microphone Placement

One of the most important steps in achieving good quality sound is to experiment with microphone placement. Take time to move the mike closer to the subject, then farther away. Change the sound volume. Move your subject away from walls and the center of rooms to avoid unwanted sound reverberations. One of the most frequently committed errors is to work the mike too far from the sound source. The rule of thumb is to work the microphone close to the speaker and to involve the microphone in the action just as you would involve the camera. The nearer the mike is to the sound source, the better the recording will be. Moving the microphone closer allows you to lower the volume and thereby cut down the background noise. Each microphone reproduces sound best when used in a particular way, and you will need to experiment to discover which position yields the best sound quality.

Monitor Recording Levels

Often, **distortion** occurs because volume levels are set so high that the recording equipment becomes overloaded. All professional video gear has audio-level meters that indicate the recording levels. Unfortunately, there is more than one type of meter and more than one way to calibrate the meters internally. Also, the maintenance and alignment of the audio portion of a video recorder generally isn't performed with the regularity and diligence devoted to the "tweaking" of the video components. This means that the same meter reading that yields a clean, well-modulated recording on one machine may indicate distortion on another. Experiment with your own equipment and listen to playback.

In general, if your recorder has a mechanical meter, that is, with a pivoting needle indicating the audio level, that meter is calibrated in volume units (VU). Speech should be adjusted to peak at 0, just before the needle moves into the red area of the meter face. If your equipment has a liquid crystal display, its meters may read peak levels and may be adjusted to indicate somewhere to the right of 0 on the meter for normal speech.

On many recorders a red light flashes when a signal level approaches (or may be intruding into) distortion. Experiment so that you know what your meters are telling you. For all their differences, most audio meters are marked in dB, a measure of sound intensity that corresponds roughly to the minimum change in sound level that the human ear can detect. Even a change in speech levels of two dB, for example, may not be noticeable to anyone who is not listening for it. Sound recorded from −10 to 0 dB generally is acceptable. To avoid further sound distortion, try to avoid automatic level controls because of the alternating levels in volume and the increases in background noise that result.

It is important to record a tone at the beginning of each session while you are recording color bars. All mixers contain a tone generator. Set the mixer so that its meters read the tone at 0 dB and then set the recorder's meters to 0 dB. This will allow the editor to calibrate the playback machine's audio output.

Monitor the Sound with Earphones

Whenever you record in the field, it is critically important to monitor the sound with earphones (Figure 6.5). Photojournalists by the hundreds fail to monitor their sound, but the practice is professional suicide. There is no other way to determine whether the sound being recorded is good enough for broadcast unless it is monitored. The best earphones enclose both ears and block out much unwanted sound, but, if you are shooting video as well as recording sound, smaller, in-the-ear plugs may be more comfortable. High-quality ear buds designed for use with Walkman-type devices can be pressed into service if full-sized headphones interfere with your shooting style.

TECHNIQUES TO REDUCE WIND NOISE

Wind makes noise only when interacting with some object. The wind in the willows or the wind roiling amber waves of grain are beautiful sounds but are difficult to record when the wind is also poofing on your microphone. The undesirable artifact we refer to as wind noise is really not the sound of the wind, but the sound of a microphone

FIGURE 6.5 To determine whether field recordings are clean and free of dropouts and distortion, continual monitoring of the sound with earphones is essential.

diaphragm literally flapping in the breeze. Obviously the windiest conditions offer quite a challenge; recording on a boat under sail or in stormy conditions on land call for elaborate measures. The lightest breeze, though, will ruin a track if you are not prepared.

The first line of defense in battling the breeze is foam. This substance is sold as *acoustic foam*, so called because it is open-celled; that is, the little bubbles in the material touch each other and thus allow air to pass through them, albeit in a convoluted path. Closed-cell foam, which may appear quite similar, will not work. The test is to hold the foam to your mouth and blow through it. Open-celled foam will allow your breath to pass through easily; note that the puff of air has lost its power after its trip through the foam. Manufacturers normally supply their microphones with **windscreens** made of gray foam or of a metallic mesh that has the same effect (Figure 6.6).

FIGURE 6.6 A microphone windscreen is the first line of defense to help dissipate the wind and absorb its shock. Here the windscreen is normally concealed beneath the metallic mesh microphone cover.

In an emergency, should the wind guard be absent, you can use the foam used to protect quartz bulbs in your lighting kit, but keeping a piece of acoustic foam in your kit is inexpensive and will come in handy. If you are having wind problems with a lavaliere mike and its tiny windscreen is not up to the task, you can try moving the mike under a layer of the subject's clothes, making a larger windscreen from your stock of foam, or repositioning the subject with her back to the wind. In high winds, the best solution might be to revert to a boom-mounted mike encased in a large mesh cage, called a *zeppelin* or *blimp*. These work in higher winds by creating a large pocket of still air around the mike. They are often augmented further by a cloth sock and further still with a jacket of long synthetic fur. You can, when installing your mike in this device, slip a foam windscreen on the mike itself and add one or more layers of foam sheet inside the zeppelin. If you still have a wind noise problem, take cover, because there's a tornado right behind you!

Windscreens can have a very slight dulling effect on the recording if you are using several layers of blocking material. The odds are, though, that if you are in a situation where you need all that protection from the wind, your subject will be shouting just to be heard.

The second step is a *filter*. A high-pass filter (or low-cut filter—two names for the same thing), so called because it sharply attenuates low frequencies and allows the highs to pass through, is almost always used in field recording. This function is usually built into a mixer, mike power supply, or into the mike itself. Some amount of high-pass filtering may also be built into a wireless transmitter—it may or may not be externally adjustable. There are simple, nonadjustable high-cut filter "barrels" designed to be placed in-line on the microphone cable (Figure 6.7), but more versatile circuits usually provide you with three choices: no filter at all and two different degrees of attenuation. The

FIGURE 6.7 A high-pass, or low-cut, filter can be installed in the mike line to diminish wind, air conditioning, and other low-frequency noises.

most severe of these settings is very useful in a stiff breeze; the more moderate setting can be handy even indoors, to lessen the obtrusiveness of furnace or air conditioning rumble. More than one filter may be used in tandem for even more pronounced effect, useful if you insist on shooting that tornado.

These filters do affect the quality of your recording, most obviously in music, but also, to a degree, when recording the voice. A low-cut filter will remove some of the depth of a resonant male voice, but the trade-off of also removing the worst of a distracting roar from a refrigerator or from a crowd of people must be considered. The conscientious recordist will eliminate as many distracting noises as possible. Turn off the air conditioner and shut off the refrigerator right before the interview starts—but remember to turn them back on before you leave! (You'll never forget if you put your car keys in the refrigerator when you shut it off.)

Bear in mind that, once you eliminate the booming rumble of wind hitting the microphone, you may still hear the wind rustling the subject's clothing. Wind can render a location undesirable even after you have solved the immediate problems with the mike. Be aware of possible problems before you become wedded to a location; the only way to know for sure is to listen carefully through your headphones. Wind in the treetops can make a terrible racket even though it is beautiful, and still, on the ground. Careful headphone listening will also reveal that most condenser microphones are so sensitive that just moving them around in still air will cause them to rumble. These mikes are therefore always used with at least a foam windscreen.

BE AGGRESSIVE

As a soundperson, be aggressive but unobtrusive. Strive to identify the small things that make sound in the environment in which you are recording. And don't give up if the sound is bad: Keep trying different variations until you get clean, usable sound. You are the person who makes the difference between unacceptable and excellent sound and between merely technically correct sound and something truly exciting. Your instincts can guide you to story elements that might otherwise be missed. If a tree falls in the forest and you weren't rolling, does it make a sound? Your audience will never know!

THE MICROPHONE HEARS DIFFERENTLY

Remember that the microphone is as different from the ear as the camera is from the eye. The microphone "hears" differently, just as the camera "sees" things your eyes and mind screen from your consciousness. Be especially aware of sound that comes from outside the camera frame. For example, it is possible for the sounds of a lawnmower to intrude during an interview conducted on a battleship berthed at dockside. Routinely, the microphone will pick up buzzing flies, air conditioners, distant airplanes, and the rumble of heavy equipment in the background, even if you fail to hear such noises while you're conducting the interview. Careful monitoring with headphones is the only way to be sure you haven't ignored a stray sound that will return to haunt you.

Sometimes there is no complete solution to a sound problem. If you are doing a feature on anti-abortion picketers and are interviewing people on a busy street in front of a clinic, you will not be able to avoid traffic noise in the sound track. If the camera chooses to frame the interviews with the fine old oak tree growing next to the clinic, your subject might appear to be standing in a peaceful glade, and the car noise will make no sense and will distract the viewer. If, however, the camera includes the traffic zooming past just two feet from the protest, the noise then becomes perfectly appropriate and will even add a feeling of tension to the scene. And, if you are prepared, your boom mike in hand and your finger on its volume control, you might even catch a shout from a passing driver that will speak volumes about the situation you are trying to document. Can you keep one eye on your surroundings and catch the first words of an irate neighbor as he crosses the street to engage the protesters?

SOUND PERSPECTIVE

Sound is a fundamental component of the editor's ability to create a sense of realism. Not only must sounds be of impeccable quality, but they should have the same perspective as the pictures they accompany. If the shot is a close-up of a basketball smacking the backboard and the mike was in the bleachers, some effect is lost. One danger of using wireless lavs is that all perspective is lost; the listener's ear is resting on the speaker's chest. If your reporter is standing on a desolate and windswept plain and the camera is pulled way back to reveal the bleak and stormy conditions, the reporter should not sound like someone speaking from an isolation booth. Either put an open mike on another channel or record some wild track of that moaning wind.

Similarly, take the case of a scene and accompanying sound of a woodpecker hard at work on a tree in the Okefenokee Swamp. If the woodpecker is photographed in a long shot or with a wide-angle lens, the bird will appear to be some distance from the camera. At that distance in real life there would be a slight delay in the sound of the tapping because it must travel some distance to the observer. In the edited video, the same delay can be incorporated into the sound track if the editor simply slips sync slightly to create a perspective of distance, even if the original sound of the woodpecker's tapping was field recorded in dead sync with a wireless microphone hidden in the tree.

STEREO

If, tomorrow, some genius invented a video camera that could record three-dimensional images that revealed detail and nuance our present flat pictures can't even suggest, it would be years before we all had three-dimensional television receivers in our homes. It would be years before the broadcast industry could agree what standards to adopt for the new medium. Yet the technology for delivering three-dimensional sound to our living rooms is already in place. Most television receivers and virtually all VCRs and DVD players sold today have stereo capability; most broadcasters are transmitting a stereo signal. Most television shows, including news programs, have stereo theme music if not surround-sound. At professional production houses, edit bays have been equipped to do stereo for years. Even the most basic of editing systems is stereo-ready, and computer-based editing systems are engineered to handle stereo audio automatically. Yet most sound in the field is recorded monophonically.

If you were to decide to produce a program in stereo, much of your field procedure might remain the same. A mono sound can always be placed in a stereo image, and an interview or standup may best be recorded in mono. But imagine yourself at an anti-war rally at the Vietnam memorial in Washington, DC. The camera shows a somber man tracing a name sandblasted in the stone. The sound records a sniffle or two, but far off to the left, you can hear a man's voice, singing a song he heard on the radio thirty years ago, and to the right, the murmuring of a crowd listening to someone speaking with anger and conviction into a bullhorn. The camera turns and moves through the crowd, and you can feel the people pass by you on both sides. You hear a yell from off-camera, but you know where it came from, and as the camera pans to the source of the shout, you can hear the crowd move past the lens. This is the potential of stereo ENG and, if you find yourself in the position to experiment, you will be rewarded with sound that will make you sure the quality of the picture has magically improved.

Many stereo microphones are available, and the ones that use a technique called M-S (for mid-side) are perfectly suited for work in television. These mikes use one unidirectional mike capsule pointing forward and another figure-eight capsule with its lobes pointed to the left and right. The mikes combine these signals in a special way to produce an accurate stereo image. Should that stereo signal be combined into mono, as in a television with a single speaker, all that will be heard is the forward-facing unidirectional mike.

COVERING NEWS CONFERENCES

One of the secrets to covering news conferences is to arrive early and stake out your territory. If a number of camera crews are expected, use your tripod to help create a buffer area for yourself. To keep other crews from moving in front of you, try leaving them a place—even make a hole for them and offer it when they arrive. You may want to be less accommodating, however, for the "radio and print people who want to get right up in front and get good shots with their pencils," advises freelance photographer Darrell Barton.[4]

Normally, news conference sound is recorded in one of three ways: You can use a shotgun mike, tap into the public address system fed from the podium mike, or you can add your handheld or stand mike to the thicket of microphones already taped to the podium. If you are taking the main sound from a common junction box or amplifier, find out in advance which adaptors you will need (Figure 6.8).

If you are the only station at the news conference, or the first to arrive, consider placing the mike where you'll want the subject. "They'll come to the mike," says Barton. "It's like bait."[5] And if possible, talk to the speaker in advance and get to know the individual. That way, when the person speaks during the news conference, he or she may look in your direction somewhat more than in the others'.

FIGURE 6.8 Recording sound at news conferences presents special challenges of acoustics and microphone placement. Come prepared, arrive early, and expect the unexpected.

RECORDING GROUP DISCUSSIONS

If your task is to record a roundtable discussion or a full circle of speakers, then a different approach is required. To mike a group of people sitting in a circle will be most simple if the individuals sit around a table. You may be able to capture acceptable sound simply by placing the mike flat on the table. If no table is present, perhaps you can dangle a microphone from a ceiling fixture above the center of the group, or else use a shotgun mike and keep it as low and as close to the middle of the group as you can. Experiment with microphone placement until the sound is acceptable.

THE TWO-PERSON INTERVIEW

The "sit-down" conversation between two people is a staple of television news and is the situation that often lends the most opportunity to control extraneous sound. Often, the crux of an issue is stated in this main interview, and the sound recorded here will be used over other pictures, so it is doubly important to eliminate distracting sounds. Check the air conditioners; close the doors; unplug the telephones; shut off the pagers. Try to make a quiet nook for serious exchange. Generally, it is best to use the same kind of mike on both parties, so the tracks will blend well. Also, because everyone is sitting down, and the camera(s) are tripod-mounted, there is no disadvantage to "hardwiring" your subjects, that is, using cables instead of wirelesses, and your chances of avoiding an ill-timed "hit" are much better.

RECORD ROOM TONE

Whenever you record sound in the field, remember to record some **room tone** or ambient noise for the editor. Room tone is the ambient sound peculiar to each environment. It is the "silence" of the forest, the calming sound of the distant river, the fan noises in a room full of computers, the sound of people breathing in a quiet classroom. During editing, gaps of silence in the sound track will draw unwarranted attention if the track suddenly goes dead. To prevent unwanted dropouts in sound, the editor has merely to insert room tone, provided the photojournalist recorded it in the first place.

THE SEDUCTIVE QUALITY OF "NAT" SOUND

The need for "nat sound"—that is, all sound other than speech that occurs naturally in our environment—as a storytelling tool is an expression of our desire for realism. Good sound is compelling, involving, and engaging. Often, good sound builds on prior experiences that viewers themselves bring to the screen. When we hear sounds on television that imitate or draw from our own life experiences, we are able to contribute to the story a more profound and intimate depth of understanding. While it is inaccurate to say that experience is the equivalent of understanding, sound is a vital component of direct observation and a source of much that we know. Always, sound serves as an equal partner with pictures in helping viewers experience the great potential of television news.

WATCH WHAT YOU SAY

Perhaps one of the most important cautions whenever you record sound is to say nothing around the microphone that you wouldn't want broadcast. Around the country, broadcast journalists compile tapes of the spoonerisms ("It's snowing tonight on Rabbit Ass Pierce" when the weather reporter meant to say "Rabbit Ears Pass") and obscenities of other journalists—and share them with peers. Some of the best-known names in U.S. television are on those tapes, and some of their utterances are an embarrassment. Even worse, in the rush of deadlines, some of their obscenities and unwarranted religious and ethnic comments, although made privately during the reporting process, have been inadvertently broadcast to home audiences, to the detriment of the profession at large. Consequently, the guiding rule must be, "If you don't want it on air, don't say it."

SOUND AND VIDEO ACCESSORIES

Returning home with usable sound is sometimes a matter of being able to fix problems that occur in the field. The following are items that many professionals deem essential to have ready access to the field. Many of these items can be especially valuable when you travel overseas or in remote areas. You will have to check many of these items, of course, whenever you travel by air. If you're worried about losing the kit if your checked luggage goes astray, consider creating a backup kit and check it through in a second bag. A carrying bag might contain the following items:

battery-operated penlight

spare batteries for everything you operate (penlight, mikes, wristwatch, microphone mixers, wireless, etc.)

spare bulbs for portable lights and your penlight

video and audio connectors and adaptors (XLR, mini, phono, etc.) (Murphy says you will either carry every adaptor except the one you need or, to make the desired connection, you must use all the adaptors you carry.)

alligator clips

straight/Phillips screwdrivers

pliers

jeweler's screwdrivers

miscellaneous small screws, bolts, nuts, pins, washers, etc.

extension cord adaptors (3-prong to 2-prong)

foreign electrical adaptors and power converter

locking needlenose pliers

small soldering iron

good electronic solder

scissors

sharp pocketknife (Swiss Army knife is de rigueur)

Allen wrench set

masking or other form of paper tape

gaffer's tape (furnace duct tape is acceptable)

nylon strapping tape

instant bonding adhesive

heat-shrink tubing

videotape head cleaner

VCR head-cleaning swabs or chamois

magnifying glass (small)

earphones (take a spare pair)

loose waterproof cover or plastic garbage bags for camera and mixer

wooden wedge or steady bag to put under the camera when shooting low angles

log books to jot down tape footage

pen/pencil(s)/felt-tipped markers

electrical wire

spare mike cables

labels for videocassettes and hard drive recorders

adjustable nylon fastening straps

75- to 300-ohm converter

75-ohm coaxial cable

in-line line-to-mike adaptors to match level from auditorium amplifiers to a mike-level input

in-line transformers to match impedance

in-line high-pass and low-pass filters

etc., etc.

SUMMARY

Sound imparts a sense of realism and life to news stories, and viewers have come to expect both natural sound and interviews in their news reports. Microphones have various pickup patterns. Some pick up sound from a full 360-degree circle; others pick up sound only from a narrow angle in front of the mike; others pick up sound both in front of and behind the mike.

Handheld microphones, although versatile and reliable, may intrude on news content when they act as barriers between the reporter and interview subjects or, in the case of standups, between the reporter and home audience. The problem is further compounded when the mike flag with station logo distracts the viewer's attention from the reporter or interview subject.

More appropriate in such situations is the lavaliere mike, an unobtrusive miniature microphone that can be clipped or pinned to clothing or taped to the speaker's chest. Shotgun microphones, which take their name from their appearance, can be used to record faraway sounds, such as at news conferences and athletic events. For the least distraction and most freedom to move about during standups and interviews, a good option is a wireless transmitter-receiver system. Sound can be transmitted over a range of several hundred feet, although wireless units are more sensitive to electrical interference than hardwired mikes.

Poor sound quality will result from improper microphone placement and from recording levels that have been set too high or too low. A dependable rule of thumb is to work the microphone close to the sound source and, as appropriate, to involve the microphone in the action. Set recording levels and monitor sound quality with earphones.

Frequently, wind noise destroys otherwise high-quality sound. Techniques to reduce or eliminate wind include foam or metallic mesh windscreens on the microphone, high-pass filters installed in the microphone line, or physically shielding the mike from wind gusts. As a further consideration, a recording should have the same perspective as the pictures it accompanies. If the picture is a close-up, the sound should be recorded in close-up, and vice versa. Almost always, sound is a vital component of the best television news stories, and in real life, a source of much that we know.

DISCUSSION

1. Of the various microphones, which types are most frequently used to cover news events? Compare the strengths and weaknesses of each type.

2. Discuss the most common microphone pickup patterns and their relative merits.

3. Explain the distinguishing features of the dynamic microphone.

4. Discuss the typical uses of the handheld, lavaliere, and shotgun microphones in news applications.

5. Discuss the major strengths and weaknesses of the wireless transmitter-receiver system.

6. When you work with news subjects, what considerations are most important to remember in concealing the miniature microphone beneath their clothing or in other personal effects?

7. Overall, what are the most important considerations to follow if you are to achieve good quality sound in the field?

8. Explain why it is essential for the photojournalist or soundperson to constantly monitor sound in the field with earphones.

9. Discuss the full range of techniques you can use to reduce wind noise in the field.

10. Explain the concept of perspective as it applies to the sound that accompanies visual images.

11. List the steps that are helpful to follow when you record sound at news conferences.

12. Discuss the potential of stereo ENG and the limitations it faces in today's production world.

13. Explain the role of nat sound in helping lend a sense of realism to television news stories.

EXERCISES

1. Attend a news conference and observe procedures that professionals use to record high-quality sound. Examine microphone placement. Determine whether cords and cables are properly taped to the floor to reduce the risk that passersby will trip or fall. Notice what techniques the professionals may use to entice speakers to look in their direction.

2. Visit with the chief photographer or a sound engineer at a television station and inspect the various microphones used for news and sports reporting. Prepare a report based on your discussions with the photographer or engineer about the uses and relative merits of each type of microphone.

3. Record a person's voice with a dynamic handheld microphone located approximately two feet or more from the speaker's mouth. Make a second recording with the microphone about ten inches from the person's mouth. Determine which microphone position results in the best quality sound.

4. Practice concealing a miniature lavaliere microphone and its cord beneath a willing subject's business and leisure clothing, on the neck of a pullover sweater, and beneath a necktie.

5. Experiment with microphone placement in a room with poor acoustics. While you monitor the sound with earphones, have a friend reposition the microphone in several locations until you find the best position to record quality sound.

6. Intentionally record sound at too low a volume, then boost volume to acceptable levels during playback. Note the distortion that results. Repeat the exercise, this time recording at too high a level and lowering volume to acceptable levels during playback.

7. Record sound outdoors in high wind. Use the mike with and without a windscreen. Block the wind with your body or other object, again with and without the windscreen. If possible, record sound with a high-pass filter installed in the mike line.

8. With and without the high-pass filter in the mike line, record the sounds from the tailpipe of an idling car or motorcycle.

9. Practice installing a wireless transmitter on a willing participant. Make practice recordings with the system, changing the transmitting antennae from the front to the back of the person, from horizontal to vertical position, and at various distances from the wireless receiver.

10. Note the variations in sound perspective that result when the microphone is involved in the action.

11. Record a series of room tones from various environments and study these respective "sounds of silence."

12. Watch editors at work as much as you can. Witness the problems caused by poor sound recording techniques.

NOTES

1. National Public Radio, 11 November 1994.
2. Ibid.

3. Murray R. Allen, "Is There a Place for Good Audio in Video?" *Follow Focus* (official journal of the Professional Motion Picture Equipment Association, Toluca Lake, CA), 3, no. 2 (Fall 1983), 24.

4. Darrell Barton, "Anticipation: The Key to Success," a presentation at the NPPA TV News-Video Workshop, Norman, OK, 16 March 1994.

5. Ibid.

CHAPTER SEVEN

THE BROADCAST INTERVIEW
Shooting the Quotation Marks

While visuals tell the story in television news, interviews provide the little moments of emphasis that punctuate the story. Without sound bites the television story is essentially barren. Interviews provide essential detail, help give stories spirit and atmosphere, and impart a sense of spontaneity that would otherwise be lost. While part of the interviewer's function is to gather facts, an equivalent obligation is to reveal the person being interviewed. The best interviews are often so strong that if the subject walked into the room days after a broadcast, viewers would still recognize the person.

While some interviews are of necessity with the mayors, ambassadors, and other authorities of the world, the most poignant and memorable interviews often are with ordinary people who have never been on television and may never be on television again. KAKE's Larry Hatteberg observes that people listen most closely when they hear folks like themselves talking.

In television news, whatever your job in the field, interviews will be a dominating fact of life. The following discussions apply whether you are a "one-person band," an employee at a station where reporters are expected to shoot video for one another, or a partner in a traditional reporter-photographer team.

ESTABLISH TRUST

Being a reporter or photographer most often means that you are an outsider, yet your job as an interviewer depends on your ability to establish trust and gain acceptance from perfect strangers quickly. The job is sometimes less difficult for print reporters, who can walk up without a camera and immediately establish rapport, than for the photojournalist who pulls up to a story burdened with camera, lights, microphone, and microwave truck.

Because your presence is so obvious, some people will be curious about you; others may be hostile, frightened, or indifferent. To achieve their cooperation, you will have to be open enough to let people come to know and trust you. "People will talk to a friend long before they'll talk to a stranger," says photojournalist Art Donahue.[1] The process can take as little as five minutes and be as simple as a brief chat over coffee, but it can never happen unless you have a genuine interest in people and have the self-confidence to reveal something of yourself. If you are afraid to approach people as you launch your interviewing career, remember that most people are flattered to be on TV even if they seem skittish about it at first.

PRACTICE HOSPITALITY

In a sense the audience will be peering over your shoulder throughout the interview. Your conduct will determine how the subject reacts, so even when you are in a rush to meet deadline, practice good manners and treat subjects with genuine courtesy. Arrive on time and take leave before you wear out your welcome. Leave the chewing gum at home, and refrain from sitting or smoking unless you are invited. Be friendly but not overly familiar. Journalists are always invited guests. Because viewers may identify more with interview subjects than with the reporter, how you treat the interviewee may translate into how viewers subconsciously feel you have treated them.

THE MOST IMPORTANT INTERVIEW QUESTION

Often the people you interview have never been on television, so your first task is to do everything you can to get their mind off why you're there. So great can be the anxiety that one of the West's most gifted poets routinely suffered bouts of diarrhea before television interviews and once fainted before the first question could be asked.

Because the objective in television news is communication of ideas through visual action, and because the most compelling stories and interviews reveal personality, it is well to remember that the interview itself is not the thing that happened. It is supporting structure for the larger story. For this reason, the most important question you can ask an interview subject is, "Show me what you do," says news consultant Bill Brown of the Coaching Company.[2]

Interviewees almost always are more at ease if they can focus on familiar work and surroundings than if they are forced to focus on themselves, their appearance, or their performance during the interview. "So many journalists interrupt reality," says Hubie Vigreux, a photojournalist at WDSU, New Orleans. "They stop the person and slap them in front of a wall for the interview, instead of talking with the interview subjects as they keep working."[3] Interview the person while he or she is engaged in familiar activities rather than standing in front of a blank wall with a stick mike thrust in his or her face. People are almost always more relaxed doing something than watching you photograph them. To avoid the appearance of staging in such situations, remember not to ask for or suggest action unless the person already routinely performs the activity in your absence.

SAVE YOUR QUESTIONS FOR THE INTERVIEW

The best interviews carry at least the illusion of spontaneity. Often, however, the reporter sets up the interview and determines in advance the subject matter to be covered, the time of day the interview will be conducted, and even the location for the interview. To help preserve the feeling of spontaneity, try not to share questions in advance of the interview. Subjects ordinarily put most of their energy into their first response. Once the camera rolls they may leave out the detail because having told you once, they assume you already know what they said. While it's natural for interview subjects to want to think through their answers in advance, the best interviews address the moment and the feelings of the moment and grow naturally from the honest interaction between you and the subject.

USE A WIRELESS MICROPHONE

When you conduct one-on-one interviews at close range with people who are unaccustomed to the bright lights and hardware of television, try to avoid the handheld mike and even the shotgun mike because such hardware reminds people they're being recorded (Figure 7.1). If you can use a wireless mike instead, subjects are more likely to forget about the microphone. When interview subjects forget the mike is on they'll be more natural and may say things they ordinarily wouldn't say.

FIGURE 7.1   Unless field crews are sensitive to the problem, the reporting hardware of television news can quickly intimidate and overwhelm interview subjects.

HELP INTERVIEW SUBJECTS FORGET ABOUT THE HARDWARE

Many of the people you interview will never have had much to do with reporters, microphones, lights, and cameras. Predictably, their first reaction will be to become almost painfully self-conscious and to direct their focus inward. To help put interview subjects at ease and keep their focus off themselves, the following strategies may be of help.

If you have the time, leave your equipment out of sight until you've had a chance to talk with the person you plan to interview.

Spend as much time as you can getting to know the subject, whether you have only a few minutes or a half hour. Often, this interaction is the most valuable time you can spend on a story because it gives you and the interviewee a way to come to know and trust one another.

Talk about things that interest the subject; try not to talk about yourself unless the subject first expresses an interest in you.

Preferably, use a miniature lavaliere microphone and wireless transmitter.

Try to avoid talking about your equipment and how much it costs.

Give the subject time to become accustomed to the camera, recorder, tripod, light case, and cables.

Let the subject do as much of the talking as possible.

When you record, turn off the tally light so people won't know the camera is rolling.

To help keep the hardware low profile, arrive early to set up the equipment. Use low-intensity lights and set them up ahead of time to give interview subjects time to adjust. Long time interviewer Bill Moyers suggests that regardless of the camera, lights, and other gear, try to operate in such a way the person forgets it's a TV interview and has a conversation.

DO YOUR HOMEWORK

The more you know about your source, the more confidence you give the person and the more you can concentrate on listening without having to worry about the next question you'll ask. Anyone can ask anyone else questions, but the interviewer can succeed only by asking informed questions that are based on knowing everything possible about the subject. Author Cornelius Ryan believed journalists should never interview anyone without knowing 60 percent of the answers. Do your homework before the interview. The person you're interviewing has, and will be prepared.

Among the resources available to most reporters are encyclopedias, almanacs and yearbooks, government manuals, directories, magazines and newspapers, the public library, the Internet, and, of course, phone calls and visits with acquaintances, friends, and relatives of the person to be interviewed. In the absence of full and certain knowledge about a subject, the reporter is virtually guaranteed an interview far beneath its potential.

HOW TO FRAME INTERVIEW QUESTIONS

So often, reporters think up the questions they'll ask on the way to the interview. The result is an interview without focus. "When you start asking questions, the other person immediately wonders, 'Why does he want to know?'" If your purpose is unclear, she may be reluctant to talk. Ask a few questions to warm up, but save the best and strongest or most controversial questions for the last part of the interview and actually build the interview to a climax. The interview must lead to a given conclusion, somewhat like a story with beginning, middle, and end. Never should it be simply a series of unrelated questions. Otherwise, the endeavor will result in a fruit salad of questions, with little clear direction.

THE ART OF LISTENING

The most powerful interviews are but conversations between two people, yet there can be no conversation without a listener. Most obviously, that job falls to the reporter. Listening, in fact, is one of the reporting arts. If you are a good listener and are truly interested in what people have to say, chances are excellent that you will come away with a good interview. People will give part of themselves to you if you give part of yourself to them, observes Larry Hatteberg.

Listening also helps you frame more meaningful questions. The interview is far more likely to be spontaneous if your questions build naturally off the other person's responses. Attentive listening also frees you from having to concentrate so hard on formulating your next question that you miss what the other person is saying.

As a further payoff, good listening can help you identify potential "edit points," even while you are in the field. When you feel something about what the person says, for example, it's generally a strong bite. "Whenever I interview someone, I try to identify the emotions I feel, and which points during the interview I feel them," says NBC News senior correspondent Bob Dotson. "Inevitably, when I go back to those moments in the interview while I'm editing, that's where I find the strongest statements."[4]

AVOID THE EASY QUESTIONS

It would be helpful for all interviewers to talk with a celebrity or two about interviewing. Whether they are screen stars or football quarterbacks, all celebrities have endured countless questions so similar and predictable that they have become clichés. Especially when you work with people who appear frequently on television, think up fresh questions. Again, the task is easier the more you know about the subject.

If your research leads you nowhere, perhaps you can call one of the subject's old college classmates for background information that may point you in new directions.

Along the way, it is perfectly acceptable to fashion questions based on your curiosity about the subject, even when they lead you beyond the subject under discussion, so long as your questions reflect good taste and reasonable restraint: "Tell me about the time you ate the box of Valentine chocolates you had given your mother."

BUILD QUESTIONS AROUND THE FIVE W'S

The strongest interview questions solicit information and most commonly arise from queries that begin with the "Five W's" familiar to all reporters: Who, Why, Where, When, What (and How). Such words have an unparalleled ability to compel informative responses. The question that begins, "Why did you oppose reinstating the draft?" is vastly superior to the question or observation that results in a simple "yes" or "no" response: "I understand you opposed reinstating the draft."

AVOID TWO-PART QUESTIONS

The strongest interviewers ask their questions one at a time, building each new question on the subject's last response. Inevitably, whenever you ask two-part questions, one of them is left on the table: "How likely are we to see prefabricated factory-built homes dominate the new home market in the United States this century, and if they do come to dominate the market, will financing be provided mostly through private lenders or through government agencies?" Most subjects will answer the first question, then having answered, will ask the interviewer to restate the second part of the question.

"HOW DO YOU FEEL?"

The question most likely to pop from the reporter's mouth at inappropriate times is, "How do you feel?" The question is asked of grieving parents, survivors of air crashes, and losers of football games. Perhaps the question is inappropriate because the answer normally is so obvious: "I feel like hell/sad/miserable/alone/scared/angry." Given story context, any viewer can fill in the blanks.

Sometimes a better approach is to make an observation, "I know it's tough for you right now," or to ask a question that probes the subject's emotions less deeply, such as "What do you think about this?" At other times, the best approach of all is simply to walk away. Some interviews are not worth the invasion of privacy and loss of dignity they would require.

ANTICIPATE QUESTIONS THE VIEWERS WOULD ASK

As a reporter, try to anticipate questions your viewers would ask the subject if they had the opportunity. You are the viewer's only representative in the field, and you will be the object of great frustration if you overlook obvious or important subject matter in your interview. Conversely, because you are the viewer's representative, remember to keep your questions in good taste and to the point.

PRACTICE THE FINE ART OF HESITATION

Silence can be golden as an interviewing technique. Mike Wallace has long believed the single most interesting thing that he can do in television is to ask a good question and then let the answer hang there for two or three or four seconds as though he's expecting more. "Typically, he says, they get a little embarrassed and give him more." Even experienced interview subjects, who have "heard it all before," sometimes give their best response to a question that was never asked.

PITCH REPORTING OPPORTUNITIES

When conducting interviews for "people stories," the professionals follow two rules. Rule #1: Don't interview people only in one location; move them around. A change of location can help rejuvenate the interview, and it provides a good chance to go from soft questions to the tough ones. Rule #2: Don't interview people. Have a conversation. Use little conversational questions and observations to which subjects can automatically respond, and in responding, define the moment. The observation "I'll bet it's cold out here" may elicit just as meaningful a response as a direct question. Remember, however, to use this technique as a way to elicit a response, not as a way to lead the subject to any particular response. Television journalist Jim Hanchett commonly uses four standard questions to foster this more conversational process:

> What's happening?
> What's going on?
> What do you think of this?
> What happens now?

Normally, the questions are asked of interview subjects as they sweep out the mud from their flooded storefront or sift through tornado debris for their possessions, while Hanchett's photographer uses a camera-mounted shotgun microphone to pick up their answers. There is no time wasted setting up a formal interview, no spontaneity lost because reality has been interrupted (Figure 7.2).

To capture responses in the aftermath of a flood, for example, Hanchett might drive the news car along a street where flood cleanup operations continue while his photographer sits on the hood of the car and takes pictures. At opportune moments, either of the two will call out to people sometimes fifteen or twenty feet from the camera: "How's it going?" Inevitably, people reply. "This is terrible. I just got flooded out of my house; I lost everything," the flood victim shouts back. Such extemporaneous questions allow no time for people to become nervous or to rehearse their answers.

FIGURE 7.2 A good way to interview people who are unaccustomed to appearing before the television camera is to carry on a conversation with them while they continue work at a familiar task.

PREARRANGE SIGNALS BETWEEN REPORTER AND PHOTOGRAPHER

A similar technique sometimes is possible even in more formal interview situations. Sometimes interview subjects will be at their most spontaneous and energetic best before the interview begins. Some reporter-photographer teams work out prearranged signals in advance so they can capture the subject's energy and feeling without interrupting the moment. Using a gesture as simple as replacing a ballpoint pen in a purse or shirt pocket, the reporter can signal the photographer to begin recording, even without the subject's knowledge. By the time the interviewee asks, "When do we start?" it sometimes is possible for the reporter to reply, "We just finished. Thank you so much."

HOW TO REACT WITHOUT APPEARING TO AGREE

Part of the art of conducting the interview is to react, but without indicating agreement or showing inappropriate displays of sympathy with the subject. Into this category fall nods of the head or responses such as "I see" and "uh huh." Most often your intent is to indicate your understanding, or to prompt your subject, through body language, to "keep going," but audiences may see such actions as agreement. As a further problem, your own utterings may make it impossible for the editor to cleanly pick up the start of a sound bite if you have stepped on that part of the audio with your voice.

To avoid such problems, some reporters tilt or cock their head slightly to one side to evidence interest in the subject's response, or perhaps even utter an occasional "mm-hmm," provided it's low enough in volume not to be recorded on the sound track. Also be mindful to blink your eyes occasionally, and to allow your interest or concern to show in your eyes as appropriate. It is also acceptable to change body position, even to lean forward to indicate your interest in the subject's responses, but do skip the "I see's" and "uh-huhs," no matter how well intentioned.

RETAIN CONTROL OF THE INTERVIEW

It is important for the reporter to retain control of every interview, even when the interviewee is assertive enough to grab the handheld mike and hold it as a means to seize control. In such instances, the best defense is a good offense. Firmly and forcefully take back the microphone. If the interviewee refuses to yield, then stop the interview with an explanation to the effect that "I hold the mike and I ask the questions. Now, if you're ready to begin . . ."

At other times you may find it difficult to interrupt a nonstop talker to ask new questions. When this situation confronts you, then you must be aggressive enough to interrupt the interview in order to ask your new question. Take a deep breath and hold it, secure in your knowledge that even interview subjects must occasionally stop talking long enough to breathe. When that magic moment presents itself, seize it as your cue to ask the next question.

INTERVIEWING CHILDREN

Few NBC *Today* viewers who watched that day will forget the report about patrolman Bill Samples, who is stationed at Philadelphia's Children's Hospital and spends his off-hours helping make the dreams of very sick children come true. NBC News correspondent Bob Dotson told of Samples and his wife, Helene, who help find money so dozens of terminally ill youngsters can see the mountains or visit the ocean before they die. The report, entitled "Sunshine Child," enabled viewers to accompany tiny Christina Wilson, who suffered from leukemia, on a visit to Disney World where she hoped to meet a mouse named Minnie.

On the plane from Philadelphia to Orlando, photographer Warren Jones showed Christina the wireless microphone that would be in her purse when she met Minnie, and he let Christina hold the camera he would be using to tell the story. The camera was valued at more than $30,000. When they landed in Orlando, the lens was covered in fingerprints. But by the next day, the lens had been cleaned and

Christina was all but oblivious to the reporting crew and the hardware that surrounded her.

"Have you seen Minnie?" Christina asked the next morning, amid the crush of children who had gathered to meet the Disney characters. Suddenly, a big black foot stepped into frame behind Christina. The little girl turned. "Hi, Minnie," she whispered. Minnie Mouse held out her arms and the two hugged each other for long moments. Once more Christina looked up at the big mouse. "Minnie, I love you," Christina said. Minnie knelt down to offer her big black nose, and a moment later Christina kissed Minnie.

Jones's technique with Christina is central to the success of reporters who interview and work with children in stories for television. Kids are fascinated by the camera and other reporting hardware, so a good approach is to sit down with them and explain the equipment, even to let them look through the camera viewfinder if possible. Soon they will be their natural selves, oblivious to the camera and sometimes even to the reporting process itself. While this approach might seem to waste valuable time, it often leads to stronger interviews and may even result in less time spent on the interview itself.

Specific questions work best with children (Figure 7.3). A usable response is more likely if the reporter asks, "What did Minnie's nose feel like?" than if the child is asked, "What did you like most about Disney World?" When vague questions are asked of children, vague answers result.

FIGURE 7.3   The strongest interviews with children commonly result when questions are specific and to the point.

THE TALKING HEAD

The viewers' inherent interest in people can help lead them to an expanded interest in news. While interviews are never substitutes for the story, they are an essential component of stories told through people. For the most part, whenever you edit interviews, keep bites short. Use them to provide emphasis rather than as substitutes for the story or for your own reporting. Many strong bites will run less than ten seconds to little more than twenty seconds, but use good judgment. Depending on content and pace, even two-hour interviews can be compelling and memorable.

While some newsrooms automatically deride the **talking head,** as though a speaker on screen is boring by definition, Robert MacNeil, who helped create the *MacNeil/Lehrer NewsHour* (now *The NewsHour with Jim Lehrer*), took exception in this discussion of his philosophy about interviews.

> We were determined to give the talking head its value. The human head is almost the only thing that appears on television close to life size. No electronic wizardry, no satellites or computers can displace the talking head as a communicator when it comes to the things that matter to us. When someone says, "I love you . . . I hate you . . . Will you marry me? . . . I want a divorce . . . You're hired . . . You're fired . . ." that talking head usually doesn't have a window frame over one shoulder, with cartoons whizzing by to distract you. TV does. If asked why, the answer from TV producers would be, "After twenty seconds, you need something different to look at." In our view, that is merely a confession of fear that unless they continuously distract with fresh visual images, the audience, like a baby, will begin to fret and switch channels. It is an assumption that is profoundly insulting to the American public.[5]

Among the attributes of the legitimate talking head are characteristics that predictably serve to further enhance the story's meaning. Such talking heads may serve to

- provide insight into the speaker's personality
- show that what is said is less important than why and how the speaker says something
- show the person as he or she is
- show speakers who are compelling and dramatic or who have dramatic statements
- help prove the visuals

By contrast, the talking head can become a handicap in the television report when it displays the peculiarities that have led to its bad reputation over the years. Such characteristics are to be seen whenever the sound bite

- substitutes for the report
- substitutes for legitimate visual communication
- substitutes for a succinct script
- fails to enhance the visuals
- is long-winded and boring

INFLUENCING HOW VIEWERS PERCEIVE THE SUBJECT

It is imperative for the reporter and photographer to represent the interview subject honestly and to make the interview technically acceptable. How you structure and photograph interviews and their environments will impact not only how viewers react to the subjects of your interviews but what is remembered about them.

Interviews by their nature are meant to reveal personality and, for the most part, call for reasonably close shots. But avoid shots that place the viewer uncomfortably close to the subject. "The viewers are entitled to look as closely at newsmakers and strangers as they look at the anchors," says WCVB photojournalist John Premack. "Yet extreme close-ups flatter no one."[6]

Lighting also impacts the interview. Avoid flat lighting and shadows on walls behind your subjects. When shadows occur, try to eliminate them by repositioning either the lights or your subject. To create softer, more pleasing lighting, and for less heat and bright light on your subjects, consider using umbrella reflectors on your lights, or at the very least low-intensity bulbs.

ONE-EYED TALKING HEADS

Also strive to compose shots so viewers can see both the subject's eyes throughout the interview. The eyes mirror the soul. They are among the most eloquent indicators of the inner self and state of mind. Too often, however, photographers compose shots so viewers see only the side of the subject's head, a shot that incorporates a full view of the subject's ear but only a single eye. Ears, in and of themselves, communicate virtually nothing.

BODY LANGUAGE

Finally, the reporter's body language and mode of dress inevitably impact how viewers perceive the interview subject, even if the reporter is unaware of such dynamics (Figure 7.4). If interviewees are open and generally friendly, no purpose is served by inadvertently portraying them otherwise. To help reflect a more accurate perception of your interview subjects, consider implementing the following behaviors as appropriate.

If the mood of the interview is open and friendly:

- Take off your coat, roll up your sleeves, and perhaps loosen or remove your tie.
- Open up visually and physically; show your friendship and your concern; move closer to the subject.
- Sit beside the source with nothing between you, not even a stick mike.
- Angle your body toward the person, rather than face the person head on.
- Create a sense of freedom by taking the person outside; communicate a clear impression that the person is with you of his or her own free will.

FIGURE 7.4 The reporter's appearance and body language can impact how viewers perceive both the reporter and the interview subject.

If the mood of the interview is investigative or adversarial, then the reporter's response changes accordingly. In adversarial situations, different body language may be more appropriate and can be reflected through the following behaviors:

- Place something between you and the source (a desk, a stick mike, etc.).
- Place more distance between yourself and the other person.
- Wear a coat and tie, or dress in a similarly businesslike way.
- Face the person straight on, instead of at an angle.

AFTER THE INTERVIEW IS OVER

By day's end, reporters who cover five or six stories a day find it difficult to remember who said what, let alone have time to preview each of the various interviews prior to writing the stories. Yet if the reporter is to write naturally into and out of sound bites and integrate them properly into packages, an exact knowledge of wording is necessary. Some reporters solve the problem by making a backup recording of the interview with an inconspicuous, handheld audio cassette tape recorder. Later, they play back the interview in the car on their way to the station or to the next story and note the exact wording of the sound bites that will be needed for the story.

The process can be streamlined even more if you train your ear to listen for sound bites during the interview itself. Listen for edit points and note the moments when you feel something about what has been said. Later, it will be a less difficult task to locate the statements you need and to communicate that information to the editor.

If your field camera is equipped with a time-code generator, you can even set the generator to correspond to the time on your wristwatch according to hours, minutes, and seconds. Then, as usable statements are made, a simple glance at your wristwatch during the interview can help you identify where on the tape the statements can be located.

INTERVIEWS ALLOW REPORTING THROUGH DIRECT OBSERVATION

In the final analysis, broadcast journalism is the art of reporting through direct observation. Through the broadcast interview, participants in news events can report even their own observations, firsthand and with an intensity and believability unparalleled in other forms of journalism. Sometimes journalists have a rare opportunity to see into a person's soul, but that moment happens only if people feel so comfortable on camera that they'll reveal their innermost selves. If you have established a comfortable working environment, prepared yourself for the interview, and allowed your source to see that you are a reasonable and caring human being, then you will have set the stage for powerful reporting.

SUMMARY

Interviews impart a sense of authority and spontaneity to television news stories and provide intimate detail that otherwise would be unobtainable. Interviews further help to reveal something of the person being interviewed. None of these goals is possible unless the reporter first establishes trust with the interviewee. An atmosphere of trust is most easily created if the reporter is open and courteous and exhibits a genuine interest in people.

Interviewees usually are more at ease if they can focus on familiar work and surroundings rather than on themselves or their "performance." Thus, interviews may progress more smoothly if a subject continues with a familiar task, and if the reporter makes observations and more nearly has a conversation with the subject rather than attempts to conduct a formal interview. Such exchanges progress even more smoothly when lights, microphones, and other reporting hardware are unobtrusive.

Few interviews achieve their full potential unless the journalist has conducted sufficient research to learn everything possible about the subject. Preparation is a prerequisite to success. Full knowledge of a subject also frees the reporter to listen closely to responses as the interview develops, another critical interview skill. As you listen to responses, react as appropriate but strive to avoid indicating agreement or showing inappropriate sympathy with the subject. Remember also that the reporter's body language impacts how viewers will perceive the subject.

Because you are the viewer's representative, anticipate the questions viewers would ask if they had the opportunity. Interview questions can be constructed around the Five W's—who, why, where, when, what (and how)—to help elicit informative responses. Questions that elicit simple yes or no responses are less desirable, as are two-part questions, which are confusing and difficult for the interviewee and audience to remember.

In all interview situations, good taste and courtesy are mandatory. If the audience feels uncomfortable with a reporter's conduct or questions, the interview may fail. When interviews are lengthy, consider interviewing subjects in more than one location. A change can help rejuvenate the interview, and it provides a good opportunity to change the subject.

Retain control of the interview, even when subjects seize the microphone or refuse to stop talking. If necessary, stop the camera or use a prearranged but unobtrusive signal between reporter and photographer to cut the sound and recompose the picture, as, for example, during a live shot.

Children represent special interview challenges. Good strategies include explaining the equipment before the interview and asking very specific questions during the interview.

While interviews are never substitutes for the story, they are an essential component of stories told through people.

DISCUSSION

1. Explain the essential role of the interview in television news stories.

2. Discuss ways that will help you establish trust with an interview source.

3. What personal conduct and manners are important to observe whenever you are in someone else's home or office?

4. What is the most important interview question you can ask in television news?

5. Discuss techniques you can employ to help put the interview subject at ease.

6. Why is it important not to reveal the questions you intend to ask until the actual interview begins?

7. Describe the most important steps you can take to help interview subjects forget the microphone, lights, camera, and other hardware involved in the reporting process.

8. Explain why research and planning are so important to the interview process.

9. Describe a good way to structure the interview questions you intend to ask.

10. Why is listening such an important part of the interview process?

11. What constitutes a "dumb" interview question?

12. Describe the difference between asking an interview question and pitching a reporting opportunity.

13. Devise and describe some prearranged gestures that a reporter-photographer team could use to signal one another during interviews without interrupting the spontaneity of the moment.

14. What are some good ways to react to an interviewee's statements without appearing as though you agree with what is being said?

15. What steps can you take to retain control of the interview, even when an interviewee seizes the microphone?

16. Explain the special challenges that arise when you interview children.

17. Describe the characteristics that make for a legitimate talking head interview.

18. Discuss how environment, lighting, composition, and even the reporter's body language can impact how viewers perceive the interview subject.

EXERCISES

1. Study professional television interviewers such as Diane Sawyer, Ted Koppel, Oprah Winfrey, Ed Bradley, Barbara Walters, and Jay Leno. Pay special attention to the techniques they use to put interview subjects at ease, elicit meaningful information, and move the interview along.

2. Arrange to interview a news source or someone who will play the role of a news source. Research the person and the topic you wish to discuss, schedule a time for the interview, arrive on time, and take a few minutes to become familiar with the interviewee. This time, take just a notebook and pencil and leave the camera at home. Concentrate on being relaxed, knowledgeable about the subject, interested, and friendly.

3. Repeat exercise 2, but with a different person. This time take the camera, lights, and microphone.

4. Interview someone while the person continues a familiar task. Make observations or offer "reporting opportunities" rather than ask formal questions.

5. Construct two lists of questions: (1) questions you would expect an informed interviewer to ask you about your life interests and activities and (2) questions of the same nature that you would like to ask a friend based solely on your existing knowledge of that person. Compare the two lists of questions. How do the questions differ? Now, experience the value of research firsthand by calling your friend's parents, old school teachers, close friends, classmates, and brothers and sisters, and ask them questions about your friend. Using this new knowledge, expand the list of questions you will ask your friend.

6. Practice listening to people more attentively, even in everyday conversations. Develop your ability to listen to people into a fine art.

7. In your everyday conversations, practice listening to people without appearing to agree. Act interested, but suppress any body language that tends to communicate agreement.

8. Practice conducting interviews and working with children until you are able to routinely elicit broadcast-worthy responses.

9. Study interviews on television to determine how interview environments, lighting, camera composition, and body language can influence the viewer's perceptions of reporters and interview subjects.

10. Listen to interviews on radio and television to practice identifying alternative "edit-in" and "edit-out" points in sound bites. Often, the routine sound bites in news stories can be shortened with no loss in meaning and sometimes can even be improved.

NOTES

1. Art Donahue, "Utilizing a Creative Eye for Everyday Assignments," a presentation at the NPPA TV News-Video Workshop, Norman, OK, 21 March 1986.

2. Comments to journalism students, Colorado State University, Fort Collins, 23 March 1987.

3. Conversation with the author, New Orleans, 23 May 1985.

4. Conversation with the author, Norman, OK, 23 April 2003.

5. Robert MacNeil, comments on the original *MacNeil-Lehrer Report*, from an address at the University of Kansas, 10 February 1982.

6. John Premack, "What's Wrong with Interviews," *RTNDA Communicator* (September 1984), 17.

CHAPTER EIGHT

TELEVISION SCRIPT FORMATS

LUAN AKIN

Few television newsrooms format scripts in exactly the same way. Even within the same newsroom, writers and reporters may use slightly different formats for the same types of stories. But as long as the people writing the scripts draw from a common pool of abbreviations and phrases, the differences won't matter. The various terms will be synonymous, and anyone familiar with those terms in general will understand the script.

The following scripts represent the various ways stories can be formatted. They're not meant to be seen as the only way each type of story should be laid out. But once you become familiar with the material here, you'll be well on your way toward reading a script from any newsroom and understanding the technical instructions that accompany the script.

READER

A **reader** is as simple as a television story can get, but it's still a valuable format for a variety of reasons. In just a few well-written lines, viewers can get an overview of a story. And by keeping the copy short, producers can increase the story count of their show and keep the pacing up as well. If a story worth running isn't visual, or if the pictures simply aren't available, a reader may be the answer.

Slug: Cabbie/Dentures	
Live Jean	-Jean-
S/Jean	
	A Denver cab driver may owe his life . . . to his false teeth.
	The driver for Yellow Cab was shot in the mouth during a robbery overnight.
	Police say the man's dentures deflected the bullet.
	The cabbie was treated at Denver General Hospital and released. No suspects are in custody.

Scripts for television are written in two columns. In simplest terms, the column on the left is primarily for instructions to the director. The column on the left does not appear in the TelePrompter. The column on the right contains information for the anchors and the actual copy to be read out loud.

The first instruction in this script, "Live Jean," indicates the story is "on camera." We'll see Jean live from the news desk or studio, looking into the camera, delivering the story. Some newsrooms may use the abbreviation "OC," or on-camera, rather than "live."

The name "Jean" at the top of the right-hand column clearly indicates to the anchors who's reading which story. This is especially important at stations that use dual anchors. The anchor's name is bracketed with hyphens or parentheses to separate it from the copy.

The only other instruction on this script, "S/JEAN," calls for a graphic, a "super," of the anchor's name. The anchor doesn't need to know his or her name is appearing at the bottom of the screen, so the super instruction appears in the left-hand column only.

VTR VO (VOICE-OVER VIDEO)

Television is pictures. They're the medium's life blood. So as often as possible, producers will include even short pieces of video that help "bring the story home." That's the job of a **voice over** (VO). VOs as short as twelve to fifteen seconds can tell a story. That's only three or four shots. But if the shots are well crafted, they can definitely leave an impression.

Slug: Kicker/Pet-a-Cure

Live Ed	-Ed-
S/Ed	Have you ever thought of giving your cat a pet-a-cure? It's not what you might think.
VTR VO	-VTR VO-
S/Jacksonville, Fla.	A Jacksonville, Florida, pet clinic is putting press-on nails . . . on cats.
	They're glued on, just like the artificial nails many women wear.
	Veterinarians say the press-on nails help cats that have been de-clawed protect themselves if they go outside.
	When the cats come back in, the artificial claws can be removed, so the furniture can't be scratched. As to polishing these nails . . . the vets say you're on your own.

"Live Ed"   In the left column, this VO begins just as the reader did: the top of the VO is live, with the anchor on camera.

"ED"   At the top of the column on the right, we see the name of the anchor delivering the story, just as at the beginning of the reader. The name must be distinguished from the copy with hyphens or some other mark to make it clear the word is not to be read out loud as part of the story.

"S/Ed" instructs the director to superimpose the anchor's name briefly in a graphic at the bottom of the screen. The anchor doesn't need to know about this super, so there's no mention of it on the right-hand column.

Next, our first instruction for video: "VTR VO," video "voice over" by the anchor. At this point in the story, the audience will continue to hear the anchor's voice, but instead of seeing the anchor on camera, viewers will see a piece of edited video—a VO.

Hyphens or parentheses are again used in the right column to bracket the indication to the anchor that the on-camera section of the script is over, and the "VTR VO" is beginning. This instruction already appears in the column on the left, but it needs to be repeated here for the anchor because only the right-hand column of a script appears in the TelePrompter.

The final instruction, "S/," calls for another super. Until now, the only graphics we've used have identified people. This graphic is a "locator." It identifies the place pictured in the videotape, in this case, Jacksonville, Florida.

VTR VO (VOICE-OVER VIDEO)
VO/SOT/VO (VO SOT OR A/B FOR SHORT)

A VO SOT or A/B is basically a VO that includes previously recorded sound, usually a "sound bite," a short piece of an interview recorded earlier. Some newsrooms edit the first video, the sound bite, and the video following the bite onto one tape. That means the script needs to be carefully timed by the anchor, so just the right amount of video can be included before the bite. If too much video is used, there will be "dead air." The anchor will have read the first section of copy, but there will be a painful silence before we hear the bite. If too little video is used, the anchor will "up-cut" or talk over the first part of the bite. Both mistakes are distracting.

To prevent such problems, many newsrooms put the first section of video (plus an extra shot or two for pad) on one tape. That becomes the A roll. The sound bite and the second section of video (plus pad) are edited onto another tape. That's the B roll.

As soon as the anchor finishes reading the first section of VO and reaches the point for the sound bite, the director calls for the videotape operator to roll the second tape, the B roll. The bite plays just where it should. There are no problems with dead air, and the anchor doesn't risk up-cutting the bite. In short, the newscast is cleaner, tidier, and looks more professional.

The use of A/Bs does mean videotape operators have more tapes to keep track of, but the results are usually worth it.

The following script is written to be edited as an A/B.

Slug: ATM Cash

Live Kathy	-Kathy-
OTS: Free Money	A bank giving away money? Sounds impossible, but it actually happened in Missouri this past weekend.
VTR VO	-VTR VO-
S/St. Louis, Mo.	Students at Washington University in Saint Louis couldn't stop cheering. A foul-up at the campus automatic teller machine left many of the students twenty dollars richer.
VTR SOT	-VTR SOT-
S/Melissa Hammond, Student	"From what I hear . . .
In: 07:14:44	. . . at the ATM." (Runs: 11)
VTR VO	-VTR VO-
	The problem happened after twenty-dollar bills were placed in the A-T-M's five-dollar bin.
	Some of the students reported the error to the bank, but most of them simply pocketed the extra cash.
	Bank tellers say the error has been corrected and the extra money has been deducted from the students' accounts.

By now, the instruction "Live Kathy" should be familiar. This script begins with the anchor live, on camera. This is the beginning of the A roll.

Instead of seeing the anchor's name appear at the bottom of the screen, for this story the producer has called for an OTS, an over-the-shoulder graphic. Quite often it's a single frame of video taken from the story—a freeze frame. It could also be a computer-generated drawing that indicates the type of story being read—flames to indicate the story's about a fire, for example. An OTS will always include a cutline, a word or two that describes what the story is about. The cutlines are simple and direct: "Severe Weather," "Police Chase," or a well-known person's last name are a few examples. The cutline for this story is "Free Money." In short, that's what the story is about.

-VTR VO-: Another familiar instruction: voice over videotape, followed by a locator graphic.

The instruction "VTR SOT" in the right column marks the top of the B roll— the point in the script where the sound bite belongs.

The graphic "S/Melissa Hammond, Student" gives us the name of the person speaking in the sound bite. Her name is Melissa Hammond. The graphic will further identify her as a student.

The instruction "In 07:14:44" tells the editor cutting this piece where to find the sound bite on the video used to shoot the interview. If the story was shot on more than one tape, the person writing the script should also tell the editor which tape to use. The director doesn't need this information, but including it on the script makes it easy to find the bite again if the story is re-written for a later show.

The short phrases "From what I hear" . . . and . . . "at the ATM" are the "in cue" and the "out cue" for the sound bite, in short, the first few words and the last few words. The out cue is the most important. It tells both the anchor and the director when the bite has finished and the anchor should resume reading. It's also helpful for both the anchor and the director to know how long the sound bite lasts.

INTROS TO LIVE SHOTS

In a sense, an introduction to a live remote is a short reader. Producers can dress up the intro with various production techniques—running a short VO that segues into the package, for example. (A *package* is an edited, self-contained video report of a news event or feature, complete with pictures, sound bites, voice-over narration, and natural sounds.) But basically, the intros are simple and straight forward. So let's make this more interesting, and cover more ground at the same time.

Instead of dissecting a plain intro to a package, we're going to look at an **anchor intro,** or **toss,** to a reporter who's live at a remote location. Then we'll examine the reporter's intro to a package shown within that live shot. These intros will contain a lot of detailed information, but don't worry. Most of it is material that we've already talked about, but here it's used in a slightly different way.

Slug: Wheat Farmers/Intro

Live Bill	-Bill-
S/Bill	Damage is adding into the millions of dollars following a powerful storm yesterday that pounded wheat crops in northeastern Colorado.
Side by Side	-Side by Side-
	Newsfour's Ann Thompson is live in Copter 4 over Washington County with more on how serious the loss is there.
Remote Full	-Remote Full-
S/Live Ann, Copter 4	
S/Live Ann, Wash. CO.	
VTR SOT Pkg	Cue to pkg:
	Through here yesterday.
Remote full	Cue to remote full:
S/Live Ann, Copter 4	In business very long.
W/Live Ann, Wash. CO.	

"Live Bill," "Bill," and "S/Bill" should be old, familiar friends by now. They show which anchor is reading, indicate the anchor is on camera, with a super of the anchor's name at the bottom of the screen.

A "Side by Side" shot is one of several production techniques a producer can use as a transition from the studio to the reporter in the field. The instruction means just what it says. The shot of the anchor live on set is switched to a shot where the screen is split down the middle, the anchor on one side, the reporter at the remote location on the other.

"Remote Full": at this point, the anchor's intro has been read and it's time to hear from the reporter. The side by side shot is switched to a full-screen shot from the remote location, and the reporter's intro begins.

Most newsrooms use what is called a "live sequence" of supers (S/Live Ann, Copter 4, S/Live Ann, Wash. CO.) for remote shots. This will include a small "live" graphic that's on screen (usually upper left corner) throughout the shot. The sequence also includes the reporter's name and location, supered during the first few seconds of each live appearance, i.e., before and after any video.

"VTR SOT Pkg" In short, roll the package!

"Cue to pkg" is the cue for the director to roll the package. The cue to package includes the final few words of the reporter's live intro. The director doesn't need to see the reporter's entire intro—just enough to call for the package when it's needed.

"Remote full," "Cue to remote full."   Once the package is over, it's time to see the reporter again in a full-screen shot of the remote. The director listens for the reporter's cue to remote full to take that shot. The cue to remote will be the last audio on the package. Usually, it's the final few words of copy or the end of a sound bite, but the cue to remote full could also be natural sound, i.e., the sound of a siren as an ambulance pulls away. If the **crossroll,** the video within the live shot, is a VO or A/B instead of a package, the cue to remote full will be the final few words of that script.

LIVE INTROS TO PACKAGES

As we'll discuss later in Chapter 12 on Live Shots and Remotes, reporters' live intros should flow easily from the anchor's toss. The reporter's intro should be brief. It's important to get to the video. But it's also important to make good use of the live presence with a meaningful reference to the backdrop or setting.

Slug: Wheat Farmers/live	
Remote full	-Ann-
	Bill, from the air, the damage is clear: Wheat field after wheat field flattened by the strong winds, rain, and hail that moved through here yesterday.

In most cases, the director won't see this script. But the information in the left-hand columnn "Remote full" is still worth including. This is a simple live shot, to and from the news set. But if this live reporter was supposed to toss to another live location, that reminder should be included in the left-hand column.

Just as with the other formats, the name of the person reading the script (-Ann-) appears at the top of the right-hand column.

PACKAGE SCRIPTS

We've seen and heard the anchor and reporter lead up to a package on the wheat damage. Now let's see the package, or more specifically, the package script. Even though this package was intended to run as crossroll within a live shot, the format for the package is the same as if the story was introduced from set. The only difference is we won't hear the reporter "lock out" or sign off at the end of the story.

In a script for a package, the instructions in the left-hand column are for the editor. If the photographer who shot the story is also editing the piece, the instructions generally don't need to be as detailed. But if there's any room for confusion, it's better to have too many instructions than too few.

Slug: Wheat Farmers/pkg

	It wouldn't be so bad if Rick Lewton's wheat field looked this flat after the harvest. But Rick hasn't harvested his wheat yet.
S/Rick Lewton Wheat farmer Tape #1, 03:50:54	"It was about 2 . . . 2½ feet tall. About this tall. But there's nothing left." :08
	That same hail storm blasted buildings and barns all over Washington County yesterday.
S/Marge Corman Wash. CO. resident Tape 2, 05:57:27	"We had brick-sized hail. It was in ice balls this big . . . Bricks of ice. It was just terrible." :07
Shot of bldg. damage Shot of wheat damage	It's no wonder weather that powerful . . . can leave a wheat field looking like this.
Rick Lewton Tape #1, 03:58:49	"You could hear the hail in the cloud. It was just roaring . . ." :04
	And once it had roared through Rick's field, not much was left.
CU Wheat as Rick talks Rick Lewton TAPE #1, 03:53:12	"This is the stem of what used to be a head. This has some of the wheat still left on it. This is what happened after the hail storm." :10

(continued)

SU Bridge Tape 2, 04:15:32	"Yesterday's storms were especially widespread. But that's not the worst of it. The hail pounded Colorado's top two wheat-producing counties." :10
	Kit Carson and Washington counties provide 20 percent of Colorado's wheat crop. The loss here will hurt statewide.
Darrell Hanavan Tape #3, 06:43:03	"We're already down to the second-worst crop in 14 years." :04
	Darrell Hanavan is the director of the Colorado Wheat Board. He says more damage like this could set a record.
Darrell Hanavan Tape 3, 06:54:59	"It could be the worst crop in 14 years." :02
	Hanavan says Colorado's wheat crop was already in trouble because of severe drought this spring.
	But for people like Rick Lewton, the hail has made a bad situation even worse.
Rick Lewton Tape #1, 03:54:59	"Most farmers can expect to have a little hail every year, and that's what they plan for. That's just part of farming. But you can't stand this kind of hail loss and stay in business very long." :10

S/Rick Lewton Wheat farmer Tape #1, 03:50:54   This instruction serves several purposes. It tells the editor who's talking in the sound bite and where that bite can be found. It also indicates that a graphic of that person's name will go here. That's important because it's up to the editor to fill out a "cut sheet" for the package, a list showing how far into the package (in minutes and seconds) certain graphics should appear. Generally, sound bites need to be at least five seconds long before a graphic is used. If the first sound bite with a particular person is too short, the graphic can wait until a second, longer sound bite from that person. If none of the sound bites are long enough, the person should be identified in the copy, as we'll see in a moment.

"It was about 2 . . . 2½ feet tall . . ."   Writing out the entire sound bite takes more time, but it's a good habit to get into. It helps the reporter remember just how the sound bite was phrased. That means the copy leading into the sound bite can flow more easily, and the reporter won't end up repeating the phrasing inside the bite.

Some reporters like to distinguish their narration track from the sound within the story by writing one in lower case and the other in capital letters. This helps the editor get a better sense of how the story is laid out. When all of the type on the page looks the same, it's surprisingly easy to overlook a section of track or a piece of sound.

It's also a good idea to note the length of the bite. It gives the reporter a better sense of how long the story is likely to run. People talk at dramatically different speeds. A bite that looks as if it should take six or eight seconds might take twice that long if it's full of pauses. Incorrectly judging the length of a package can force a sloppy re-write or re-edit at the last minute.

Shot of building damage Shot of wheat damage   When the reporter has a certain shot in mind for a particular phrase or sentence within the copy, it's best to tell the editor. Here, the reporter has called for a certain type of shot: video of building damage in one case, and wheat damage in the other. There will be times when the reporter wants a very specific shot. When that happens, the editor needs to know exactly what that shot is and where it can be found.

SU Bridge Tape 2, 04:15:32   At this point in the script, the reporter has called for a standup bridge recorded earlier when the story was being shot. A "bridge" implies that the reporter's standup is within the story, rather than at the beginning or end. A package used as crossroll for a live shot shouldn't have a standup open or close.

"Darrell Hanavan"   Notice there's no "S/" in front of this name. The name is there to help the editor identify the speaker, but neither bite from this speaker is long enough for a graphic. Instead, the person is identified by name and position in the copy.

It's actually a good habit to identify the people speaking within a story even if you do plan to super their name. That way, if the graphics computer fails, and they sometimes do, the story can stand on its own without supers.

REPORTER AND ANCHOR CLOSES

Generally, reporters will close out their live shots with another sentence or two live, then toss back to the anchor on set. Quite often, the reporter close is only loosely scripted, if it's scripted at all. The director doesn't need written instructions to know when to return to the camera on set. The reporter will make it clear by using the anchor's name at the close of the live report.

THE CASE FOR CAPS AND LOWERCASE

Some television writers prefer to write their stories entirely in capital letters, as demonstrated in the following story.

> THERE MAY BE TROUBLE AHEAD FOR A PROPOSED CITIZEN REVIEW PANEL TO OVERSEE JOHNSON CITY POLICE. MAYOR WEBB SAYS CITY COUNCIL APPEARS LIKELY TO VOTE DOWN THE IDEA IN WHAT MAY BE A STORMY MEETING TONIGHT. THE MEETING BEGINS AT 7 O'CLOCK AT THE CITY AND COUNTY BUILDING.

Other writers and anchors prefer their scripts in "caps and lowercase," as the following story demonstrates.

There may be trouble ahead for a proposed citizen review panel to oversee Johnson City police. Mayor Webb says city council appears likely to vote down the idea in what may be a stormy meeting tonight. The meeting begins at 7 o'clock at the City and County Building.

Station policy or the preference of on-air personnel may answer the question as to which format is "best." Otherwise, you will have to choose which format you most prefer. Some journalists find that caps and lowercase helps them find their place in the copy more easily, regardless of whether they record voice tracks in a sound booth or present the news live from a studio. Other journalists seem to find all caps easier to read, although if that were actually the case it might seem as if newspapers, magazines, and book publishers would print their stories in all capital letters. Ultimately, the choice seems to boil down to which style can help make on-air presentations the most seamless and flawless. Which format makes words that demand special emphasis most obvious? Which format reveals the strength and meaning of individual words most definitively? Your answers will help determine which style you select.

SUMMARY

Script formats vary from one station to another, but virtually all stations follow some variation of the prototype formats described in this chapter. From the simplest voice-over script, to VO/SOTs, and to the most complex scripts for packages, every writer needs an understanding of script structure.

In addition to the formats discussed in this chapter, you may wish to include features from other formats you are familiar with to custom design a script structure that is most comfortable for you.

EXERCISES

1. Obtain samples of television news scripts from one or more local stations. Compare the scripts with examples provided in this chapter, and with each other, if you have samples from more than one station. Determine which formats you most prefer and analyze the reasons for your preferences.

2. Following the example in this chapter, write five separate television news "readers," each on a different newsworthy topic. Limit each of your stories to twenty seconds in length. You may wish to use a newspaper or news magazine as your source of information for this assignment.

3. Following the example in this chapter, write three separate VTR VO stories of approximately thirty seconds in length, each on a different newsworthy topic. Follow the format of the VTR VO example in this chapter. You may wish to use a newspaper or news magazine as your source of information for this assignment, or use information from

any other legitimate source. Assume you have at your disposal all video you would need for each story.

4. Write three separate VO SOT stories for broadcast, following the format of the VO SOT example in this chapter. You may wish to use a newspaper or news magazine as your source of information for this assignment, or use information from any other legitimate source. Determine an appropriate length for each story you write. Assume you have at your disposal all video you would need for each story.

5. Write intros to three live shots, following the format example in this chapter. Determine an appropriate length for each intro. You may wish to use a newspaper or news magazine as your source of information for this assignment, or use information from any other legitimate source.

6. Write a video news package, following the format example in this chapter. Use quotations from newspaper or magazine stories as the source for your "sound bites." Assume you have all video you would need for this assignment.

CHAPTER NINE

WRITING THE PACKAGE

__Package.__ An edited, self-contained video report of a news event or feature, complete with pictures, sound bites, voice-over narration, and natural sounds. The package is a form of narrative storytelling with a beginning, middle, and ending.

Some reporters start with the pictures whenever they "write" a package. Others start with the words. But the most efficient reporters first block the package as a story with a beginning, middle, and ending. The blueprint looks something like this:

1. Focus (the story stated in a sentence)
2. Beginning (lead)
   a. Studio lead-in
3. Package lead
   a. Visual lead
   b. Voice over (VO)
4. Middle (three or four main points)
   a. Main point A
   b. Main point B
   c. Main point C
   d. Main point D
5. End (close)
   a. Final visual
   b. Strong closing sound
   c. Final VO

Following this approach, you first emphasize the ideas you wish to communicate, and only then begin the search for images and words that will most effectively tell the story. You structure the story through four distinct stages of development: (a) existing knowledge and new information obtained from story research before you leave the station; (b) field research and interviews; (c) viewing and editing field video and sound bites; and (d) writing the final package. Structuring a package thus becomes much more a way of thinking than of writing.

DEFINE YOUR FOCUS

Once you understand the story, you can define your statement of **focus.** The focus is a simple, vivid, declarative sentence expressing the heart, the soul, of the story as it will appear on air.[1] Until you know the story yourself, it will be difficult to tell it to anyone else.

In the following example of how to structure a package, assume you are assigned to cover a story on smart ways to lose weight. Perhaps as you research the story, you begin to understand that the story focus is, "The secret to weight loss lies in eating a healthy diet from the four basic food groups."

WRITE THE BEGINNING (STUDIO LEAD-IN)

The package, like all stories, will need a lead-in. Audiences are best served if the studio lead-in instantly and intrusively begins the story, rather than serves merely as an introduction to a story yet to come. The package then continues the story as the story cuts from studio lead-in to first video and voice over.

STUDIO LEAD-IN:
If you want to lose weight and become healthy for life, you'll never need a fad diet again. In fact, you never did. You learned the secret in elementary school. (Reporter) has the story.

The anchor has disclosed the heart of the story in the studio lead-in. At this point the package begins to air and audiences see the story's first video.

WRITE THE PACKAGE LEAD

Again, as you plan the "visual lead," or first video of your package, identify the central idea you wish to communicate before you worry about the words. In general, the thought process focuses first on (a) an idea to communicate; (b) images to prove the idea visually; and (c) words as necessary to interpret and explain the images.

If you want to indicate in your first visual that healthy diets are instinctive, you may decide your first video should be of children eating healthy foods. You might further decide to emphasize close-ups that show healthy faces and foods. Now that you have the images defined, you can write the voice over.

VOICE OVER TO ACCOMPANY THE "VISUAL LEAD":
Nutritionists now tell us the only diet we ever needed is to follow the four basic food groups, and to eat a variety of food from those groups. It's how healthy people just naturally eat . . . and it can become a way of life for almost anyone.

(Video [close-ups]: Children eating healthy foods: apples, vegetable snacks)

WRITE THE MIDDLE OR MAIN BODY

After the package lead, begin the middle or main body of your report. In a 1:10- to 1:30-minute package, try to limit yourself to no more than three or four main points. Again, focus on the ideas to be communicated before you worry about the images or words.

In this example about healthy diets, perhaps after finishing your research you know that you wish to emphasize four main points, as follows:

1. You can eat anything you want, just not everything (eat in right amounts).
2. Exercise plays a role, although you don't need to be obsessive.
3. Healthy diets and foods are tastier. Fatty foods actually are less satisfying. If you cut fat in your diet, you begin to crave healthy foods.
4. If you find you can't control your eating, you may be using food as a substitute to fill other needs in your life.

Again in the main body, focus first on (a) the idea to communicate; (b) images to prove the ideas visually; and (c) words as necessary to interpret and explain the images.

Now that you have your idea clearly focused for *point one*, "You can eat anything you want, just not everything (eat in right amounts)," you begin the search for images. Perhaps you decide to visit a supermarket and are able to photograph a shopper as she buys apples and whole grain foods. As part of your report you interview the woman and she admits to having the occasional urge for a hot fudge sundae. In the bite, the woman tells you, "I've found that diets based on deprivation will not work, so I try to eat healthy foods but also occasionally reward myself with a hot fudge sundae. It's no big deal that way."

Even while you are in the field, you decide to build off the woman's interview as a way to incorporate a reporter standup at this point. "Try to integrate the reporter standup so the story doesn't come to a stop," advises network freelance television producer and photojournalist Ray Farkas. "Make it flow visually."[2] In this story, perhaps you decide the standup gives you an excellent transition from point one ("Eat reasonable amounts of whatever you want") to *point two* ("Exercise plays an important role"). You "script" the standup either in your mind's eye or perhaps jot down the main idea on a note pad and deliver your standup to camera. Normally, in a 1:10- to 1:30-minute story, two or three sentences will provide sufficient length for a standup.

> **STANDUP (AT FAST-FOOD TAKE-OUT):**
> "So the occasional indulgence in a healthy lifestyle is normal . . . and inevitable. Just one caution: Know when to say enough . . . and remember to exercise."

The standup in this example helps introduce *point two:* "Exercise plays a role, although you don't need to be obsessive." Again, after you define the main point, look for images that will help prove it. In this story, perhaps you decide to photograph people walking along the exercise path; people running around an exercise track; and a basketball game you happen to spot as you drive by. Perhaps you decide to interview a person walking along the exercise path and record the following sound bite for the report.

> **BITE:**
> "Five months ago, I weighed thirty-eight pounds more than I do now. Once I started working out, my body began to crave healthier foods."

Remember to block in visual transitions as you move from one main point to the next, and remember to insist on "visual proof" for each of your main points. Because *point three* states that "Healthy diets/foods are tastier," you will need one or more shots that prove this idea. The transition shot that begins point three after the sound bite could be of an ultra close shot of mist-covered red delicious apples. As the shot holds on screen, a hand comes into frame. The next shot, in matched action, shows a shopper reaching into the fruit bin at a natural foods store as she selects apples. The next shot, a close-up, might show the woman's hand coming into frame. In a matched-action shot, this time a medium or long shot, the woman places an apple on the kitchen counter at home. As the sequence continues, she cuts the apple, arranges it on a plate with some cheddar cheese, and hands the plate to her four-year-old daughter.

Voice-over narration throughout this sequence would make the following points: natural foods, those without much processing, often are the healthiest and the tastiest. Further, when people cut fat in their diets, they begin to crave healthy foods; fatty foods actually are less satisfying.

At this stage, you begin *point four* in your package: "If you find you can't control your eating, you may be using food as a substitute to fill other needs in your life." Because point three ends on the idea that fatty foods actually are less satisfying, you could launch point four with video of fatty foods. The shot might be of dessert cakes on a bakery shelf, rows of potato chip products in a supermarket, fried chicken in a deli display, or any other shot that proves the main point visually. If you use such a shot, you will need voice over narration that helps you make the transition to point four: "While fatty foods won't kill you, they can leave you craving more. Worse yet, with high-fat temptations around, it's easy to lose control with these foods." At this point, you might cut to another sound bite that helps prove point four. Perhaps during your field interviews, someone told you:

> **SOUND BITE:**
> "Food is a powerful drug. Often we eat to satisfy needs that have nothing to do with food. To live a healthy life style, you may have to learn why you're eating when you're not hungry."

The person who gave you such a sound bite might be a dietician, a specialist in addictions or eating disorders, a dieter you meet at a weight-loss clinic, or some other person with the close knowledge or experience to make such an observation. A word of caution: The bite must occur spontaneously in the field during the interview process, without coaching from the reporter. Ethical reporters never steer an interviewee into making a statement to help substantiate a main point in a story. Based on your own research, however, it might be permissible during an interview to observe, "I suppose some people use food almost like some people use drugs." In this way you have suggested subject matter, but not the response itself. Every interview question follows such a process.

WRITE THE CLOSE

Next, write the **close** to your package. The close makes it obvious to your audience the story is ending. Without a strong close, the package will stop but it will not end. As soon as you arrive in the field, begin your search for a closing shot—a visual close you can build toward throughout the entire piece, something so strong it's obvious the story is finished. Lazy reporters tend to end stories with interviews or standups, but such endings are the visual equivalent of an unsigned letter.

If you must write from video someone else shot in the field, search it carefully for a closing shot. If you are under extreme deadline pressure, ask the photographer or editor to help you identify a strong closing shot. Once you have identified a closing shot on tape, you can then build every component of the report toward that final moment.

In this example, you might want to leave audiences with the idea, "If you learn how to eat and live healthily, you will live a happier life, and possibly a longer life." The close not only wraps up the story but reinforces the story's focus. In this example we stated the original story focus to the effect, "The secret to weight loss lies in eating a healthy diet from the four basic food groups." Note how the story close, "If you learn how to eat and live healthily, you will live a happier life, and possibly a longer life," reinforces the focus and brings the story to a decisive ending.

Again, in the close, give your audience visual proof of the point you wish to communicate. Images that show an elderly person playing with a grandchild might address the idea of a longer, happier life. You also might photograph senior citizens having the time of their life at a square dance, or perhaps find a fit, trim couple in their 70s jogging in a park. The more articulate you can make your images, the more memorable your message will become.

PREPLANNING THE PACKAGE

Often, you can plan many elements within a package before you even enter the field, based on your existing knowledge and new information obtained from story research. We are not talking about making a story, or writing the story in advance, but rather about nailing down all the information you can before you enter the field, then filling in the holes as you shoot field video and conduct your field research and interviews (Figure 9.1).

The term **preplanning** thus refers to planning that occurs before you leave the station. "You can do a lot of effective reporting without leaving where you are—kitchen or station—by letting your fingers do the walking," says reporter Chuck Crouse. "The more extensive your use of the phone, the more finesse you may need to

FIGURE 9.1   The most complete and authoritative reports build on the reporter's research, planning, and knowledge of the community.

apply. For instance, your city councilors are probably experienced at talking to you, and see each call as a chance to communicate with their constituents. An attorney involved in litigation, however, may be wary of talking to you."[3]

You also can gather information by reading newspapers and magazines, talking with friends and acquaintances, and just from living. "You must reflect on the story before the need to write it occurs. Otherwise it will be difficult to speak with authority," says Bob Moon, national correspondent for AP Network News. "As a given, we assume you know everything you can about the local community: what crops come from the fields, what goods emerge from the factories, and the like."[4] The same need for reflection and understanding applies even when you are covering institutions and issues. "I became convinced many years ago that prior acquaintance with developing country issues—not to mention knowledge of the tastes and smells in those lands—is indispensable to covering the news these days," says Peter Jennings, news anchor and senior editor of ABC *World News Tonight.* "It simply isn't possible to catch up with the events by quickly reading official reports and calling government officials—not that one shouldn't use every resource available."[5]

In such discussions, note the distinction between preplanning and "prewriting" the story. "Planning is essential. But it is no substitute for the reality of what a reporter finds on location," says NBC's Bob Dotson.[6] Basically, when you preplan a story, you plan the story on paper or as a **storyboard** in the mind's eye that treats only those elements you feel reasonably certain about. But if conditions change in the field, you must change with them. "Prewriting is an easy way to laziness," said WCVB's Martha Bradlee. "Skill in reporting comes from the ability to rapidly organize your story once you've arrived and had time to digest what is happening."[7]

Another form of laziness occurs when reporters wait to understand the story until they return from the field and actually sit down to write. By then, it's too late because the story happens in the field and can never be more than you bring back from the field. "A good television news story is made in the field by competent reporters and photojournalists," says KAKE's Larry Hatteberg. "Reporters must be concerned with the story and not the standup and how it will play. You have to cover the story to write it."[8] Using this approach, you focus first on ideas, then on images and words.

SPOT-NEWS PACKAGES

Spot-news packages can follow the same planning process, although fast-breaking news offers less time for contemplation and reflection. Often the reporter and photojournalist do well to capture what's happening. Still, once the breaking event has ended, some time usually remains to identify the story and its focus, assess what happened, and record pickup sound and additional video. Even while covering spot news, the reporter and photojournalist can identify (a) story focus, (b) the story's three or four most important main points, and (c) how the story will close. If raw field material is unavailable to prove the story's crucial beginning, middle, and ending, or if the field crew has insufficiently identified these points before they return from the field, the story will suffer. In the following spot-news story, note how the package has a beginning, middle, and ending, and how the visuals "prove" every main point. The studio lead-in has been omitted to help make the package's essential structure more obvious.

Grain Elevator Explosion (Field Report)

(VTR WITH VO NARRATION)

:04 LS Rubble & firemen	The explosion occurred about nine o'clock this morning at the McMillan Grain Company just outside Abilene.
:03 MS Fireman scales tower	Police say five workers were inside one tower at the elevator when the explosion occurred.
:04 CU Grimy faces	Four of the men were killed instantly. One survived.
	(SURVIVOR ON CAMERA)
:18 Sound bite	We were leveling out wheat by hand at the top of one of the storage towers. I heard one of the guy's shovels hit another shovel. There must have been a spark because all of a sudden that dust exploded. Why I'm not dead, I'll never know.

	(QUESTION FROM OFF-CAMERA) How did you escape?
	(SURVIVOR) The west side of the tower was still standing . . . and that's the side with the emergency ladder. When I came to, I was being hauled out by a fireman who'd come up the ladder to look for survivors.
:04 Reporter standup	(REPORTER STANDUP) The explosion shook buildings and rattled store-front windows in a five-mile radius around Abilene. Officials estimate property damage at more than two million dollars.
:04 LS Damaged trucks :03 CU Driver inspects damage	(VTR WITH VO NARRATION) Trucks from the summer wheat harvest were dumping their loads when the explosion occurred. Falling debris damaged 15 of these trucks.
:05 Injured driver sits on running board	Several truck drivers suffered minor injuries.
:15 Trucks drive past damaged elevator	Farmers who had been using these facilities will now have to deliver wheat to storage elevators in surrounding towns. At the McMillan Grain Company in Abilene, Tina Roberts, 9-News.

SET A HIGH STANDARD FOR PACKAGES

If you do make your story into a package, you are obligated to set high standards for your work. Not every story justifies a package or even a reporter's presence, and many stories work well as simple anchor VO or VO with previously recorded sound (VO SOT). Conversely, if you are assigned to write, report, or photograph a simple VO but think the story would make a good package, tell your producer or assignment editor you think it should be a package. To help guide your decision, you can think of stories as falling into two categories:[9]

1. A video story that can be told by the camera and through sound bites. Into this category fall spot news, fires, overturned tanker trucks, and similar "event-driven" stories.
2. Stories that require explanation, analysis, or the reporter's observations of the environment—stories the camera alone cannot tell without a reporter to help tell it.

If the anchor can do what the reporter is doing, and do it better, then you have to make the reporter justify his or her presence in a package. "When reporters tackle a complex story, they chronicle the sequence of events, flesh out the personalities, explain the issues and the implications, and put all the pieces of the puzzle together," says journalist Peter R. Kann.[10] Although Kann describes the essential qualities of a print reporter, they apply equally to television reporters who know more about the story than the anchor, and who have a gift for bringing stories to life. Such television reporters can almost always justify their presence in the story. Furthermore, if the television reporter experiences the story, senses it, and serves as an eyewitness in some way to explain the smells and sights of an event, then audiences may feel they need the reporter in the story.[11]

Ultimately, it's not how many stories you crank out that counts, but how memorable you make them. "You pick timeless subjects and treat them properly, and people are going to be looking at them 200 years from now. We are stockpiling history," said the late Canadian documentary filmmaker Donald Britain.[12]

Fifty or a hundred years from now, for example, historians may look back on Ron Mitchell's reports about construction of Denver's International Airport, the last U.S. airport to be built in the 20th century. When construction began, Mitchell, a KUSA reporter, took viewers into the empty fields east of Denver. In subsequent reports, using standups and even the routine sounds from public address systems at other airports, he crafted reports to "show" viewers where the various concourses, taxi ramps, baggage claim areas, and concession stands would someday be located. Today his series chronicles the airport as it rose from an empty field in the 1990s to become a hub for international travelers.

USE NATURAL SOUND LIBERALLY

To help involve viewers and listeners in your story, and to help them feel as if they're experiencing the events you show on screen, remember to use natural sound throughout your package (Figure 9.2). Natural sound up full at the very start of a package, even before the first voice over, can help draw viewers into the story. Such natural sound could be an athlete's labored breathing, a young boy yelling "Ice cold lemonade, 25 cents!," or the purr of electric clippers at a pet grooming boutique. "When we go out, we don't often enough listen for the little sounds," says Ray Farkas, network freelance television producer and photojournalist. "Too often, we go for the bite at the sheriff's news conference versus the sense of what it felt like to be in the sheriff's office or the marriage license bureau."[13]

In the end, every package should capture something of the news environment and communicate that experience to viewers. Universally, storytellers seek to communicate a sense of experience as they communicate with their audiences. The news package is simply another form of narrative storytelling with a beginning, middle, and ending. "Television journalism is uniquely a combination of storytelling, photographic, and cinema-editing skills which can be specifically learned and clearly articulated," says news producer John Haydock.[14] Routinely, at television organizations

FIGURE 9.2   Images and natural sounds from the environment lend a sense of realism to news packages and help viewers feel as if they're experiencing the event.

around the world, some of the most memorable journalism takes the form of compelling news packages.

SUMMARY

The package can be defined as an edited, self-contained report of a news event or feature, complete with pictures, sound bites, voice-over narration, and natural sounds. It is a form of narrative storytelling with a beginning, middle, and ending. Before they write the words for a package or shoot the pictures, the most efficient reporters first create a blueprint or structure for their packages. Ideally, the reporter's thought process will concentrate first on the main story idea, then on images to prove the idea visually, and finally on words as necessary to interpret and explain the images.

Typically, a 1:10- to 1:30-minute news package includes a focus statement (the story stated in a sentence), a beginning or lead (including the studio lead-in and a visual and voice-over lead for the package), a middle section with three or four main points, and an ending or close. The strongest packages normally begin and end on visuals from the news environment rather than with reporter standups.

The package takes form during four stages of development: existing knowledge and facts obtained from story research before you leave the station; field research and interviews; viewing and editing field video and sound bites; and writing the final package.

To tell the story effectively, you must first understand it yourself. A good way to crystallize your thinking about a story is by defining your statement of focus. The focus is a simple, vivid, declarative sentence expressing the heart and soul of the story as it will be on air. When you can distill your understanding of a story this succinctly, you are ready to report it. The best reporters routinely exchange ideas for the story with other people involved in the storytelling process so that everyone works toward a common goal.

The strongest packages begin with a studio lead-in that instantly and intrusively begins the story, rather than serves merely as an introduction to a story yet to come. The story then continues as the package begins to air. The main body of the package typically contains three or four main points, each with visual proof, and with a visual transition to help the package flow smoothly from one main point to the next. Use sound bites to help prove the visuals and to reveal more about the people in your stories, and work to integrate reporter standups to help make your packages flow visually.

As soon as you arrive in the field, begin your search for a strong closing shot. Once you have identified the closing shot and know how the story will end, you can build the package to an obvious and definitive ending.

As you structure the package, planning is essential. Often you can plan many elements within a package even before you enter the field, but never go so far as to write the story in advance: The goal is to gather information and reflect on the story before the need to write it occurs. If you wait to understand the story until after you return from the field and sit down to write it, the story may fail. Breaking news offers less time for reflection and contemplation. Your first obligation is to capture the action in breaking spot news. Sometimes all you can do under those conditions is react, not think. But often you will have time after the main action subsides to identify the story and its focus, assess what happened, and record pickup sound and additional video.

Not every story justifies a package or even a reporter's presence. Often packages would work just as well as simple anchor VO or VO SOT. At other times, VO SOT stories would better serve audiences as packages. To guide your decision, you can think of stories as falling into two categories: The first category includes video stories that can be told by the camera and through sound bites. This category includes spot news and "event-driven" stories. The second category includes stories that require explanation, analysis, or the reporter's observations of the environment. These stories cannot be told without a reporter to help tell them.

If the anchor can do what the reporter does in a package, and do it better, the reporter may be unnecessary. If the reporter experiences the story, or knows more about the story than the anchor, then the reporter's presence in a package can be justified.

Use natural sound liberally in all packages as a way to help involve audiences, and to help them feel as if they're experiencing the events you show on screen. The use of strong sound helps storytellers communicate a sense of experience to their audiences.

Appendix B, "A Reporting, Writing and Editing Checklist," is provided to help you plan the package and concentrate your energies for the hard work this form of writing and storytelling demands. Remember, the more articulate you can make your images, the more memorable your messages will become.

E X E R C I S E S

1. Videotape a television news package and analyze its structure. Prepare a two-page, typed, double-spaced report that addresses the following considerations:

   Length of the studio lead-in, in seconds

   Your analysis of how effectively the studio lead-in discloses the heart of the story

   How effectively the first video communicates the story to come

   Whether the package lead-in continues the story as expressed in the studio lead-in or actually begins the story

   Number of main points in the story, listed individually

   Use of visual transitions between main points

   Use of sound bites

   How well the story integrates a reporter standup, if any, without disrupting the package's visual flow

   How well the story builds to an obvious, definitive conclusion

   The presence of an obvious and easy-to-articulate story focus

2. Using a newspaper story that contains quotes from one or more sources, write the script for a 1:10-minute television package. Include all elements for the package: a studio lead-in, all VO narration, scripted sound bites transcribed from quotations in the story, a script for a reporter standup, and a brief description of all visuals you would use, complete with visual transitions between all main points in the body of your package. Follow the script format example in Chapter 8, "Television Script Formats."

3. Record a television news package and write a script that reflects how you would make the package more informative and interesting. Change any components of the package as it now exists: you may want to rewrite the studio lead-in, for example, so that it's more interesting and addresses a wider audience or to disclose the heart of the story more immediately. You may wish to indicate changes in the existing video, or perhaps you may want to eliminate or shorten some sound bites. You may want to build a stronger close for the package. You may decide even to shorten the package itself. All changes you make should serve to make the story more interesting, more informative, and more memorable.

4. Record and view five television news packages and write a one-sentence focus statement for each, based on what you understand about the story after watching it. Next, analyze how an even stronger focus statement could have made each story even more memorable and relevant to viewers.

5. On a given day, study a front-page newspaper story and decide to what extent you could preplan the various story elements before you enter the field. Choose a story you think a local television story will cover that day. Identify the story, try to write a focus statement for it, list what you already know about the story, all the facts you still need, and what sound bites you might use. Include a reporter standup, if possible. Next, write a script that contains everything you know about the story, leaving holes as necessary in the script for missing information. That evening, watch the story on television. Compare your treatment of the story, based on your own preplanning, with the station's field coverage.

6. Compare the structure of a spot-news package with the structure of a package that addresses a nonbreaking news event. Discuss how package structure differs between the two examples, and what influences might account for the differences.

7. Apply the "Story Checklist" on page 349 to the script you wrote for assignment #2. Rewrite the original script as necessary to incorporate as many of the checklist elements as possible.

N O T E S

1. Fred Shook and Don Berrigan, "Glossary: Television Field Production and Reporting," Atelier Sur le Récit Visuel, Service National de la Formation et du Développement, Bureau de Montréal, Société Radio Canada, Montréal, Canada, 1991.

2. Ray Farkas, "Looking through the Lens Differently," a presentation at the NPPA TV News-Video Workshop, Norman, OK, 21 March 1991.

3. Chuck Crouse, "Doing It by Phone," *RTNDA Communicator* (September 1987), 66.

4. Bob Moon, "Bringing the World to Main Street," a workshop for students and professional journalists at Colorado State University, Fort Collins, CO, 9 November 1990.

5. Peter Jennings, "Foreword," in *Main Street America and the Third World*, 2nd ed., by John Maxwell Hamilton (Cabin John, MD: Seven Locks Press, 1988).

6. John Premack, "Straight from the Shoulder," *RTNDA Communicator* (December 1985), 28.

7. Ibid.

8. Ibid.

9. John Haralson, in remarks to students at the Talent Performance Development Workshop, Colorado State University, Fort Collins, CO, 22 February 1992.

10. Peter Kann, quoted in an undated letter to *Wall Street Journal* subscribers.

11. Bob Kaplitz, "Managing Creative People," a presentation at the NPPA TV News-Video Workshop, Norman, OK, 19 March 1991.

12. Terry Kolomechuk, ed., *Donald Brittain: Never the Ordinary Way* (Winnipeg, Canada: National Film Board of Canada, 1991), 54.

13. Farkas, 21 March 1991.

14. John Haydock, "Developing an Evaluation System for Daily News Packages," *RTNDA Communicator* (November 1987), 17.

■ ■ ■ ■ ■

CHAPTER TEN

HOW TO IMPROVE YOUR STORYTELLING ABILITY

Audiences with access to a multitude of viewing choices have come to expect certain standards from their favorite newscasts. At the very least they want their stories and storytellers to be interesting and appealing. While every journalist is acutely aware of the limitations of the medium, and the impact of human frailties on the final result, the audience can only judge your work by what you put on the screen. In the end, nothing else matters. "The ability to appeal, whatever the subject matter, separates the successful creator from the artistic failure," writes filmmaker and author Edward Dmytryk in his book, *On Film Editing*.[1] Survival and professional advance depend, then, on a commitment to produce stories with a style and substance that are consistently solid, unique, and appealing, even on those days when you would willingly trade your job for a dead mouse or two.

SEEK GRADUAL IMPROVEMENT

As you strive to make your stories more attractive and compelling, you will be surrounded by competitors who may seem more capable than you. Perhaps they have more experience and confidence, or their stories just seem more inviting. While it's useful to study the techniques of others, it's important to realize that you are in competition primarily with yourself. "You are only as good as your last story, so you have to compete with yourself to improve the story each time out," says Rick Hessel, former director of electronic news gathering for NBC News, Chicago.[2]

Implicit in the process of self-improvement is the very real possibility of failure, a hazard that keeps some people from realizing meaningful accomplishments in their careers. You can't fail if you don't try, after all, but neither can you succeed. "Don't be afraid to fail," says KAKE's Larry Hatteberg. "You don't learn unless you fail."[3] Given that outlook, an occasional failure can be seen as a virtue in the journalist's professional development, with each new success building on some past failure.

SEEK MINOR VICTORIES

Improvement is a gradual process, and as such, subject to frustration. The trick, says NBC senior correspondent Bob Dotson, is to go for the minor victories. "Don't try to hit a home run every time out, just get on first base every time at bat," says Dotson. "You find the right word, or write a phrase that works, or shoot a scene that tells the story."[4] A similar approach is advocated by photojournalist Lou Swierzowski, whose philosophy is, "Sometimes great, sometimes a bit less, but always solid."[5]

The commitment to slow, steady development can result in significant improvements over time, so great that long-time CBS news anchor Dan Rather told *Washington Journalism Review*, "I really believe what moves a career along—not just in journalism—is not doing the one big extraordinary thing, it's doing the routine things extraordinarily well time after time."[6]

EXCELLENCE VERSUS PERFECTION

Every artist seeks perfection. Some even delude themselves that they have found it. There is the cabinetmaker who drives nail holes into an otherwise exquisitely sculpted work to render it obviously imperfect, thereby seeking to underscore his feat by imposing an obvious flaw. Elsewhere the film director orders take after take until his actors have achieved perfection in their performances. Bringing order and perfection to the world, and trying in some small measure to control it, is the natural urge of most artists. But carried to extremes, perfection can become a disease that robs the creator of vital energy. No one is perfect, and no one can become perfect.

The alternative is to strive to achieve *excellence* rather than perfection. Be as good as you can be, but realize your limits. This approach allows you to direct the energy you might otherwise have spent trying to become "perfect" on more productive endeavors. You may even choose to expend some of that energy reporting extra stories on your own time. "Some of my best work has occurred during the times when I was not on the company payroll," says NBC's Bob Dotson.[7]

HAVE A STORY

Storytellers, of course, need stories. But often in television news, reporters and photojournalists confuse their accounts of events with stories. Routinely they can be heard to identify the story subject, but not the story itself: "My story is about consumer spending." But until you sum up the story in your mind it will be difficult to tell the story to anyone else. For this reason a story **focus** or **commitment** is one of the storyteller's most potent tools. It is simply a summary statement that identifies the story to be told, a concept known variously in literature and theater as theme, story line, premise, or point of view. In the reporting process, commitment is the story stated in a complete sentence: "A decade of excesses in consumer spending is ending as consumers begin to spend more defensively" or "Mental health workers say loneliness is an American epidemic." The focus statement provides a way to give the story life and help drive it forward.

Typically but erroneously, the reporter is left to identify the story, but in reality that job falls to everyone involved with the story. Because you may see the story differently than the **assignment editor** or the person who accompanies you into the field, whether that person is the reporter or the photographer, remember to communicate your ideas to one another so that all agree on a single focus. If you will invest just two or three minutes to develop a focus statement, you can have a stronger story and spend far less time in the field. Even when the action is moving quickly all around you, and it seems as if you must purely and simply react, force yourself to take time to think. Relax, take a deep breath, and become aware of your surroundings. Mentally sift through the action around you, decide what's important to the story and what can be ignored, and most of all decide on the story you will tell your audience. Recognize that you must be flexible enough to change your story commitment if the event changes. "We're all visitors to worlds of fantasy," says freelance photographer Darrell Barton, "but there's no reason to become a resident."[8]

THE ESSENCE OF STORYTELLING

The essence of all storytelling is conflict. There is no very good story in the premise "He wanted her and he got her; the end." Conflict—the quest for a goal against opposition—keeps the story going.

The 82-year-old woman who nurses heroin-addicted babies back to health is engaged in one of life's greatest conflicts: life and health over death and suffering. The runner who has lost his leg to cancer but rides across America in a wheelchair to raise money for handicapped athletes illustrates his character under pressure. Because so many journalism stories are accounts of things gone wrong, conflict and struggle are inevitable components of television news. To ignore them is to ignore the nature not only of news, but life itself.

EXCUSES

In the face of deadline pressure, budget restraints, and equipment breakdowns, virtually every broadcast news story is imperfect, and some are made to be outright forgettable. As a memo at a television station in Texas reminds news personnel, "We have some decent stories that we are making average."[9] Inquire at any newsroom why a particular story failed, and inevitably you will encounter The Excuse—the common tendency we have to invoke self-exoneration whenever we fail to achieve the standards of which we are capable.

Some excuses, of course, are legitimate. They are explanations of something that went uncontrollably wrong. But other excuses are masquerades for indifference and procrastination. Note that some of the most common excuses are admissions of failure:

- "It was a dumb assignment. The producer didn't know what he wanted."
- "I don't have enough time to do a good job. I have to cover six stories a day."
- "My equipment is no good."
- "I didn't have time to set up the camera on a tripod."

- "They don't pay me enough that I have to do everything around here."
- "You can't shoot sequences in spot news."
- "It's the photographer's job to take the pix. I don't feel I can suggest shots."
- "Audiences don't expect that level of quality."
- "It's not my job, that's up to the reporter."

The work of people who make such excuses fades quickly into oblivion, so professionals leave such excuses to the competition. The more excuses the competitors make, the less impact their reporting will have. Ultimately, on every story, the choice comes down to a simple yes or no whenever you ask yourself, "Am I going to do my best job on this story or not?"

KNOW THE COMMUNITY

The smaller the market, the more broadcast journalists you will find who are on their way through town to a better job. At one time market hopping may have helped further careers, but today tenure in the marketplace seems to hold greater rewards. Stations need employees who want to live in the community and are willing to stay long enough to learn something about it. No reporter who arrives in town and leaves eight months later can discover very much about the community, and even two years is little enough time for a reporter to learn about an area, its politics, and its people. Generally, assuming acceptable pay and working conditions, the longer the journalist can stay in an area the better. Tenure in the marketplace allows journalists to develop more recognition and acceptance among viewers and to report stories about the community with a depth and sensitivity not found in the work of reporters who are on their way through town.

■ ■ ■ ■ ■ ▬

COMMUNITY-ORIENTED JOURNALISM

Traditionally, journalists have struggled to make their accounts objective, but inherent in all stories is a point of view. The job of determining *which* point of view falls to the journalist. Will a particular news story be simply an account of an event or situation, or of how the event affected people and how they responded? Will Durant, the American educator and historian, typically addressed such questions from the philosopher's point of view.

> Civilization is a stream with banks. The stream is sometimes filled with blood from people killing, stealing, shouting and doing things historians usually record, while on the banks, unnoticed, people build homes, make love, raise children, sing songs, write poetry. The story of civilization is the story of what happened on the banks. . . .*

*Jim Hicks, "Spry Old Team Does It Again," *Life* (18 October 1963), 92.

In a sense you are a historian for the market area you serve. You tell the stories of the soldiers, the boatbuilders, the archaeologists, the miners, and the musicians of your region. Someday, should you reach the network level, you still will tell those same stories, but you simply will share them with a larger audience.

CURIOSITY PAYS

Curiosity is a prerequisite if the journalist is to develop an understanding of the market in which he or she works. One broadcast executive tells of a reporter who spent nearly eighteen months in town. A week and a half before she was to leave town for another reporting job, she came to him to ask directions to the nearby mountains, which she had never visited. After a year and a half on the job, she had yet to explore the streets or to learn in which direction the freeways ran.

Cities and communities reveal themselves to explorers, so soon upon your arrival in town, come to know everything you can about street names, geographical oddities, regional pronunciations, community leaders, and Saturday night dances. Introduce yourself to the municipal court judge and walk along the riverfront. At restaurants, pass up the cheeseburger and sample the regional specialties like alligator tail and armadillo steak. Attend or visit area churches and synagogues and take in a movie at the local drive-in. In short, immerse yourself in the area's history, culture, commerce, and religion, and your knowledge will lead you to become a more effective storyteller.

SEE BEYOND THE OBVIOUS

Every day reporting crews reaffirm the axiom that if the journalist doesn't care about the story, neither will the audience. If you can find a new way to tell the routine story, even those you have covered repeatedly over the years, then it will be more interesting and memorable for your audience. Typically, if five reporting crews are sent to cover a ribbon-cutting ceremony, four of those crews will cover the story in about the same predictable fashion. Perhaps one or two crews will look for a fresh new way to tell the story.

"It's the Boy Scout motto, 'Be Prepared,' " says Art Donahue, whose awards include National Television News Photographer of the Year. "Make things look a little more interesting; try to think of everyday stories in a different way, not just as a standup and two talking heads on every story."[10] Donahue, a master at showing familiar subjects in a new light, once told the story of freeway traffic jams caused by a bridge under repair using only pictures and off-air sound recorded from trucker's conversations over CB radios.

SHOW AUDIENCES WHAT THEY MISSED

Your obligation as a visual storyteller is to show viewers what they could not see for themselves. In other words, show viewers what they would have missed, even had they been eyewitnesses to the event. Search for unique story angles that other reporters may have overlooked in their rush to cover the story. While the competition is shooting the smoke and flames at the apartment house fire, look around you. Perhaps you will notice an elderly man next door trying to fight back the fire with a garden hose to save his modest home. The observant seem to encounter such "lucky breaks."

NBC correspondent Bob Dotson notes that after a tornado strikes, reporters seem to gravitate to the governor touring the area and ask how things look. But when Dotson covered the aftermath of a tornado in South Carolina, he found a man even more articulate than the governor. "'Well, it got my teeth, but it didn't get me,' the man said. And he reached down in the debris and held up his mud-covered dentures. This guy crystallized it for me," says Dotson.[11]

There are critics of this approach, of course, who charge that the technique can inject unnecessary drama and emotion into news reporting. But life is dramatic, and honest journalism demands honest human reactions.

INVOLVE THE CAMERA

In 1939 David Sarnoff called television a "new art," with the implication that it was a medium whose potential was yet to be fully explored and perfected. Today we have come to realize that part of the power of television's "art" is its ability to involve the viewer by transmitting a sense of experience. "As viewers, we thirst for first-person experience," observed Bill Moyers in his PBS series, *A Walk Through the Twentieth Century*. The promise of a sense of first-person experience is one reason we turn to television, even for news.

The involved camera helps create the experiential illusion and thereby provides a way to help differentiate your reporting from the competition's. Try to involve the camera more directly in the action, in order to place the viewer in the very heart of the story. If the camera is physically and intimately involved in the action, the viewer will be too (Figure 10.1).

Look also for unique camera angles to help tell your story and to make it more visually memorable. Be aware, however, that if the angles are too drastic, your technique may call attention to itself and thereby destroy the viewer's sense of direct involvement in the story.

SEQUENCES ADVANCE THE STORY

Sequential video produces a continuous, uninterrupted flow of action that tells the story. A series of shots are edited together to create for viewers the illusion of continuity and a sense of having experienced the event. Sequential video allows the flow of the action to speak for itself.

A commonly used, but much less effective, alternative is called **illustrative video.** This reporting approach simply uses video that illustrates the script, roughly in the proportion of one scene per sentence of voice-over narration. It is similar to a series of unrelated slides or scenes that fail to provide a sequential series of shots. Conti-

FIGURE 10.1 When the camera is involved in the action, so is the audience.

nuity is not present. There is little regard for the order or rhythm or even for the meaning of individual shots working together. Illustrative video rarely tells a story.

DON'T TRY TO SHOW ALL OF NEW ZEALAND

A frustration of every broadcast reporter is the lack of air time available to tell complex stories. "If only I had a couple more minutes," pleads the reporter. "You can have five more seconds if you'll give up a week of your summer vacation," the producer replies. At such times it is useful to remember the strong messages and nuances that can be communicated by a thirty-second or even a fifteen-second commercial. The best commercial messages are simple, yet powerful and memorable. And the typical television news story can be just as memorable if you can find ways to tell your story briefly but eloquently.

One approach in the face of insufficient air time is to follow the maxim that "less is more." Photojournalist Larry Hatteberg has crystallized the concept in his advice, "Don't try to show all of New Zealand."[12] Hatteberg forged this conviction while on assignment to portray New Zealand in a four-part series. Confronted with showing the nation's overwhelming complexity in only four two-minute reports, Hatteberg dramatically narrowed his focus. In the end he chose a sheep rancher, a street magician, a fishing boat captain, and a railroad engineer, and told his stories through them. Still, after viewing the stories, there is a sense that we have seen all of New Zealand after all, because the treatment is both wide-ranging and powerful. Hatteberg's approach mirrors the sentiments of John Grierson, the British documentary historian and filmmaker, who once observed that you can write an article about the mail service, but you must make a film about one single letter.

LEVELS OF VIEWER INVOLVEMENT

Viewers experience three levels of observation when they watch television news:

Level 1   Subject is seen in an activity, accompanied by natural sounds and spontaneous comments.

Level 2   Subject is shown in an activity with voice over from a script. Accompanying sound bites are accomplished by stopping the action or event in order to conduct the interview.

Level 3   Reporter on camera describes what someone else did or said.

While each of the levels is appropriate to certain stories, the strongest reporting occurs at Level 1. Natural sound and spontaneous action lend a powerful sense of realism to broadcast news reports. A sheriff saying, "Move along folks, water's rising fast," inadvertently becomes part of the reporting process itself. The reporting techniques embodied in Level 1, and to a lesser extent in Level 2, allow levels of subject familiarity so great that viewers would know a person in your report if the individual were to walk through the door days later.

PURSUE YOUR INTEREST IN PEOPLE

Obviously, it's important to care about the people in your stories. Caring simply means that you are interested in your subject and that you listen hard to what the person has to say (Figure 10.2). In a quite different sense, caring can mean to become emotionally

FIGURE 10.2 The strongest television news stories normally result when the journalist is interested in the subject and pays attention to what the person has to say.

involved. Sometimes, the reporter can care too much and carry too much of the emotional burden, and that may show.

The key is to report honestly and with appropriate feeling. "[The story] has to come from the heart if it is going to work well. For in the end, I have to feel the story if I am going to reflect it with feeling," writes television journalist Tim Fisher.[13] "Storytellers must have compassion, and compassion can only grow out of familiarity," observed the late author Jack Bickham.[14]

MAKE VIEWERS WATCH

In helping viewers want to watch your stories, it is important to avoid telling them everything they need to know in the voice-over script. Rarely, in the newscast built on words, will you have to watch a story to understand it. You can become more aware of this truth if you will take the time to "watch" a television news story with your back turned. Often, in fact, you can listen from the next room with little loss in meaning. This kind of television, of course, is radio with pictures and is neither involving nor engaging.

A more powerful reporting method is to help people watch through voice over that invites the viewer to re-engage with the screen constantly. It is a "This" versus "This tea ceremony" approach. If you read the next two sentences aloud, the distinction will be made clear: "Every hiker should carry one of these in his backpack" versus

"Every hiker should carry a compass in his backpack." Only the first sentence acknowledges a need to help viewers watch the screen during the report.

DEVELOP VIDEO FLUENCY

In this word-oriented culture, the effort to express the story visually without stating it flatly, in words, is a trick easier said than done. And the less the reporter has to say, the worse the problem can become. For all its eloquence, the visual image receives short shrift among print-oriented journalists, even in the face of generations of filmmakers who have proven the power of visual communication. "Very early . . . I discovered that viewers are more attentive to silent sequences than they are to dialogue scenes," writes filmmaker Edward Dmytryk. "When the screen talk[s], so d[oes] the viewer. Silent scenes command attention."[15]

The same realities persist today. *Time* magazine noted that after screenings of *Ryan's Daughter*, director David Lean was wounded by reviewers "who so often tend to listen to movies more intently than they look at them, thus missing much of [Lean's] special grace and subtlety."[16] Happily, film and television viewers are more astute consumers of visual information than critics whose obsequious devotion to words blinds them to the larger meanings and experiences that visual fluency could offer them.

Time and again we learn that the viewer would rather see it than hear it, a lesson that even network reporters must learn. As reporter Linda Ellerbee observed, "Pictures, I came to learn . . . were different from words; as different . . . as smells are from sounds."[17]

ACCOMMODATE YOUR REPORTING TO STORY DEMANDS

Unthinking enslavement to pictures can be just as devastating as an unreasonable loyalty to words. Strong storytelling demands that the most effective means of communication be used from moment to moment. If pictures and natural sound are the best way to tell a story, then use them. If the story can more effectively be told through a reporter, or through silence, then shape the story accordingly.

REPORTING THE NONVISUAL STORY

Many of the stories you are assigned will be static and nonvisual, unless you can engage your imagination and find a way to make them move. Into this category fall city council meetings, public hearings, empty fields to be used as major building sites, and vacant buildings that have just been designated as historical landmarks. To lend essential movement and interest to such reports, a number of approaches are possible:

- Look for preshot video, file film, and old newsreels, which show the subject in action.
- Look for life and for things that move in the scene, be they rippling flags, flying birds, or people riding by on bicycles.

- Research the story so that you have a more complete idea of the story's visual potential.
- Try to humanize the story by focusing on people, people-related subjects, or symbols of people and how they live. (In the aftermath of a house fire, perhaps the close-up of a charred box of Valentine candy can remind us that people like ourselves were left homeless by the fire.)
- Find a hook for the nonvisual story. Try to relate this event to a larger event or to an existing interest or issue.
- Shoot and use sequences in your report: To see is to believe, but to see sequentially is to experience.
- Use art, models, or, if ethically warranted, re-creations.
- Pick out the main issue and do a story on that.
- Use digital video effects (DVE), as CBS once used in the story of a man's death after a police dispatcher had refused to send an ambulance. Through the use of a squeeze zoom, a freeze frame of the victim's house was shown on one side of the screen; a still shot of the dispatcher was shown to the other side of the frame. These two images were connected with an artist's rendering of a telephone cord as viewers listened to a recorded tape of the fateful conversation.
- Work a reporter standup into the story, preferably as a sequence.
- Create imagery in the mind's eye through sound.
- Write to create imagery.
- Touch feelings through little surprises and moments of drama.
- Use innovative lighting that helps define the story's mood and environment.
- Pitch reporting opportunities to people in the news—let them define and describe their environment, the event, and the moment.
- Shoot pictures that share experience.
- Challenge yourself. Improve your attitude. Remember that your audience will never care more about the story than you do.

PERSONAL APPEARANCE AND CONDUCT

Whenever you are in public, you not only represent the station for which you work, in many ways you are the station. How you conduct yourself and how you dress can influence not only how the community thinks of your station, but the quality of your stories. "You can gain access to stories or be denied access, based on how you dress," says Rich Clarkson, former photographic director of *National Geographic*.[18]

Clarkson recommends at the minimum that photojournalists wear sneakers, blue jeans, a nice shirt, tie, and a very good-looking sports jacket. With such attire, the photojournalist can appear presentable while covering every situation from an apple harvest to a governor's conference. "Do the dirty work without the jacket," says Clarkson.[19]

Stations commonly provide reporters and anchors with a wardrobe allowance, on the grounds that appearance and station image matter. But aside from the typical jackets, caps, and golf shirts that display the station logo, photojournalists rarely receive such benefits. If the photographer ruins clothes covering a story, or if the black rubber from the camera shoulder mount ruins a shirt, stations may pay the cleaning bills or replacement costs. If the station won't pay, perhaps the photojournalist can persuade management by saying, "My acceptable appearance is really for the good of the station." If the station refuses to pay the cost, consider paying it yourself in order to maintain your own standards of appearance. After all, maintains Clarkson, "It is up to each of us to create a better situation for ourselves."[20]

ETIQUETTE

Reporters around the country are making a name for themselves as pushy, rude, and aggressive. Deservedly or not, the public has begun to think of journalists as uncaring and unsympathetic. Competition and deadline pressures are partly to blame, but sometimes the problem can be a simple lack of sensitivity.

At funerals, or in similar stories that involve death or illness, first seek the family's permission before you shoot any video or conduct interviews. Most of all, as you cover the story, conduct yourself according to the considerations you would expect from a reporter or photographer if this were your family. Dress appropriately for the occasion and try to shoot the story with a longer lens to remain as far away and inconspicuous as possible.

SHOOTING AND REPORTING SPOT NEWS

Spot-news reporting encompasses events that are not under the photographer's or reporter's control. They are events that break suddenly and without warning and cannot be predicted. Because spot news is such a pervasive part of everyday reporting, the following discussion addresses some of the major factors that can lead to improved coverage of spot-news events.

Seconds Count

Timing can be everything when you cover spot news. Those first on the scene usually get the best video and the most awards for spot-news coverage. Early on, people are still excited (and exciting) and events are still happening.

Learn to Shoot by Instinct

Equipment familiarity is essential if you are to develop an instinct for shooting fast-moving events. The equipment should become such a natural extension of yourself that your reactions are automatic; you don't have to stop and think about it. In this, as in most other endeavors, practice makes perfect. During lulls in the news day, practice rack-focusing from one object to another. Imagine shots. Think about how to cover stories, even when you're at home sitting in the easy chair. And learn to listen when the interviewee speaks so you'll know whether to move in for a close shot or pull back for a shot of the speaker's husband.

Be Ready

The Scout motto "Be Prepared" is the first rule in shooting and reporting spot news. That means having batteries that are charged and connected to the camera, proper filters clicked into place, recording media loaded and cued, camera white-balanced, and the mind switched to "think." One photojournalist is said to have photographed five planes crashing, over the course of his career, because he's always ready.

Avoid "Sticks"

When you shoot spot news, tripods are impractical. Get off the tripod and shoot hand-held, but remember the rules that affect handholding: Don't handhold on telephoto; to minimize shakiness, set the lens at wide angle and even consider leaving the lens on wide angle; determine the near plane of focus for the lens you are using and don't go closer to your subjects than that distance.

Anticipate

Covering spot news means working ahead in your mind and asking what you will need to shoot as your next shot. Although no rehearsals are possible when you shoot spot news, you can try to understand in advance what is likely to happen or to imagine what may happen. "If you see something you like you've probably missed it," says freelance photographer Darrell Barton. "Don't think with the camera on, think before you turn it on."[21]

Shoot the Essentials First

Shoot the essentials first when you cover spot news; you can't go back and ask for re-takes. As you shoot, edit in your head. Previsualize and shoot what you know you'll need. Think of three shots at a time: the shot you're taking, the shot you just took, and the shot you'll take next. Pick up cutaways and other "editing fodder" after the event.

Shoot Sequences

Shoot sequences, especially on spot news, or you'll wind up with a slide show. You can't always shoot spot news sequentially, but you can create the illusion of sequences by shooting one firefighter's face, another firefighter's hands, and yet another firefighter's feet. Or you can photograph a basketball player shooting the ball, then cut to a CU of a basketball photographed at another time during the game as it goes through the hoop. You also can "snap zoom" while you're shooting (a long shot, for example, fol-lowed by an instant zoom to a medium shot or a close-up). During editing, the few frames of the snap zoom can be eliminated from the scene to create the illusion of a three- or four-shot sequence.

Tell a Story through People

Impose a theme on your story. Good spot-news coverage is partly a product of the journalist's insight and ability to feel. You may choose to show the human effects of a tragedy, for example. And although you don't control the event, you can shoot the essential scenes and sounds that reflect the event in meaningful symbols. Explain the event and how it affected people. Look for shots that tell us about people: the charred luggage at a plane crash, improperly installed electrical wiring at a mobile home fire, or perhaps the photograph of a child who is the subject of a mountain search and rescue.

Be Considerate . . .

. . . of authorities at the scene. It's the old saying that you can catch more flies with honey than with vinegar. If an official won't let you into the scene of a spot-news event, try to talk your way in. Sometimes you can begin to shoot without permission—and continue to shoot—with a statement to the police/fire/military authorities as simple as, "Let me know if I get in your way." Such a statement implies you're willing to cooperate with those in charge, and sometimes that's all they need to hear. A word of warning: Don't be intimidated; don't be shooed away from the event too easily. Many of the best scenes may occur soon after you have been told to go home.

Be Considerate . . .

. . . of people in spot-news events. Spot-news subjects, be they mine rescue workers or helicopter pilots, are under intense pressure. They are under stress; they may be experiencing grief; they may be in physical shock. Learn to "read" the physical and psychological signs of stress and fatigue to know when it's better to press ahead or to stop pushing.

People in spot-news events are less aware of the camera than they would be in slower-moving stories. Often, the reporting crew is the last thing on the minds of those who are victims of tragedy or are caught up in emotional, stressful times. Sometimes they will not even be aware of your presence, until someone tells them days or months later that you covered the story. Still, to avoid upsetting people, don't crowd or otherwise violate their personal space, but do work in close enough to get good close-ups, and remember to treat people—and their privacy, dignity, and emotions—the way you would want to be treated in similar circumstances.

Play It Safe

You face an element of risk each time you cover spot news. You may encounter downed power lines, smoke, dioxin, asbestos, pcb's, bare electrical wires, high water, toxic spills and chemicals, heat, fire, cold, high winds, explosions, falling walls, ice, and people with knives, guns, and explosives. And if those don't get you, you can even be run over by a parade float while you're shooting a cutaway of the onlookers.

Carry everything you will need to cover the story, because you may be unable to return to the news car or helicopter for spare tapes, a first aid kit, protective clothing, a change of clothes, food, or adequate lights for night shooting. Be prepared, and remember: No story is worth your life.

Don't Try to Be an Emotional Superperson

Some spot-news events are hideous. Others are gory. Others are unimaginable. And some events can affect you more than you realize or will admit. So be conscious of your feelings, and if your feelings are bothering you, talk them out with somebody who understands. Otherwise, they can build up inside you . . . and explode.

Remember Good Taste

When you report spot news, show what is appropriate and nothing more. You may decide to show only the photograph of a drowning victim rather than the covered body, or a very long shot of a resuscitation effort rather than close shots. Some shots, such as a sequence of someone putting a gun into his mouth and pulling the trigger, should never make air. How does one know whether to record such footage? Some journalists make the shot, regardless of content, then decide later whether it should be aired, or else leave the decision to the producer, anchor, managing editor, or news director. While the practice of "shoot now, decide later," often is valid, it can lead to charges of invasion of privacy and other legal entanglements (see Chapter 15, "Law and the Broadcast Journalist"). Often, the best response in such situations is to follow the adage, "If you don't want it on air, don't shoot it." While the competition may air shots you consciously chose not to make, remember propriety and its role in helping you protect your credibility.

TOWARD A NEWS PHILOSOPHY

Journalists have commonly defined their job as information gathering and delivery. "We deliver the information; it's up to the audience to understand," the reasoning went. Journalists could practice such elitism in the days when viewing options were limited. But today, audiences have gained control of the medium. Viewers with remote control units, satellite dishes, cable TV, and digital recorders even control the program schedule. They decide whom they will watch, when, where, and for how long. If the stories in a newscast are powerful, compelling, and engaging, viewers may stay. But if stories are dull, routine, and predictable, it's good-bye viewer. As always, the heart of television news remains the story, with true celebrity achieved through mastery of the storytelling process.

SUMMARY

The most successful journalists produce stories that appeal to audiences, regardless of the story's subject matter. Improving storytelling ability is a gradual process of learning to do the routine things extraordinarily well time after time. While some journalists seek perfection in their work, a more feasible alternative is to seek excellence.

Because storytellers need stories, a good approach is to summarize the story to be told in a simple, declarative sentence, which photojournalists call their commitment or focus. Once the focus or commitment is defined, the storyteller, even in journalism, must look for elements of opposition or conflict. Active conflict, such as a person's drive to overcome a handicap or fight illiteracy, helps illuminate the essence of individuals and even communities. Not every story contains conflict; some stories are merely accounts or announcements of events and fall outside this discussion.

As a photojournalist, avoid excuses. Audiences can judge your work only by what you put on the screen. While some excuses are legitimate, they can too easily become cop-outs. Strong storytellers try to show familiar subjects in a new light. Some even succeed in showing viewers familiar with a subject what they have overlooked. In such endeavors, the more the camera is involved in the action, the more realistic the story will be.

Other devices to strengthen the storytelling effort include telling the story through people, the use of matched-action sequences, and narrowing story focus to a manageable level. As John Grierson, the British documentarian, observed, the goal is not to write an article about the mail service, but to make a film about a single letter.

While words are crucial to the storytelling process, too many words can overwhelm a report. Use words, pictures, sounds, and silences sometimes by themselves, sometimes together—in whatever combinations best tell the story. Through such dedication, even so called nonvisual stories can be made compelling and interesting. Many of the same considerations apply to spot-news reporting, with the important proviso that reporters and photographers must anticipate fast-developing action and be extraordinarily conscious of personal safety. In the course of all conduct, television journalists are public figures. Their actions reflect not only on themselves, but on their employers and their profession.

DISCUSSION

1. Discuss steps the photojournalist can take to make the style and substance of news stories more appealing while still preserving the story's fundamental accuracy and integrity.

2. What is the difference between excellence and perfection in the reporting process? Which of these options is the wiser pursuit?

3. Explain why it is important to identify the story you're reporting and to state it aloud, or at least sum up the story in your mind, before the reporting process begins.

4. Why is communication between the reporter and photographer so vital throughout the reporting process?

5. Discuss the role of conflict in storytelling and how the concept applies to television news stories.

6. When excuses become a habit, a way of life almost, they can erode the photojournalist's ability to produce work of consistent excellence. Identify the attitudes and personal practices that can help you avoid making excuses about your work.

7. Identify a half-dozen or more activities in which you can engage to learn more about your community. Explain why those activities are important to help make you a better reporter, photographer, or storyteller.

8. What steps can you, as a photojournalist, take to show viewers what they might have missed, even had they been eyewitnesses to the story you're reporting?

9. Why is it important for the photojournalist to capture and transmit a sense of experience about the story being reported?

10. Discuss the approaches you can follow when you must tell complex stories briefly, yet with power.

11. Why is it important for you to care about the people in your stories, or at least to be interested in them? If you care too much about the people in your reports, can you remain detached and objective when reporting their stories?

12. Describe a good reporting method that can help make viewers watch stories by frequently inviting them to re-engage with the television screen.

13. Discuss ways you can make so-called nonvisual stories more visually appealing and informative.

14. Photographers have to work in all manner of environments and weather extremes, so to what extent should they have to maintain a well-groomed, well-dressed appearance in public? As part of your answer, describe the proper attire that you believe a photographer normally should wear on field assignment.

15. Describe effective reporting practices and considerations for personal safety that can be applied when covering spot-news stories.

16. When all is said and done, what is the journalist's most important obligation in reporting the news?

EXERCISES

1. To help improve your ability to develop focus or commitment statements, choose a very simple object or phenomenon, such as a pumpkin, a Christmas tree ornament, or a spring breeze, and identify a focus statement that will help you generate a visual story about the subject. Example: "The spring breeze is a trash collector." Further identify two or three main points you want to communicate about the subject and find visual proof for those main points. In a story centered around a car wash, for example, a main point might be, "Every time you clean something, you make something else dirty."

2. Find an ordinary subject and strive to make it more appealing through your photography or reporting.

3. Construct a television story that uses only pictures and sounds, but no voice-over narration, to tell a visual story complete with beginning, middle, and ending.

4. Study books, films, and compelling stories for the presence of conflict. Analyze the role of conflict in storytelling.

5. Take a fresh look at the community in which you live. Learn more about the area's history, culture, commerce, and religion. If you can do so safely, jog or take walks through areas of the community that are unfamiliar to you. Find a story to photograph and report based on your new awareness of some aspect of the community and its people.

6. Take a complex subject such as the issues that surround no-smoking ordinances and shoot two or three simple reports that illustrate the principle that "you can write an article about the mail service, but you must make a film about a single letter."

7. Write a script to accompany a story you have photographed and/or reported that constantly re-engages viewers with the screen. Use phrases such as, "Be sure to include one of these in your backpack," rather than "Be sure to take a compass."

8. Choose a "nonvisual" story subject, such as a historic cabin or other building in your community that is open for public tours. Strive to make your photography and reporting about the subject powerful, compelling, and engaging.

9. Study spot-news stories for evidence of the photographer's and reporter's ability to tell such events through people. Note how often sequences are present in the spot-news stories you view. If sequences were absent, would they have been possible to photograph?

10. Interview police, fire, or sheriff's authorities and inquire about their greatest frustrations when working with television reporters and photographers.

11. Visit a federal, state, or local environmental safety official and learn more about toxic chemicals and other environmental hazards you can expect to encounter during spot-news coverage.

NOTES

1. Edward Dmytryk, *On Film Editing* (Stoneham, MA: Focal Press, 1984), 78.
2. Rick Hessel, "Telling the Visual Story—Network Perspective," a presentation at the NPPA TV News-Video Workshop, Norman, OK, 22 March 1984.
3. Remarks at the NPPA TV News-Video Workshop, Norman, OK, 17 March 2003.
4. Interview with the author, Fort Collins, CO, 26 April 1981.
5. Lou Swierzowski, "Working by the Rules," *News Photographer* (November 1984), 20.
6. Mark R. Levy, "WJR Readers Name the Best in the Business," *Washington Journalism Review* (February 1986), 26.
7. Bob Dotson, Conversation with the Author, Norman, OK, 23 February 2003.
8. Darrell Barton, "Gangbang Journalism: A Photojournalist's View," a presentation at the NPPA TV News-Video Workshop, Norman, OK, 19 March 1986.
9. A newsroom memo from Jim Prather, then news director, KRIS-TV, Corpus Christi, TX, January 1986.
10. Art Donahue, "Utilizing a Creative Eye for Everyday Assignments," a presentation at the NPPA TV News-Video Workshop, Norman, OK, 21 March 1986.
11. Dotson, 2003.
12. Larry Hatteberg, "People-Oriented Photojournalism," a presentation at the NPPA TV News-Video Workshop, Norman, OK, 18 March 1986.
13. Tim Fisher, "Television Is a Trust," *News Photographer* (November 1984), 21.
14. Jack Bickham, "The Line between Fiction and Non-Fiction, and How to Improve Your Storytelling," a presentation at the NPPA TV News-Video Workshop, Norman, OK, 23 March 1984.
15. Dmytryk, 79.
16. Richard Schickel, "A Superb Passage to India," *Time* (31 December 1984), 55.
17. Linda Ellerbee, "And So It Goes: My Adventures in Television," *Playboy* (April 1986), 196.
18. Rich Clarkson, "TV News Photographers as Professionals—Some Believe You Have a Long Way to Go," a presentation at the NPPA TV News-Video Workshop, Norman, OK, 21 March 1986.
19. Ibid.
20. Ibid.
21. Darrell Barton, Connects to Journalism Students at the University of Oklahoma, 5 November 2002.

CHAPTER ELEVEN

THE ROLE OF TALENT PERFORMANCE IN FIELD REPORTING

One of the photographer's responsibilities is to help make the field reporter look good, even when the field reporter is the photographer. That responsibility extends from the photographer's choice of angles and lens settings through lighting and helping to augment the field reporter's on-camera performances. At first, it might seem that considerations of talent performance are outside the photographer's domain, yet shooting interviews and standups are two of the most predictable assignments in a photojournalist's life. Moreover, at stations where reporters must shoot their own footage, or where reporters are required to shoot footage for one another, interlinking photojournalism and talent performance is axiomatic.

If the photojournalist is to be an equal partner in the reporting process, then one of the photographer's vital roles is to help the reporter achieve compelling and informative standups. For the photographer to contribute meaningfully at that level, however, requires of the photographer a detailed understanding of the principles and practices involved in talent performance and development.

In this chapter, particular attention is paid to the field reporter's interaction with the camera and with ways to enhance that interaction through demonstration standups that are more compelling and visually literate. Without the photographer's involvement, the realization of such goals is unlikely.

BENEFITS OF DEVELOPING PERFORMANCE POTENTIAL

The manner in which we present information influences how well our ideas stick in other people's minds as much as the information itself. Consequently, the best television news originates when performance derives as a natural outgrowth of news content. Ideally, everything we observe about the anchor or reporter on air—from inflections and gestures to facial expressions—is clearly derived from the content of the report.

The presentation of news on television calls into play most aspects of the psychology of human communication. When you master these principles, chances are greater that you will be more comfortable in front of the camera and microphone, more appealing to news directors and to your viewing audience, and that you will be a more polished and professional reporter. Ultimately, such qualities will make you a better and more marketable reporter and a better communicator in every area of life in which you interact with others.

To an extent, good performance, like good writing, is imitative. Professionals who have gone before us show us the way, and at both the local and network levels much of their work is worthy of emulation. As you begin your career, you may do well to experiment with techniques you observe, adopting what works for you and discarding what doesn't. While it is legitimate to study the work of others, it is of even greater consequence to identify the qualities that make you and your performances interesting and unique.

HOW TO DEVELOP THE QUALITIES THAT MAKE YOU INTERESTING

One of the most difficult questions to answer about yourself is, "What is it that makes me interesting?" Part of the answer lies in your appearance and physique. Fat, tall, short, or skinny, we all are unique. Perhaps you have freckles. Maybe you drag out the vowels in your words and clip your consonants. Maybe you scowl or blink too much or hide your emotions so well that your inner self is inaccessible to others. How you dress will make a difference. Where you grew up, and with whom, also matter, as do your personal beliefs and convictions, your education, your value system, and your life experiences. In a word, you are unique. That is the first quality that makes you interesting.

Be aware that trying to see yourself through the eyes of others can be counterproductive, for much the same reason it can be detrimental to share audience research with news talent. This is because the key to behavior lies not in how we see ourselves, but in how we see others. It may be more useful to consider how you think about others and how you treat those around you.

Determine What Interests You

To be interesting, you must be interested. Elsewhere in this book, the proposition has been advanced that your audience will never care more about a story than you do. As a way to learn to care more intensely about every story that you report, you can use a model that Barry Nash,[1] a Dallas-based talent development consultant, shares with field reporters and news anchors throughout the country. "Ask of every story you report whether the community wins or loses with this event," says Nash. Using this approach, every story is about winning or losing. To some extent then, every story is about communicating that win or loss.

The principle is obvious if you imagine the absolutes of destiny with which each individual, each community, typically concerns itself. "Winning and losing has to do with every minute in our lives," says Nash. "Either we're celebrating victory, or we're pursuing it—trying to figure out what went wrong." News is about a society's pursuit of winning.

THE IDEAL FUTURE

TOTAL HELL

FIGURE 11.1   Every news story lies somewhere along a continuum that moves the news viewer toward a sense of greater happiness and self-actualization or toward a sense of despair and failure.

At one end of the continuum is "The Ideal Future" in which there is no sadness, no unemployment, no disease or unpleasantness of any form. In this ideal world lie happiness and self-actualization. At the other end of the continuum lies "Total Hell," in which everything goes wrong. Here lie misery and failure (Figure 11.1).

In this model, derived from *Acting Power* by Richard Cohen, every story moves the viewer (or the viewer's community) closer to one end of the scale or the other.[2] A victory over inflation moves us up the scale: the explosion of a space shuttle with astronauts aboard moves us toward the bottom. Some stories won't be on the scale: Their predominant message may simply be "Here, take your mind off your trouble for a while." Such stories serve us much like comic relief in a good play: They provide momentary diversion without necessarily advancing the plot. But even these little stories may not belong in the newscast if they don't affect the community in some way.

Using the Cohen model, part of your job is to communicate how you feel about the direction the story is taking you and your audience. Another part of your job is to expect your audience to react and for you to look for that reaction. In human communication, after all, there is no such thing as a neutral transaction.

WHY WE COMMUNICATE

The main reason we tell anybody anything is to elicit a response, to see how he or she will react. Yet when you present information to the television camera, the lens gives you no reaction. You are, after all, talking to a piece of glass from which you expect no reaction, so it's little wonder if you feel your presentation is flat and uninteresting.

To improve your performance in front of the camera, begin to treat the lens as if it were a person. All of us want people to react to us when we speak, so expect and even demand reaction from the lens. Use whatever device works best for you. Maybe you tape a picture of your best friend to the camera lens and talk to that one person. Perhaps you imagine someone in the viewing audience and speak through the lens to that one individual.

Whatever you do, believe that someone is there to react to you and to your story—whether you are addressing a microphone in the announce booth or the front lens element on a field camera. The key to eliciting audience reaction is simple: Learn to predict in your mind's eye how the audience is going to react to you and to your story. Look for audience reaction, expect it, and let us see what you think about the reactions you know you are eliciting from the viewing audience.

Remember that anchors and reporters actually lead audience reaction by demonstrating how they want the audience to react. If you want viewers to smile, for example, it is imperative that you smile. This is another reason why you must interpret your vocal delivery from a visual point of view. If you say "We're glad you could join us," then visually you have to prove to your audience that you really are glad for their presence, especially through your facial expressions.

COMMUNICATE WHAT YOU FEEL ABOUT THE STORY

Much of the energy in your reporting comes from what you feel about the story, both from the standpoint of your emotions and your sensory experiences. Expressing your *emotional experience* is valid, so long as you report honestly and with appropriate feeling. Virtually always, though, *extreme emotion* is unwarranted. It would be inappropriate, for example, to show extreme emotion when reporting a story in which a close friend has been killed or seriously injured.

From the standpoint of *sensory experience*, what you feel can be more important than what you do in reporting that story. "The important thing is the feeling, the experience of the moment," says Nash, "and the sensory experience is vital."

To communicate that vital sense of experience to your audience, you must first understand the event you are reporting in all its dimensions. Imagine for a moment that you have been assigned to report the outcome of a hockey game. Ask the following questions of yourself for this exercise—and for every story you cover.

1. **What do I SEE?** Perhaps you see tons of fans yelling, sweating, drinking, and cursing. You see the spray of powder as skate blades knife across the ice, and you see the scoreboard and areas on the playing surface where the ice glistens. You see the rhythm of the skaters and the grimaces on their faces.

2. **What do I HEAR?** Now you hear the echo of the public address system, the crash and grunts of players. The crowd is screaming and there are occasional obscenities. "PEANUTS, get your red hot PEANUTS," a vendor in the crowd yells. "That son of a bitch!" the coach yells, and in the background an organ punctuates the night.

3. **What do I SMELL?** Waves of scent wash over us from the cigarette smoke, the beer, the player's sweat, and the popcorn. The air smells cold and crisp. The aftershave on the fellow next to you shouts for your attention. On the other side of you, a woman's perfume lurks quietly, still waiting to be discovered.

4. **What do I FEEL?** Now, almost subconsciously, you become aware that your face is cold. There are goose bumps on your arms and you feel the adrenalin pump through your body and you feel flushed with excitement. You also are aware that beneath your warm coat you are, for the most part, cozy and warm.

5. **What do I TASTE?** We taste the cigarette smoke in the air and the afterbite and maltiness of the beer. There is the sharp, acid taste of the mustard on our hot dog and the crunchy, toasted flavor of the almonds in our chocolate bar.

PUT A FEELING OF EXPERIENCE
INTO YOUR REPORTS

When you understand the experiences of a moment or an event, you can fill in with words and your own actions those experiences and information the pictures don't communicate. It is a technique that NBC correspondent Bob Dotson has called "writing to the corners" of the picture. It is a sensual, tactile, and descriptive form of reporting that transcends two-dimensional imagery. "You could smell the storm's path before you could see it," Dotson once wrote in describing the path of a hurricane that had snapped tall pine trees and released their resinous fragrance.[3] Writing to the corners of the picture ranks as an unparalleled technique when you have static pictures or shots of aftermath.

When you set out to make your reporting experiential, create accurate mental pictures and experiences and speak to your audience of those moments. Try to make your story a report of what we see, hear, smell, taste, and touch. Relate experience and fill in the holes for your audience. To a great extent your excellence as a reporter or photojournalist lies in your ability to capture the moment and to communicate the texture of that moment, for when we experience an event we are more likely to understand it.

MULTIDIMENSIONAL REPORTING

So often, reporters concern themselves more with how they look and sound in front of the camera than with how they think about the story and how well they understand it. This is why the secret to being great lies not in being polished or slick, but in how effectively you are able to communicate the story through **multidimensional reporting.** This means that you communicate with every reporting tool available—the camera, the microphone, the spoken word, the video editing process, and even by portraying the actions and behaviors of news subjects as warranted.

Audiences only become interested in the story if you do. They become interested when they see you think about the story and interpret and react to it. They also respond to your physical presence and appearance as you report the story.

THE BODY LANGUAGE
OF EFFECTIVE REPORTING

Once again, the audience will be interested in the story only if you are, so show them your interest. TV is first and foremost visual. If we don't see it, we don't believe it. So, be *visually aggressive*. If you are sitting down when you report, sit on the edge of your chair and incline toward the camera with your body.

In other words, use your body to communicate your interest and enthusiasm for the story and your audience. Gesture with your hands, if it feels normal to do so (Figure 11.2). Whether through the position of your body, the light in your eyes, or the animation of your gestures and facial expressions, much of the message you communicate will be visual.

FIGURE 11.2 Handheld microphones can impede the reporter's ability to gesture and interact spontaneously with the story subject or environment. More natural and spontaneous standups can result when the reporter uses an inconspicuous lavaliere microphone, ideally in combination with a wireless transmitter-receiver system.

GIVE THE STORY'S MEANING SOME THOUGHT

As an on-air anchor or reporter, you will face two immediate problems:

1. sounding spontaneous and conversational, and,
2. if you are an anchor, making sense of other people's writing.

To overcome these problems you will have to understand the story, know how to draw on your energy, and learn to talk to the audience not only with your body but with your whole self.

Words are your first ally, because the way words are built helps to convey their meaning. Just for a moment, say the words *bowling ball* aloud. Roll the sounds around in your mouth, and as you say them aloud, throw the ball down an imaginary bowling alley. Notice how "heavy" the words sound when compared, for example, to the words *ping-pong ball*. Now say *ping-pong ball* aloud and toss it lightly as you "hold" it in your hand.

Having gone through this exercise, were you now to stand in front of a camera and say these words aloud, you could make your audience feel the difference because you've given your words some thought. You've felt the meaning of the words before you tried to communicate them. Quite correctly, there is not a right or wrong way to deliver words to an audience, but there are degrees of commitment and involvement in how you report stories that can distinguish you from your competition.

MARKING COPY

Whenever we speak, our natural inclination is to emphasize contrasts and new ideas. When we emphasize a word, we imply a contrast. We subdue old and less important ideas by deemphasizing them in our delivery. One of the quickest ways to improve your voice performance, then, is to go through your copy and underline the *ideas that contrast* ("angry crowd"—"did not react"; "human labor"—"machine-made goods"), as well as *ideas that are new.*

Some other considerations:[4]

- Pronouns almost never are stressed unless they're used for contrast.
  EXAMPLE: "They voted for *you*, not *him*."
- Don't stress any word you can eliminate without changing the meaning.
  EXAMPLE: "The course you recommend leads to *progress*, but the policy he sanctions leads to *disaster*."
- When an adjective modifies a noun, it's often more reasonable to stress the adjective.
  EXAMPLE: "It was the *smallest* turnout in the county's *history*."
- Seldom stress anything in a parenthetical expression.
  EXAMPLE: "He was (said the chairman) the last to leave the meeting."

■ When you read a construction that contains a preposition with a personal pronoun for its object, stress the word before the preposition, perhaps stress the
preposition, and subdue the pronoun.
EXAMPLE: "A night in jail will be *good* for him."

Some exceptions:

■ When the pronoun is contrasted with something.
■ When the pronoun is followed by a restrictive modifier.
EXAMPLE: "They *sent* for *him* before the votes had been counted."
■ When the object of the pronoun is compound.
EXAMPLE: "We have reporters standing by *here* and *there.*
■ Normally you would not stress when the word immediately preceding the
preposition is a personal pronoun or some other word.
EXAMPLE: "Take it *with* you."
■ Stress verbs infrequently.

Reporters tend to fade or lose energy in their delivery at periods in news copy.
As you read copy, let your voice stay up and keep it up until the thought you are expressing is complete. Regardless of your inflection, pitch, or volume, the key is to
maintain your energy through the ends of thoughts and sentences. As a rule, try not
to let either your momentum or your inflection drop. When either flags, so does audience attention.

ERR ON THE SIDE OF "OVERDOING IT"

If you are to reach your audience and touch their minds and hearts, you must pass
through a series of filters, each filter acting as something of a choke point in the transmission line. Your physical presence will be converted to light rays and sound waves
and passed through lens elements and magnetic coils. Records of these conversions will
reside for a time on disk or videotape, then be reconverted to electrical impulses, shot
through transmission cables and into the airwaves and possibly to satellites in outer
space. Antennae will grab replications of you and your voice and shoot them through
still more air space and wires. Even after a reconstruction of your physical self appears
on the viewer's home screen, your metamorphosis is unrealized until someone is interested enough in you and your story to turn and watch.

For these reasons, as you develop your performance ability, it may pay you to
be a little wild and crazy with your voice and your face and to push your presentation
and delivery a little harder than feels comfortable or even normal. Over and over
again, experiment with and critique your performances. A good method is to study
video or audio recordings of your past performances. They will quickly reveal your
foibles.

Soon you will find what works best for you, even if at first your approach feels
awkward and abnormal. Along the way, don't forget to feel good about yourself. It is a

great gift to discover the wonderful things in life that are around us. It is an even greater gift to discover your own self-worth, and to enjoy it and share it with your audience.

HOW TO RELAX

None of this will be possible, however, until you feel at ease as a reporter. In order to communicate effectively, you will need to feel comfortable and relaxed. Pause now for a moment and reestablish an awareness of your body. From head to toe, check out which of your muscles are tense and which are relaxed. If your muscles are tense, relax. Tense muscles tell your brain, "Hey, I'm not relaxed, I'm tense." If your muscles are tense, the same will be true of your on-camera performance.

Pause also to become aware of how you breathe. One secret to performance success is to let your tummy pooch. Breathe with your diaphragm instead of your chest. You may notice that you tend to breathe differently when you sleep and after you first awake than during the rest of the day. If you do, begin work to establish more effective breathing patterns that will help you relax.

If your on-microphone, on-camera delivery tends to be rushed and pushed, relax. Strive to feel so good, so comfortable, that you relish everything you're saying and doing on camera. Begin to enjoy the experience. Begin to allow yourself to relish what you are doing.

DEVELOPING CONVERSATIONAL DELIVERY

Whether you are before a field or studio camera, or sitting at a microphone in an announce booth, one of your primary obligations is to establish an intimate connection with your audience. Television, after all, is such an intimate medium that it can place the reporter visually closer to an audience than the reporter could approach in real life. "Television puts you as close to your audience as if you were kissing them with their eyes open," says Barry Nash. When you are that close to an audience, your voice will have to be close to an ideal level in conversational delivery, a process made easier if you follow three rules of thumb:

- The pitch of your voice goes up when you are tense, so strive to relax.
- The pitch of your voice goes up as volume increases, so lower the volume of your delivery.
- The message we communicate has to do with how we think about others, not with how we think about ourselves.

To help reporters keep vocal pitch at conversational levels, voice coaches often have them first rehearse then read a real script into the microphone. As the practice session begins, the first advice is to lower volume to help keep pitch at conversational levels. As script delivery progresses, the voice coach may urge, "Softer, still softer, down-down-down" or may even recommend that the reporter read the script in a half or full whisper. Whispering serves two purposes in this exercise: First, it emphasizes the need to lower volume in order to lower pitch; second, it helps to reveal the nature of intimacy. We sometimes tend to pay more attention to people who whisper than to those who shout.

Another valuable exercise is to practice standup delivery at varying distances from the field camera. The farther you are from the camera, the greater is the danger that you'll try to yell to it. This is true even when the field mike is clipped to your lapel. When yelling occurs, up goes tension, up goes pitch, and out goes intimacy. The problem occurs in part because we are "talking to the camera," not to the audience. Outside, you may have to yell if there's a bulldozer at work behind you, but in that case the environment will tell you what to do.

In standups, just as when you write voice over, remember to keep it conversational and to incorporate moments of silence or "white space." Even in standups, you can be silent if you're doing something meaningful. If you are tasting a new food in your standup, it is acceptable to taste—savor—exclaim—swallow, and then, finally, to speak.

In order to communicate intimately with your audience, the bottom line is to keep your focus off yourself. This is because the messages we communicate have to do not with how we think about ourselves, but with how we think about others. If you wish to make an audience laugh, it will work better to tell yourself "I'm going to make the audience laugh" than to say, "This is funny." The goal is to have a relationship with an unseen audience and to elicit a response—if only from the camera.

GIVE YOURSELF SOMETHING TO DO

Even in field settings, some reporters may not sound or appear natural, comfortable, and relaxed. They break character and lapse into sing-song delivery. The problem may worsen during on-set appearances in the studio or whenever reporters cut voice overs in the announce booth. To solve such problems, it may help to give yourself something to do when you are on camera or in front of the microphone. This approach can help you transfer your focus from yourself to the story you are telling and will relieve your anxiety and give your natural tension somewhere to go. Your on-camera appearance will thus be more comfortable and natural.

REASONS TO DO STANDUPS

Sooner or later in every reporter's career the questions arise: "Why do we do standups? Why must we? What purpose do they serve?" Elsewhere it has been written that reporters are not the story, and this truth is fundamental. But it also has been suggested that you try to tell the story through people. Because reporters are people, and you are a reporter, it is valid to try to find activities that let you use yourself to help tell the story more effectively.

Often, for example, **standups** can be used to enhance otherwise nonvisual stories. At other times, in the absence of appropriate visuals, they may constitute the most effective means of communication at your disposal. Standups also help to establish the reporter's credibility. Reporters who have been first-person, on-site observers can be assumed to know more about the story than those who get their facts from the news service and telephone without ever having set foot in the field. Without your standups, viewers may assume the anchors do most of the field reporting. Even the people who sign your paychecks need to be reminded occasionally who's out there on the "front line." At contract renewal time, recognition of you and of your work is vital. While not every story needs a standup, many stories and almost every career can benefit when standups are incorporated judiciously into the reporting process.

THE DEMONSTRATION STANDUP

When you do a standup, keep it simple, stick to the basics, and give yourself something to do. Work to make every standup a little visual story and base everything you do on your story. Commit yourself physically and mentally to selling your story, and where appropriate strive to be physically and actively involved in its telling, a technique called the performance or **demonstration standup** (Figure 11.3). The standup activity can be something as simple as a reporter pointing out the rusted bolts and flaking paint on an old bridge for a story on highway safety. Or it can be something as

FIGURE 11.3 Reporters can give themselves something to do when they are on camera as a way to transfer focus from themselves to the story they are telling. The technique is called a demonstration or performance standup. In this standup, the reporter shows a community book depository.

complex as huffing and puffing your way up a steep mountain road to illustrate the difficulty of reaching a recluse who is the subject of your story. On another day, perhaps you can wipe the grease from your hands after you eat a hamburger for a story on high cholesterol in American diets, or climb into sports clothes for the soccer game standup.

When you do standups, allow yourself to look at the environment, to interact with it, and even to turn your back to the camera as appropriate. In a feature story, if you have followed itinerant farmworkers on their rounds for most of a long, hot, grueling day, perhaps it will be appropriate for you to do a "sit-down" standup as you remove your hat and conclude for the audience that no one would work such long hours for such low pay if other employment were available.

In the case of all such activities, an obvious precaution is to avoid the melodramatic. The point is to communicate meaning, and to have a good time doing it. Make your time on camera relaxed, natural, and easy to watch, and use every action to help illustrate the story. Remember never to ignore the environment, but to work within it.

A good way to evaluate your standups is to ask two questions of yourself: "Did my audience enjoy watching it?" and "Did I enjoy doing it?" When standups are most successful, the answer to both questions is *yes*. Another way to determine whether your standups are working is to look at them without sound. If you look like someone we'd like to watch, even with the sound off, your standup probably works.

AVOID STAGING IN THE DEMONSTRATION STANDUP

Regardless of the activity you give yourself in demonstration standups, the cardinal advice against staging still applies: *The story should in no way be altered by your presence in a standup.* If, in your standup, you are operating the controls on a ham radio and speaking to the eyewitness of a volcanic eruption in Alaska, then your activities as a reporter have become the story. The story has been altered because the event is no longer what it would have been in your absence. On the other hand, no harm should result if you merely pause to shake the loose railing on a rusty old bridge as a way to show how fragile and dangerous the bridge has become.

DRESS FOR THE ENVIRONMENT

Appearance is a good way to enhance your credibility as a reporter, so it pays to dress for the news environment or, more simply expressed, to dress appropriately for the story. This advice is important to all television reporters, because if viewers are worrying about your tie or your scarf, they will be missing the story.

If you are reporting from the scene of a landfill site, you may want to loosen your neckwear and hold your jacket over your arm or shoulder. If you are reporting from the ski slopes, trade your trench coat for a ski jacket. On skid row, a silk business suit may be out of place, both because it doesn't fit in and because it may psychologically distance you from your news sources.

    This same advice applies when you are conducting interviews: Dress to reinforce your credibility. If the moment is relaxed and informal, your demeanor and the way you dress should help reinforce a sense of informality, so take off your coat and roll up your sleeves. If the story is investigative and confrontational, a dark coat and professionally knotted neckwear may help reinforce the meaning of your story. If the setting is a hospital lab, you may want to wear a lab coat so that you don't look out of place.

YOUR APPEARANCE

    In dressing for television the cardinal rule is to focus attention on your face, not on your clothes (Figure 11.4). Even the length and style of your hair will impact how the audience perceives you. Generally, women can dress the part of the professional, which

FIGURE 11.4   Dressing appropriately from one story environment to the next is a good way for reporters to enhance their credibility. In all on-camera appearances, an important consideration is to choose clothing and accessories that will help keep attention on the face.

means choosing clothing that is both feminine and elegant—blouses and silks, for example, and clothing with softer lines. And generally speaking, women may want to try raising their hair off the shoulders for a more mature, credible look.

Accessories for men and women reporters should be subdued so as not to draw the viewer's attention away from the face. If you are a woman, for example, consider avoiding huge, distracting earrings. If eyeglasses are a problem, consider substituting contact lenses. In numerous markets, the advice to female reporters is to avoid glasses. Although audiences seem to be more tolerant of eyeglasses on men, think twice before wearing them on air. Remember that the camera comes so close to you that sometimes all you have to communicate is what's in your eyes. Eyeglasses add another filter to distract the audience and yet another barrier through which you must project yourself. At times, when glasses reflect the glare of the lights or when dark glasses hide your eyes, they can create an impenetrable barrier between you and your viewers.

Whenever you appear on camera, dress so that you avoid "disappearing into the background." If the background of trash against which you appear at the landfill is bland and brown, a jacket of the same tone will do you no favors. Similar problems arise if you wear "cool" colors for an appearance on a "cool" set. If you know in advance what colors are present, you can dress to create at least some contrast between you and the background. Remember, too, to take textures into account when you dress. Some texture in clothing generally is desirable when it helps to communicate a more tactile sense of environment to the viewer.

While it may seem that set design, clothing, cosmetics, hairstyles, and accessories have little to do with journalism, they are in some ways identical to the problems of newspaper layout, design, and format that confront print journalists. If newspaper layout is sloppy, confusing, or unattractive, the very message of the story can be damaged. In television news, the story is just as vulnerable to the vagaries of aesthetics.

LET THE AUDIENCE KNOW YOU AS A FRIEND

As you develop as a reporter or anchor, viewers will come to evaluate you the same way they evaluate their best friends. When we first meet strangers at parties, part of our evaluation is based on their appearance. If you were asked to talk about your best friend, you could describe your friend's voice, dress, manner, and speech patterns. You could tell us something about your friend's birthplace and background, his or her age and approximate income. All these things we come to know about people we like. And all these things are what make each of us so uniquely individual.

Your individuality, then, is one of your greatest strengths in a medium that communicates through people. To really succeed, you must take the risk of allowing the audience to come to know you as a friend. You will have to let the things that make you unique come through, so that others can see what makes you special. Such a task takes time and can hardly occur if you are a "market hopper" who moves from one job to another every year or so. And it must be said that the community in which you work is equally special; it, too, will require some time to reveal itself and for you to come to know it. Tenure in the marketplace is thus vitally important if you are to build this special relationship with the community—and it with you.

COMMUNITY ANALYSIS

One way to learn more about the community and the viewers you serve is to conduct a news audience analysis. If you know the people who watch your reporting, you are better qualified to serve them as a professional interpreter of issues and events.

The analysis in this example is completed by responding to the following items after research has been conducted:

PART I: *Research and complete the following Work Sheet for Audience Analysis.*

    A. physical environment
        1. geographic location
        2. climate
    B. economic environment
        1. principal industries
        2. secondary industries
        3. average income
        4. white-collar population
        5. blue-collar population
    C. political environment
        1. party participation
        2. principal local referenda in last five years
        3. principal political ideologies
        4. type of city government
        5. elected officials
    D. social environment
        1. recreational activities
        2. cultural organizations
    E. religious environment
        1. types of religions
        2. percentages of religious affiliation
    F. names of communities in the market

PART II: *Profile a group of "average viewers" in your market. Presume that your newscast is watched by ten people. Use the ratings demographics to break down the group by sex and age. Construct an average viewer profile on each type. This list can be as long as desired. The point is to profile each member of the average viewing group as specifically as possible. Some questions to be considered:*

- How old are they?
- What gender are they?
- Are they married?
- Do they have children? How many?
- Where do they live?
- Where do they work?
- What do they wear?

- What pleases them?
- What makes them angry?
- How do they spend their spare time?
- How much money do they make?

PART III: *Put together a sampler reel of your packages. Study each package from the perspective of each of the average viewers profiled in Part II. Questions you might ask yourself include:*

- Is the package relevant to my viewers? Which ones? Why?
- If it does not seem relevant, could it have been altered to work better? How?
- How could the anchors be used to enhance the impact of each package on my local audience?

IMPACTING HOW PEOPLE PERCEIVE YOUR NEWS SOURCES

Body language, whether inadvertent or purposeful, impacts how viewers perceive the people you interview. If you "open up" the interview, both visually and physically, the interview will appear to be more casual and relaxed. If, through body language, you communicate your friendship for and concern about the news source, your audience will more likely feel a sense of friendship and concern toward him or her.

As a general rule, interviews carry a more "adversarial" tone when the following visual elements are present:

- Something physical separates the news source from the reporter. The object may be as obvious as an office desk or something as seemingly innocent as a handheld stick mike.
- Reporter and interviewee wear coats and ties or other business attire.
- Physical distance is great between reporter and interviewer.
- Interviewee appears to be "trapped" or "pinned" behind a desk in a corner or against a wall, with nowhere to go.
- Reporter and interviewer face each other squarely, almost head-on.

Conversely, reporters and interviewees appear to be more relaxed and friendly when the opposite visual elements are present:

- Reporter and/or interviewee take off coats or at least unbutton them.
- Interview is taken outside where the visual message is a sense of freedom, a clear impression that the interviewee has agreed to the interview of his or her own free will.
- Reporter sits beside the interviewee with nothing between them, not even a stick mike.
- Reporter angles in toward the other person, rather than facing the individual straight on in a confrontational manner.

It may appear that such concerns should occupy no place in the mind of the conscientious journalist. Influencing how the audience perceives a news source might appear to be somehow biased and to smack of staging. But whether in television news or any form of human expression, there is no such thing as a neutral transaction. If an interviewee is kind at heart, honest, and friendly, no purpose will be served by inadvertently communicating an opposite impression. Television is a medium with which people interact. Television news does not lie quietly on the coffee table, passively under our control as are newspapers; rather, it is a medium that provokes reaction and emotion. No matter how hard we strive to be neutral, objective, and unbiased, it is well to remember that in television news, and in all human communication, even no action is a reaction.

Rather than failing to react, the key to being objective is to unerringly cover all sides of an issue with equal energy. In other words, aggressively pursue all sides of the story so that your delivery remains just as committed and just as energetic throughout coverage of all the issues. If the story you deliver is about taxes going up, you may observe that it's great news for folks who live on the east side of town where new schools are needed, but bad news on the west side where elderly people need that money to pay their medical bills. At a minimum, every journalist seeks assurance that messages have been communicated accurately. If meaning has been communicated accurately, by virtue of the journalist's familiarity with the language of visual communication, then understanding has been served.

USE YOUR BODY MORE EFFECTIVELY

Whenever you deliver standups, be aware of your body and your posture. If you are not using one or both arms to gesture, hold them naturally at your side, but remember always to use your body to help tell the story. Angle your body toward camera, rather than confront your audience straight on and leave the impression that you are somewhat adversarial. At the very least, slap the wall or the side of a building in your report on building code violations. Better yet, use your whole body to shake a support beam to better illustrate the flimsy construction. If your report is about a new, two-pound, portable laptop computer, you may want to heft the computer and look at it as you say, "This two-pound baby [*Heft the computer and look down at it*] is destined to change the way America does business."

Consider more active standups whenever you plan your stories. Plan to ride the escalator, to slap the side of a wall, or to shake the stick on a training jet, if such actions are appropriate and will help tell the story more effectively without resulting in melodrama or staging. And consider moving not only horizontally, as when you do an into-frame/out-of frame standup, but vertical movement as well. Perhaps you can start on your knees as you pick up a baby rabbit for your report on neglected animals, rise up, then finally stand before the camera with rabbit in arm.

POSTURE MATTERS

Your posture—how you hold your body—is obvious to the audience and will impact how viewers perceive you and your reporting ability. Often, immediate improvements in posture can be made by concentrating on how you hold your head and shoulders. Stand, run, and walk as if a string is attached to the very crown of your head and is lifting you—almost as if you were a puppet on a string. This technique helps you keep your chin in, helps make the crown of your head go up, and helps prevent the appearance of "leading" with your head as if you're about to fall forward when you walk. Remember, too, to keep your shoulders down and to keep them rounded. You should feel relaxed and natural whenever you are on camera, and your appearance should reflect that feeling. Study the appearance of reporters you respect; most often you will discover that their posture is impeccable.

HOW REPORTERS EVOLVE INTO ANCHORS

For most reporters the dream of becoming an anchor remains a dream, yet many reporters do evolve into anchor work. If management thinks of you primarily as a reporter, your aspirations may come to nothing, so the first trick is to give yourself opportunities to be perceived as having anchor potential. This can most easily be accomplished by producing stories that need on-set follow-up and amplification. Whenever practical, suggest to the producer that your story is of such a nature that you should appear on set to discuss ancillary issues with newscast anchors. When you make it on set your performance will be crucial, so follow the advice of the pros:

- Hone in on the anchor with your eyes and ears.
- Listen intently.
- Gesture appropriately, perhaps with a pencil, and even tap on the desk to make your point.
- Be natural and energetic.
- Be interested and interesting.
- Remember to focus on something outside yourself and to enjoy what you're doing.

SPLIT-FOCUS PRESENTATION

Throughout your on-set interaction with the anchor, the audience normally will look at whichever of you is speaking. If the anchor is talking, you also should be looking at the anchor. When you speak, the anchor should be looking at you. As you speak, remember to divide your attention between the anchor and the audience, a practice known as **split-focus presentation,** which helps to make the audience part of your conversation. This technique is vastly preferable to the method in which both anchor and reporter resolutely face the camera and take turns speaking without ever turning their heads to acknowledge one another.

THE ANCHOR DEBRIEF

Going into your report, the anchor normally will set up your story with a brief remark or two, then turn toward you and comment briefly so that the two of you can interact. When you finish interacting with the anchor on set, be looking at the camera as you begin your introduction to the story. After your report has aired, you will need to return control of the show to the anchor. In your transition back to the anchor as you finish your presentation, be looking at the anchor. At this point the anchor normally will ask a follow-up question or two, a form of debriefing that serves to reestablish the anchor's command of the show. This interchange is known as the **anchor debrief.** Most often, you will be expected to have a question for the anchor to ask when you come out of a story back to the set. In formulating your questions, remember that good anchors will want to ask questions that represent the viewers' interests as well as the community's perspective. Ideally, you will take time to discuss your anticipated responses briefly with the anchor prior to airtime.

WHEN YOU ARE BEFORE THE CAMERA

Anytime you are before the camera, whether in the studio or in the field, your work will demonstrate to your viewers the extent to which you are well groomed, conversational, professional, and incisive. Resolve, therefore, to develop a consistent and recognizable visual style and prove that you are a good journalist who knows what your audience is thinking and needs to know about the stories you report. As *Time* columnist Hugh Sidey observed, "Journalists were originally created to enlighten, not to threaten; to inform, not to perform; to know, not to show."[5]

To prove these things, do what a good journalist does. Ask questions, process information, show that you are a team player, and prove that you care about the community in which you work. Finally, show us that you care about us as viewers and, yes, even that you like us. If you do all these things, you may become the person in your market that viewers most often seek out as their most authoritative and likable source of news.

SUMMARY

The reporter and photographer are partners in helping tell stories through the reporter's on-camera performances in the field. Routinely, the most effective and memorable television news occurs when performance originates as a natural outgrowth of news content. To be interesting on camera, the reporter must be interested—in stories, in the subjects of stories, and in the community and its residents—and be photographed in such a way that the interest is communicated to home viewers.

Most communication is an attempt to elicit a response. On-camera presentations can become flat and uninteresting if the reporter becomes accustomed to the lack of reaction from the camera and lens. One solution is to treat the lens almost as though it were a person and to expect and even demand reaction from it. Other good approaches are to imagine you're talking to a friend or to predict in your mind's eye how the audience will react to you and your story.

Performance is further enhanced when the reporter and photographer strive to capture the sensory experiences of stories—the sights, sounds, smells, tastes, and textures—and to fill in with words and actions what the pictures don't communicate. Because audiences become interested in the story only if the reporting team is interested, let viewers see the reporter think about the story, interpret it, and react to it.

Reporters can use body language to communicate interest and enthusiasm for the story and the audience. To be more visually aggressive, the reporter can sit on the edge of the chair or other object, lean forward toward the camera or interview subject, make hand gestures, and alter facial expressions as appropriate.

Always, effective performance depends on thorough knowledge of the story and its subjects. Voice delivery can be enhanced by studying and practicing with words and by giving their sounds and meaning some thought. The way words are built helps to convey their meaning: "For years, Florida citrus growers have likened the tang of grapefruit juice to the crisp smack of a wave." For natural voice delivery, emphasize contrasts and new ideas, and mark copy accordingly.

While it's important to be relaxed on camera, it's also important to project a sense of energy. Proper breathing and vocal techniques can help the reporter achieve energetic yet conversational delivery. A valuable exercise is to practice standup delivery at varying distances from the field camera. The goal is to overcome any tendency to yell to the camera, even when it is some distance away. When yelling occurs, tension and vocal pitch increase while intimate connection with the audience decreases.

Even in standups it is acceptable for the reporter to stop talking occasionally in order to do something meaningful, such as shake a bridge railing or taste and savor a food. Demonstration standups, in which the reporter has an activity to perform while on camera, can help the reporter appear more natural and relaxed. No story should be altered by a reporter's presence in a standup.

Beyond their ability to enhance otherwise nonvisual stories, standups help establish the reporter's credibility and remind viewers just who actually does the field reporting. Viewers might otherwise mistakenly credit anchors for originating many of the reports they see. Reporters and photographers can work as a team to help make standups visually prove and reinforce the story to be told.

It is important for the reporter to dress appropriately for the story and to dress to keep attention on the reporter's face rather than on clothing, hair, or jewelry. Accessories should be subdued, and the reporter may want to avoid eyeglasses altogether. To succeed as an on-air reporter, you must allow the audience to come to know you as a friend and see the qualities that make you special. Your individuality is one of your greatest strengths in a medium that communicates primarily through people.

Just as important is the need for photographers and reporters to understand the people who watch news reports. You are better qualified to serve audiences when you know their needs, interests, concerns, and aspirations.

Some reporters may evolve into anchors more quickly by producing stories that need on-set follow-up and amplification. When practical, suggest to the producer that you should appear on set to discuss your report or related issues with the anchor. Techniques for interaction with the anchor include split-focus presentation and the anchor debrief.

Tenure in the marketplace serves most reporters well. After serving for years as a trusted friend in the community, most reporters are welcomed as authoritative and likable sources for news.

DISCUSSION

1. To what extent is the photojournalist a partner in helping reporters develop their on-camera performance potential?

2. What are the qualities that help make on-camera reporters and anchors "unique"?

3. What is the basic motive behind most acts of communication? How can this motive be used to enhance the reporter's on-camera performance?

4. Why is it important for reporters to communicate something of their emotional response to stories?

5. Why is it important to communicate some of the sensory experiences to be found in the environments of the stories being reported?

6. Describe what is meant by the "body language" of effective reporting.

7. What is the importance of learning to relax while presenting information on camera?

8. List the practices you can observe to help develop conversational on-camera delivery.

9. Describe the demonstration standup and provide two examples of effective use of this technique.

10. Take a news director's point of view and respond to a reporter who asks, "Why do we do standups? Why must we? What purpose do they serve?"

11. What considerations govern the reporter's on-camera appearance and dress?

12. How do the reporter's posture and body language impact on (a) story content and (b) the viewer's perceptions of the reporter?

13. What considerations are important to keep in mind whenever the reporter appears on set with the studio anchor?

EXERCISES

1. Practice speaking to the television camera. Strive to be truly relaxed, conversational, and natural. Show your imaginary audience how you want them to react through your own reactions to the material you are delivering. If a camera is unavailable, talk to the end of a peanut butter jar taped to a camera tripod or use any other device that will work for you. Even try talking to yourself in the mirror.

2. Set up a television camera and record yourself as you taste and savor a food, think about the experience, and react to it.

3. Take a walk, go to the museum, or bake a cake and note all the physical sensations you encounter, including what you see, hear, smell, taste, and feel. As a television reporter or photographer, practice using the camera and microphone as well as your own presence on camera to communicate such sensations to an audience.

4. Make a series of voice-over recordings or else appear on camera and practice breathing with your diaphragm rather than your chest during delivery.

5. Practice controlling the pitch of your voice. As you read a script, lower pitch and volume until you reach a half or full whisper, then raise pitch and volume to conversational levels. When you lower volume you also lower your vocal pitch, a good way to establish a greater sense of intimacy with your audience.

6. Practice speaking to the camera from various distances. Strive to keep your voice pitch and volume at the same conversational level, regardless of the distance you are from the camera.

7. Study how words are built as a way to communicate their meaning more effectively. Practice enunciating such words as *butterfly*, or *ping-pong ball*, or even such phrases as *My name is Bond . . . James Bond* to determine their weight and feeling.

8. Read a television script or newspaper story aloud and practice marking and delivering the copy to better emphasize contrasting ideas and words as well as new ideas.

9. Work to develop a more acute awareness of your body and an ability to relax tense muscles, especially when you are in front of the camera or when you are handholding the camera.

10. Research and complete the work sheet for audience analysis on pages 223–224 for the community in which you live.

11. Analyze how you can most effectively dress to focus attention on your face, not on your clothes or accessories. Practice making presentations in front of the camera and videotape your appearances for analysis and critique.

12. Watch a television newscast. For each story that contains a reporter standup, think of a demonstration standup activity that might have been more effective to help enhance the story.

13. Devise and deliver three demonstration standups on camera, using your choice of subject matter.

14. Videotape a series of practice standups under the following conditions: (1) while holding a handheld microphone, then using a miniature lavaliere microphone attached to the reporter's clothing; (2) while wearing a jacket and tie or scarf, then with the jacket removed; (3) with no jacket, but with the shirt sleeves rolled down and buttoned, then with the shirt sleeves pushed or rolled up; (4) with the reporter's body facing the camera straight on, then angled slightly.

15. Practice improving your posture when you walk, run, stand, and sit. Keep your chin in and hold yourself as if a string is attached to the very crown of your head and is lifting you. Ask someone to videotape your posture for analysis.

NOTES

1. Barry Nash is a professional talent consultant. The remarks in this chapter are derived from his work with students at Colorado State and with professional talent in markets of all sizes throughout the country. He is a partner in The Coaching Company, Dallas, TX (http://www.coachingcompany.com).

2. Richard Cohen, *Acting Power* (New York: Kampmann, 1982. Originally published by Mayfield Publishing, 1978).

3. *NBC Nightly News*, 29 March 1984. Reporters still "borrow" this line. The author has heard it parroted in Texas, Maryland, Louisiana, and Colorado.

4. The "Guide to Marking Copy" and "News Audience Analysis" used as a general reference for this chapter were provided courtesy of Barry Nash, The Coaching Company, Dallas, TX.

5. Hugh Sidey, "The Mick Jaggers of Journalism," *Time* (5 October 1987), 28.

CHAPTER TWELVE

LIVE SHOTS AND REMOTES

LUAN AKIN

Television journalists routinely craft live reports, even as events unfold before their eyes. Today, television audiences have come to take such immediacy for granted. As eyewitnesses to news events, television viewers frequently become participants in the reporting process, sometimes as knowledgeable about the developing story as the field reporter. This chapter details the live reporting process, tells how to organize and write the story in the field, and examines the traits and abilities that help make television reporters "live capable."

Luan Akin works as a helicopter specialist and general assignment reporter for KCNC-TV, the NBC owned-and-operated station in Denver. Every year she originates hundreds of live remotes from virtually any location the KCNC helicopter can fly to, whether high in the Rocky Mountains or even from a bird's-eye view of fierce storms above the high mountain plains. Her pilot is Mike Silva.

I never will understand why I didn't spot the tornado myself. Denver's forecast on this June day called for severe weather—heavy rain, lightning, hail, and possible tornadoes. That meant the helicopter crew of pilot Mike Silva, photographer David Gregg, and myself would be chasing storms. Only this time, the storm found us.

As I drove to the airport, the cloud layer overhead clamped down on the city, growing darker, lower, and more ominous. I caught up with Mike and David as they half-walked, half-ran to the helicopter. I yelled to Mike that we needed to get in the air right away. A funnel had been sighted over Denver. Without missing a beat—without even looking up—Mike jerked his index finger and pointed to the sky. A towering funnel was dead overhead.

It wasn't large by midwestern standards, but it was the biggest funnel our city had seen in a long time. It turned out to be one of seven tornadoes that hammered Denver that afternoon.

For the next four hours, we were part of a "live" marathon. Mike, David, and I did one shot after another. We were live (from a respectful distance) as a twister snapped power lines and ripped up huge trees, tossing them half a block away. When we weren't live, other KCNC crews were. One team on the ground walked viewers through a neighborhood that had been especially hard-hit. The photographer shot "off the shoulder" as the reporter stepped over downed tree limbs and the live truck engineer helped guide the long run of cable. Yet another crew was going live ten miles away, in a business district that had been torn apart. The shots went round-robin, intermixed with weather bulletins and live updates from the newsroom.

It was one of those times when all the teamwork and the technology paid off. It was also one of the most grueling afternoons I've had in television. But it was one of the most rewarding, thanks to the challenge of "going live."

WHAT DOES IT TAKE TO "GO LIVE"?

All the general skills important in TV news are doubly important for successful "live" work. Among them are a well-developed vocabulary, good news sense, experience as a general assignment reporter, and strong interviewing skills. They all add up to the ability to tell a story clearly and accurately under what can be chaotic conditions (see Figure 12.1). But perhaps the single most important skill in a good live reporter is a knack for writing and talking conversationally. Many reporters make the job of going live much more difficult than it needs to be. They try so hard to look and sound serious and professional, and end up sounding stuffy and awkward.

If you're in the habit of writing conversationally, telling stories in a simple, straightforward style, you'll find it much easier to talk that way, too. Short sentences filled with everyday words can help make even the most complicated story something your audience can understand.

SPOT NEWS

"Spot news" and "live shots." For broadcast news reporters, they go together like ham 'n eggs. To less-experienced reporters, going live from the scene of a breaking news

FIGURE 12.1 Live reporting demands not only an ability to write and speak conversationally, but an ability to tell the story clearly and accurately under field conditions.

story can seem like trial by fire, but developing a system of your own can help tame the madness. It's basically a matter of knowing what to expect. We'll take it from the top.

Gather as You Go

The wheeler-dealers of the world are always telling us time is money. But if you're a broadcast reporter on your way to a spot-news story, time is information, or at least it should be. You can't afford to wait until you arrive on scene before you begin asking questions.

There are all kinds of information-gathering possibilities in the average news van. The station's two-way radio is a good example. Often, the assignment desk or someone else at news base hears of the story first and lets you know on two-way that all heck's breaking loose somewhere. If you have a cellular phone, make good use of it, but coordinate with your newsroom. Avoid duplicating calls to the same sources, such a police dispatchers. Stations that make a habit of that may find the dispatchers are less patient or cooperative during future emergencies.

Scanners can be especially helpful as you're racing to the scene of a breaking story. Lock out (eliminate from the scan) all frequencies except those carrying radio traffic relating to the story you're working on. Handle the information you hear on scanners carefully. Treat the information as fact only after you or someone in your newsroom has verified it. And always be careful to attribute what you're reporting to the appropriate source. My helicopter crew and I once were dispatched based on the following scanner traffic:

> "A DEAD HIPPOPOTAMUS HAS BEEN SPOTTED ON THE SHOULDER OF PEÑA BOULEVARD NEAR DENVER INTERNATIONAL AIRPORT . . ."

Clearly, this one required a bit of skepticism. Fortunately, as we flew toward the scene, what I reported was:

> "POLICE SAY A MOTORIST CLAIMS THERE'S A DEAD HIPPOPOTAMUS ON THE SHOULDER OF PEÑA BOULEVARD NEAR DENVER INTERNA-TIONAL AIRPORT . . ."

It turned out to be a cow . . . apparently, a rather ugly cow.

Don't forget to listen to "the competition," i.e., competing radio or TV stations, as you head toward a spot news story. You can bet they'll be listening to you. If you think you're on to something they haven't heard about yet, be careful how much you say on two-way.

TV reporters can monitor the AM or FM radio stations with the best news departments in their market. Updates or cut-ins from those stations can provide still more background information. Just remember that you or someone in your newsroom needs to confirm that information before you use it.

LIVE/REPORTER INTROS

One of the first things a reporter should do at the "top" or beginning of a live shot is clarify the location of the scene. Some stories might require only a general description of the location:

> "WE'RE HERE NEAR THE BASE OF SUGARLOAF MOUNTAIN WHERE FIRE FIGHTERS SAY THEY'RE GETTING THE UPPER HAND ON THIS WILD-FIRE . . ."

If a newsworthy element of the story involves a specific location, the reporter should make that location clear.

> "WE'RE ON LOST ANGEL DRIVE NEAR THE SUMMIT OF SUGARLOAF MOUNTAIN. FIRE FIGHTERS NOW TELL US THE WILDFIRE HAS DE-STROYED EVERY HOME ALONG THIS HALF-MILE ROAD."

If a specific location is newsworthy, it's important to make sure the audience is told just where that location is. Any crossroll (video run within a live shot) the reporter is using also will need graphics. If the scene of the live shot is the same location as the first video in the crossroll, there may be no need to repeat the locator graphic. But if there's room for confusion, don't hesitate to list the location twice.

Immediacy versus Information

Once on scene, one of the first issues to deal with is obvious: When is your newsroom expecting you to go live? If the story involves a threat or major inconvenience to the public, news reporters are obligated to get the information out as quickly as possible. But what if the situation is less urgent? Newcomers to news might assume it's standard procedure to spend several minutes at the scene gathering vast amounts of information before the first live report. Not necessarily.

Sometimes uncertainty is the price of instant news. The news business is especially competitive. There can be lots of pressure to be first with a breaking story. That's when you may have to fall back on the adage: "Go with what you have."

By the time radio reporters reach a breaking news story, they may have already gone live over the two-way radio or cell phone. TV helicopter crews face the same challenge—heading toward a scene and going live at the same time with little information. Reporters with TV ground crews may be expected to jump out of their car and step up to the camera, ready to present whatever information has been gathered enroute to the scene. Reporters should have the right to postpone a live shot if for any reason they don't trust the information they've been given. But don't assume you need to have every detail down pat before a live shot is justified.

In fast-breaking stories, where initial information is thin and there's pressure to go live right away, let these two simple rules of thumb be your guide:

Guideline #1: Tell the Audience What You Know.   It sounds obvious, but you'd be surprised how easy it is to overlook information that's right in front of you.

- Where are you? Use a specific address only if it's pertinent to the story. Otherwise, use a junction or landmark that viewers or listeners will recognize.
- What's happened? Perhaps a body's been found. Or a building's on fire. Or a child appears to have fallen through thin ice. At the very least, you should be able to explain what type of call or alarm brought emergency crews to the scene.
- What can you see from your vantage point? Clearly, radio reporters routinely have to help their listeners visualize the scene. But even with the added benefit of live pictures, TV reporters need to remember that viewers will see only what the camera can shoot.
- Describe the broader picture outside that TV frame: the effect of freezing weather on fire-fighting equipment, or a traffic jam caused by police cars blocking access to a murder scene. Just be careful what conclusions you draw from those observations. In the chaos of a rapidly unfolding story, it's easy to add 2 + 2 and get 5.
- Be careful to qualify what you say, especially when the information is sketchy. Make liberal use of terms such as "still unclear," "at this time . . . ," and "unconfirmed reports."

Guideline #2: Tell the Audience What You Don't Know.   More precisely, acknowledge questions the audience might have that you simply can't answer . . . yet. But be sure to tell them you're trying to get the answers, and then get them:

"NO WORD SO FAR ON HOW THIS FIRE BEGAN OR WHETHER ANYONE MAY BE TRAPPED INSIDE . . ."

or

> "FOR NOW, THERE'S NO INDICATION WHERE THE CHILD'S PARENTS
> WERE WHEN THE LITTLE BOY WANDERED OFF AND FELL THROUGH
> THE ICE . . ."

Acknowledging unanswered questions is far better than having your audience assume you've overlooked important parts of the story.

Hit the Ground Running

If the spot news story is slightly less chaotic than the scenes described above, then hopefully you've arrived with several questions already answered. For example, is there a command post, and if so, where? In larger towns and cities, many police and fire departments are becoming increasingly sophisticated in their dealings with the press. During emergencies, these agencies will often establish a command post, an on-scene headquarters, and have a designated "PIO" or Public Information Officer available there. That person's duties include gathering information for news reporters.

An effective PIO is especially important when the media is kept at a distance—outside of a roped-off murder scene or at a dangerous fire. If they're willing, PIOs can help clear the way for better access to a story, arranging to help TV photographers move in briefly for closer pictures of the scene. The command post is often the best place to send TV microwave or satellite trucks, at least in the early stages of a breaking story. That will put the TV crew closest to the PIO, a vital source of information.

Remember that the command post, indeed, the general scene of the spot news event, may not be the only scene your station needs to cover. Try to determine what other locations are important to the story, locations that another news crew should check out. Examples would be a hospital where the injured are being taken or a staging area where people have been told they can wait for an "all clear."

While PIOs can be valuable, no self-respecting reporter will be satisfied with only the "official" information such a spokesperson provides. Be on the lookout for other sources of information: neighbors who might have known the murder victim, a fisherman who may have seen the now-missing child playing near the water's edge.

Look for People "Once Removed"

In the section on Television Live Shot Formats, we'll talk about live interviews with people such as eyewitnesses and bystanders. For now, just remember to pay attention not only to the obvious players in the story, whether the emergency command personnel or the immediate victims of a crime, but also to the people "once removed." They may be the men and women actually fighting the fire or the neighbors who used to babysit for the children who have apparently died in that fire. If time permits, and the people are willing, record an interview. It's a lot safer than assuming you'll be able to find them later.

TELEVISION LIVE SHOT FORMATS

Creativity as much as technology limits the "look" of TV live shots, even spot-news live shots where the pace is fast and furious. Live reports can be broadcast in several formats, but often, if time permits, you can enhance the live shot's production value by combining parts and pieces of different formats. The point isn't to set a new world record on the number of roll cues needed within one ninety-second live shot. The goal is to use different elements to communicate more information more effectively. Just as an entire newscast needs to be produced with attention to production techniques and pacing, live shots should have a "finished" look, too.

"Blue Eyes," "Naked Live," or "Thumb Suckers"

As unappealing as they may sound, these TV slang terms all refer to remotes that have no "crossroll," no video or interviews within the shot. It's just the reporter and his or her imagination. So let's put that imagination to work. One of the best reasons to go live is to make the viewer an eyewitness to a story as it unfolds. If the scene has a lot of different elements, why not take the viewers on a tour?

Say you're doing a live shot on a winter storm that's dumped two feet of snow on the city. Don't just stand there! Ask the photographer to shoot off the shoulder if necessary. Make sure the photographer understands what you plan to do, and which direction you'll be going so you'll be framed properly in the shot. Then walk around in this knee-deep snow, live. Dig through what appears to be a snow drift and uncover a mailbox. Shovel snow off of the sidewalk. Give the viewers the feeling they're right there, standing in the snow next to you.

Wireless lavaliere microphones are ideal for this kind of walking shot, but even a lavaliere hard-wired to the truck will work. Lavs leave your hands free to handle your notes, or gesture and refer to the scene around you. You might also want to use a hand prop, something pertinent to the scene, that helps put the story into better perspective. Just don't get carried away. It's important to get to the video quickly. Remember, pacing within a live shot is just as important as pacing within the overall newscast.

As long as noise levels permit, lavalieres are usually better than stick mikes for all TV live reports. One clear exception is remotes with live interviews, which takes us to our next topic.

Live Interviews

If you like a good challenge, you'll love live interviews at the scene of a breaking news story. Live "Q and A" with officials will generally go one of two ways:

1. Either they're comfortable dealing with the press and know they should give fairly short, straightforward answers, or
2. They lapse into "officialese," and talk about "extricating" people instead of freeing them, or "extinguishing the blaze" instead of putting out the fire.

Try to talk with the person first, well before you're both in front of a live camera or microphone. Get a sense of what to expect, and whether a live interview would help your coverage or hurt it. Give the person an idea of how much time you have for the live interview, and generally what subjects you plan to cover. During the interview itself, listen carefully to their answers. Don't be so focused on your next question that you miss an important detail worth pursuing.

If your live interview is with an eyewitness or bystander, be especially careful. You could have a loose cannon in your midst and not know it until it's too late. And there's always the chance the most talkative person off camera will freeze or revert to one-word answers as soon as the live shot begins.

Avoid using lavaliere microphones during live interviews. When you're holding the mike, you have more control over what happens. You may want to record the interview for use later. Discuss your plans with your photographer, too, so he or she can zoom in for tighter shots if time allows.

Say the person's name and relationship to the story at the beginning and end of the live interview. And don't forget to give that same information to your producer so a key can be ordered to superimpose the person's name at the bottom of the screen during the live shot. If you want your photographer to remain wide, on a **two shot,** tell your producer whether the person's name and title should be superimposed screen right or left.

Live/VTR VO/Live (Live/Voice-over-Video/Live)

At last! Let's get some video into this live shot! With a little planning, it's amazing how quickly video shot at the scene of a breaking news story can be "turned around" and appear as crossroll just minutes later. One trick is for photographers to "edit in the camera." Shoot the basics: wide, medium, tight—clean, simple shots that can be microwaved back to news base and edited in the same order they were shot.

The use of crossroll comes at a price. It means the reporter's job just became more complicated. Now, the producer is going to need specific cues—three- or four-word phrases that indicate when the reporter wants the video crossroll to start and stop. The "roll cue" is the cue to start the video. The "cue back to remote" is the cue for the director to switch back to the remote camera, that is, the camera shooting the live shot.

Be precise with your roll cues. If you get sloppy or paraphrase them, the producer and director might miss them, and the crossroll may never run. To make sure you don't forget the cue or change it accidentally, write it down if necessary so you can refer to it during the live shot. If your intro includes detailed facts or figures, write those down, too. Otherwise, try to avoid reading your intro. It can drain the energy and immediacy right out of the shot.

Reference Video in the Live Shot

One of the first rules of writing for television news is to "reference your video." Make sure what you're saying complements what the viewers are seeing. That can be tough if you're voicing over video you can't see. If you don't have a TV monitor at your live location, or for any reason you can't see the crossroll, keep your references general. If you want to make more specific references to certain shots, you'll need to relay editing instructions based on the script you plan to read.

For example, editing instructions for crossroll at a serious apartment fire might go something like this:

"OFF THE TOP, GIVE ME EIGHT SECONDS OF THE BEST FLAME FOOT-AGE. FOLLOW THAT WITH SIX SECONDS OF FIRE TRUCKS ROLLING ONTO THE SCENE. NEXT, GIVE ME SIX SECONDS OF THE VICTIM BEING LOADED INTO THE AMBULANCE, THEN EIGHT SECONDS OF THE CROWD WATCHING. CLOSE OUT WITH AT LEAST TEN MORE SECONDS OF VARIOUS SHOTS OF THE BURNING BUILDING."

It's a rough outline, but it lets you reference several different visual elements in your crossroll even when you cannot see the video. If the video rolls on cue, you're in business.

Live/VTR VO/SOT/VTR VO/Live (Live/Voice-over-Video/Sound on Tape/Voice Over/Live)

Ah, the plot thickens! The live shot becomes more complicated, but hopefully more interesting with **SOT**. It may be part of an interview shot earlier with an eyewitness or an official. Or it may be "nats," natural sound, perhaps a police officer shouting instructions or demonstrators chanting. Natural SOT could even be nonverbal, such as the countdown and explosion at a building demolition.

Let's say you're going live from the scene of a small-plane crash. You've interviewed an eyewitness to the crash, and you want part of that interview, a sound bite, used as crossroll. The editors back at base will need to know what video you want for the voice over going into the bite: general shots of the crash scene, or something more specific, perhaps an ambulance pulling away, then close-up shots of the wreckage. Some stations will edit the VO/SOT/VO onto one tape. Some stations will use two tapes. The advantages of each method are discussed in Chapter 8, "Television Script Formats."

Either way, the editors will need to know how much video to lay down before and after the bite, and which bite to use. It's up to the reporter to supply that information. Assuming time is tight, don't feed significantly more video or sound than you'll need for crossroll. Streamline the process for the editors as much as possible.

Make sure the SOT serves a purpose, and don't forget pacing. Don't take an otherwise high-energy live report and bring it to a screeching halt with a forty-five-second sound bite that puts your audience to sleep. Remember, most TV live shots will run from one to two-and-a-half minutes long, including crossroll. Make good use of your time.

Cues for crossroll that includes SOT are basically the same as cues for voice-over crossroll. Make your roll cue and your cue back to remote clear and specific. Be sure not to duplicate the wording for your cues in other parts of your script. If the video starts or stops at the wrong time, it can be hard to make a graceful recovery.

When it's absolutely necessary, crossroll can consist of SOT alone, with no voice over before or after. In other words, Live/SOT/Live. It's generally not pretty, and you should have a reason for doing it. But if it's important to convey certain information, and if the person giving that information can't or won't give a live interview, SOT alone is an option.

Live/VTR SOT PKG/Live (Live/Video Package/Live)

Thankfully, having to feed back all the elements needed to package a news story isn't as common as it once was. Most satellite trucks include editing facilities (Figure 12.2). By the time a news crew gathers enough material to package a story, a satellite truck can usually be in position at the scene, and editing can proceed much as it would at base. If the distance between the scene of the story and the TV station isn't that far, the piece can be edited back at the station.

Still, for one reason or another, a reporter may sometimes need to feed a narration track and video for an editor to cut back at the station. As the reporter, you can do several things to make that process easier and more efficient.

NARRATION

Once your package script is written, your narration can be fed back live or prerecorded and fed back with the video. When the editor at the station is ready to record the feed, send the track first. Remember, the editor will most likely be working without a written script. By sending the track first, the editor can listen to the track as it's being fed, and become familiar with the story. Once the track's in and the video feed begins, the editor can watch for the people and events you've included in the script.

As you cut the narration, refer to each portion of track between sound bites as "section 1, section 2. . . ." That will help give you a way of referring to the script when it's time to give editing instructions. And just as you do when you record in the audio booth at the station, give a clear 3-2-1 countdown before you begin each section of track.

There is one big exception to the argument that the narration track should be fed first. If time is running out and your photographer is done shooting, the video can be fed in while you're writing the script. Doing two things at once can mean your package will make its slot in the show.

Sound Bites

Before you feed or record your narration track, make sure you've written within your script the in-cues and out-cues of the sound bites you plan to use. Then, after a clean pause in your narration, read the cues as well, giving the speaker's full name and title for *keys* (words or graphics electronically inserted into the video scene) or *cg's* (words electronically produced on a computerized "character generator" and superimposed

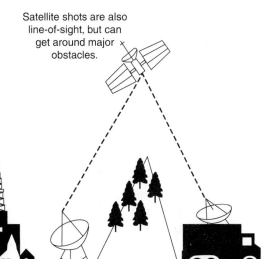

Helicopter

Equipped with microwave pod
Requires line-of-sight to receiver
Program audio and video usually available
Two-way communication available
Usually equipped to feed tape
Can serve as relay for ground unit

Satellite shots are also line-of-sight, but can get around major obstacles.

Microwave signals are line of sight.

Portable Transmitter

Small transmitter often used by news bureaus
Requires line-of-sight to receiver
Availability of program audio and video depends on location
Two-way (radio) or cell phone communication depends on location
Usually capable of feeding tape

ENG (Electronic News Gathering) Truck

Equipped with transmitter on telescoping mast
Requires line-of-sight to receiver
Program audio and video usually available
Two-way or cell phone communication usually available
Fully equipped to feed tape

SNG (Satellite News Gathering) Truck

Dish mounted on large van or truck
Requires line-of-sight to geo-stationary orbiting satellite
Program audio available, usually no program video
Cell phone available, two-way radio depends on location
Reporter hears producer through earpiece
Usually fully equipped to edit tape
Special satellite window needed to feed tape prior to shot

FIGURE 12.2   The method of transmitting the microwave signal to the station affects how the reporter works in the field. The ability to communicate with the station, and the reporter's access to "air" or "program" audio and video, can simplify or greatly complicate a live shot.

over a scene). You might even describe the person so the editor can find the bite more easily. The same guidelines apply to any natural sound breaks you've called for. Explain within breaks in your narration, just which "nats" you want and where they can be found. Don't make the editor's job harder than it has to be.

Video

You want to make sure the editor has enough video to make the piece look as good as possible, but not so much it overwhelms the editor. Just because your photographer has shot three tapes doesn't mean all three tapes need to be fed for your package.

If possible, talk with the editor on two-way radio or cell phone as the video is being fed. You can describe the scene and the players as you go. Try to point out people and places that require careful referencing, e.g., criminal suspects or the exterior of a home where someone's been found murdered. Saying the right thing over the wrong picture can be disastrous.

If it's impossible to talk to the editor, additional editing instructions can be recorded at the end of the narration track. Again, be as specific as necessary to make sure referencing within the package will be correct.

HELICOPTER LIVE SHOTS

Any live shot format that will work on the ground will work from a helicopter, though some are more cumbersome than others. Shooting, narrating, and feeding an entire package from a helicopter would be awkward, but it's certainly possible. The one exception is the "walking" live shot discussed earlier.

When technology allows, live interviews from helicopters can be effective. The interviewee may be on the ground, at a scene where aerials add to the story. For example, a reporter in a helicopter could use audio patched through a cell phone or a two-way radio to interview a fire fighter on the line of a forest fire. This technique can also be used when two reporters are covering the same story. The producer can have them "toss" live to one another, air to ground, for example. A news source can also be interviewed live as he or she views the scene from the air. The questions could come from a reporter who's also on board the helicopter, from a reporter at the scene on the ground, or even from an anchor on set.

During any live shot, it's important to keep in mind the transition between the live shot background and the first video at the top of the crossroll. It can be confusing if the scenes look too similar. This is especially true with helicopter live shots if the photographer is shooting out the window and the crossroll begins with another aerial. Avoid that if possible. At the very least, warn the producer, and ask for a dissolve or another effect to help distinguish between the live remote shot and the videotape.

Because of their mobility, helicopters can often get to the scene of a breaking news story long before a ground crew arrives. Even if aerials are of no value in covering the story, the producer may ask the helicopter crew to "go live" with whatever tidbits of information are available. In effect, the helicopter crew is simply breaking the story. The challenge for the reporter is to make the aerial perspective of the scene as meaningful as possible, emphasize that a news crew is enroute on the ground, and tell audiences that more information should be available shortly.

LIVE IN THE NEWSROOM

With TV's emphasis on having a "live" look, some stations originate entire newscasts from a set in their newsroom. Even more common is a "news desk" in the newsroom, an alternative to the set in the studio. A news desk live shot is an option when producers want a reporter to present a story live but don't have a feasible live location, or don't have the time or technology to make the remote work.

Live shots from the newsroom also may be the best way to bring a late-breaking national story home to local viewers. An example would be a major plane crash in another part of the country. Live updates from the newsroom can be aired throughout the local news show. **Phoners,** live telephone interviews with eyewitnesses or officials on scene, can be dramatic and informative. The phoners can serve as the next best thing until video of the scene is available. The telephone interviews can also run over video that's already in house, with the local anchor or reporter at the news desk asking questions related to the scenes that are showing.

It's a matter of opinion as to whether these shots are being overused. They can certainly be an easy way out of investing the time and energy needed to go live at the scene of the story. But they can also be an effective and legitimate way to maintain or reinforce a reporter's identification with a particular story. Crossroll options for a newsroom live shot are basically the same as for any remote shot.

LIVE GRAPHICS

Stations have different guidelines governing the use of graphics (keys and cg's) during remote broadcasts. But it's standard procedure at many stations to maintain a small "live" graphic in the upper left-hand corner of the picture. Because the graphic may remain on screen throughout the report, photographers must frame live shots so the graphic doesn't obscure important action. That action might look cluttered and confusing with the word "live" keyed over it.

Remember, the name and title of people being interviewed live should also be relayed to news base. If the live interview will be on a two-shot, make sure the graphics operator knows who will be on which side of the screen.

LIVE/ANCHOR INTROS

The sense of immediacy surrounding a live shot begins with the anchor's introduction or toss. Ideally, the reporter in the field will have written the intro and dictated it to the news base. This approach can prevent some problems and create others. First, the advantages: The most obvious reason for having the reporter write the anchor's intro is accuracy. The reporter, after all, is on the scene. For the most part, writers, producers, and anchors back in the newsroom are getting a distilled version of what's going on. That can leave too much room for error.

When the reporter writes the anchor's intro, it's easier to coordinate information. The flow between the point where the anchor leaves off and the reporter begins is built in, or should be, so the "toss" from the studio to the field becomes stronger.

> **Anchor:** Some business owners along South Broadway are fuming tonight . . . angry that city hall has scheduled extensive road construction during the last two weeks of the Christmas shopping season.
>
> Newsfour's Kathy Walsh is live in that shopping district with more on why the store owners there are so mad.

> **Reporter:**   BILL, I'M STANDING AT BROADWAY AND CEDAR. BARRICADES LIKE THIS CLOSE THE TWO RIGHT-HAND LANES OF BROADWAY FOR NEARLY HALF A MILE. THAT'S SIX BLOCKS OF STORES . . . AND DOZENS OF STORE OWNERS . . . WHO SAY THEIR CUSTOMERS CAN'T FIND A PLACE TO PARK.

The anchor's intro flows logically and smoothly into the reporter's intro. The reporter could strengthen her presentation further by using a wireless mike, walking around the barricades, as the photographer pulls out to a wider shot to show the extent of construction.

Realistically, reporters often don't have time to stop and write an intro for the anchor. The best approach then is for the reporter to suggest information for an intro. That way there can still be a strong transition from the news set to the remote. Reporters who haven't written the anchor's intro, and certainly those who haven't even suggested an intro, should make a point to find out what has been written before the live shot begins. Surprises are one of the last things you want in live television.

The anchor's introduction to a live shot is like a well-written intro to any TV story. It needs to establish why the audience should care about the information coming up. But the purpose for the intro doesn't end there. When anchors are setting up a toss to a live report, they should make it clear why the story is being presented live. Is the situation changing and evolving? Do unanswered questions require the reporter's continued presence at the scene? Such references in the anchor's intro will add to the sense of urgency about the story. (We'll discuss the debate about "live for the sake of live" shortly.)

A few final points about anchor intros to live shots: They should be brief, but substantive, i.e., no vague references to "some sort of police problem somewhere in the city." On the other hand, if the anchor's going to use all the information available about a breaking news story, the reporter on scene without anything to add can look pretty foolish.

And should the anchor toss to the reporter in the field with a question? Some news directors discourage it. Still, a tightly written intro followed by a simple, direct question can be a clean and effective transition. But questions that aren't well delivered or that sound "canned" can be deadly. If a question is included as part of the anchor intro, it's vital the reporter knows the question, so the response can be accurate and natural.

REPORTER CLOSE

Like a well-produced story, a well-produced live shot should have a beginning, middle, and end. A strong close to a live shot will play off the final shots and sound in the cross-roll. The reporter's live close should "tie up" the story. If appropriate, refer to the next likely event or development. And remember, there's a big difference between assuring the audience (and the anchor) that you'll be following the story, and promising an update. Refer to a follow-up live shot only if the show's producer has agreed to make room for one.

Most newsrooms have abandoned the practice of having the reporter give his or her own sign-off at the end of the live shot. These days, that's usually left to the anchor. The cleanest, simplest way for the reporter to toss back to the anchor is to use the anchor's first name somewhere in the reporter's final sentence.

ANCHOR CLOSE

Whether the anchor asks the reporter a question at the end of a live shot is usually a function of how much spare time the newscast contains. If the producer wants "Q and A" to wrap up the shot, it's best to have the reporter suggest a question. That doesn't mean the question has to be scripted. Like questions going into a live shot, questions coming out of a live shot can sound phony.

Some anchors seem to feel the reporter at a breaking news story is duty-bound to answer any question the anchor comes up with. Realistically, it doesn't work that way.

Even reasonable questions sometimes don't have timely answers. That means reporters have to learn how to say "I don't know," but say it gracefully. If it's a good question, say so, and perhaps acknowledge that you've been wondering the same thing. Then explain why the information isn't available yet.

If it's a stupid question, answer with as much tact as you can muster. It might be tempting to respond otherwise, but it wouldn't be professional.

WHY GO LIVE?

One of the most obvious reasons to go live is simple: timing. A significant spot-news story is breaking and the only way to cover it during the regular newscast is with a live shot. A truck and crew are dispatched and the live shot is scheduled into the show. But many stories that don't qualify as spot news still deserve live coverage.

Ongoing events that can change rapidly often make good stories for live shots. Jury deliberations in a big murder case or a train wreck are but two examples. The wreck would initially be handled as spot news, but the live crews are kept on scene to cover the story as it unfolds: the search for victims, removing the mangled cars, reopening the track, and the on-scene investigation into what went wrong.

Perhaps the greatest strength of live coverage is that it enhances what television already does best: make the audience an eyewitness to the news. Live coverage can "bring a story home," even if it's happening halfway around the world.

Remotes can enhance much smaller stories, too. Take a strike, for example. A picket line can be a strong visual backdrop for a live shot (though it quickly becomes cliche). A reporter can use a picket to represent the larger story, then personalize the dispute and bring it to life with crossroll profiling one of the workers on the picket line. How is the strike affecting that worker's family? Do the striker's young children understand what's going on? How long can the worker afford to hold out?

WHY NOT GO LIVE?

It's easier to determine when we should go live than when we shouldn't. The benefits of live coverage of major breaking stories are obvious. Knowing when not to go live is a more subtle matter.

Newsmakers are increasingly savvy about orchestrating live coverage. Routinely, politicians, union officials, and leaders of special interest groups make announcements or hold demonstrations during regularly scheduled newscasts. Or they create a well-timed "dog and pony show," making a non-event especially visual in hopes of luring live TV coverage. Some of these stories warrant live coverage, but many do not. News producers may be especially vulnerable on weekends when they often have to struggle to fill their shows.

There are no handy rules to determine whether going live with a scheduled event is playing into the newsmakers' hands. Basically, it comes down to a matter of public interest. How much do your viewers care about this story? If the interest is there, then live coverage is probably justified. When timing is the problem, there's always the option of sending a live truck to feed back video of the event without going live at the scene with a reporter. It gets the story in the show, without giving the event more "play" than it deserves.

What about those shots that are clearly "live for the sake of live"? We see reporters all the time at remote locations leading into stories that an anchor on set could just as easily have introduced. Night after night, even at the network level, we see correspondents reporting live from their desks, telling us about the latest goings-on at the Pentagon or the White House. The network reporters' live introductions and closes are often just one sentence long, hardly so weighty the anchor couldn't have said as much. So why go live with these stories?

The goal is to give viewers a sense of confidence in what the reporter is saying. A correspondent becomes a familiar face, explaining time and again what the Pentagon is up to. If the audience becomes familiar with a station's reporting staff, and sees them routinely in live shots and standups, viewers may relate better to those reporters and listen more closely to what they say. Presumably, they may even be more likely to tune in. You may have the greatest story of all time, but it's not worth much if no one's watching.

PHONERS

There will be times when a station can't send a reporter to cover a story live. Perhaps there aren't enough people or the story's too far away. This is the time to reach for your trusty telephone.

If the story is especially important, live telephone interviews are an option. Phoners that have been recorded are a bit safer, but they may also lose some of their drama. Some reporters try to avoid phoners with officials like dispatchers, for example, who haven't actually been to the scene of a breaking story. But most emergency crews have cellular phones in their cars. If dispatch will give you the phone number for one of the units on scene, you have a good shot at "live" coverage, once removed.

LIVE TEASES

You have to snag viewers before you can inform them. In the best of worlds, you'll have compelling video that will grab the audience like a 300-pound linebacker. But always you need to snag viewers, and that's where teases come in.

Live teases delivered from live remote locations let you pique interest and keep your audience hanging in there through brief breaks in programming. As with all teases, remember the cardinal rule: Never promise more than you can deliver. If you hint at high drama or significant developments that don't exist, viewers will come to distrust you. Your teases will lose their impact, and you may lose your audience.

Mechanics of a Live Tease

You can master the basic logistics that make live teases work without much experience. Once you have the mechanics down, you can concentrate on showcasing tease content, certainly the more creative and challenging part of the job.

Teases within an overall newscast generally promote three to five stories. A standard format might include a couple of video teases voiced over by the anchors, a live tease or two from the reporters in the field, followed by quick references to up-coming weather or sports stories.

If your live shot includes a tease, make sure you know what comes immediately before your tease. If the item just before you is a scripted tease delivered by an anchor, ask for the specific words that will serve as your cue. If *you* follow another live tease, the producer may not have a scripted phrase to give you. Just be sure you know what story and reporter come before you, and listen for the obvious break. Either way, be looking at the camera, not the field monitor, from the moment your shot is "hot." Establish strong eye contact immediately.

Plan for noise. If your live location makes it difficult for you to hear your cue, ask your producer to give a "go" to your photographer when your camera's hot. Make sure your photographer knows that cue is coming, and is ready to give you a clear visual signal to begin.

Clarify with your producer whether a specific "toss" is needed at the end of your tease. Should you simply complete your tease and stop talking or pitch to another reporter or anchor?

Content of Live Teases

Like all teases in television, live teases should hint at a story's content but stop well short of revealing the story itself. Your goal is to raise a question in the viewer's mind during the tease, and then to answer that question in your live shot that follows. That doesn't mean teases should be delivered in the form of a question. Once in a while, questions are okay if they're compelling: "How does it feel to fall two-thousand feet from an airplane and live to tell about it? We have a live report, next." Inane questions, though, annoy viewers: "How could getting a simple haircut kill you? Find out after the break." A better practice is to begin your tease almost like a compelling lead to a news story.

Example #1

"There's a new store in town that can help you look like a million bucks . . . without spending a dime. I'm Tom Russell. We'll take you there live."

This tease lets viewers form the obvious questions, "What store and where is it?" As an added bonus, it promises the viewer a benefit: The viewer will learn how to look great while saving money. The tease and story content compel, engage, and benefit viewers. They realize from the tease they'll miss something important if they don't watch. By contrast, the following story tease offers fewer reasons to stay tuned.

Example #2

"Where can you get a really good deal on clothes in Denver? I'm Tom Russell. I'll have a live report."

Ho hum. Pretty boring. Not much energy. The phrase "live report" is accurate, but not very exciting. Guess I'll head to bed.

Incorporate Your Surroundings in the Tease

Whenever you report live from the field, show your surroundings. Use what viewers can see in the background, or as you move through the background, to energize the story. In our story about the new clothing store, maybe we can show two hundred customers waiting in line on opening day.

Motivate Movement in the Tease

Movement in a tease can help make the story come to life, but the movement has to make sense. Just like your scripts and ad-libs, your movement and delivery need to be crisp and conversational. Any movement should be natural, too. If it feels awkward or forced, odds are it will look that way.

Check out all the reporters who do the "walk to nowhere" in standups, and you'll get the idea. Simply walking from Point A to Point B in a standup for no reason except to add movement makes little sense. Walking from Point A, where a runaway truck swerved to avoid kids in a crosswalk, to Point B, where the truck overturned, looks natural and helps viewers better understand the story.

Tease length is more a matter of common sense than rules. On average, good, tight teases will run from five to ten seconds. Much shorter, and you risk the old "World ends. Film at 11." caricature. Much longer, and the show's pace will drag. These are guidelines, obviously, and not rules etched in stone.

Begin now to watch other newscasts and reporters with a critical eye and ear, and figure out what works best and why. Experiment. Add your own signature. Follow your own sensibilities and instincts, and soon you'll develop an effective style that others will try to emulate.

SOME PARTING ADVICE

Many of the guidelines that will help make your stories more effective are equally important when you go live. Be conversational. Tell the story naturally, in the sort of clean, simple style you'd use if you were talking to a friend. Reporters should also make the live introductions and closes that wrap around their packages smooth and natural.

Try using newspaper stories to practice ad libbing live shots. Jot down notes from a story that might have made a good remote. Use those notes to practice telling that story live, without a script. Challenge yourself further and imagine what the overall scene of that story would have been like. Describe those surroundings if it adds to the story. Remember, TV viewers can see only what's within the camera frame, and sometimes must depend on the picture the reporter paints in their imagination.

Credibility isn't just a matter of sounding as if you know what you're talking about. You also have to look like you know what you're talking about. In other words, dress appropriately. It's distracting to see a reporter in a three-piece suit and Italian shoes going live from a muddy wheat field that's been flattened by hail. To some viewers, that reporter will look so foolish that the story's point is lost. That doesn't mean you need to invest in bib overalls and a straw hat. Just don't clash with your live background.

The same guideline applies for reporters covering bad weather. If you're not dressed for the part, your message may not get through. Most reporters who do a lot of live shots keep spare clothing handy. It just makes sense.

A FINAL THOUGHT

One of the best tips for any broadcast reporter is to be human—in your approach to a story, in the way you write it, and in any live work surrounding that story. If you're curious about something, odds are your audience will be curious, too. If grotesque or tragic events at a spot-news story shock you, it's okay to let some of that show. You have to be professional and keep a certain distance between yourself and the events you cover. But there's such a thing as being so overly emotionally objective the story becomes sterile. At that point, many in the audience may begin to wonder why the story matters or why they should care.

SUMMARY

Using live reporting technology, television journalists report news more swiftly than at any time in history. All the general communication skills important in radio and television news are doubly important for successful live reports. Such skills include a well-rounded vocabulary, good news judgment, solid reporting experience, and strong interviewing skills. Of all these skills, the most important remains a knack for writing and talking conversationally.

Specialists in live reporting gather information even while enroute to the scene. The average news car or van allows journalists to monitor police, fire, and civil defense frequencies; communicate with the newsroom; and often, speak with news sources via a cellular phone.

You may have to go on air on arrival, with no opportunity to gather information beyond what you collected en route to the scene. In such situations, follow two rules of thumb: (1) tell the audience what you know, and (2) tell them what you don't know. In all cases, qualify what you say, especially when the information is sketchy, using such terms as "still unclear at this time" and "unconfirmed reports."

Hit the ground running when you arrive on scene. Look for a command post and public information officer, or PIO, who can help clear the way for better access to a story. Also search for other locations and ways to report the story so your report will contain more than the "official" information such a spokesperson provides.

If you feed raw material back to the station, narration can be fed live or prerecorded and fed back with the field video. Because the editor may have to work without a written script, try to send the voice track first. This lets the editor listen to the track as it's being fed and become familiar with the story.

Almost any live shot that will work on the ground will work from a helicopter. You can do virtually anything but the "walking" live shot from a helicopter, including shooting, narrating, and feeding an entire package.

The sense of immediacy surrounding live shots begins with the anchor's introduction or "toss." Ideally, because the reporter in the field knows most about the story, the reporter will write the intro and dictate it to base. This approach also strengthens the flow of the "toss" from studio to the field. If the reporter lacks time to write an anchor intro, another approach is to suggest information for an intro.

The reporter's live close should "tie up" the story. If appropriate, refer to the next likely development. Remind the audience and the anchor you'll be following the story, but promise a follow-up live shot only if the show's producer has agreed to make room for one.

Whether through coverage of spot or breaking news, or by updating the news as it unfolds, live reports make audiences an eyewitness to the news. While the benefits of live coverage are obvious, knowing when not to go live is a more subtle matter. If the story doesn't warrant live coverage, the newsroom can send a live truck to feed back videotape of the event without going live at the scene with a reporter.

Whenever you report live from the field, dress appropriately to the environment. Whether in the field with news sources, or on screen as a television reporter, you have to look and sound like you know what you're talking about. The goal in every instance is to avoid distractions, so that you can keep news sources and audiences focused on story content. Most of all, be professional, but also be human in your reports—in the way you approach the story, in the way you write it, and in any live work surrounding that story.

EXERCISES

1. Assess the general writing, reporting, and communication skills you possess to conduct successful live reports for radio or television news. As part of your assessment, determine to what extent you have a well-developed vocabulary, good news judgment, ade-

quate reporting experience, and strong interviewing skills. Also make an honest assessment of your writing and speaking skills, especially your ability to write and speak fluently and conversationally under pressure. Develop a multiphase plan to strengthen skills or abilities you feel deficient in, and establish a regular schedule to practice writing and speaking under pressure.

2. Practice gathering information "on the run." Take notes as you listen to a breaking story on a radio or television newscast. Study your notes briefly, then step before a radio microphone or television camera and record a practice live shot. Replay the recording and critique your performance.

3. Monitor live reports on your favorite AM or FM radio station. Analyze those qualities that make live reports on your favorite station so effective. Prepare a two-page report, double-spaced, and discuss your findings in class.

4. For practice, ask a friend to shoot video in at least three locations as you locate yourself at the beginning of a live shot. At each location, alternatively provide a description of the location, a specific description of a junction or landmark that viewers or listeners in your area would recognize, and finally the location's exact address if available. If help is unavailable, set up the camera and record yourself.

5. For practice, record the introduction to a live report, using background notes from a newspaper article or a broadcast news story. Include as much of the following information as possible in forty seconds or less: your location, what's happened, what you can see from your vantage point, and the "broader picture" that exists outside the TV frame. Qualify your information as necessary, and use terms such as "still unclear," "at this time," and "unconfirmed reports" as warranted.

6. Record the live close to a practice report, this time telling your imaginary audience what you don't know. End the close with a toss back to the studio anchor, including as part of your last line the anchor's first name.

7. Interview a Public Information Officer at a police or fire department about his or her dealings with the press, protocols the PIO follows during emergencies, how the command post operates, and the procedures and guidelines reporters are expected to follow. Submit a report of not more than five double-spaced pages and discuss your findings in class.

8. Record yourself delivering a :50 to :60 "thumb sucker" to camera. Play back the result and critique your performance. Note especially the sense of urgency you communicate, how fluid and extemporaneous you sound, and your ability to develop and maintain eye contact with the audience.

9. Using your own or donated footage, produce a practice live/SOT/live report not to exceed 1:20. Play back the result and critique your performance.

10. Using your own or donated footage, produce a live/VTR/live report. As part of your script, note the roll cue and cue back to remote for the crossroll.

11. Using the newspaper as a reference source, write a practice "live" report that includes editing instructions for crossroll on a spot-news story. For guidance, see pages 238–240.

12. Using your own or donated footage, produce a live/VO/SOT/live report, including all necessary roll cues for the producer. Record your own live intro and close.

13. Write the script for a spot-news package, using any source of information you wish. Prerecord all voice-over narration as though it were to be fed live back to the station. Refer to each portion of track between sound bites as "section 1, section 2 . . ." and give a clear 3-2-1 countdown before you begin each section of track.

14. Record a practice live report from a real or imaginary television newsroom. This can be a late-breaking story or one or more live updates from the newsroom.

15. Based on any of the live intros you have written for any of the exercises above, write anchor intros that flow smoothly from the anchor to your own report. Keep the anchor intro brief but specific. For additional practice, record the anchor intro on tape and use it to introduce your own live intro.

16. Ad lib a reporter close that includes a smooth toss back to the anchor. Reference the final shots and sound in the crossroll as you tie up the story. If appropriate, refer to the next likely event or development and assure the audience, if appropriate, that you'll be following the story. Include the anchor's first name as part of the last line in your close.

17. Practice preparing and delivering three versions each of a radio voicer, a radio news wrap, and if practical, a live interview in which you report and update a spot-news story over time in the field, including interviews with significant sources.

CHAPTER THIRTEEN

THE ASSIGNMENT EDITOR AND PRODUCER

Architects of the Newscast

At the most successful news operations, an astutely defined news philosophy serves as the underpinning of a daily operational guide. This philosophy shapes collective staff judgment about what is news, how it is to be covered, by whom, and how it is to be packaged and showcased. It is a philosophy born of a genuine understanding of the community, and it serves inevitably to help make the assignment editor and producer partners in building the daily newscast. Since both the assignment editor and producer are such key players in deciding the station's destiny, their partnership is essential.

THE ASSIGNMENT EDITOR

The assignment editor's job is to cover everything that happens, a responsibility some broadcasters consider to be the toughest job in the news department. Not uncommonly, assignment editors may have held previous jobs as reporters or producers, but whatever their background they evidence a certain psychological profile and temperament. At minimum everyday, these folks will have to

- read newspapers
- monitor broadcast news competitors
- monitor police, fire, sheriff, and emergency radio transmissions
- maintain close communication with the news director and producer
- know the reporter's egos, peculiarities, writing styles, and internal clocks
- know who can work with police, who has great interpersonal skills
- nurture the best general assignment reporters, the true prizes of the newsroom
- know whose stories are working, whose stories are failing
- help producers find the f-l-o-w to stories and transitions
- know what stories and story treatments will appeal to viewers
- know what stories are important to the community
- know what stories justify live reports
- follow breaking news, faster and better than the competition
- communicate with the promotion department

- know what stories need updates
- identify relevant feature stories
- based on current research, know what kinds of stories viewers are least likely to watch
- realize how the producer and reporter's writing complement the anchor's job of introducing stories
- know how to make any story more compelling, more understandable
- know which anchors would do the best job of introducing specific stories
- know how to make stories more instant and interesting, while preserving accuracy, polish, and professionalism
- be able to protect time for research and constant updating
- excel in outperforming the competition, the driving force in every newsroom
- define relevant news—the news people want to know
- know how to improve what anchors and reporters do
- establish commonality with the audience
- stop smoking
- drink enough water
- spend enough time with family and other loved ones
- have a life outside the newsroom
- develop an informed, healthy mind
- get enough exercise and rest

The assignment editor also assigns crews, answers the phone, checks the news wire, sorts and reads the mail, reads scripts of previous newscasts, keeps a news file, develops story ideas and sometimes helps write the stories, makes and adjusts schedules, helps organize the newsroom, and negotiates conflicts between staff members. Assignment editors read everything, always looking for another story, another angle, and they bear the greatest responsibility should the station miss a story. In a real sense, the assignment editor is a co-partner, along with the producer, in helping shape the station's destiny (Figure 13.1).

NEWS ASSIGNMENT SHEET

Every news day assumes a life of its own. Often, it seems, it's either a slow news day or "all hell is breaking loose." Regardless of market size, there is an ebb and flow to the news that assignment editors must anticipate. Here is an assignment sheet from a typical news day at a station around market size 50. The left column indicates time of day the assignment is to be covered.

> **9:00**   **City Budget**   The city is holding a public hearing Friday morning so that the citizens can speak their minds on city budget proposals before they vote on them June twentieth. Many of them have been doing that for the past several weeks, but this includes all the budget-cut proposals, so there should be a large turnout.
>   Paul/Miles Pkg.

10:00	**JOB TRAINING** Sam has the report on funding problems at the Private Industry Training Council, which tries to find jobs for people as well as provide incentives for companies to hire them.
	Steve/Sam Pkg.
12:00	**MOZART FESTIVAL** The big festival begins tomorrow and continues through the twenty-first. It is being held at the community center and will feature several concerts by some of the best musicians celebrating the music of Wolfgang Amadeus Mozart.
	Curt/Danta Pkg.
1:45	**LAST LEGISLATIVE WRAP-UP** Possible story on what the legislature did and didn't accomplish this session . . . kind of a legislative report card.
	Tim/Rick Pkg.
9:30	**HOME REFINANCING** Terry reports on what homeowners should do if they are contemplating trying to refinance loans on their homes.
	Andy/Terry Pkg.
8:00	**STUDENT LOANS** Sam will finish his story on the cost of going to college. Many students are getting large loans to pay for their educations. The IRS is already cracking down on former college students who have never paid off their loans.
	John/Sam Pkg.
1:00	**SHERIFF DAY** The mayor proclaims Friday as Johnny France Day and makes him an honorary sheriff. He's the guy who tracked down the father-and-son mountain men who kidnapped an Olympic athlete.
	Andy/Glenda VO/SOT
10:30	**SPIRIT OF TEXAS** Feature on a lake patrol officer honored for his service
	Jeff/Wendy Pkg. Hold

Joe Comp Day
Jill Comp Day
Mary and Cathy Edit

8:00	**McIntyre Trial**	Eddie/Randy	Pkg.
	Murder Arraignment	TBA/Glenda	VO
	Bellman		VO
	Judges Sworn In		VO

ASSIGNMENT EDITORS HELP CONCEPTUALIZE THE PACKAGE

Most reporters have worked with an assignment editor who sends crews to everything. Some assignment editors may think of packages and even newscasts as holes to fill. They tend to treat reporters and photographers as folks who bring home the fill dirt.

FIGURE 13.1 An assignment editor at the news assignment board schedules reporting crews to cover the day's news.

In actuality, only news that is important to the viewer needs to be covered. Such a simple axiom demands that the assignment editor be a good judge of what is truly newsworthy, and to know the community's pulse. A decision about which stories should be covered also can be shared with other newsroom employees (Figure 13.2). Effective newsrooms often use a beat system in which reporters share more news coverage responsibilities with the desk; this encourages more enterprise reporting and followup.

Since assignment editors are in effect the "first reporter" on many stories, they, too, share a responsibility in helping determine the focus statement for many of the stories they assign. Although it may be too early to make a theme statement at the time a story is first assigned, the opportunity certainly exists for those stories on which planning and research are well underway.

The Futures File in an Organized Newsroom

One device that helps assignment editors know which news to cover is the **futures file.** This file is a collection of story ideas, notes, and news releases about upcoming events. The futures file contains information about predictable news, so it helps create better newsroom organization. Better organization in turn can help reporters anticipate stories and how best to cover them rather than simply react to them.

The News Planner

Most commonly, reporters are given story assignments on the day their stories will air. Reporters who may originate from three to six stories a day, or even a single story, have little time to unearth sources or spend on in-depth research. But in some newsrooms,

FIGURE 13.2 As a new shift begins, reporting crews consult with their assignment editor about the day's field assignments.

assignment editors and news planners try to plan story coverage far in advance so as to give reporters lead time to develop stronger stories. The job of news planners is to think ahead, research stories, and generate story ideas not only for next week's newscasts but also for series that may be aired in coming months. Reporters work on these advance assignments as time permits throughout the news day, in addition to their daily reporting assignments.

Stringers

Even on slow news days when nothing seems to be happening, the station is likely to be awash in a sea of news, with access to material from sources as diverse as its own field reporters, feeds via satellite, network and local microwave sources, cooperating regional stations, news syndications, and the like. Problems may arise, however, in covering fast-breaking news in nearby local communities, unless the assignment editor has access to a news stringer network that is already in place.

Stringers are private individuals who agree to photograph breaking news for the station for average payments of twenty-five to fifty dollars per story. Stringers may receive a telephone call from the assignment editor to cover a story, or they may cover a story "on spec" with payment forthcoming only if the story is aired. If the story occurs within twenty-five miles of the station, the stringer may be asked to drive the tape to the newsroom at no additional compensation. Beyond twenty-five miles, the station may arrange a pickup point at the sheriff's office or a shopping center. Some stringers are paid mileage, others receive mileage only if they drive in excess of fifty miles.

Stringers usually supply their own cameras and tape, commonly in mini-DV format. Stations transfer the stories to hard drive for air and return original material to the stringers.

Sometimes the stringer's most important job will be to provide coverage until the station's own crews can arrive on scene. Normally, stringers serve as a supplement to existing staff rather than as a replacement. They also help expand the station's ability to project an image of covering news throughout the market at relatively little investment.

THE PRODUCER

Every day the newscast starts out as a blank page and a gleam in the producer's eye. If you think of the newscast as a house that must be built from the foundation up every day, then the producer can be thought of as its architect. As stories filter back from the field throughout the news day, as scripts are written, and as editors assemble VO/SOTs (voice-over/sound-on tape) and packages, the producer works to structure and define the newscast. The job is an amalgam of deadlines and creative decisions. And occasionally there are opportunities to impact the newscast in ways that can help shape the station's destiny (Figure 13.3).

FIGURE 13.3 News personnel, including the news anchors, show producers, and assignment editors, interact during a daily budget meeting to help plan the day's news coverage and determine probable lead stories of the day.

TOWARD A NEWS PHILOSOPHY

Unless viewers are involved in the newscast, they are vulnerable to raids from the competition. Yet night after night across the country, multitudes of viewers are served a kind of news hash, a mishmash of good news/bad news/irrelevant-dull-pointless news. The problem tends to be especially acute in the smaller markets, where viewers are in a sense sacrificial audiences who must either submit themselves to the available fare or go without. At the most proficient news operations, news is presented with an identifiable style. News treatment at these stations imparts relevancy to the day's events. Stories and production values build and hold audience interest. Shows have an identifiable mood and feeling, and reaction to news content is evident. Audiences leave these newscasts feeling a sense of connection not only with the station and its anchors and reporters, but with the information itself. At such stations, informed audiences are among their foremost legacies.

The station's news philosophy and how it positions itself against competitors can help build market dominance. The station's philosophy becomes a tangible force over time as station management and staff begin to ask and answer of themselves: "What are we all about? How do we want people to think of us? What do we stand for?" Such questions help the station determine its image, its values, and its edicts.

Incorporating a Sense of Community

Communities are made up of people, their dreams, triumphs, and struggles. To understand a community, you must be part of it. One way to be more in touch with viewers and their needs and interests is by developing a broad foundation of first-person knowledge. This means activities as simple as taking time during days off to drive into various areas of the community, visit a cafe for a cup of coffee, or walk through a new residential area. Extending that same principle, broadcast journalists can be encouraged to involve themselves in community events and civic affairs, whatever their scope. Perhaps one day a month can be devoted to charitable or volunteer activities or to pay a visit to senior citizens at the local rest home. Whatever activities you choose, the payoff is greater understanding of and empathy with viewers who look to your station for an accurate portrayal of the happenings and life within their community—from a station whose employees are themselves contributing and involved members of the community.

Winning Stations Care about Their Communities

Care about your community, and it will show. Fail to care about your community, and every viewer will know. With that motto apparently in mind, WUSA-TV, Minneapolis-St. Paul, changed its station call letters to KARE-TV. Even the call letters imply an attitude about the station's commitment to the community.

In a real sense, viewers help dictate the definition of news. Useless news, after all, is very often unviewed news. Every night, viewers come to the station's newscast with certain expectations. They expect to see the big stories of the day and to be informed about the truly interesting and significant happenings of the day. They expect to encounter a certain range of experiences and for a while to inhabit certain emotional territories. They seek an identifiable presence in the show's primary and secondary talent (anchors and reporters), and they look to these people—people they have learned they can trust—for help in understanding the day's news. Most important, they look for interest and relevancy in exchange for the half-hour or more of life they will invest in the station's newscast.

The Good News/Bad News Syndrome

Journalism has evolved as a profession that addresses "things gone wrong," with emphasis on issues and problems that need to be addressed and solved. By that definition, journalism would seem to be mostly accounts of "bad news." Yet among the most important roles of journalism, as Walter Lippman has argued, is that of showing us the way. The world is gray, neither all good nor all bad. Typically, audiences want their newscasts to reflect a similar balance of content, made up neither of all good news nor all bad, but news that fairly represents what is happening in the viewer's many worlds.

Given that understanding of audience needs and interests, it is useful to examine the typical half-hour newscast. Look at each story and each element of production and rank it for emotional weight according to whether it can be categorized as "plus," "zero," or "minus." Determine for each component in the newscast—be it the story, standup, anchor reaction, or graphic, whether you feel positive, neutral, or negative toward it. As you rank stories in the news lineup, you may discover a long string of "bad news" stories, a common occurrence at stations where a news philosophy is absent or only vaguely operable. Some newscasts may go heavy on bad news for most of the hour, with a good news kicker at the end.

Placed in proper perspective, even so-called bad news can sometimes be converted from a minus to a zero, or even to a plus. Arguably, then, news is drawing the line. There is no such thing as good news or bad news, no such thing even as hard or soft news. "There is simply news and how you treat it," says Bill Brown, consultant and managing partner of The Coaching Company, Dallas. "It's whether you report fairly, with balance and perspective, and how you clue in your viewers."[1]

Brown cites as an example a story in which a woman's body was found years after her murder. Some stations in the market chose to emphasize the agony and tragedy of the event; other stations emphasized family members who expressed relief that they could now get on with the rest of their lives. In stories about Mexico City earthquakes, some stories of necessity dealt with the great loss of life and related tragedies. Other stories, however, dealt with the renewal of life expressed in accounts of the city's efforts to establish makeshift nurseries to accommodate the hundreds of newborn babies who arrived during the earthquakes. Such balance and perspective may help a station achieve dominant position in the ratings far more easily than when stations consider journalism to be predominantly accounts of "bad news."

Sources of News

As a station strives to initiate a better balance of content, staffers can find it useful to examine how news stories (and ideas for stories) originate. In the case of journalists, the observation that applies to the rest of humanity is operable: Most people seek the easiest solution to a task; most people take the easy way out. The most obvious stories, therefore, are those that present themselves, and the easiest stories are those that take the least thought and are the most accessible to cover. This is one reason stations within a market tend to report the same stories and the same general types of stories.

Two types of news routinely offer the type of accessibility journalists must rely on if they are to meet their profession's incessant daily deadlines. The first type is made up of that predictable menu of events with which viewers have become so familiar. This menu includes both spot news, which occurs suddenly and without warning, and the more predictable happenings such as public hearings, trials, and press conferences that can be scheduled and covered as developing stories. Spot news encompasses such happenings as explosions, murders, robberies, air crashes, and bridge collapses. Information about such events is available around the clock to any station with police and fire scanners and to reporters who have cultivated their connections with local dispatchers and law enforcement agencies (Figure 13.4).

The second common type of news source is the person who represents a special interest. In one way or another this person seeks to promote a particular point of view or otherwise capitalize on public exposure of a deed or message. In this category are press secretaries, public relations practitioners, publicity agents, branches of the U.S. military, a university research project or fund-raising effort, a candidate for mayor, and a nuclear power plant just down the road. Typically, special interest sources schedule events and press conferences at times and locations as convenient for the reporter as possible. These

FIGURE 13.4 An assignment editor tracks crew locations during coverage of a breaking news story.

sources try to provide events that are both visual and timely and can be pegged naturally to "real" news events. Some firms go so far as to provide the visuals themselves and sometimes even pre-shot and edited packages with well-written scripts that a station's reporter can voice as his or her own. These "electronic press releases" imitate local news formats; often they are aired "as is" at smaller stations, with no way for viewers to know the originator was someone with a product, service, or point of view to promote.

With little time for assignment editors and producers to plan newscasts or to develop enterprise stories, it's small wonder that newscasts around the country tend to be event driven, a phenomenon that Bill Taylor, senior consultant and managing partner at NuFuture.TV, calls "clutch and brake" news. The newscast is filled with one event after another, with little sense of connection between stories or sections within the newscast or of the themes that may be present among the day's stories. One way to break out of the syndrome is to begin to look for the meaning behind events and situations and to generate interpretive stories even when there is no event per se.

Story Followup

Another need is to pay more attention to story development and story followup. In reality, few stories just happen and fade away. They keep going. Audiences have an extraordinary hunger for followup, and they look to stations to keep track of all the things that they, as viewers, can't keep up with. This means that a key element of reporter survival is story ownership and initiative. At most stations, many more stories contain valuable followup potential than actually receive it.

Nowhere is it written that reporters must wait for someone to assign them a story. In fact, the best reporters try to establish story ownership and to update their reports whenever new developments warrant. Story ownership is not a hallmark of the reporter who ambles up to the assignment editor every day to ask, "Uh, what do you have for me today?" but it can become such a reporter's byword if the newsroom demands followup.

Some news operations require that reporters generate a certain number of enterprise ideas each week and insist that reporters maintain a file on every story they report and follow up on them periodically. "If you're dissatisfied with your assignments, then come up with your own. There is no reason to always be reacting to other people's story ideas. We are all news people and we should understand what is important in our respective commuinities," says Scripps Networks executive John Lansing.[2]

Lansing also advocates that photographers become involved in story development and followup. "It should be remembered that TV photographers are in the news business just as much as the reporter sitting next to us in the car," he says. "There is a lot of satisfaction in originating a story, then setting it up and grabbing a reporter to go along."[3]

Determine Your News Philosophy

The destiny of any newscast hinges at least as much on the producer's news philosophy as it does on news judgment. If the producer has a valid news philosophy and community orientation, the newscast will typically represent a more palatable range and treatment of the day's news. The news will evidence more emphasis on people and less emphasis on institutions. Better balance in the news will be evident, and the producer may even begin to de-emphasize the next event/next event, clutch/brake syndrome and begin to produce the newscast more as though it were a half-hour news package with a definable theme, with logical transitions, and with a logical beginning, middle, and end. Perhaps best of all, the newscast will begin to have a distinctly identifiable look. One look at this newscast and most viewers will know instantly which station they are watching. At a majority of stations, such goals are neither impossible nor unrealistic.

Viewer Mood

Throughout the newscast, viewer mood must be at the forefront of the producer's mind. Typically, stories carry an "emotional charge" of plus, zero, or minus, so most producers try to avoid strings of any given type of story within the newscast, just as they strive to avoid "Ping-Pong" story order, which results in a rapidly alternating series of good news/bad news/good news stories. For one thing, a long string of negative stories will leave viewers with a bad taste in their mouth. No one enjoys being subjected to an unending series of stories whose predominant emotional impact is negative. Conversely, if the story lineup ping-pongs back and forth between positive and negative stories, viewers may be unable to change their own moods so quickly, not to mention anchors who must ride an emotional roller coaster that requires smiles one instant and doleful faces the next.

As the person in charge of the ebb and flow of viewer mood, be mindful that a story's emotional charge can be altered, based both on your news philosophy and on your commitment to stories and newscasts that provide balance and perspective. At the very least, try to make the final story in every segment an upbeat one. This technique helps the audience place viewing experiences in a positive or at least neutral frame of mind and helps them be more receptive to stay tuned through the commercial breaks. Additionally, if the range of viewer emotions is predominantly negative, some viewers may tend to blame the anchors or the newscast itself rather than accept responsibility for their own feelings.

Monitor Story Count in Each Segment

Occasionally, one story is allowed to stand alone in a segment, but this practice short-changes both the segment itself and the viewers at home. Pace falls off, commercials bunch up, and suddenly the lone story seems somehow gratuitous. The problem is especially acute in newscasts in which a franchise report is isolated as the sole story within a segment. The franchise might be a consumer report or health watch segment that airs every week at a scheduled time.

Often these reports are treated as the "odd man out"; they're stuffed where they least clutter up the newscast lineup because of newsroom attitudes toward franchises: "If you say I have to air Dr. Duke Reed's Medical Report, I will, but I don't have to like it or spend much time on the setup."

The key is to integrate franchises so that scheduled news stories flow naturally into them. If Dr. Reed's syndicated report covers ways to avoid skin cancer, the producer can precede the report with something as simple as reader copy on a cancer-related story from the news services. A line or two of copy can then be used as a transition to the skin cancer report: "Despite breakthroughs in some forms of cancer treatment, skin cancer is a more serious threat than ever. Dr. Duke Reed tells how we can reduce the risks in our everyday lives."

Another goal is to end stories and segments with content that's "talkable," in other words, for the anchors to join in as appropriate on the last moment of stories and segments. At the end of a cooking segment in the noon newscast, the technique can be something as simple as one anchor saying to the other, "That looks good. I'm glad it's lunchtime," followed by the co-anchor's acknowledgment, "Me too." The idea is to reach closure on stories and to close out segments with a definitive gesture that indicates "the end of this section is at hand."

Closure is important because we need to see anchors confirm the reactions we have as viewers. If anchors fail to acknowledge stories and packages, or to cleanly end each segment, viewers may see the anchors as callous, humorless, insensitive, unthoughtful, or any of a host of other unflattering descriptions. Since anchors show viewers how to react by their own reactions, some acknowledgment of stories is essential—even if the reaction is nothing more than a tilt of the head or a nonplussed expression. Gratuitous, vacuous happy talk continues to be verboten.

Work with the Anchors

Depending on such factors as market size and the magnitude of the egos involved, producers can sometimes impact the look of the newscast by working more closely with anchors and reporters. Anchors can't react candidly or confidently to stories they haven't seen, for example, so a bit of grounding about the package the anchor won't have time to preview may result in a more spontaneous newscast. A moment or two spent on story setup can help to eliminate anchor uncertainty on the air. Or perhaps the producer can suggest that the anchor use simple, on-set props to better tell the story. Into this category fall such simple props as copies of mail order catalogues used by area shoppers to avoid paying in-state sales tax.

The dual or tandem anchor format can slow a show's pace if interaction becomes ponderous or if both anchors insist on "owning" the story. In this case the newscast can be helped if interaction between anchors is kept friendly but precise and if story setups are kept to a minimum. Even the little half-beat hesitations that occur when the anchor comes back on air and waits to be cued or to affirm on-air status can be eliminated by using a floor director who gives the anchors tight, crisp air cues. More spontaneous interaction can result if the technical director is given permission to do live edits from one camera to the next during anchor interplay in the studio.

Within the news operation, reporter and anchor education also is important as the station strives to help employees focus and refocus on station goals and news philosophies, which can lead to improved newscast content and appearance.

TEASES

Most producers either write or assign the teases that are meant to tantalize viewers into staying tuned for the news to come: "Next, advice from the experts on the safest suntan of all. We'll have that story when we return, and more about the cheapest ways to travel this summer, wherever you're headed." Just as a newspaper headline reflects the essence of a print story, the broadcast tease tells us a tantalizing tidbit about the story to come, but doesn't give it away: "Some day all the medication you need may come in a glass of milk." This tease, which aired on KCNC, Denver, promoted a story that told viewers that scientists have genetically altered milk to produce a human heart drug.

Teases should reveal just enough about the story to keep viewers tuned in, but not so much information as to render the upcoming story unnecessary. "Tease the teasable reasons to watch a show," says NuFuture.TV's Bill Taylor. "Keep telling late night viewers why it's important to stay tuned, and remember to include, not exclude, the audience," says Taylor.[4]

When you write teases, try to find a way to communicate a sense that all viewers will need to know about/be interested in/be entertained by this next story. Often, it is possible to sell people who appear in the stories you are teasing and let them sell the stories. Even in teases the maxim is operable that if you can sell the person, the person will sell the story.

Fulfill the Promise of the Tease

Night after night, year after year, it is imperative for the package to fulfill the promise of the tease. Viewers quickly grow tired of unkept promises. The same criterion applies to the story lead-in. Avoid generic teases and lead-ins. The more specific, engaging, and compelling you can make them, the better.

HELP MAKE THE STATION A REGIONAL FORCE

To build larger audiences, a station may seek to establish itself as the one that does the best job covering regional news. Even stations that work zealously to cover regional news over the years may still be identified as serving primarily the community in which they physically reside. In either case, the producer can help the station achieve greater recognition as a regional force in covering news over a wide area.

One way to help establish a reputation for regional coverage is to "regionalize" the open to the newscast. The idea is to prove to viewers that you're covering their area. As warranted, stories from particular viewing areas can be featured in newsbreaks and teases. Besides the mention of other towns in headline stories, town names can be mentioned in weather and sports. In fact, the more mention of town names in weather, the better. Note that news coverage in other communities creates a need for more locator maps, for viewers who may be unfamiliar with another community's location. In themselves, however, the locator maps also show you're covering those areas.

To project a more regional presence, newscast opens can also contain visuals of identifiable personalities, sports teams, architecture, and geography. Obviously, however, the station cannot become a regional force unless it makes a comprehensive effort to cover news of the region. That means the news operation must pay attention to communities whenever something happens in them.

Today, given high levels of cable TV penetration, viewers can easily receive most major stations in their state of residence, regardless of their location. For this reason, and because state coverage is important to all viewers, more stations are expanding to statewide coverage and incorporating it under their umbrella of "regional" coverage. Stations routinely establish "bureaus" in outlying areas that employ at least a resident reporter and photographer, and resident statehouse reporters are commonplace.

Some reporters may contend that a given event in an outlying community isn't "news" because of its narrow focus or limited appeal. But narrow story focus does not automatically exclude a wide audience. When the reporter develops a story with the viewer's interests in mind, everyone wins. Producers also can remind reporters that audiences will never care more about a story than the reporter, and that the only thing that makes a story dull is a dull reporter.

Producers also can lean on reporters to use the telephone, and can use it themselves, to universalize the story. "If false alarms or bridge safety are a problem in one community, pick up the phone and find out if similar problems exist in other communities—including your own," says NuFuture.TV's Bill Taylor.[5] If you remember to followup on more angles than just "the" story, and insist on more followup from your reporters, you may soon be airing background stories on how false alarms are investigated, or why money in the road and bridge fund is collecting interest instead of being spent on bridge repairs.

IMPROVE AUDIO-VIDEO LINKAGE

Viewers are the clear winners when script content matches the pictures on the screen—that ideal marriage of words and pictures known throughout the industry as audio-video *linkage*, or *referencing*. Producers and reporters alike have an obligation to monitor linkage within all stories in the newscast and to make the linkage as consistently on target as possible. The goal is to reduce audience confusion by eliminating wallpaper video. This goal can be accomplished by following two simple rules. The first rule is: "Write the pictures first." The second rule is: "Don't talk about it unless you show it: See dog, say dog." The opposite approach, also valid, is expressed in the truism, "Say dog, see dog," although this approach may tend to place undue emphasis on the script with visuals serving as an afterthought.

VISUALS

Often the producer has little control over visuals that are returned from the field. The producer can exercise control, however, in which visuals make air. One consideration is to avoid video stories that begin with shots of a blank wall rather than "visual leads," or images that instantly and more obviously communicate the story to come. If the story is about child abuse, for example, little purpose is served in opening the story with a shot of the courthouse wall.

Another visual pet peeve of producers is **BOPSA**, or "bunch of people sitting around." Reporters and photojournalists who are at a loss for more meaningful visuals to tell the story frequently bring home lots of BOPSA. Members of their audience with remote controls just as frequently tune out of the newscast at the appearance of BOPSA. Producers also can work with reporters to avoid going "head-to-head" from standups or interviews at the end of packages when the camera cuts back to an anchor on set. If the shot of the person seen in the last shot of the package (the head) is nearly identical in registration with the studio shot of the anchor (the other head), the show has a problem.

FRESHEN FILE VIDEO

In monitoring the visual appearance of the newscast, producers should try to avoid constant reruns of file video. Often, the station may have only a few seconds of video showing a murder suspect walking to court, or of the shootout in which a prison escapee was killed, so the shot tends to be used cover and over ad nauseum as story updates are aired. Among the offenders in this category are file shots of the lamentable space shuttle explosion, shots of navy frigates under missile attack in the Persian Gulf, and stale footage showing the aftermath of airline crashes as the investigations advance over weeks, months, or even years. The solution is to use file video sparingly and to update file video so that audiences are exposed to somewhat fresher images as time progresses (Figure 13.5).

USE TALKING HEADS WITH PURPOSE

Another way to improve the newscast's look and reduce viewer confusion, is to re-examine how talking heads are used. Viewers are frequently subjected to sound bites in which a person can be seen talking while the reporter's voice continues at full volume but with sound from the bite low under and barely audible. Each night viewers by the tens of thousands struggle to make out what the person is saying, while the reporter's voice-over narrative makes such comprehension impossible. Reporters practice the technique somewhat automatically, perhaps having never considered the effect on viewers. But during editing no reporters have ever turned down the sound of their own voice-over narration, while allowing sound bites to continue full up over the narrative. Yet reporters daily perpetrate on viewers in virtually all markets the same travesty in reverse.

To correct the problem, the producer can insist on the elimination of all competing sound when bites are on screen and can recommend as a matter of policy that anchors and reporters never talk over video of talking heads. Allowing speakers to be heard is simply a matter of courtesy and common sense. If a person can be seen talking on screen, he or she also should be heard. If the talking head imparts information more effectively than any other means, then it should be used.

The most gratuitous use of talking heads occurs when they are used as visual chewing gum to illustrate a sentence of voice-over copy in which the person's name is mentioned, or as the mandatory sound bite within a package because nothing better is available. If the sound bite lends nothing other than visual identification of a person mentioned in the script, then perhaps it should be converted to a stiff-frame graphic in a window alongside the anchor, or even be eliminated.

FIGURE 13.5 File video provides a valuable resource to illuminate otherwise nonvisual stories. Care should be taken to use such video sparingly, update it whenever possible, and identify it in the broadcast as file footage, with a super.

WEATHER AND SPORTS

Weather and sports provide unusual challenges for the producer because often these sections of the newscast are treated as little "islands" somehow separate and apart from the main show. Frequently, weather and sports talent act as their own producers and may not even be accountable to the news producer. Such autonomous identity can produce a "hands-off-my-show" mentality and a sense of "us–them" rather than the more desirable "us–us" view in which everyone contributes to help achieve commonly held goals.

At the very least in such situations, the producer can negotiate to keep emphasis on the weather in perspective. On days when severe weather has struck or is imminent, it may be appropriate to lead the newscast with weather-related stories and even to bring the weather anchor on set to report weather developments that constitute hard news. At other times when there are only a few, thin, scattered clouds and another week of temperatures in the mid-70s to report, the weather may even be shortened to make room for more important breaking news.

Audiences are usually most interested in local temperatures, current conditions, and an immediate forecast that covers weather for the next couple of days. Such information usually can be communicated in two to two-and-a-half minutes. If the weathercaster insists that four minutes are required, it may be time for the producer to initiate more serious negotiation.

Sports anchors also are accountable for the time they devote to sports. The justification can be based on the amount of interesting and significant sports news available that day. Some news operations even require that the sports department justify its selection of stories in the sportscast, just as news must justify its selection. The goal is to keep the sportscast pace moving and its content relevant to viewer interests.

Because of network coverage, local stations are almost forced to compete with an industry look in sports. Viewers accustomed to the professional polish and pace of network sportscasts have come to expect similar use of pictures and comparable pacing in local sports coverage. To compete more effectively, stations can make greater use of video in sports and can create more compelling sportscasts by concentrating more on the people angle in their stories.

While sports is about winning and losing, and about scoreboards and won-and-lost columns, the most interesting sports (and news) has always been about the small human dramas inherent in athletic competition. Audiences still want to know who won the game, but if the sportscast is to appeal to the widest possible audience it must become more "people oriented," with less emphasis on scoreboards and more emphasis on storytelling and human drama.

Producers and assignment editors are journalists, and in a real sense they are reporters. Often the assignment editor is the first reporter on a story, sometimes the primary reporter. Just as important is the role of the producer, who must place stories within the context of the newscast, suggest graphics that will better tell the story, and help orchestrate that overwhelmingly complex information assembly line called the newsroom. While many are called to try their hands at these sometimes perplexing occupations, only the best qualify to be chosen.

SUMMARY

Successful news organizations operate by news philosophies that reflect understanding of the communities they serve. This community understanding serves inevitably to make the assignment editor and producer partners in building the daily newscast.

The assignment editor monitors the news day, helps conceptualize news packages, and schedules and assigns reporting crews to cover stories. The producer is the architect of the newscast who helps determines story selection, the news lineup, and the use of various production elements within the newscast.

Both the producer and assignment editor may help write newscasts. At some stations, a news planner assists the assignment editor by generating ideas for stories and series and by conducting research and helping plan story coverage. Private individuals called stringers may be paid to shoot stories in outlying areas that would otherwise be difficult or impossible to cover.

At face value, journalism would seem to be mostly accounts of "bad news." Often, however, news is neither good nor bad, but simply a reflection of how it's treated. Most viewers want a balance of news that fairly represents what is happening in the viewer's many areas of interest and concern. Some "bad news" stories that start out with a negative emotional weight can be reasonably and fairly converted to a neutral or even a positive emotional charge. Of great importance is the need for assignment editors and producers to avoid long strings of negative or bad news stories.

Historically, newscasts have been built on a foundation of spot-news stories and information from special interest groups, including business, governments, and other public and private institutions. Such stories are relatively easy to identify and cover. But of at least equal importance in building a community newscast are enterprise stories, which result in a sense of story ownership and the need for followup on the part of both reporters and photographers. No one must wait for the assignment editor to assign a story.

As the station proves its worth to the community, management may seek to build larger audiences by establishing the station as a regional force. At such times, it is incumbent on the photographer and reporter to universalize stories from outlying regions and to relate them to the interests and concerns of viewers from the more immediate viewing areas.

Also important is the need to integrate sports into the newscast, rather than allow it to remain an island unto itself.

Communication between the assignment editor and producer is vital, as is their willingness to maintain communication with all members of the reporting team, including anchors, photographers, and reporters.

DISCUSSION

1. Describe the typical duties of an assignment editor and discuss the assignment editor's role in the reporting process.

2. Describe the job of the news planner and contrast it with the duties of the assignment editor.

3. Describe the duties of the newscast producer and discuss the producer's role in the reporting process.

4. Define a personal news philosophy that incorporates a sense of responsiveness to the needs of the community in which you reside.

5. In what sense do viewers help dictate the definitions of news at their favorite stations?

6. Discuss the philosophy that contends there is no such thing as good news or bad news, but simply news and how you treat it.

7. Describe and provide an example of how the content of a story with an emotional weight of minus can be converted to an emotional weight of zero or even plus. Is the change of emphasis in your example ethically and professionally valid?

8. List and describe the most common sources of news. Contrast the impact of traditional news sources on news content with stories that originate by virtue of reporter enterprise.

9. Discuss the importance of story followup and story ownership as the concepts relate to television photographers and reporters.

10. Enumerate the most important considerations influencing news content, treatment, and story lineup in the typical newscast.

11. To what extent should news anchors interact with reporters and photographers and be considered as members of the reporting team? To what extent should anchors adhere to the concept that "all performance follows content"?

12. What is the role of the news tease in attracting and holding news viewers? Provide at least two examples of visual news teases that a photojournalist could originate for stories being shot in the field and that could be aired without the need for reporter or anchor voice-over narration (such as a shot of sheriff's officers breaking down the door to enter a suspected illegal gambling casino just outside the city limits).

13. How can the photographer and reporter help to make a television station a more regional force?

14. How can producers, reporters, and photographers work together to eliminate "wallpaper video" and achieve more precise audio-video linkage?

15. In your role as a photojournalist, describe steps you can take to freshen or update file video of one-time news events in which only a few seconds of video could originally be photographed.

16. Discuss the steps a station might take to better integrate the sports and weather departments into the daily news operation, rather than allow them to remain as islands unto themselves. Why is such integration important?

EXERCISES

1. Invite a television assignment editor and newscast producer to class to discuss their respective duties.

2. Arrange to visit a television station to observe activities on the assignment desk. It may be possible for you to arrange a weekend visit, when the assignment editor may have more time to spend with you.

3. If you have access to a broadcast-quality camera or to a good quality home video camera, contact your local station about appointment as a news stringer.

4. Interview community leaders and television viewers in your community to identify what they feel are the most important problems and issues in the community. Determine the extent to which these same individuals believe that local media, especially television news operations, are partners in the problem-solving process.

5. Conduct exercise #4, but instead of interviewing community leaders and television viewers, talk with local news directors, assignment editors, and producers. Further, ask them to describe their news philosophies and attitudes about the community.

6. Interview a random but representative selection of ten or more television viewers in your community and ask them what they expect of their favorite newscasts, and the extent to which they expect the station to become involved in the community.

7. Write a position statement no longer than three double-spaced, typewritten pages outlining the news philosophy that you recommend a station to follow. Define your views of how station employees should think of their obligation to the community. Determine an identifiable style and mood for the daily newscast, and identify proper values for news treatments, production, and promotion activities that will help attract, hold, and properly inform news viewers.

8. Test the concept that "there is no good news or bad news, but only news and how you treat it." Using a "bad news" or otherwise negative newspaper or television story as your starting point, try to fairly and accurately convert story emphasis to an emotional weight of zero (neutral) or even plus (positive).

9. List ten enterprise stories that you could assign yourself or another reporter or photographer today without having to wait for an assignment from the assignment editor.

10. Consult back issues of your local newspaper to find a story that was reported several weeks or months ago, and do a followup story on your own.

11. View a local television newscast to determine (a) the content and number of stories in each of the news segments between commercials and (b) the approximate emotional weight of each story (minus, zero, or plus). List each story and its emotional weight in a table for easy comparison.

12. Be alert for news teases that may appear "on the half-hour" during daytime and evening prime-time hours. Record or write down, verbatim, any teases you hear. After you have watched the stories on the late evening newscast, rewrite the original teases to improve them. In each instance, include both the original tease and your rewrite.

13. Record an off-air story from a television newscast. Identify a shot or short sequence that could be used on the air as a visual tease, or else go out and shoot a visual tease that would have worked for the story that aired. Consider choosing a noncontroversial story, and avoid imposing on any of the subjects who appeared in the original report if you decide to retrace a story.

14. Watch your favorite television newscast for a week and assess the extent to which the station attempts to project a regional presence. List any devices the station uses to project itself as a regional force.

15. Record and study a local newscast to determine how precisely the audio-video linkage is controlled in stories. Also be on the alert for the use of stale or outdated file video. If you encounter obviously out-of-date video, think of ways to freshen the images.

16. View a sportscast and describe in two or three double-spaced, typewritten pages the steps that could be taken to improve the cast. Include observations about such considerations as length of the cast, individual story length, story count, graphics, production values, effective storytelling methods, emphasis on scores versus people, coverage of major and minor sports, use of visuals, quality of writing, and the sports anchor and reporters.

NOTES

1. Bill Brown, "How to Survive as a Reporter," a presentation at Colorado State University, 23 March 1987.

2. John F. Lansing, "Develop Good Habits," *News Photographer* (12 December 1985), 27.

3. Ibid.

4. Bill Taylor, comments at a television news workshop, Columbia, SC, 14 June 2003.

5. Taylor, conversation with the author, 5 March 1987.

CHAPTER FOURTEEN

SPORTS PHOTOGRAPHY AND REPORTING

BOB BURKE AND MARCIA NEVILLE

Sports reporting and photography sometimes are treated as islands unto themselves, somehow separate and distinct from news or the rules and philosophies that govern news reporting. While distinctions exist, this chapter acknowledges the common ground on which compelling sports highlights and sports feature reporting are based. It is the work of Bob Burke and Marcia Neville, a husband–wife team at KCNC-TV, Denver. In the first part, chief photographer and sports producer Bob Burke shares essential observations about effective sports photography. In the second part, sports reporter Marcia Neville follows up with a comprehensive guide to sports reporting. Most of the ideas apply to virtually all sports and assume that you know something about the sport you intend to photograph or report. If you know little about a particular sport, either read up on it or have someone explain it before you shoot a single frame.

HOW TO BE A GREAT SPORTS PHOTOGRAPHER

Too often sports coverage is all about production these days. It's all eye candy. Storytelling really takes a backseat, and that makes me crazy. My message is to challenge yourself to do more than simply shoot highlights.

The great sports photographers can capture what happened, why it happened, and what it all means. The "greats" focus on the essence of sports—the emotion, the competition, the pain, and the glory. Highlights and music are fun, but there's so much more if you look for it.

Take it another step. Break down the action that makes the highlight happen. Capture the emotion. Get the pictures that allow viewers to make the connection with an athlete or a team. And to do that you have to understand sports. It's not necessary that you have played the sports you will cover, but it helps. In this job, you have to know a little bit about a lot of things. When you shoot a city council meeting, you have to know what the format is, what the issues are, and what sides the participants are on. Same with shooting sports. You have to know what the game is, how it will be played, and who the players are.

I'm so disappointed when job applicants show up with a montage of football highlights and music and pass it off as a "story." Sports afford us so many opportunities to tell great stories! You can't help but have a beginning, middle, and end. It's like the "idiots guide to storytelling," it's so easy. So I go crazy when I see a sports story that's nothing but highlights and dissolves and talking heads.

FIGURE 14.1   Bob Burke, photojournalist, KCNC Denver.

I'll never forget one of my first sports assignments. I was sent to shoot a feature on a record-setting high school shot-putter at a local school. "No problem," I told myself. The reporter and I found our subject on the practice field, throwing the shot. I set up the camera and asked the athlete to go about his normal practice routine while I took pictures for the story. The shot-putter walked into frame, spun around a couple of times and lofted the heavy metal ball into the distance. I looked down at the counter time on the tape deck and found that I had a great eight-second shot. I asked the athlete what else he did during practice. 'That's it," he said. Panic set in. How was I going to make a two-minute story out of an eight-second act? I would have shoot the young man throwing the heavy metal ball fourteen or fifteen times, just to have enough tape to cover the story. But if you take pride in your work, you know that type of reasoning just won't cut it.

Ultimately, the same elements that make for a good news story make for a good sports story. Like news stories, sports stories need a beginning, middle, and end, sequences, natural sound, and matched action. If anyone ever hands you the line "Don't worry about it, it's just sports," don't buy it. Sports are just as important as the news and deserve just as much attention. In sports, like news, professionals dare not ignore the fundamentals of photojournalism nor break the rules that govern the art of storytelling (Figure 14.2).

THE BIGGEST PROBLEM IN SPORTS PHOTOGRAPHY

The biggest problem you will encounter in most sports photography occurs when you look through the viewfinder and try to follow people or objects moving at high speed

FIGURE 14.2 Sports photojournalists follow many of the same photographic practices and reporting fundamentals as the news photographer.

in unpredictable directions. If it is hard to follow a hit baseball with the naked eye, imagine how much more difficult it is to follow it while you're squinting into a viewfinder. Without practice, it can be almost impossible. And not only must you follow that tiny speck, you must keep it in focus, properly composed in the frame, and correctly exposed.

The first time I shot a sports story, I ended up shooting such a wide shot of the field that no one could tell what was happening. When I tried to edit the footage, I found I had so worried about following the ball that I overlooked some of the most important hallmarks of a well-told story—the cutaways, sequences, and matched action. Experience will be your best teacher, but there are a few tricks of the trade.

How to Follow Sports Action

The wider the shot, the easier it is to follow action. But the wider the shot, the less exciting the pictures will be. Consider the example of a quarterback who drops back to throw a pass. It's easier just to shoot a wide shot of players running around while a tiny speck flies across the screen (Figure 14.3). But it's more exciting if you begin with a tight shot of the quarterback's face as he drops back to pass, follow the ball in the air as it's thrown, and stay with the ball until the receiver gathers it in.

When you first start to photograph such shots, begin with a tight shot of the action and gradually widen out until you find the composition that best shows the bal-

FIGURE 14.3 An important responsibility of the sports photographer is learning to follow the ball smoothly and fluidly.

ance of the action. Most important, follow the action. You don't want to miss the game-winning touchdown because you were so tight you couldn't follow the play.

The sports photographer typically receives three types of assignments: (1) shoot **highlights,** (2) shoot a feature story, or (3) shoot highlights and feature at the same time, the toughest assignment of all. The amount of risk you can afford to take when following action depends on the assignment and the type of story you are covering.

HOW TO SHOOT SPORTS HIGHLIGHTS

When you are assigned to shoot baseball highlights, your job is to come back with the big plays of the game. In this case your risk factor is high. If the game is decided by a home run in the ninth inning and you miss it, everything you've shot up to that point is worthless.

To protect yourself, find a shooting location that gives you an unobstructed view of the entire field. Since all action flows from home plate, the best position is directly behind and, preferably, above the backstop. From this position the angles at which the ball comes off the bat are less severe, so the ball is easier to follow.

Almost any other position results in action that moves right to left, or vice versa. Such action is more difficult to follow because it tends to travel out of your

...s easiest to follow when it is coming at you or moving away
...rself accordingly.

) Capture the Play

...) shoot sports, photograph the beginning of most play with a fairly
...gain more confidence, you can tighten your shot. Avoid shots that
...ever, since your first priority is to capture the play. When you shoot
...ning the shot around the pitcher and batter. Such composition allows
...low the ball.

...e ball is hit, try following the ball instead of the batter, just as though
you are a fan in the stands. While some photographers like to follow the batter, most
fans follow the ball. Similarly, in football, it is more natural to follow the ball after the
quarterback throws it than to follow the quarterback. It is, however, easier to follow
the batter or the quarterback, and if you don't have success following the ball (don't
feel bad if you don't), then follow the batter or quarterback instead. Usable shots are
the goal.

Follow the Action Smoothly

Jerky, sudden camera movements distract the viewer, so strive to make whatever you
shoot look smooth. If a ball hit to left field disappears from frame as you move your
camera to follow it, your tendency may be to panic and to start panning and tilting in
an effort to find it. A better approach is to stay on course and look for signs that indicate where the ball is headed. Players may be running or looking in a certain direction,
for example, and will actually "point" you toward the ball.

If that approach fails, stop where you are for a moment to create an edit point. A
cut from a moving shot makes for a rough-looking edit. Once you have created an edit
point, look for your next shot, usually the batter running the bases or turning back to
the dugout after he realizes he's out. The need for smooth movement and edit points
also applies if you've been lucky enough to follow the ball.

Protect the Plate

Remember, also, to "protect the plate." Assume you have a runner on third base and
the batter hits a single to right field. The fielder gathers in the ball and throws it to the
infield. Meantime, the runner at third has scored. In this case, follow the ball until you
realize it's a base hit and the runner can advance. Pause for a second to create an edit
point, then as fast as possible, find home plate and wait for the runner to score. Shots
of scoring runs are important to highlights. Obviously, you can edit out the abrupt
camera movement that enabled you to focus the camera on home plate.

Shoot Cutaways

Protect yourself against jump cuts by shooting plenty of cutaways, such as shots of fans,
the scoreboard, and players in the dugout. Jump cuts are offensive wherever they show

up. Cutaways also will help cover any problems you may have had while trying to follow the ball.

HOW TO SHOOT SPORTS FEATURES

Shooting a sports feature involves all the skills you need to shoot highlights, as well as an ability to create sequences, shoot matched action, and develop a beginning, middle, and end for your story. Surprisingly, it is easier to do these things when shooting a sports story than on most any other assignment.

Sports are custom-made for sequence shooting and matched action. In baseball, the pitcher is always on the mound and the batter is always at the plate. In football, the center always snaps the ball to start the play, the linemen always crash into each other, and the quarterback always gets the ball. Whatever sport you are shooting, take a moment to think about the basic action and break it down into its elements.

Say your assignment is to shoot a story about a baseball player who leads the league in home runs. Since your focus will be his ability to hit, the most important shots will happen when the player is up to bat, and it is then that your risk factor will be highest. When he's batting, shoot nothing but the subject so that you are on the shot if he hits a home run. When he's not at bat, shoot cutaways and the other elements you will need for sequences and matched action.

Each time your subject prepares to bat, for example, he may pull his bat from the rack and rub rosin on his hands to get a good grip. He then walks from the dugout to the on-deck circle, swings the bat a few times to warm up, and watches the game until it's his turn to bat. At that point he walks to the plate, knocks the dirt off his cleats, takes his batting stance, and awaits the pitch. Even before he's taken a swing, you have a nice eight-second sequence. And the batter will do the same things next time he's up, so you can photograph further matched-action shots, such as a wide shot of the batter in the on-deck circle and a tight shot of his face as he walks to the plate. Remember to allow the player to move into and out of your shots as a way to smooth the flow of action during editing when you must condense the action to fit a one-and-a-half minute story.

Even when the batter is in the dugout, you can continue to make shots of action on the playing field that can later be incorporated into matched action sequences of the batter. Most basic sports action is repetitive and chances are good the same pitcher will be throwing to the next batter. This means you can make a shot of him throwing to the next player as part of a sequence involving the real subject of your story.

Again, in feature stories, cutaways are essential. Whenever someone else is at bat, make shots of the catcher, fielders, the manager, fan reaction, and wide shots of other players at bat. When you edit together all these shots, along with the shot of your subject at bat, it will magically look as if you had five cameras shooting the story. You will find yourself with a story that moves quickly and is visually exciting.

A final precaution whenever you shoot sports features is to move in as close to the subject as possible. Often, a field-level location is ideal for such stories. Remember, however, to move around. Shoot as many different angles of the action as you can. A variety of angles helps in editing and make your story more visually interesting.

HOW TO SHOOT A SPORTS FEATURE
AND HIGHLIGHTS SIMULTANEOUSLY

The most difficult assignment is to shoot a sports feature and highlight the same time. Although sports action is repetitive, it also is unique. The batter will hit that five-hundred-foot home run only once, and the shortstop will make that game-saving catch only once. So how do you keep from missing the biggest play of the game while you take all those shots you will need to make a good feature story? The answer is to take calculated risks.

Shoot nothing but game action during critical situations, such as when bases are loaded with two out in the ninth inning. Shoot your other shots when things aren't so crucial, and hope nothing big happens while your attention is diverted. Above all, try to be aware of what's happening in the game at all times. Don't just turn on the camera and shoot pictures. Know why things are happening. This approach helps ensure that you won't miss the big plays you need for the highlights and that you know what pictures you will need to tell the feature story.

You can take advantage of the time when one swing of the bat won't turn the tide of the game, for instance, or of the time between innings. Use this time to shoot cutaways, or to make isolated shots of your subject and other players. Show the batter stepping up to the plate or the pitcher throwing the ball or perhaps the infielder poised for action. Next, you can show the batter again, either swinging at the pitch or letting it go by. Such shots will be useful in both your highlights and the feature story.

Anticipate the Action

Whatever sport you photograph, anticipation is important. When the quarterback looks ready to make a pass, be ready to move with the ball. Here, two considerations are important. First, have your body already turned slightly down field so that you can turn to follow the ball's flight more smoothly. Second, when the quarterback cocks the ball behind his head, place the ball in the bottom of frame. This technique gives you more room in the frame to follow the ball once it is released.

Use Natural Sound to Lend Interest

Sports have great natural sounds that photographers and editors can use to get away from that tiresome routine of narration/sound bite/narration in sports stories. Sounds of the fans and of bodies crunching together can help bring a sports story to life. Music also can be added to a sports story, but just like the use of slow-motion in sports, a little often goes a long way (Figure 14.4).

Interest also can be added to sports through changes in camera angle and perspective. Take the camera off your shoulder or tripod occasionally and shoot from a different perspective than eye level. Viewers like to see the action from different angles.

Be Aware of Danger

Shooting sports can be dangerous. In most cases the photographer is close to the action, and the action usually involves bodies and objects flying around with great force

FIGURE 14.4   The sounds of game action, from the crack of a bat to the roar of a crowd, lend realism to sports reports. Here, the sounds are captured with a parabolic dish.

and speed. If you get in the way, you lose. Who among us has not seen a photographer run over on the football sidelines?

The sports photographer's potential for injury is further heightened because vision is limited to what can be seen in the viewfinder. Your peripheral vision is eliminated. If you are zoomed in to a tight shot of the quarterback twenty yards downfield, you have no way of knowing what is happening right in front of you. An ugly scenario can quickly ensue: The quarterback drops back and throws a pass right toward you. You have anticipated the pass and are able to follow the ball. A great shot is in the making. Gradually, you pull back to a wide shot to show the receiver catching the ball, when—BAM—the receiver runs into you. You were watching the ball and couldn't tell that it was headed out of bounds. Neither could the receiver, who followed it until he collided with you.

To prevent such endings, have your reporter or someone else you trust to watch out for you while you're shooting. And if you sense the action may be coming too close, pull your eye from the viewfinder and see what's happening. There will be other shots and it's most important to protect yourself and the athletes. And remember that if someone runs into you and is injured, it's your fault. Keep a safe distance from the action; your lens will bring it to you.

Most important whenever you're in the field, remember to think for yourself all the time. Don't wait for the reporter to tell you to take this or that shot, but do work as a team and communicate with one another. It's a much better story when the words and pictures mesh.

WHY I HAD TO BE A SPORTS REPORTER

I was two weeks into my first job as a night side television news reporter and my assignment was city council. The meeting had already begun as we entered the room and discussion was heated. But, who was that talking and what were they arguing about? I froze. No one wore numbered jerseys to identify themselves and there was no scoreboard to show which side was winning. Here, there were no rules I could understand, but somehow I muddled through. That's when I knew I had to be a sports reporter. After three hours' effort, I don't need to hear that the council will delay its decision. I need to know that some team won the game. I need sports action and its excitement. More than anything, I need pictures. Ever try telling a minute-and-a-half story with nothing but meeting video? Nothing is more boring. In contrast, sports with its instant winners and losers is action-packed, a story full of visuals just waiting to be told. In a good sports report a good sports reporter conveys that excitement through both pictures and sound. Athletics rank pretty low in the scheme of worldwide events, but that's exactly why viewers are so intrigued by them.

FIGURE 14.5   Marcia Neville, sports reporter, KCNC Denver.

ORIGINALITY COUNTS

Now, more than ever, the teams and their games are an escape, so it's our job to keep the fun in our coverage. What a sportscaster is not allowed to be is boring. The sports report is the portion of the newscast that begs for personality, even irreverence! So, add a spark of originality to every single story you report. Find a new angle on an old story. Be a little "off center." Make a commitment not to take yourself, or your subject, too seriously. And, reignite that spark each time you get a new assignment. Most of all, work hard to find a different way to tell the same story everyone else is telling. Some time ago a Denver Broncos place-kicker was in the midst of a tough string of games. Not only had he missed some crucial field goals, he kept hitting the uprights. Most reporters asked him about the problem and did slow-motion replays of the misses, but one reporter added the "spark." He invited the kicker out on the field to try and hit the uprights! That's the kind of storytelling that makes an impression, and viewers remember.

BE PREPARED

Sports have an impact beyond the playing field which means that, like it or not, every reporter in a newsroom will end up on the sports beat at some time. Whether it's minor league baseball in a small town, or the NBA in a large city, the games and the players are important to fans, politicians, and the Chamber of Commerce. Because so many people are affected, assignment desks often send general assignment reporters out to cover news angles on sports stories. So, even if your beat is city council and you have no interest in athletics, you will end up covering sports. Don't let the prospect intimidate you, just be ready. Read the sports section. Stay current. Know who runs things and keep an updated list of contacts. More than anything, you're a reporter. Whether you're covering city economics or the bankruptcy of a ball team, it's just another story. And, if you get that dreaded "game story" assignment, relax. Go in with as much knowledge as possible and don't be afraid to ask questions. Even when the veteran sports reporters are doing interviews about plays you didn't even notice, you can usually get everything you need from one of those broad "What do you think made the difference?" questions.

IN-FIELD SPORTS REPORTING

Once you work your way up to covering the big leagues and major colleges, your job becomes easier. At that level, you're always provided full rosters, updated statistics, and play-by-play running accounts of the games. But, on the minor league or high school level, it's a whole different story. Here, you're on your own. And, since most of us begin our careers on this local level, we have to be ready for the challenges. Consider the coverage of a high school football game, for example. Your assignment is to cover the night's big game between the undefeated cross-town rivals and to provide a one-minute package for the late 11 p.m. newscast. The game is scheduled for 7 p.m. and should end around 9:30, leaving you plenty of time to conduct interviews and pull the story together under deadline (Figure 14.6).

Arrive Early

Ideally, you beat the crowd and avoid parking hassles by arriving at the stadium well before kickoff. As your photographer relaxes and settles in, you head off in search of rosters. If you're lucky, you were handed a program at the gate, but typically we're told there are no programs. That's when you're on your own and should be ready to suffer writer's cramp!

Identify Every Player

There's really no option here but to write down every single name and number, not just the starters. That way, when the third-string defensive lineman scoops up the fumble and scores the winning touchdown, you're covered.

And, if you do receive one of those precious programs, don't depend on it to be correct. Take the time to head up to the press box and ask about any roster changes.

FIGURE 14.6   Sports reporters must often rely on their own initiative in compiling game rosters, statistics, and other crucial information, especially when covering sports at the minor league or high school level.

You're much better off finding out about them at the stadium instead of later back at the office. Life becomes difficult at 10:45 p.m. when your notes show #83 catching the game-winning touchdown and your roster only lists #82 and #84. Once everyone's identified, it's game time! Depending on conditions, you and your photographer will choose to shoot on the sidelines or from a high location. While sideline photography provides the more exciting shots, not all photographers are comfortable shooting there, and deciding to shoot high almost guarantees that you won't miss any of the action. Whichever location you decide on, it's important to stay with your photographer. In sports, as in news, reporters and photographers are a team.

Keep a Play-By-Play Log

By now you've synchronized your watch with the camera time code and you're ready to keep track of the game. Reporters use different systems for taking game notes. Some jot down only the "highlights," such as quarterback sacks or touchdown runs. Others advise a more complete approach where you're actually keeping a play-by-play account of the game. It may be more work but, in the end, making a note of every single play provides the extra information that makes you a better storyteller. For example, let's say it's midway through the second quarter and the quarterback completes a pass. Using your logbook you confirm that this is his first completion and the team's only first down so far. It's good information that could make its way into your story later on, and the kind of fact you're not likely to get from anyone but yourself. Remember, on the local level, you're on your own.

Write Down Each Play

Keeping the log is reasonably simple. Come up with your own code to keep track of downs, yardage, and the ball carrier. On big plays, jot down a simple description of the play and the corresponding time code. When you return to the station you won't have time to look at the play before writing the script, so it helps to have a reminder on paper of how the play developed. The log will tell you that the player cut left and broke two tackles. In your notebook the play might look something like this:

>   1 + 10W:30W   7W>10W (left) far brk 2Ts** (7:20) w/5:40 2Q
>   1 + 10W:30B

Decipher the code and this is what you get: first and ten for the white team on its own thirty, quarterback #7 hands off to #10, who cuts left toward the far sideline and shakes off two tackles. We know he picked up forty yards because the play started on his thirty and the next play begins on their thirty. According to time code, the play can be found at 7:20 on the tape and, in case it's important later, the play happened midway through the second quarter (Figure 14.7). The two asterisks are also part of the "code." The first indicates that this is a potentially big play. The second confirms that the photographer has a good shot of the play and it is available for broadcast.

Always remember to check with the photographer about shot availability *while you are still in the field.* When you write a script that calls for a play that's not on the tape

FIGURE 14.7 Logging important plays when photographing sports allows the editor to quickly locate key plays.

or not good enough for air, editing under deadline becomes even more pressure-packed than normal. Remember, too, that the photographer's input is a big part of the creative process. Communication in the field helps ensure that you air the best product possible (Figure 14.8).

Communicate with the Photographer

Often the reporter is the photographer's "eyes." If the viewfinder is focused on a close up of the coach, the photographer doesn't know that a player is limping off the field. Without the reporter's help, the photographer may not realize that the injured player is a star lineman. And, unless the reporter speaks up, the photographer won't know to shoot more than a five second shot of the player leaving the field. When you know you're going to need a particular shot, tell the photographer. Don't assume you're both thinking the same thing.

Shoot the Standup Bridge

Now, it's halftime. And, since there's nothing worse than doing your standup during the game and missing a big play, this is a great time to do a bridge from the first half to the second. Keep your on-camera time short and informative. For a one-minute package eight to twelve seconds should be enough. And, try to be active. If your energy level

FIGURE 14.8 Throughout the reporting process, strong reporting requires ongoing communication between all members of the sports reporting team.

and delivery don't match the excitement of the game you'll slow down the pace of the entire package.

Conduct Postgame Interviews

Let's assume that the team that struggled in the first half managed to come back to win. The quarterback threw for 200 yards in the second half including the game-winner in the game's final minute. Time for the postgame interviews. If you need to talk to the losers, it's always a good idea to round them up first. They tend to disappear, while the winners will stick around. When you talk to the winners you'll want to ask the quarterback what changed from the first half to the second. You'll want to know what was said at halftime and you'll want to ask about any specific plays you plan to use in that night's report. It's always a good idea to ask participants to describe key plays (Figure 14.9). In this case you can ask both the quarterback and the receiver to describe the winning pass play, with the intention to run video of the play over that description in the finished story.

You'll find that high school athletes can give a pretty good interview, and if they give you strong responses, interviews with the coaches are usually unnecessary. It's the players and the excitement of their moment that will impress viewers the most.

Ask "Next-Day" Questions

Since this is such a big game, you will probably be responsible for a followup package on tomorrow's evening news. Prepare for that report with "next-day" questions during your interviews. Find out what the win means for the rest of the season and ask

FIGURE 14.9   Postgame interviews are an important part of the sports report.

what's next. Simple questions that look ahead are often enough to add a new angle for the day after.

Plan the Story

Now, it's 9:45 p.m. and you're headed back to the station, thinking about the story, and writing in the car. You've been allotted only one minute for action, stand-up, and interview. So, decide what's most important. In this case, it's the comeback. You'll set it up by showing the losing team taking the lead, go to the halftime bridge, and finish it off with the winning throw and the sound of the players describing it. If there's time, throw in a "Gee, it's great to win" sound bite, and you're done for the night! On game nights that don't feature undefeated cross-town rivals, it's a challenge to give same-night, quickly edited, highlights packages a "spark." That's when it's important to look for ways to tell a solid story from the game rather than just running down a list of highlights.

Next Day Follow-Up

To make your day-after report stand out from the competition, you may want to head out to afternoon practice the next day, or even better, physical therapy the next morning. Talk to the quarterback about the pain of success as he ices down his arm, or, head to the other side of town and find out what next week's opponent thought of the win. It always helps to find a truly new element to keep viewers informed and interested, even entertained.

FEATURE REPORTING

If the same game were to be played out of town, with no live capability, the result would be a feature story rather than a same-night highlight package. The two approaches require different video because a good feature includes more than just game action. That's why you would probably choose to shoot the feature story from the sidelines. On the field you can record natural sound from the game and the crowd while capturing the creative images that bring a feature story to life. For added spark, you may want to concentrate on one player. If you stay with the quarterback after he releases the ball, for example, and he gets hit hard, you have a new angle on how tough he is. Or, if he's well protected, you can visually show how good his offensive line is and focus the story in that direction. A play-by-play log is less important for a feature story, but you still need to stay in the game. As the photographer's rushing around to get all those great "color" shots, it's up to you to get him or her in position for the big plays. Then, before you write the story the next day, log the video yourself. Be aware of pictures and sound and write your story around both elements.

WRITING AND VOICING SPORTS

Sports is action, action is excitement, and excitement must come through in the audio portion of your story, both in style and delivery. Consequently, sports relies on a more rapid-fire approach to storytelling. In sports our scripts are written and narrated with a different energy than a traditional news report. Often what appears to be "bad" writing on the page sounds perfectly natural when it's voiced. There's no need to say, for example, "We're in the bottom of the second inning with a man on first base and another man on third base." Instead, while avoiding clichés, we go with some standard baseball patter, "Bottom of the second, runners at the corners. Joe Smith skies the ball. Homerun! 3–0 Crusaders." With a strong and enthusiastic delivery the writing comes alive and matches the energy of the moment. The unique story angles you initiate get an added spark through a fast-paced script and delivery.

AVOID PERSONAL INVOLVEMENT

Just as in the job of a news reporter, your job is to observe and report. But, in sports, it's very easy to get too dose to the teams and players we report on. So, be aware of the danger and avoid it. Know the players, love the team, but don't let your personal involvement interfere with your objectivity. There are days this job's not all fun and games. Reporting on cheating scandals or drug abuse cases is hard enough. Don't complicate it by allowing yourself to get too close to the people involved. But, with that said, I think you'll agree that TV sports reporting is one of the very best jobs around. I mean, look at how much people have to pay to get into sporting events . . . while we get paid to be there. I wouldn't trade it for the world!

SUMMARY

Sports reporting and photography follow rules and philosophies similar to those that govern news reporting. A prerequisite for all reporters and photographers is to know the sport they intend to report.

Sports Photography

One of the biggest challenges in sports photography is to look through the viewfinder and follow people or objects moving at high speed in unpredictable directions. Wide shots make it easier to follow action but are less exciting. An alternative is to begin the play on a tight shot and widen out to show the action as it progresses.

The sports photographer routinely receives three types of assignments: shoot highlights, shoot a feature story, or shoot highlights and a feature story at the same time. Shooting highlights means shooting the big plays of the game. A clear view of the entire playing field, preferably above the action, is essential if every potentially important play is to be photographed. In baseball and football, most photographers imitate the fans and try to follow the ball rather than the batter or quarterback.

Sports features call upon all the skills and techniques used to shoot highlights, as well as the ability to shoot sequences and matched action and develop a beginning, middle, and end for the story. When sports action is repetitive and predictable, these tasks are sometimes easier to accomplish. Smooth camera movement and the need for edit points apply in sports photography, just as in news. To protect against jump cuts, remember to shoot plenty of cutaways.

The most difficult assignment is to shoot a sports feature and highlights at the same time. A good approach is to shoot nothing but game action whenever a score appears to be imminent and to shoot the feature material when play is less critical. Just as in news photography, it pays to anticipate the action and to be aware of danger. Think for yourself, but remember to communicate with the reporter and to work as a team.

Sports Reporting

The best sports reports convey interest and excitement through both pictures and sounds. If the sports reporter is to outdistance the competition, every story needs a fresh angle or a similar spark of originality. One of the most important suggestions when covering sports is to be prepared. Know the team, the league, and the big rivals, know the club manager, and know something about the individual players. Never be afraid to ask questions.

Often, the biggest difficulties occur in covering the minor leagues and high school sports. Big league and major college athletics supply full rosters, updated statistics, and quarter-by-quarter running accounts. If you're on your own, arrive early at the stadium, settle in, and make ready for kickoff. Check at the press box for any roster changes either before the game or at the half. If there are no programs, copy down every player's name and number. Throughout the game, stay with the photographer and keep track of the game with a play-by-play log. Remember to check with the photographer about shot availability while you're still in the field.

At halftime, shoot a short, informative standup bridge from first-half action to second. Interviews can be conducted after the game. If you plan to run a followup package on tomorrow's evening news, remember to ask next-day questions in your interview—questions such as what the game means for the rest of the season. Plan the story both in the field and during your return to the station. Decide what's important and what setup you need to introduce the big plays, and try to personalize the story.

For next-day followup stories, you may want to attend afternoon practice the next day and interview key players or possibly even the team's next opponents.

If the same game were to be played out of town, the result would be a feature story, as opposed to a same-night highlight package. You may want to shoot the feature story at field level and focus more on coaches, cheerleaders, fans, and players on the sidelines.

In sports, both the writing of scripts and voice-over narration can be carried out with greater enthusiasm than might be found in straight news reporting. But avoid becoming personally involved with the team you're covering, and be careful to avoid letting your feelings interfere with your objectivity.

DISCUSSION

1. Describe the important similarities between sports and news stories.

2. Discuss approaches that can help the sports photographer more easily follow people or objects moving at high speed in unpredictable directions.

3. What special considerations should be observed when shooting sports highlights action?

4. Describe useful techniques you can use when shooting sports feature stories.

5. What special considerations come into play when shooting a sports feature and high-lights simultaneously?

6. List the precautions to observe to protect your personal safety when you photograph sporting events.

7. Describe the most important hallmarks of the good sports report and the good sports reporter.

8. Why are big league sports sometimes easier to cover than minor league or high school athletics?

9. Describe the process and any special considerations involved in reporting a typical sports highlights story.

10. Describe the process and any special considerations involved in reporting a typical sports feature story.

11. Describe the practices and philosophies specific to writing and voicing sports copy.

12. Why is it important to avoid becoming personally involved with the players or coaches of the teams you cover?

EXERCISES

1. Attend a high school or college athletic event, such as a baseball or softball game, and practice photographing the action. Develop your ability to follow the action smoothly, and remember to create edit points in your shots. Use a home video camera if necessary.

2. Attend an athletic event and shoot a sports highlights story.

3. Attend an athletic event and shoot a sports feature story.

4. Try your ability to simultaneously shoot a sports feature story and game highlights.

5. Attend an athletic event, but this time leave the camera at home. Identify all players, keep a play-by-play log, and script a standup bridge at halftime. Later, write a voice-over script in which you identify the locations of any interviews you would use if this were an actual report.

6. Repeat Exercise 5, this time with a photographer and camera. Conduct postgame in-terviews and edit together a one-minute package of game highlights complete with voice-over narration and game interviews. Remember to ask next-day questions during your interviews. Re-read Chapter 11, "The Role of Talent Performance in Field Re-porting," before you begin this exercise.

7. From the materials you generated in Exercise 6, create a one-minute, next-day package complete with interviews and voice-over narration.

8. Prepare a sports feature report on a team's outstanding quarterback, pitcher, center, or other player, complete with video, interviews, a reporter standup, and voice-over narra-tion. Re-read Chapter 11, "The Role of Talent Performance in Field Reporting," be-fore you begin this exercise.

CHAPTER FIFTEEN

LAW AND THE BROADCAST JOURNALIST

Journalists are delegated responsibility each day to make ethical and legal judgments that hinge on familiarity with First Amendment guarantees of *freedom of press and speech*, Fourth Amendment guarantees of the individual's *right to privacy*, and Sixth Amendment guarantees of the *right to a public trial by an impartial jury*. Many legal transgressions—including invasion of privacy, libel, trespass, and contempt of court—occur in the field during the process of *gathering* the news. *Reporting* the news initiates still other legal questions.

The Internet brings even more questions to the table, such as who owns the rights to published or "repurposed" material, and whether journalists should observe a print or a broadcast legal model, or both, when using the Internet. If a site defames an individual or institution, who is responsible? Is it the original author, the on-line service, and/or the journalist who quoted the information? These questions are being answered in courts around the country.

ANYONE CAN SUE FOR ANYTHING

As another consideration, journalists who are unfamiliar with the state and federal statutes that govern news coverage are sitting ducks for those who seek to coerce through legal manipulation. Human imagination is boundless; people can sue for anything. Some news sources may use their apparent command of the law to censor or otherwise influence news reports and their timing.

This chapter discusses many of the legal questions journalists face routinely and offers guidelines to help journalists know when to seek advice. Although a generous application of fairness can help eliminate the need for some routine media advice from attorneys, the guiding rule should always be "If in doubt, seek help."

THE FOUR ESSENTIAL QUESTIONS

Broadcast journalists consequently need answers to four questions that occur frequently during the news gathering and reporting process:

- Does what I'm about to do violate state or federal law? Federal guidelines are different and usually tougher than state guidelines.
- Is what I'm about to do sanctioned by virtue of prior legal precedents as established through interpretations of the First Amendment?
- Can anyone stop us from what we're about to do?
- Could we go further?

Self-interest requires that you stay abreast of changes in the law that affect the answers to these questions. Even when you're on solid legal ground in reporting a story, if a suit is filed you remain at the mercy of human sympathy and emotion: Although what you've reported—and how you've reported it—might be safe in a perfect world, in a practical world the judge may well say, "Tell it to the jury." Because some judges and many juries are unfamiliar with media law, you and your station could face a lengthy, costly appeal to defend your right to report the story.

THE CHILLING EFFECT OF LITIGATION

Escalating court costs, damage awards, and attorney fees produce what has been called the "chilling effect" of litigation. The tendency of any reporter or station that's been burned by a jury is to become overly cautious. The probable consequence of two or three trials is that for the rest of your life, you'll restrict your hard-hitting journalism to very complimentary restaurant openings.

GATHERING THE NEWS

The right to speak and publish is usually considered to be protected by the First Amendment. Gathering news, however, is not always automatically protected, although the courts have generally held that if journalists are to report news they must also have the right to gather it.

As a general rule, when gathering news, journalists are free to go anywhere a person can go without special permission—so long as their equipment doesn't get in the way. Although journalists may attend a theatre opening, a political rally, or a courtroom trial, they virtually never can light, photograph, record, or transmit live pictures of these same events without first obtaining special permission.

The Journalist's Right of Access

The question of where television can go with all its hardware is being answered by the hour; as equipment becomes smaller, more inconspicuous, and less disruptive, the right of access to news events becomes less of a problem. Until the art of equipment miniaturization reaches its ultimate state of grace, however, journalists must rely on the time-honored customs of tact, diplomacy, decency, and common sense if they are to gain access to stories before they become history.

Defamation and Privacy

Nowhere in the law are reporters and photojournalists more likely to cost their stations money than in matters of libel (defamation) and invasion of privacy.

Libel is the use of factual information (as opposed to opinion) that holds someone in hatred or contempt, subjects the person to ridicule, or otherwise lowers our esteem for the individual. Defamation can occur as soon as you communicate a false statement of fact to a third party, even if you never broadcast the statement.

Invasion of privacy is any act of intrusion, including trespass and publication of embarrassing facts, even if true, that violates an individual's reasonable expectation to privacy (Figure 15.1). Invasion of privacy is actionable as soon as you intrude into someone's private area. As in the case of defamation, invasion of privacy suits can be brought against you and your station regardless of whether you publish a story.

Libel

Libel has been defined in the courts as malicious defamation, although in a broader context libel can be any statement that holds someone in hatred or contempt, subjects the person to ridicule, or lowers one's esteem for the person and therefore damages the individual's reputation. Property, businesses, and institutions also can be libeled.

FIGURE 15.1   The Fourth Amendment to the Constitution guarantees the individual's right to privacy. Violations of state or federal privacy laws can lead to a journalist being charged with invasion of privacy, trespass, eavesdropping, and unauthorized surveillance.

Although oral defamation might qualify as slander, in television news it's considered to be libel, even if the alleged defamation is made orally.

In the United States, media lose between 70 to 80 percent of defamation suits that go to jury, although historically about the same number of guilty verdicts have been reversed in appellate courts.[1] Even so, the great expense of jury trials is in itself a penalty that must be paid even if the station is vindicated.

Know the Statement Is True.   Because libel is a statement of information that constitutes defamation (as opposed to a statement of opinion), an excellent protection against liability is to have good reason to believe the statement is true. Few reporters can know with certainty that a statement is false. All most journalists can know about the allegations they report is what they see in a document or hear from a source. If the reporter is using valuative judgment words, they probably would fall under the heading of opinion, which cannot be false in the same sense that a statement of fact can be false.

Fortunately, for journalists to be liable for defamation, they must normally know the statement is false or be aware that it is probably false. Such latitude offers a heady measure of legal protection.

In some states a common test for defamation is negligence. In other words, courts look for evidence that the journalist used "due care" in evaluating the truth of the defamatory statement. To protect yourself against charges of negligence, always adopt a higher standard than the law sets. Ask yourself, "Do I believe the statement to be true?" This is a much easier and more practical question to ask than, "Do I believe the statement to be false?" This approach implies the need to go as far as possible to investigate the facts and to be certain that you've "jumped through every hoop" in determining the truth of your reporting.

Another test is to ask, "Whom am I talking about? Might what I report in some way lower our esteem for that person?" In applying such a test, it's important to remember that most substantive news is derogatory to someone. Still, if you can answer yes to the question "Does this look and feel authentic?" you'll probably be safe even if the statement later proves to be false. As yet another safeguard, ask yourself, "Does the public have a right to know this?" Perhaps the information addresses some aspect of public business, for example, or comes from sworn testimony or from subpoenaed information that is part of the court record.

Evaluating Sources to Eliminate Malice.   Whenever someone makes derogatory statements about another person, try to evaluate the person's motives. Was he just fired? Is he bitter? Perhaps you interview a woman whose sister has been beaten to death, and the woman tells you, "Her husband was a no-good bum. He beat her for years." In that moment, you are helpless to know whether the statement is true or false.

Only if the statement is made during a live broadcast, and only if you used due care to stop it, might you escape liability should the broader standards of defamation be applied. The woman could make the statement; you could say what the woman told you; you could make the statement without attribution; but in all three instances the court would typically consider your responsibility for the allegation to be the same.

Later you may be able to establish the woman's malice, but if you air the allegation without first evaluating your source you may one day regret your decision. The court may ask whether there was something further you should have done—and there usually is—to establish the source's motives.

Note the distinction between the two concepts of malice that are applied in this discussion. An older, common-law version of malice applies in establishing the malice of the news source. As a result of the 1964 U.S. Supreme Court ruling in *New York Times v Sullivan,* however, a second concept of malice is operable as it applies to the journalist. This newer concept, called "actual malice," or the Sullivan Rule, as later modified, results from the Court's opinion that "Constitutional guarantees require, we think, a federal rule that prohibits a public official from recovering damages for a defamatory falsehood relating to his official conduct unless he proves that the statement was made with 'actual malice'—that is, with knowledge that it was false or with reckless disregard of whether it was false or not."

The ruling applies to public figures or to persons who have voluntarily placed themselves in the public view. The issue of actual malice as it applies to private plaintiffs is left to state law. Some states allow reporters to repeat charges they suspect are false. Other states require that reporters investigate such charges before they repeat them.[2]

Assume the Highest Standard.   Actions for libel can be brought in any state in which a station's signal is received. A Pennsylvania resident libeled by a New York station could bring suit in his home state, for example, although Pennsylvania courts normally would use the libel standards that apply in New York. This offers some protection against individuals who might otherwise bring suit in a state where chances for settlement are more favorable. Consequently, attorneys generally advise that you assume the standard for your own state, or preferably an even higher standard.

Dealing with Police.   Use caution any time police serve as your primary source for potentially defamatory statements, or any time you're tempted to publish information obtained from the police radio. A street cop may tell you on the record, "This looks like it could be a gangland drug-related shooting," but to protect yourself check further. Otherwise, simply through inference, you could be defaming an innocent person.

Generally, you can rely on police, although not always. In one libel action, a reporter aired police-supplied photographs of alleged "thieves and burglars" at a flea market. One of the persons clearly identified in the photographs had no police record and sued for libel. A court ordered the police to pay a penalty for libel.

HOW TO AVOID COMMON LEGAL PROBLEMS

An area of great danger to journalists is unsuspecting defamation. The problem occurs most frequently at the hands of reporters who approach television as an illustrative medium, using pictures to illustrate a script that in turn carries most of the reporting load. Each of the examples that follows conceivably might lead to claims of an alleged invasion of privacy called *publicizing in a false light.*

- The camera shows a reporter on a crowded street corner, then pans over to show a hapless passerby as the reporter says, "Is there a cure for herpes? Obviously not."

- Voice-over narration discusses the problem of overweight Americans while the television screen shows generic cover footage of women walking along a street. The women, through "guilt by illustration," are implicated as being overweight.
- Reporter voice-over narration says, "Drug dealers are using their profits to buy huge homes like these." The narration is unwittingly married with generic cover footage that shows the home of a respected commodities exchange executive. A lawsuit follows.
- Several young women walk along a street against voice-over narration that charges that the area being shown is full of prostitutes. The women, not surprisingly, sue the station.

The use of generic video, which some attorneys call "inadvertent cutaways," is a dangerous journalistic practice that leads not infrequently to libel and invasion of privacy suits. When suits are filed against reporters who shoot a street scene, then use it generically for two years to illustrate scripts about herpes victims, thieves, and tax evaders, judges are likely to say, "When you were talking about the mad rapist, you could be understood to have been talking about the person you showed on the screen. Let's let the jury decide."

Many court rulings and jury verdicts are as predictable as a coin toss. To avoid the coin toss, apply good judgment and discretion. Stories with impact, significance, and far-reaching consequences may be worth the risk, even though they may result in legal action against your station.

Use of the Word *Alleged*

A time-honored way to handle criminal cases is to remember the adage, "No charges, no name." In criminal cases, a person's identity should be withheld until charges are filed. At the point charges are filed, the word *alleged* can be one of the reporter's most important legal protections. This is because how much you can say (and sometimes show) about anyone associated with a crime or a criminal depends on the level of that person's involvement.

There are at least three critical levels to consider:

1. Material witnesses: Some people are brought in as material witnesses, nothing more.
2. Suspects: Other individuals are brought in as suspects, or material witnesses may become suspects.
3. Arraignment: Only at arraignment does actual "alleging" begin; at this point someone charged with murder becomes an *alleged* killer.

In a sense, even someone *convicted* of murder remains an alleged killer. The jury says he was the killer, but the journalist can never know with absolute certainty. While the conventional wisdom in many newsrooms holds that the word *alleged* is a useless word under the law, it may help to establish the journalist's "state of mind" that existed toward the suspect when the story was reported.

Invasion of Privacy

The Fourth Amendment to the Constitution protects the individual's right to privacy, including the "right of the people to be secure in their persons, houses, papers, and effects." As defined in the courts, invasion of privacy is any act of intrusion that occurs without an individual's consent, including trespass and publication of embarrassing facts, even if true, and that violates an individual's reasonable expectation of the right to privacy. As the concept affects journalists, it has parallels with libel law, but note the distinction about truth. Libel is actionable only if the report is false. Invasion of privacy can be actionable even if the report is true. Exceptions occur if the information is already part of the public record or if the report concerns activities that occurred in public. Such information is privileged, even though it might be false, provided it is reported completely and as accurately as it was made available to the journalist.

In gathering television news, one of the most common forms of invasion of privacy is **trespass.** What problems can there be, journalists sometimes ask, if we shoot first, then talk things over? The problem must be addressed before you shoot, because you invade privacy and incur potential liability when you first enter a private or semiprivate area.

Often, trespass is inadvertent. Someone with apparent authority gives you permission to enter the scene of a news event; later, someone with greater authority threatens you with a lawsuit and tells you to leave. What are the damages for walking into a person's home and invading privacy? The answer can be anything from one dollar in actual damages to clean the carpet you soiled, to punitive damages that are anyone's guess for causing "emotional distress."

Apparent Authority

Technically, you are liable for trespass if you're in the wrong place at the wrong time. Typically, however, courts determine a journalist's guilt or innocence on the basis of **apparent authority.** The following examples illustrate some of the everyday challenges journalists are likely to encounter.

Fatal Fire.   You seek permission to shoot video of a fatal fire at a rest home. The angle on your story is that many of these homes in your area may not be fireproof. The manager of the home is on duty and tells you, "Go on in." The fire chief, at your request, later also grants you access to enter the home. You shoot video until the fire is almost out, but as you prepare to leave the owner of the home arrives. The fire chief has long since left, but the owner tells you to leave immediately. The moment the owner tells you to leave, you must leave, of course, but the most immediate question is whether you're liable for trespass for having entered the home in the first place.

Courts generally answer this question on the basis of apparent authority. If someone on the scene says, "I own or lease this property; come on in," and you have no reason to doubt that person's authority, you normally are safe to enter the premises. If you are unable to find the owner or manager and the fire chief gives you permission to enter, you may still enter the premises. Once inside, you might still be liable for trespass or invasion of privacy if, for example, you inadvertently shoot into a private room and show an elderly resident in an embarrassing situation.

Assuming you did not invade anyone's privacy, you're probably safe to air any footage you shot while you had apparent authority to shoot, that is, from the home's manager or from the fire chief. If the owner, the last to arrive at the scene, tells you not to use any footage you've shot, even under the fire chief's apparent authority, you're probably still safe to go ahead and air anything shot before the owner's arrival. In this example, if anyone is to be sued, it probably will be the fire chief. If in doubt, consult your station attorney.

Day Care Center.   You receive permission from a city building inspector to enter a day care center that has been cited for safety violations. The city building inspector is the apparent authority, although you must leave if the manager or owner (either of whom have greater authority than the building inspector) tells you to leave.

Landlord–Tenant Dispute.   You're covering a landlord—tenant group dispute. You normally may enter someone's private apartment at that person's invitation, even if the landlord tells you to leave, because in many states tenancy rights give the individual greater apparent authority than the landlord. You also may stand on public property to photograph the apartment complex and you may also be able to stand on a common area of the apartment grounds, again with a tenant's permission, and shoot video.

Entering a Restaurant.   You learn that your state health department may close a local restaurant if unsanitary conditions aren't corrected. As part of your report, you enter the restaurant with cameras rolling, walk to the manager, and begin to ask questions. The restaurant is open to the public, you reason, so anyone can come in. A further question is whether you're liable for what you shoot before the manager tells you to leave.

Limited Invitation

In the last example, the courts have held that in the case of restaurants (or even car dealerships), the public has a **limited invitation** (see *LeMistral, Inc. v Columbia Broadcasting System*, 402 N.Y.S.2d 815, 817. N.Y. App. Div. 1978). The invitation is to come in to eat (or look at and buy cars). The public, a term that includes journalists, is not invited to come into the business with cameras rolling to shoot video. Such practices in your state may therefore fall under the heading of invasion of privacy.

Often, normally private homes, businesses, and institutions assume quasi-public status because of some event. As a general rule, you can shoot anything your eyes can see if you have permission to shoot in the first place. Be aware, however, that examples are simply that. Check state laws to be certain where you stand and where you can stand. In one incident, reporting crews from two television stations sought permission to enter leased land to photograph horses that were said to be starving. The crews obtained permission from the land owner but not from the individuals who had leased the land. In this case, the overriding question was whether the reporters had reasonable belief that the owner had apparent authority, an answer that will vary from one state to the next.

TECHNOLOGY

Technology has created new opportunities for trespass. The news helicopter is but one example. In numerous states, property lines are considered to extend from the boundaries of the property to the heavens. Technically, any time a helicopter or airplane flies over someone's property it may be trespassing. Practically, however, the damages of such an act are minimal—unless, of course, a news helicopter hovers for too long above a burning home and fans the flames.

As a general rule, journalists have been able to record anything they could see, even with a telephoto lens and a shotgun mike, but the rules may change as more photographers acquire 1,000 mm lenses and ever-more-sensitive microphones. While it's true no one has yet determined the maximum focal length you can use to record a news event, it's equally true that some judge, somewhere, will also ask whether subjects of the long lenses and shotgun and parabolic mikes had a reasonable expectation of privacy.

Hidden Microphones

If someone stands unclothed before an open living room window in a crowded city, that individual might be expected to know someone could be lurking in the distance with a telephoto lens. But if that individual is holding a private conversation inside the home, that same person should have a reasonable expectation to privacy, which extends to protection from "snooper" microphones or even from normal shotgun mikes, which can pick up hushed conversation from great distances.

Recording Third-Party Conversations

Recording conversations to which you're a third party presents yet another dilemma. You may get by with airing portions of the district attorney's comments you recorded at opening night of a new theatre presentation, even if the D.A. said he didn't like the play and even though you recorded his comments without his knowledge and as a third party to his conversation.

In some states, intrusion with shotgun mikes can constitute eavesdropping, a transgression governed by state and federal statutes. Hence, the recording of a restaurant conversation that could be overheard passively by any third party might constitute intrusion because of the patron's reasonable expectation of privacy while dining.

Obviously, the use of concealed microphones for any purpose should be undertaken with great care if journalists wish to avoid lawsuits for intrusion. And no journalist should plant a microphone in a flower pot or make secret recordings of any kind without first checking with the station attorney.

ROUTINE TELEPHONE USE

Telephone recordings have great potential for legal devastation because they can so easily be misused to invade someone's privacy. Recordings do help to ensure exact quotes, and they are commonly used as the electronic equivalent of a reporter's notes (something to consider should you ever be subpoenaed), but sometimes their use can backfire (Figure 15.2).

FIGURE 15.2   Even routine telephone use can lead to lawsuits for invasion of privacy. No recordings or broadcasts of a conversation can be made unless the source is so advised.

To prevent problems, it's mandatory that you always advise the person on the other end that you intend to record a conversation, regardless of who initiates the call. Federal Communications Commission (FCC) rule (47 C.F.R.S73.1206) governs the broadcast of live and recorded telephone conversations. Before a telephone conversation is recorded for a future broadcast or before a telephone call is broadcast simultaneously with its occurrence, broadcast reporters must inform any party to the call of their intent to broadcast the conversation. The notice must be given before any portion of the conversation is recorded or broadcast live. The notice must also occur before the recording or live broadcast *begins*. It is not sufficient to give notice just before the broadcast of a recorded call.

Even if you intend to record the conversation only for your records, you should advise the person, preferably before the conversation begins. For maximum protection record not only your statement of intent, but the other person's verbal consent. If you intend to air excerpts of the conversation on air, you should advise the person before the primary conversation begins—again, as near the start of the call as possible.

Common sense dictates, and a jury may agree, that any caller can reasonably expect not to have his or her voice extend beyond the other end of the line, unless that person is advised to the contrary. An exception exists when the party is aware, or may be presumed to be aware, that the conversation is being or likely will be broadcast, as in the call placed to a broadcast program that features call-in telephone conversations.

Surveillance in States with One-Party Consent.   Regulation of recorded conversations is federally governed by Title III of the Omnibus Crime Control and Safe Streets Act of 1968. The act allows law enforcement agents to conduct electronic surveillance, provided a judge has reviewed the plan and agrees. In many states and under federal law, an exception can be made for the reporter, provided the reporter doesn't intend to damage an individual's reputation falsely or to violate someone's privacy without newsworthy justification. Generally, under such laws, it is legal to monitor telephone calls or make surveillance tape recordings when one party to the conversation knows what is happening.

Hidden Voice Recorders

Although using a hidden voice recorder where a person has a reasonable expectation of privacy may not violate federal law, in some states the practice might add to a plaintiff's claim for invasion of privacy or trespass. In states with one-party consent and under federal law, a person acting in the reporter's place may be able to record a conversation without the reporter's being present, provided the person who carries the recorder understands what is happening. To be safe, always check with legal counsel.

Two-Party Consent.   At least twelve states (California, Connecticut, Delaware, Florida, Illinois, Massachusetts, Maryland, Montana, Nevada, New Hampshire, Pennsylvania, and Washington) require that all parties to conversations, even if there are more than two, give their consent if the conversations are recorded. Unless consent is obtained from all parties, severe criminal penalties are possible. Reporters who wish to record conversations in states with two-party consent should seek knowledgeable counsel to avoid the possibility of severe criminal penalties. For the most recent list of one- and two-party consent states, see The Reporters Committee for Freedom of the Press (RCFP) web site at www.rcfp.org, or write or call RCFP, 1815 N. Fort Myer Drive, Suite 900, Arlington, VA 22209, (800) 336-4243 or (703) 807-2100.

ACCESS TO CHILDREN AND JUVENILES AS NEWS SOURCES

With some exceptions, a child is defined as anyone under eighteen years of age. Normally, you can use juvenile names and pictures if you obtain them legally—and if the identities are already part of the public record. But to be on the safe side it's always wise to consult your state law for the exceptions. Children's right to privacy is protected from the streets to the home to the courtroom. Although reporters normally cannot be thrown out of adult trials except for gross misconduct, they can be routinely excluded from juvenile trials. Even when a reporter wishes to interview a child on a public street, there is no guarantee of the child's legal consent to talk unless the person is at least eighteen years of age.

The same caution extends to news coverage in schools. Because of the principle of limited invitation, a school principal may legally refuse a reporting crew the right to take pictures or to conduct interviews with children in the school unless the crew first obtains parental permission. Without such permission, the principal has the right to keep reporters out altogether.

From one state to another, juvenile law varies. A juvenile charged with murder, habitual crime, or other felony may forfeit his or her right to privacy. Occasionally, stations may jointly decide not to air a child's identity, even though the child's name has been legally obtained and can legally be broadcast. When the choices are difficult and competition a factor, a guiding principle is to ask, "What does the public need to know?" and "Does the public have a right to know this child's identity?" Your own sense of fair play and humanity will doubtless provide the proper answer.

SUBPOENAS AND SHIELD LAWS

A reporter's sources, conversations, notes, and outtakes are sacred, although some members of the legal community may believe otherwise. The mildest form of **subpoena** is for an on-air tape; the most severe is for a reporter's notes or the names of sources. What the reporter must learn above all else is how to keep quiet. Tell no one the identities of secret sources or of the content of notes or outtakes. Once you've revealed such knowledge, you've forfeited your right to withhold the same information from the courts.

If your attorney or news director asks whether you have source material, you may answer that you have the material but never divulge the contents, even to them. Attorneys and news directors are paid to fight the good fight for you. They're the ones who are paid to say, in court, "Yes, there is material, but we're not producing it."

In protecting sources, the key to the ball game is never to promise a source complete confidentiality unless you're willing to go to jail indefinitely. Generally, no one has the right to determine a reporter's editorial judgment, so notes, outtakes, and sources are normally protected. In a number of states, this protection is formally extended through **shield laws.** But remember to treat the material as confidential in the first place; otherwise you may have problems withholding that same information from the courts. And remember that shield laws, in the final analysis, offer the journalist only scant legal protection.

ACCESS LAWS

Whereas shield laws allow the journalist to protect confidential sources under certain circumstances, *access* or *sunshine laws* protect the journalist's right of access to judicial, legislative, and executive records, extraordinary school board and city council proceedings, and the like, which otherwise might be kept off limits to the public. Such open meeting and open records laws may apply to state government but not to local government.

Journalists are routinely excluded from closed sessions of sensitive personnel and legal matters at all levels of government, although some officials may invoke such exclusionary rules as a way to bar journalists from meetings that should be open to the public. Advice from legal counsel may be necessary to gain permission to attend such meetings or even to learn of actions taken during meetings that should have been conducted in public.

COURTROOM TELEVISION

Because the Sixth Amendment to the Constitution guarantees defendants in criminal cases the right to a *public* trial, television journalists have fought for decades to bring television cameras into the courtroom. "We have watched wars live on television," the argument goes, "so perhaps it's time that American news viewers are able to see what happens in American courtrooms." Slowly, in state courts at least, they are winning the battle.

Most States Allow Courtroom Coverage

Some form of extended media coverage, meaning coverage by television, radio, or still photography, is permitted in forty-eight states, with a majority allowing cameras in a criminal trial. Consent of the presiding judge is almost always required, and many states require advance written application for permission. Nearly all states routinely prohibit coverage in cases that involve juveniles, victims of sex crimes, domestic relations cases, and trials that involve trade secrets. Coverage of jurors normally is either prohibited or restricted, to prevent juror identification. To stay abreast of changes in your state, or for a comprehensive summary of TV cameras in state courts, see the Information Resource Center of the National Center for State Courts web site at www. ncsc.dni.us/is/clrhouse/tvcams99.htm.

Television Cameras Banned in Federal Courts

After a three-year experiment in six U.S. district courts and two appeals courts, the Judicial Conference of the United States ruled in late 1994 to ban television cameras in federal courtrooms. The proposal exempted criminal trials from the experiment, but allowed coverage of civil proceedings in the district courts of Indiana, Massachusetts, Michigan, New York, Pennsylvania, and Washington, and in federal appeals courts in New York City and San Francisco.[3] "[The] basic concern was the potential impact on jurors and witnesses; potential distraction of witnesses; and whether jurors were made nervous by any fear of possible harm," said David Sellers, a spokesman for the twenty-seven-member panel of judges that issued the ruling.[4]

Criminal trials were excluded from coverage, and during the first two years of the experiment, media covered only a handful of civil cases. Judges repeatedly cautioned against media apathy, warning journalists the experiment might fail unless they increased coverage of federal court proceedings.[5] Still, the ban surprised many observers who fully believed the experiment had been a success. News organizations, among them CNN in Atlanta, believed the decision ran counter to the trend in U.S. society to open institutions to more rather than less public scrutiny.[6] Today, television and radio coverage of federal criminal and civil proceedings remains effectively banned both at the trial and appellate levels. In 1999, 2001, and 2003, the Senate Judiciary Committee introduced legislation that would allow federal trial and appellate judges to permit cameras in their courtrooms on a three-year trial basis.[7] You can find continually updated information on the current status of cameras in federal courts at the Radio Television News Directors (RTNDA) web site, http://rtnda.org/foi/cc.shtml.

The Role of Cameras in the Courtroom

Journalists believe cameras in the courtroom help audiences better understand the judicial process. "Legal experts say that people watching the action on television are getting a glimpse of the excitement of trial work performed by articulate, competent, and hard-working attorneys," observed Harriet Chiang, as legal affairs writer for the *San Francisco Chronicle*.[8] But Chiang and other legal experts note that both sides may become preoccupied with publicity rather than the quest for justice, engaging in "sandlot style" lawyering.[9] For years media observers have argued that televised trials help ensure that public trials are indeed public and that they subject judges and other public officials to greater public scrutiny.[10] Edward Estlow, as president of the E. W. Scripps Company, said, "A trial committed to videotape is a trial more accurately reported because the cameras create a record that both newspaper and broadcast representatives can then consult in order to verify their reportage."[11] Television coverage may indeed enhance the public's access to the judicial process," (see Figure 15.3). Today the flipping of pages and scratching of artist's pens may be more disruptive in the courtroom than the occasional soft clicks of the television camera turning on and off (Figure 15.4). Even so, federal judges and the Supreme Court have declared themselves not yet ready for prime time.

Once cameras are allowed in the courtroom, still more concerns must be answered. If the camera is within the jury's view, will jurors be influenced as to what the reporter and photographer feel is the most newsworthy or most significant testimony? Will undercover police be publicly identified should they be called to the witness stand? Will journalists use the camera to cover only the most sensational trials or to record only the most sensational testimony (i.e., the star witness breaking down on the witness stand)? What if the rape victim's name is inadvertently spoken, or her face shown, during a courtroom broadcast? What if a prisoner is called to testify, then later faces retribution from prison cellmates? What if perspiration on the judge's bald head is unsightly? What if the prosecutor can't match the defense attorney's performance? What if . . . ?

Standards for Courtroom Coverage

Gradually, judges, attorneys, and journalists are establishing the standards that answer such questions. Today's journalists do not propose an unlimited number of cameras, lights, and microphones inside the courtroom. In fact, they normally operate with one television pool camera and one still camera for combined newspaper and wirephoto coverage.

With **pool coverage,** an otherwise unyielding judge may open the way for TV coverage of a court trial. Similarly, a pool arrangement may answer the question of how many stations can interview a prisoner on death row or cover his or her later execution

FIGURE 15.3 The Sixth Amendment to the Constitution guarantees the individual's right to a speedy and public trial by an impartial jury. The issue of free press–fair trial involves such considerations as shield laws, subpoenas, and television in the courtroom.

FIGURE 15.4 Television cameras in the courtroom are becoming a more common sight as technology reduces the levels of disruption that were once common in broadcast trial coverage.

without disruption by the presence of camera crews and hardware from a dozen or more stations.

Under the pool arrangement for trial coverage, a single camera is set up at a stationary point in the courtroom, and its signal is fed live to the station, to video recorders just outside the courtroom, or to a central receiving location elsewhere within the courthouse. All stations that wish to cover the trial are provided access to the video signal from the courtroom camera, a method designed to create the least distraction. Sound can be supplied simply by tapping into the public address system commonly found in most courtrooms (Figure 15.5).

In many states the judge is the absolute authority when it comes to cameras in the courtroom. Although challenges to the presence of cameras at a trial may be made by jurors, attorneys, witnesses, or the accused, the judge most often has sole discretion. Each judge handles the procedures differently. Some judges will not allow zooms or camera movement. Others will allow zooms, but not pans—so as not to distract the jury with camera movement.

The judge may require the photographer and reporter to wear coat and tie or other suitable dress. Some judges require that once set up, the photographer and reporter must remain in the courtroom—even though the next three days of testimony may not make a newsworthy story—so jurors won't be influenced by the reporter and photographer's judgment of what is the most newsworthy or most significant testimony.

Some Do's and Some Don'ts. When a broadcast news organization wishes to originate trial coverage, the first step is to submit a written request for camera coverage to

FIGURE 15.5 Pool coverage minimizes disruptions in the courtroom through the use of a single camera to feed signals to all stations that wish to cover the proceedings.

the judge at least twenty-four hours in advance. If the judge denies access, the judge's word is final: There usually is no appeal process. If the judge allows trial coverage, rules will almost certainly be imposed—undoubtedly similar to those that follow.[12]

DO'S:

- Do pool all TV and audio coverage.
- Do use only one operator for TV coverage using only one camera set in one location.
- Do dress and conduct yourself in a manner consistent with the dignity and decorum of the courtroom.
- Do use the existing court audio system for sound recording if technically feasible.

DON'TS:

- Don't leave media identification on cameras or clothes.
- Don't take close-ups of jury members.
- Don't use auxiliary TV lights.
- Don't take audio recordings of attorney–client conversations or conferences held at the bench.
- Don't change tape or disk drives while court is in session.
- Don't use portable voice recorders.
- Don't ask the judge to referee a media dispute such as over pooling.

A judge may also require that some individuals—a rape victim, for example, or a juvenile witness, an informant, or an undercover agent—not be photographed in the courtroom. At any point in the trial, a judge may terminate coverage if it hinders the judicial process or appears to jeopardize an individual's right to a fair trial.

Cameras normally are excluded from pretrial hearings in criminal cases, from jury voir dire (a preliminary examination to establish a prospective juror's competence), and from proceedings in the judge's chambers. Depending on the state and the judge, cameras may be allowed at other proceedings such as trial hearings, sentencing, resentencing, and the like.

In some cities where new courtroom facilities are under construction, facilities to conceal the television camera are an ordinary part of courtroom blueprints. Two-way windows at the back of the courtroom conceal the camera so no one in the courtroom is aware of its presence. If cameras cannot be seen it is more difficult for them to influence the trial's outcome, though it is not impossible, especially if courtroom participants know the proceedings are being televised.

Judges and lawyers being human, their concern about how they'll appear on television the first day or so of a new trial is to be expected. But almost without exception, the camera's presence is quickly forgotten. Soon, the TV camera is old hat, as common a fixture as the gavel or the witness stand.[13]

Should attorneys appeal the verdict in a televised trial, their first request may be for video recordings of the trial. The station's own rules should apply in governing whether the request is honored. Some stations might supply whatever footage has been aired, but no outtakes. Other stations might supply nothing at all—even in the face of a subpoena. The reasoning is that if pool coverage is allowed, bar associations, watchdog groups, and attorneys can record the trial themselves, even with a home video cassette recorder, unless coverage is limited to news organizations as it sometimes is.

After the Verdict Is In

Once the verdict is in and the jury has been dismissed, courthouse reporters traditionally have been free to question jurors about the verdict, their secret deliberations, and why they voted as they did. Still, individuals called to jury duty remain private citizens, and today some courts are extending the right to privacy to jurors as they return to everyday life. In 1982 the 5th U.S. Circuit Court of appeals, in *re Express-News*, ruled that "jurors, even after completing their duty, are entitled to privacy and to protection against harassment."

A LEGAL PERSPECTIVE

Questions about the law and its interpretations confront every journalist, frequently under the pressures and deadlines of field reporting. While legal counsel may not be immediately available, every journalist can rely on a powerful ally called common sense. The answers to many legal questions are products of nothing more than a sense of good judgment, fairness, taste, and a concern for the dignity—and privacy—of others. Beyond these guidelines is a prescription that has proven itself through the centuries: Treat others as you would expect to be treated in the same situation. Your audience expects nothing less. Above all, remember: When in doubt, consult an authority—either station or legal.

SUMMARY

Self-interest requires that journalists stay abreast of laws that apply to the reporting process. While the act of reporting the news can lead to legal challenges, many legal transgressions occur in the field during the process of gathering the news. Even when journalists are on solid legal ground, defending against lawsuits can be costly and time consuming and tends to make reporters overly cautious in covering subsequent stories.

Two of the most important areas of concern to journalists are libel and invasion of privacy. Libel is the use of factual information, as opposed to opinion, that holds someone in hatred or contempt, subjects the person to ridicule, or otherwise lowers our esteem for the individual. Invasion of privacy is any act of intrusion, including trespass and publication of embarrassing facts, even if true, that violates an individual's reasonable expectation of a right to privacy.

Normally, to be liable for defamation, journalists must know that a statement is false or be aware it probably is false. An excellent protection against libel, therefore, is to have good reason to broadcast only statements you believe to be true, and to use due care in evaluating the truth of defamatory information.

When a news source makes defamatory allegations in a broadcast, it is imperative to evaluate the source and the source's motives. In the case of public figures and persons who have placed themselves in the public view, the U.S. Supreme Court's Sullivan Rule prohibits recovery of damages for defamation unless actual malice is proved, that is, "with knowledge that it was false or with reckless disregard of whether it was false or not." The issue of actual malice as it applies to private plaintiffs is left to state law.

Use caution when broadcasting information obtained from police, because in the early stages of investigation their statements may be only personal opinion. Another problem area is unsuspecting defamation, which can occur when generic or file video is used to illustrate a script that carries most of the reporting load, as in the case of pictures of an unknown woman used against voice-over narration that talks about the high incidence of prostitution in the area.

One of the most common forms of invasion of privacy is trespass. The guiding rule is to obtain permission to enter any private or semiprivate area before you shoot, not afterwards. Often, trespass is inadvertent and occurs because someone with apparent authority, perhaps a police officer or fire official, gave the photojournalist permission to shoot. Generally, the footage can be aired up to the point that someone with greater authority, perhaps the building owner, arrives and tells the photographer to leave.

The principle of limited invitation prohibits journalists from freely entering quasi-public businesses and institutions, such as restaurants and supermarkets, to report and take pictures. In such examples, the public, a term that includes journalists, is invited only to eat or shop, not to take pictures.

Technology has created new opportunities for trespass and eavesdropping. Telephoto lenses and tiny microphones that can pick up hushed conversation from great distances are but two examples. In no case attempt to use concealed microphones or make secret recordings without first obtaining competent legal counsel.

Some states require that both parties to conversations give their consent if the conversations are to be recorded. In other states a person acting in the reporter's place may be able to record a conversation, provided the person who carries the recorder understands what is happening.

Telephone recordings can easily be used to invade an individual's privacy. To help prevent problems, always advise the person on the other end that you intend to record the conversation, even if you intend to record it only for your records. Courts are extra sensitive about protecting children's right to privacy. Be especially cautious about broadcasting children's names, pictures, or other information that would allow them to be identified, even when such information already is part of the public record.

Shield laws help protect the reporter's confidential sources, conversations, notes, and outtakes, but attorneys routinely try to subpoena such information. For maximum protection, tell no one the identities of secret sources or of the content of notes or outtakes. Once you reveal such knowledge, even to your news director, you've forfeited your right to withhold the same information from the courts. When protecting sources, never promise a source complete confidentiality unless you're willing to go to jail indefinitely.

Whereas shield laws allow the journalist to protect confidential sources under certain circumstances, access or sunshine laws protect the journalist's ability to inspect records and other vital information that otherwise might be kept off-limits to the public.

Although most states allow television cameras and microphones into trial courts, permission normally is granted at the sole discretion of the trial judge, who may also require the defendant's or the attorney's consent. To help preserve the right to televise courtroom trials, reporters and photographers are obliged to dress appropriately to the courtroom environment, and they must strive to create the fewest distractions possible and follow the judge's rules and instructions to the letter.

In all matters regarding law and the gathering and reporting of news, the best guide to the proper course of action is to be found in good judgment, fairness, taste, and a concern for the dignity and privacy of others. Beyond these considerations, remember the adage "When in doubt, seek help."

DISCUSSION

1. At what point during the reporting process must journalists be concerned about considerations of law? Explain your answer.

2. Discuss the potential chilling effect that litigation or the threat of litigation can have on news content. Provide an example or two as part of your response.

3. What right, if any, does the journalist have to gather the news?

4. Explain the customary definition of libel as it applies to television journalists. Is it possible to "visually libel" a person with the television camera or through a television graphic?

5. What actions on the part of journalists might constitute invasion of privacy?

6. What steps can the journalist take to avoid libel suits?

7. What are the most important actions a journalist can take to protect against charges of negligence in libel suits?

8. Discuss the Sullivan Rule as it applies to public figures or persons who have voluntarily placed themselves in the public view.

9. Why is it important to use caution when using police information as the main source of potentially defamatory statements?

10. Discuss the potentially dangerous journalistic practice of using generic video, also known as inadvertent cutaways, which can lead to libel and invasion of privacy suits. Suggest alternatives that can help the journalist avoid unsuspecting defamation or "guilt by illustration."

11. Discuss the principle of apparent authority as it applies to invasion of privacy.

12. Explain the role of technology in creating new opportunities for trespass and invasion of privacy.

13. Even routine telephone use can lead to lawsuits for invasion of privacy. Describe steps the journalist can take to avoid legal problems, especially when making telephone recordings.

14. What precautions are essential for the journalist to observe in reporting news that involves children or juveniles?

15. While shield laws may help the journalist protect a source's identity, that right can easily be forfeited. Explain how.

16. Discuss sunshine laws and the degree of protection they typically afford journalists and the public.

17. Discuss your views about the role of television in the courtroom. To what extent do you believe journalists should have an unqualified right to record and report courtroom trials? How do you respond to the Judicial Conference of the United States ruling in late 1994 to ban television cameras in federal courtrooms?

18. What standards of conduct and dress should the photojournalist observe when photographing courtroom trials?

19. What considerations should govern a journalist's relationship with jurors both during and after the trial?

EXERCISES

1. Invite a television news director or general manager to class to discuss steps the station routinely takes to avoid libel suits and other legal challenges. A number of stations conduct ongoing legal seminars to help news employees stay sensitive to legal issues and aware of changes in the law. Some stations may allow you to attend such seminars.

2. Seek to identify and interview a newspaper or television reporter whose story has resulted in litigation.

3. You can request personal copies of pocket-sized legal references from many state bar, press, and broadcast associations. Such references commonly cover libel and invasion of privacy laws (including trespass and eavesdropping), and state laws that help protect the journalist's right of access to public records.

4. Attend a trial where television cameras are allowed in the courtroom and observe the procedures that reporters and photographers follow.

5. Watch television newscasts for the use of generic video or inadvertent cutaways that might potentially lead to libel or invasion of privacy suits.

6. Write a short letter to an imaginary trial judge requesting permission to shoot video at an upcoming criminal trial. Attempt to anticipate and answer whatever objections a judge might have to your request.

NOTES

1. KCNC-TV Legal Seminar, Denver, CO, 19 May 1984.

2. Frederick Shook, Dan Lattimore, and Jim Redmond, *The Broadcast News Process*, 6th ed. (Englewood, CO: Morton Publishing Company, 2001).

3. "Out of Order," *Denver Post*, 22 September 1994, 18-A.

4. "TV Cameras Barred from Federal Courts," *San Francisco Examiner* (22 September 1994), A-11.

5. Tony Mauro, "Use It or Lose It," *RTNDA Communicator* (August 1993), 9.

6. Harry Rosenthal, "Cameras of Little Import in Courts, Study Finds," *Denver Post* (22 September 1994), 18-A.

7. http://www.rtnda.org/news/2003/052303.shtml, downloaded 02 June 2003.

8. Harriet Chiang, "Ito's Snakepit," *San Francisco Chronicle* (12 February 1995), 1.

9. Ibid.

10. "Shop Talk at Thirty: A Case for Courtroom Cameras," *RTNDA Digest*, as reprinted with permission from Editor & Publisher, from a speech delivered 18 May 1984 by Edward Estlow, president of the E. W. Scripps Company, before the Judicial Conference of the Sixth U.S. Circuit, 3.

11. Ibid.

12. Excerpted from "Cameras in Colorado Courtrooms," (Aurora, CO: Colorado Broadcasters Association), 1983.

13. Radio-Television News Directors Association Legal Seminar, "Broadcast Coverage of the Courts," Denver, CO, 2 June 1984.

CHAPTER SIXTEEN

JOURNALISTIC ETHICS

The field of journalism is strewn with ethical land mines. Sometimes there are explosions, with great loss of public trust and confidence in television news. Some journalists use deception to expose deception, citing occasions when it may be both necessary and ethical to break the law to expose a larger wrongdoing—to obtain false identities, for example, to show how easily false documents can be obtained. Elsewhere a reporter practices misrepresentation to gather evidence of nursing home fraud by posing as a patient's relative. Other journalists, equally committed to serving the public good, leap from dark shadows with cameras rolling to ambush unsuspecting adversaries. Later they will march with those same cameras, unannounced, into offices, businesses, and other private property.

The defense for such practices can be persuasive. "How else could we prove fraudulent practices at the cancer clinic unless we posed as cancer patients ourselves?" they ask. "If I hadn't sneaked a look at documents in the D.A.'s office, our community might never have learned of prostitution kickbacks to local police," another maintains. "Television is a visual medium; how else can we demonstrate the national problem of illegally obtained passports unless we misrepresent the identities of crew and misrepresent the reasons we're shooting this footage?"

A DEFINITION OF ETHICS

As such discussion implies, law and ethics are intertwined. Often, unethical activities also are illegal. Breaking and entering, theft, trespass, and intentional libel are but a few examples. The distinction between law and ethics, however, is clear. Laws are rules of living and conduct that are enforced by an external authority, usually by means of penalties. Ethics are the rules of living and conduct that you impose upon yourself, or that your profession strongly suggests you should impose upon yourself.

While there are guidelines for ethical behavior, few enforceable penalties exist. There is no law against arrogance or bad taste, for example, or against allowing yourself to become obligated to another person or institution and thereby influenced. Ethics is an internal philosophy of what is right and acceptable. At its core is your own determination of what is fair, truthful, accurate, compassionate, and responsible conduct.

THE EFFECTS OF COMPETITION

Many of the ethical problems reporters encounter come from knowing the competition is in head-to-head combat—and pushing hard (Figure 16.1). Such pressure tends to make reporters overdo, and the problem worsens as management insists on ever-higher ratings and on reporters whose faces and stories must garner instant recognition in the TV news marketplace. In their zeal to be first with the best story, some reporters overstep the boundaries that define ethical behavior. Inevitably, their sins become known to the world.

Every few years a reporter gains national notoriety for faking news stories or plagiarizing the work of other reporters. Other reporters trample lawns, snoop in mailboxes, misrepresent their identities, speak falsehoods to reticent news sources to force responses, stage news events, and generally conduct themselves unprofessionally. The public takes note of such transgressions and, over time, journalists and their profession suffer because of such behavior.

Roughly twenty years ago a third of U.S. citizens believed news reports were often inaccurate. In 2000 that number jumped to almost two-thirds of those polled, primarily because of the post-presidential election controversy in Florida that year. Gallup Poll interviews since then find that nearly 60 percent of those interviewed rated news stories as "often inaccurate," with only 39 percent rating them "accurate."[1]

FIGURE 16.1 The pressures of competition to be first with the best story can significantly influence the journalist's ethical and professional conduct.

As always, the reporter's most valuable asset is not simply the headline-making story, but credibility itself. Without credibility, as expressed by the degree of trust and faith the audience is willing to assign to the journalism profession at large, nothing else matters.

SITUATIONAL ETHICS

One story after another invites the reporter and photojournalist to redefine what is ethical conduct and what is not. The practice of judging a situation on the basis of the good that will likely come from a particular course of action is called **situational ethics.** As a philosophical theory, situational ethics can either help the journalist determine the tough call or act as a siren's beckoning to professional self-destruction. Will coverage of a suicide attempt help illuminate the helplessness of unemployment, or is the journalist's first obligation to help save the person's life? Is the photographer's duty to help rescue victims from an overturned school bus or to shoot footage of the rescue for a story that addresses the larger issue of school bus safety? The answers to such questions inevitably vary according to the story, its treatment, and which journalist is covering the story.

Given that journalists as a class adhere to no universally accepted code of ethics, who then is to regulate the journalist's conduct and who is to establish the norms for journalistic competence and ethical behavior? Traditionally, individuals and institutions throughout most levels of society have searched for methods to force journalists to conduct themselves ethically and to license them, if necessary, to achieve that objective.

On first inspection, the call to license journalists may not seem extraordinary. Before doctors or lawyers can practice their professions, they must complete rigorous study, demonstrate their competence before peers, and be licensed in the state in which they practice. By contrast, anyone can become a journalist by assigning oneself the title; no license or formal review of competence is required. Yet journalists remain as accountable to their clients as lawyers and doctors, and their ethical behavior must be equally above reproach as it must be in law and medicine. Why, then, should journalists not have to meet the same standards as other professionals?

THOSE WHO DISSEMINATE IDEAS
CANNOT BE LICENSED

Although in most other professions such an idea might border on heresy, the responsibility to establish and enforce norms of ethical conduct falls to the individual journalist. In the United States, which fosters free speech and free press, a predominant attitude has been that journalists cannot be licensed, because to do so would be to license their ideas. Only journalists who disseminated an approved doctrine might qualify for licenses. If a journalist's point of view differs from that of a review board, who can reasonably say such difference constitutes "incompetence"?

Because every administration and special interest group wants to cast itself in the most favorable light, and wants its views heard above all others, "competence" and "official doctrine" are concepts that vary according to who is in power. If licensing were imposed, whose versions of truth should be used as the foundations on which to license journalists? Republicans? Democrats? Socialists? Protestants? Moslems? Jews? White supremacists? Abortion rights advocates? Right-to-life advocates? Whites? Blacks? Chinese? Hunting groups? Environmentalists? Conservative courts? Liberal courts? Ultimately, the most reasonable answer would seem to advocate the responsible dissemination of all ideas. It is difficult to know what our opponents and those of different persuasions believe if they are prevented from speaking freely or if their messages are silenced. Ultimately, the engine that drives a democracy is precisely the freedom to debate and to adopt and promote differing philosophies and points of view.

Even journalistic "competence" is not as verifiable as legal and medical competence. Spelling and grammatical and other communication skills can hardly constitute sufficient evidence on which to determine a journalist's competence. Even the most celebrated network anchors occasionally mispronounce words.

THE JOURNALIST'S CONTRACT IS WITH THE PUBLIC

In the end, journalistic conduct in the United States is governed by a far more powerful review board than any public agency or congressional law could establish. Each hour of each day this same entity—the public—extends and renews the journalist's license to operate, by virtue of its patronage. David Halberstam, former *New York Times* correspondent who received the Pulitzer Prize for his Vietnam War reporting, once likened the journalist's press card to a social credit card that is subject to periodic renewal. While this social credit card is nothing so tangible as a formal document, it is nonetheless an extension of trust that the viewer can withdraw at will and without advance notice.

Even when the public is willing to overlook a journalist's indiscretions, there remains a group of peers, employers, and even advertisers who can bring powerful sanctions against that journalist. All citizens of the world are accountable by virtue of their deeds. Journalists, whose reputation is only as good as their last performance, are no exception. Loss of patronage is only a click of the remote away.

As the late CBS reporter Edward R. Murrow once observed, "to be believable, [journalists] must be credible." Today a nation whose citizens include stern faces in black robes looks down its nose at journalistic malpractice. As suspicions of malpractice increase, reporters are branded as arrogant, deceitful, intrusive, insensitive, sneaky, biased, and a host of other references that spell poor citizenship. Magazine and newspaper advertisements ask why reporters don't at least practice the Code of Ethics of the Society of Professional Journalists (Sigma Delta Chi), a code outsiders sometimes view as a rough equivalent of the Hippocratic Oath for physicians.

Because ideas are always at stake in journalism, no code of ethics can answer every dilemma the journalist will face in covering the news. A far better option may be for each journalist to adopt an individual code that, regardless of the dilemma at hand, will preserve that journalist's credibility and ensure the continuation of that publicly granted license to operate. Without public trust, respect, and credibility, any journalist is mute.

LAW AND ETHICS ARE INTERTWINED

Ethics is a branch of philosophy, not of law, but the two are inseparably linked. Although numerous laws protect against threats to First Amendment guarantees of free press and free speech, for each protection there exists a potential abuse. When the journalist abuses First Amendment rights, the law offers still other protections for the individual.

As one example among dozens, journalists do have the First Amendment right to report information, although nowhere in the Constitution is the public guaranteed the "right to know" anything. The right to report is preserved through sunshine and access laws, and through shield laws, which help reporters obtain information from otherwise reluctant sources through guarantees that source identities will remain anonymous.

If a journalist were to abuse shield law protections by attributing information to a nonexistent source, a judge might then invoke subpoena powers to establish the source's identity, under threat of a jail term should the journalist refuse. The subpoena power in this example exists as a public protection, although it too can be abused by courts or police who seek to use journalists as unpaid information gatherers or to conduct fishing expeditions.

TOWARD A PERSONAL STANDARD OF ETHICS

Ethical behavior can be thought of as promoting fair play, even for those individuals and institutions we dislike. In *New York Times v Sullivan*, the U.S. Supreme Court ruled that journalists can report about the actions of public officials unless malice is present, that is, if the journalist knew the facts were false to begin with or published the information in reckless disregard for whether or not the information was false.

While this ruling means public officials may have to grin and bear some intrusions into their private lives on behalf of the public good, it offers a measure of protection against reports that are patently unfair and possibly malicious.

On occasion, the concept of fair play poses dilemmas as the journalist walks the fence between obligations of fairness to the news source and a responsibility to provide the public with essential knowledge. The process can be less confusing if you stop to consider the consequences of your actions. Be fair, of course, and strive to determine who will be hurt or helped by your report. As a further consideration, try to determine whether the hurt is necessary.

CASE STUDIES IN ETHICAL DILEMMAS

With few opportunities to define ethical standards under the pressure of deadlines and instant reporting, journalists must already have established solid editorial and ethical philosophies before those dilemmas arise. The situations that follow are offered to help the reporter and photojournalist accomplish that objective. They encompass such situations as trespass, illegal surveillance, and invasion of privacy. As in most ethical deliberations, there are few answers, mostly questions.

As you begin your own deliberations of the issues that follow, you may be interested to know that, during panel discussions of these issues,[2] professional journalists have tended to divide about equally on whether to proceed in the following situations or to avoid becoming involved. The panel discussions that addressed these issues at the NPPA Television News-Video Workshop for professionals included news directors, photographers, and reporters. Videotapes of the first four panels are available from the National Press Photographers Association, 3200 Croasdaile Drive, Suite 306, Durham, NC 27705. The legal principles raised here are addressed in Chapter 15, Law and the Broadcast Journalist. A discussion of each situation can be found at the end of this chapter. For more case studies, see www.journalism.indiana.edu/Ethics.

Trespass

Case 1.   Safety officials have condemned an abandoned, privately owned building and posted it as unfit for human habitation. The owner has constructed a fence to keep out transients and children who might otherwise enter. "No trespassing" signs are prominently posted.

Last evening a child died and two others were injured when a stairway collapsed inside the building. A community citizens group says the building is one of dozens that pose such dangers. You are assigned to shoot video and a reporter standup inside the building. You can't locate the owner to obtain permission to enter the building, but police suggest they might look the other way should you decide to trespass. Will you enter the building illegally or stay out?

Case 2.   You are researching an investigative report about a palm reader who is said to con elderly people out of their life savings. You visit the palm reader at her place of business and she tells you to get lost. Later you decide to visit her at her residence. A "No trespassing" sign is posted on the front gate of the fence around her property. Will you go up to her house and knock on the door? Will you jump the fence if the gate is locked?

Surveillance Photography

The palm reader regularly invites elderly people to her residence, where you believe she conducts many of her con operations. One night you notice she has left the curtains open and the shades up, and you can see her sitting at a table with people who appear to be clients. Will you stand on the street and photograph the woman's activities through the open window? Will you try to obtain sound with a shotgun or parabolic microphone?

Hostage Coverage

Case 1.   An emotionally disturbed man holds hostages inside a sleazy bar. He says he'll kill one of the hostages unless he can broadcast a message to his wife. Police ask you to loan them your video camera so two of their officers can pose as a reporter-photographer crew to gain entry to the bar. You don't have time to contact the assignment desk or news director for advice. What will you decide?

Case 2.   A distraught father holds his children hostage in a private home. Through the window he can see your camera. He opens the door and shouts that he'll kill himself unless you leave the area. Unknown to the man, police plan to rush the house in about fifteen minutes, and your assignment editor has told you not to miss the action.

Do you retreat? When police rush the house, do you follow right behind them to photograph this dramatic, if unpredictable and possibly dangerous, moment?

Entrapment

To show how easy it is for minors to buy liquor, you send a seventeen-year-old minor into a couple of liquor stores, record video of the purchases through the store windows with a long lens from a van across the street, then walk into both stores, camera rolling, to interview the clerks. The clerks protest that you are guilty of entrapment and ambush journalism. How do you reply?

Invasion of Privacy

You wish to tape a historic medical procedure in which your cameras would peer inside the patient's body. The patient is too ill to respond to your request. The doctors will give their approval, provided the patient's family doesn't object. You tell the family your audience has the right to see this moment of history unfolding. The family says, "Sorry, but we don't want our relative to become a sideshow for TV news people. Permission denied." What should you (and your station) do next?

Violence

Case 1.   You cover a demonstration that turns violent. Four persons are injured. Your camera is rolling as a demonstrator steps into frame, shoots, and kills a police dog. Police club some demonstrators. Elsewhere, demonstrators threaten police officers with baseball bats. Will you show this violence on the evening news to give the audience an accurate portrayal of the event?

Case 2.   You're photographing a federal informer as he walks along a courthouse hallway between two marshals. Suddenly a man steps from a telephone booth and shoots the informer dead. You capture the event on video. Will you show the scene of the killing on tonight's news? if your competition shows it?

Protecting Confidential Sources

You're preparing a story on a radical terrorist group. You promise not to reveal sources or confidential information when you first talk with the terrorist leader. Later he tells you the group has lost control of one of its members who plans to plant a bomb at the federal court building tomorrow night. Will you go to the police or FBI with your information?

Breaking and Entering

You're producing a half-hour special on drug use in your city and have learned the address of a drug dealer. You go to the house, but no one answers when you knock on the door. You then notice that a window is open. Will you climb inside to check out the place or will you not enter the house?

Destroying Police Evidence

A person has been stabbed to death in a hotel. You arrive with your camera just as police arrive. The detective, an old acquaintance, tells you to go in, shoot your video, and leave before crime lab technicians arrive. He says if you don't act now, the technicians won't let you in for fear you might disturb evidence, perhaps even destroy clues to the murderer's identity. The detective doesn't seem all that worried that your presence inside the room might destroy evidence. Do you shoot the murder scene or not enter the room at all?

Televising Executions

Your state has approved your right to televise live broadcasts of executions. Your news director tells you he doesn't believe the public is ready for live broadcasts, but he wants to record the execution for broadcast during the late evening news for what the news director believes will be the event's "deterrent value." The general manager has also endorsed a delayed broadcast of the execution, citing his belief that if capital punishment is a societal value, then society's citizens have an obligation to view the consequences of their decision. What do you say—and do?

Covering Suicide Attempts

Case 1. You're enroute to work when your assignment editor radios you about a woman who's threatened to jump from a bridge with her one-year-old child in her arms unless her estranged husband returns immediately and makes up his arrears in alimony. You're one of the first people on the scene. When you arrive, the mother makes a further demand that your station broadcast a live appeal from her to her husband. A woman who identifies herself as the distraught woman's mother runs up to her daughter, clutches her, and says, "Put down that damn camera and help me grab her!" Do you put down your camera, or do you continue to record video?

Case 2. A mentally disturbed man has perched himself atop an office building and says he plans to jump to his death because his protracted unemployment has made it impossible for him to provide for his family. He's telephoned your station and competing stations to advise newsrooms of his planned suicide. Do you cover the event?

Illegally Obtained Information

You're at the district attorney's office. He leaves the room to find some information you've requested. While you wait, you notice an interesting file folder lying open on his desk. Do you look at the top page? the top three or four pages? Do you make notes if the information appears to be of interest? If the file folder is closed, would you open it, especially if you believe it could provide information that appears to be critically important to a story you're doing?

Yielding Editorial Control of News Content

A truck carrying nuclear warheads overturns on a highway in your area. The defense department prohibits any photographers at the area on grounds of safety and national security. Defense department officials say they will escort reporters into the area and permit them to photograph selected views of the accident, on condition they submit all video recordings for defense department screening before they are aired. Should you agree to these conditions to obtain footage?

Cooperating with Police

Inside an office building, now surrounded by a police S.W.A.T. team, is an armed man who has shot out several windows and asked for a live television interview so he can broadcast his message to the public. Officers say that unless they can impersonate your crew, they may have to storm the building with resulting injury or loss of life. They promise you can air any of the footage they manage to record. Assuming that you hand over your credentials and camera to the police, will you air any footage or interviews the police manage to shoot?

Private Lives of Public Officials

What will you do if you are the first to confirm information that a prominent individual, perhaps a state senator, is having an affair? has been diagnosed as having a serious but not life-threatening illness? is undergoing psychiatric counseling for marital difficulties? is showing early signs of senility in everyday conduct, which, although not evident to the public, is readily apparent to a loyal staff? is an alcoholic or abuses other drugs? is a homosexual?

Misrepresentation

Case 1. You are sitting in a bar where you happen to engage in a conversation with the new city attorney. The attorney thinks you're just another person at the bar and begins to open up, pouring out information that would make a great story. At this point do you tell the attorney you're a journalist or do you hide the fact?

Case 2. You're investigating the death of a person who has died under mysterious circumstances. Relatives won't talk, but someone in the newsroom suggests you obtain information from the victim's relatives by posing as a coroner's assistant. Will you act on this suggestion?

Under such circumstances as the case studies we've just posed, concern for truth and fairness can help the journalist determine not only whether to publish, but how the facts should be gathered and how the story should be covered. Another consideration is to ask how the public would react if they could view your news gathering and reporting methods before the story airs.

Accepting Favors

Few news operations allow their journalists to accept favors from news sources. In the past such favors have included free airline, sporting events, and concert tickets; books; meals; magazine subscriptions; taxi fares and limousine service. Freebies are dangerous precisely because of their intent: to obligate journalists to news sources in the hope of at least some coverage or of more favorable coverage.

Today the general wisdom is that if the public pays, so does the journalist. If the story is newsworthy, the station can afford to cover it. Most journalists would agree that it is permissible to accept something as insignificant in value as a cup of coffee or an hors d'oeuvre at a charity ball that is equally free to the general public.

Reporting in Context

The television camera is notorious for its ability to isolate events from the larger environments in which they exist. The camera, focusing naturally on the drama and the spontaneous evolution of a news event, can turn the reality of a few flooded streets into the illusion of a flood-ravaged city. It can make the angry faces of a few hundred protesters seem like a mob of thousands, or the towering flames of an apartment house fire seem like a reenactment of the burning of Atlanta.

No news report makes its journey into the minds of all viewers intact, and the potential for misunderstanding increases when events are reported out of context. The next time protesters chain themselves to a railroad track to keep trains from carrying nuclear warheads through an urban area, it may be appropriate to contrast the protester's viewpoint with the majority opinion of the rest of the city's residents. While it is essential to show the event, and to provide a vicarious experience of what happened, it is equally important to place the story in perspective.

REVERSE-ANGLE QUESTIONS

As in all questions of ethics, the overriding precaution is to do nothing that would unjustifiably inflict damage on others or that anyone could misperceive and later use to damage the journalist's credibility. The advice applies to the practice of shooting reverse-angle questions after the interviewee has left the scene. Perhaps the reporter has phrased the question ineptly and wishes to restate it more articulately, this time on camera, or perhaps the reverse-angle question will be employed as an editing device to condense the interview with no loss of visual continuity.

To preserve one's journalistic integrity, reverse-angle questions must be asked while the interviewee is still present. The reporter may wish to give the interviewee a simple explanation of the need for such a shot. Otherwise, an increased likelihood exists of accusations that the interview was edited out of context or that through slick editing the interviewee was made to appear to say things he or she never said and in fact does not believe.

STAGED NEWS EVENTS

Occasionally you may need to stage an event to be photographed. In fact, numerous news events are staged. Interviews and news conferences are among those events in which the time, location, and even the content and context are determined in advance (Figure 16.2). This form of staging is normally acceptable because it's so apparent to the viewer. The audience recognizes that no one can force interviewees to answer questions against their will, although unethical reporters have been known to coach persons to answer interview questions with predetermined answers. When we stage

FIGURE 16.2 News conferences are one example of stories that are staged in the sense that the time, location, and even the general content and context of the event are determined in advance.

unfairly, we create something that did not exist. It would not have happened in our absence. When we stage fairly, we recreate what already existed, what would have happened even in our absence.

Not every instance of staging needs to be identified. No breach of ethics should occur if you ask subjects to perform some action common to their everyday routine that, even in your absence, they would normally perform anyway. You might, for example, wish to ask a person to come through the door to her office again, so you can reshoot the scene from a more appropriate angle. Perhaps an artist is not working in her studio the day you wish to shoot. No loss of public confidence should result if you ask the artist to sit down in the studio and paint for a few minutes, so you can shoot some video for your story. It is perhaps less ethical to tell the artist where to sit, how to sit, or what to paint, or to rearrange any part of the studio or any other environment to create a more pleasing composition for your own shots.

Use Reenactments Sparingly

Reenactment also is occasionally permissible. Perhaps you want to show how psychiatrists treat child abuse victims, for example, but don't wish to invade the actual victim's privacy or to interrupt therapy. Use reenactments sparingly, and any time you do reenact an event, tell your audience. They will respect your candor, and their belief in what you show and tell them will increase. Even file video should be so identified to prevent any possibility of misunderstanding.

Another example of reenactment, potentially far more damaging to the reporter's credibility, is illustrated in the following scenario:

Reporting crews from three television stations have just arrived to interview a presidential candidate's state campaign manager the morning after the candidate's victory in the New Hampshire primary.

While the crews are still setting up but not yet rolling, they hear the campaign manager tell someone on the telephone, "I think we're going to take this state as easily as we took New Hampshire." All three stations miss the bite, but start rolling in hopes they can capture a similar statement before the campaign manager hangs up.

The conversation continues, but now the campaign manager is voicing a series of "uh huh's" into the telephone. Finally, one reporter hands the campaign manager a note that reads, "Talk about New Hampshire."

Finally, the campaign manager tells the person on the other end of the telephone, "Some reporters here want me to talk to you about New Hampshire," and he proceeds to talk about the previous day's primary victory. That night, some of the stations air the comments as if they were made during a spontaneous telephone conversation.

Of the numerous questions that surround such reporting methods, two are paramount. First, should the reporter have prompted the campaign manager to restate his original comments? Second, should reporters from the other stations have aired those comments as if they originated spontaneously? Some reporters would air the comments. Others would avoid airing them altogether. Still others answer the first two questions by asking a third: Would the audience have approved if it could have peered over the reporter's shoulder as he handed the campaign manager that note?

IDENTIFY FILE VIDEO PROMINENTLY

Always identify the use of file video to prevent any possibility that viewers believe the old video is current. Many stations label such video "File," "File Video," or "Library Footage" and often include the date it first aired. Often, you may have only a few crucial seconds of video to illustrate a story that advances over time (stale footage showing the aftermath of an airline crash as the investigation advances over weeks, months, or even years, for example, or perhaps old footage of a murder suspect walking to court as the trial, sentencing, and appeal processes run their course). Ideally, use such file video sparingly and try to advance it over time to avoid endless repetition. Most important, always remember to identify file video to avoid misleading your viewers.

IDENTIFY MATERIAL PROVIDED
FROM OUTSIDE SOURCES

Equally important is the need to identify all video that comes from any source outside your newsroom. Normally, the origin of network and news syndication stories is self-evident. In everything from mike flags, screen graphics, and reporter signoffs, the authorship and logos of network and syndication services receive obvious and prominent treatment. The biggest problem occurs with video news releases and footage from businesses, public relations firms, government agencies, and other special interest groups. Such stories arrive at the station free of cost, and reduced budgets make their use tempting. Stations frequently produce their own stories from such footage, updating and localizing the material as warranted, and may use their own reporters and anchors to voice such stories from the studio.[3] Unless stations identify the source, audiences have no way of knowing the story represents a special interest point of view. Some news organizations air even the video that amateurs shoot without identifying its source. But the most responsible news organizations clearly label video from outside sources.

TOWARD AN INDIVIDUAL CODE OF ETHICS

Ethics can be thought of as promoting fair play, even for those individuals and institutions we dislike. Often the best response to a news situation is detachment, the hallmark on which objective reporting is founded. But ethical reporting is more than the simple transmission of facts and truth, and it is more than fairness and accuracy. It is also the dedication to good taste and to a regard for human dignity and life. Not infrequently, ethical reporting is possible only when the journalist has made a much broader ethical commitment to be sensitive in reporting how others live, believe, and behave.[4] Sensitivity and compassion are not frequently mentioned as journalistic virtues or as prerequisites for employment, but they are qualities the public can rightfully demand from a profession often noted, and occasionally disdained, for its cynicism.

As you develop a personal code of ethics, you may wish to take into account some of the guidelines that follow. They form the basis for many individual codes of ethics in journalism.

- Broadcast only information that you know to be accurate, fair, and complete.
- Tell your audience what you don't know.
- If you make a mistake, tell your audience.
- Respect the privacy of others.
- Do nothing to misrepresent your identity.
- Whenever you disclose information that damages a person's reputation, disclose the source.
- Leave the making of secret recordings to authorized officials.
- Respect the right of all individuals to a fair trial.
- Promise confidentiality to a source only if you are willing to be jailed to protect the source.
- Pay for your own meals, travel, special events tickets, books, and CDs.
- Accept only gifts, admissions, and services that are free of obligation and equally available to the general public.
- Avoid outside employment or other activities that might damage your ability to report fairly or might appear to influence your ability to be fair.
- Avoid making endorsements of products or institutions.
- Guard against arrogance and bad taste in your reports.
- Stay out of bushes and dark doorways.
- Never break a law to expose a wrong.

Many news organizations also encourage employees to follow the guidelines in the Radio-Television News Directors Association (RTNDA) and National Press Photographers Association (NPPA) codes of ethics.

CODE OF ETHICS AND PROFESSIONAL CONDUCT
RADIO-TELEVISION NEWS DIRECTORS ASSOCIATION

The Radio-Television News Directors Association, wishing to foster the highest professional standards of electronic journalism, promote public understanding of and confidence in electronic journalism, and strengthen principles of journalistic freedom to gather and disseminate information, establishes this Code of Ethics and Professional Conduct.

PREAMBLE
Professional electronic journalists should operate as trustees of the public, seek the truth, report it fairly and with integrity and independence, and stand accountable for their actions.

PUBLIC TRUST
Professional electronic journalists should recognize that their first obligation is to the public.
  Professional electronic journalists should:

- Understand that any commitment other than service to the public undermines trust and credibility.
- Recognize that service in the public interest creates an obligation to reflect the diversity of the community and guard against oversimplification of issues or events.
- Provide a full range of information to enable the public to make enlightened decisions.
- Fight to ensure that the public's business is conducted in public.

TRUTH
Professional electronic journalists should pursue truth aggressively and present the news accurately, in context, and as completely as possible.
  Professional electronic journalists should:

- Continuously seek the truth.
- Resist distortions that obscure the importance of events.
- Clearly disclose the origin of information and label all material provided by outsiders.

  Professional electronic journalists should not:

- Report anything known to be false.
- Manipulate images or sounds in any way that is misleading.
- Plagiarize.
- Present images or sounds that are reenacted without informing the public.

FAIRNESS
Professional electronic journalists should present the news fairly and impartially, placing primary value on significance and relevance.
  Professional electronic journalists should:

- Treat all subjects of news coverage with respect and dignity, showing particular compassion to victims of crime or tragedy.

(continued)

CODE OF ETHICS AND PROFESSIONAL CONDUCT RADIO-TELEVISION NEWS DIRECTORS ASSOCIATION   Continued

- Exercise special care when children are involved in a story and give children greater privacy protection than adults.
- Seek to understand the diversity of their community and inform the public without bias or stereotype.
- Present a diversity of expressions, opinions, and ideas in context.
- Present analytical reporting based on professional perspective, not personal bias.
- Respect the right to a fair trial.

INTEGRITY

Professional electronic journalists should present the news with integrity and decency, avoiding real or perceived conflicts of interest, and respect the dignity and intelligence of the audience as well as the subjects of news.

Professional electronic journalists should:

- Identify sources whenever possible. Confidential sources should be used only when it is clearly in the public interest to gather or convey important information or when a person providing information might be harmed. Journalists should keep all commitments to protect a confidential source.
- Clearly label opinion and commentary.
- Guard against extended coverage of events or individuals that fails to significantly advance a story, place the event in context, or add to the public knowledge.
- Refrain from contacting participants in violent situations while the situation is in progress.
- Use technological tools with skill and thoughtfulness, avoiding techniques that skew facts, distort reality, or sensationalize events.
- Use surreptitious newsgathering techniques, including hidden cameras or microphones, only if there is no other way to obtain stories of significant public importance and only if the technique is explained to the audience.
- Disseminate the private transmissions of other news organizations only with permission.

Professional electronic journalists should not:

- Pay news sources who have a vested interest in a story.
- Accept gifts, favors, or compensation from those who might seek to influence coverage.
- Engage in activities that may compromise their integrity or independence.

INDEPENDENCE

Professional electronic journalists should defend the independence of all journalists from those seeking influence or control over news content.

Professional electronic journalists should:

- Gather and report news without fear or favor, and vigorously resist undue influence from any outside forces, including advertisers, sources, story subjects, powerful individuals, and special interest groups.
- Resist those who would seek to buy or politically influence news content or who would seek to intimidate those who gather and disseminate the news.

- Determine news content solely through editorial judgment and not as the result of outside influence.
- Resist any self-interest or peer pressure that might erode journalistic duty and service to the public.
- Recognize that sponsorship of the news will not be used in any way to determine, restrict, or manipulate content.
- Refuse to allow the interests of ownership or management to influence news judgment and content inappropriately.
- Defend the rights of the free press for all journalists, recognizing that any professional or government licensing of journalists is a violation of that freedom.

ACCOUNTABILITY

Professional electronic journalists should recognize that they are accountable for their actions to the public, the profession, and themselves.

Professional electronic journalists should:

- Actively encourage adherence to these standards by all journalists and their employers.
- Respond to public concerns. Investigate complaints and correct errors promptly and with as much prominence as the original report.
- Explain journalistic processes to the public, especially when practices spark questions or controversy.
- Recognize that professional electronic journalists are duty-bound to conduct themselves ethically.
- Refrain from ordering or encouraging courses of action that would force employees to commit an unethical act.
- Carefully listen to employees who raise ethical objections and create environments in which such objections and discussions are encouraged.
- Seek support for and provide opportunities to train employees in ethical decision-making.

In meeting its responsibility to the profession of electronic journalism, RTNDA has created this code to identify important issues, to serve as a guide for its members, to facilitate self-scrutiny, and to shape future debate.

Adopted at RTNDA 2000 in Minneapolis September 14, 2000. Reprinted by permission of the Radio-Television News Directors Association.

NATIONAL PRESS PHOTOGRAPHERS ASSOCIATION CODE OF ETHICS

STATEMENT OF PURPOSE

The National Press Photographers Association, a professional society dedicated to the advancement of photojournalism, acknowledges concern and respect for the public's natural-law, right to freedom in searching for the truth and the right to be informed truthfully and completely about public events and the world in which we live. NPPA believes

(continued)

NATIONAL PRESS PHOTOGRAPHERS ASSOCIATION
CODE OF ETHICS   Continued

that no report can be complete if it is not possible to enhance and clarify the meaning of the words. We believe that pictures, whether used to depict news events as they actually happen, illustrate news that has happened, or to help explain anything of public interest, are indispensable means of keeping people accurately informed; that they help all people, young and old, to better understand any subject in the public domain. NPPA recognizes and acknowledges that photojournalists should at all times maintain the highest standards of ethical conduct in serving the public interest.

CODE OF ETHICS
1. The practice of photojournalism, both as a science and art, is worthy of the very best thought and effort of those who enter into it as a profession.
2. Photojournalism affords an opportunity to serve the public that is equaled by few other vocations and all members of the profession should strive by example and influence to maintain high standards of ethical conduct free of mercenary considerations of any kind.
3. It is the individual responsibility of every photojournalist at all times to strive for pictures that report truthfully, honestly and objectively.
4. As journalists, we believe that credibility is our greatest asset. In documentary photojournalism, it is wrong to alter the content of a photograph in any way (electronically or in the darkroom) that deceives the public. We believe the guidelines for fair and accurate reporting should be the criteria for judging what may be done electronically to a photograph.
5. Business promotion in its many forms is essential, but untrue statements of any nature are not worthy of a professional photojournalist and we severely condemn any such practice.
6. It is our duty to encourage and assist all members of our profession, individually and collectively, so that the quality of photojournalism may constantly be raised to higher standards.
7. It is the duty of every photojournalist to work to preserve all freedom-of-the-press rights recognized by law and to work to protect and expand freedom-of-access to all sources of news and visual information.
8. Our standards of business dealings, ambitions and relations shall have in them a note of sympathy for our common humanity and shall always require us to take into consideration our highest duties as members of society. In every situation in our business life, in every responsibility that comes before us, our chief thought shall be to fulfill that responsibility and discharge that duty so that when each of us is finished we shall have endeavored to lift the level of human ideals and achievement higher than we found it.
9. No Code of Ethics can prejudge every situation, thus common sense and good judgment are required in applying ethical principles.

Reprinted by permission of the National Press Photographer's Association.

SUMMARY

Ethics is a philosophy of what is right and acceptable as it governs the rules of living and conduct that impact on professional deportment. They are the rules you impose on yourself or those your profession strongly suggests you should follow. Laws, by contrast, are rules of living and conduct that are enforced by an external authority, usually by means of penalties.

The pressures of competition tempt some journalists to commit unethical practices. Sooner or later, however, such acts end up reflecting unfavorably on the profession at large. Other problems can result when journalists practice situational ethics, the practice of determining what to do from one situation to the next on the basis of the good that will likely result from a particular course of action.

In the absence of a universally accepted code of ethics, it falls to the individual journalist to determine what is good and bad, right and wrong, fair and unfair. Given the indiscretions of some journalists, ranging from accepting favors and staging news to trespass and entrapment, some groups and individuals would seek to impose their own notions of ethical behavior on journalists and to license them. The predominant tendency is for each special group, the largest being the federal government, to presume the ultimate authority to license. Ideas, unlike pharmaceuticals and vending machines, are difficult to license.

In the end, nevertheless, the public extends to journalists somewhat the equivalent of a license to operate through its trust and patronage. Without these fundamental components in place, no journalist can be heard.

DISCUSSION

1. Describe the essential differences between ethics and law.

2. Based on your observations of television news coverage and promotion, discuss how the pressures of competition can influence the journalist's ethical decisions.

3. Discuss what role situational ethics should play in your professional career.

4. Describe from personal observation any television news practices with which you disagree.

5. Discuss your views about the wisdom of licensing journalists to (a) certify journalistic competency and (b) help ensure fairness in reporting.

6. In the absence of review boards and licensing boards for journalists, what other forces exist to help ensure that the journalist reports fairly and competently?

7. Under what circumstances, if any, are reenactments of stories ethically defensible?

8. Should a journalist refuse all gifts or just those above a certain value (ten dollars and higher? twenty-five dollars and up?)? What about a cup of coffee at a restaurant? a drink at a bar? a meal? a movie ticket?

9. Under what circumstances is it acceptable for a journalist to hold another paying job, say as a speech writer for a public relations company or as a video editor for an industrial telecommunications company?

10. As a journalist, when is it acceptable for you to accept pay from a special interest group for a speech you make? to shoot tape for a paid political spot?

11. When is it acceptable for you to publish information about a public official that you learned secondhand because your spouse or friend works in close association with that public official?

12. Under what circumstances, if any, is secret recording ethical?

EXERCISES

1. Respond to your choice of any five of the ethical conflict situations that begin on page 319 of this chapter, and defend your answers.

2. Choose five class members to play the roles of (1) assignment editor, (2) news director, (3) person in the news, (4) photographer, and (5) reporter. Ask penetrating questions to prompt the various individuals to respond to the ethical conflict situations beginning on page 319 and lead them to defend their responses.

3. Invite working journalists, perhaps a reporter–photographer team from a local station, to describe how they would react to the ethical conflict situations outlined in this chapter.

4. Make a list of favors you would accept without reservation from news sources and those you would refuse to accept under any circumstances. Explain your decisions.

5. Construct a personal code of journalistic ethics that you will follow as a working professional.

DISCUSSION OF ETHICAL CONFLICT SITUATIONS

Following are discussions of possible scenarios in response to the ethical conflict situations posed on pages 319–322. Your answers may vary, and you can expect a spirited defense of differing points of view whether you raise these issues in class discussion or with working professionals. In the end, there is no "right" answer, unless the response you advocate runs counter to humanitarian considerations; would harm an individual's safety, reputation, or mental well-being; results in the breaking of a law; or runs contrary to your station's ethical guidelines.

Trespass

Case 1.   Discussion. You could be guilty of trespassing unless you obtain permission to enter the building. If you are unable to locate the owner, ask a police officer to give you permission to enter the building. If you are later challenged, you can at least cite your decision to act on the basis of "apparent authority."

Case 2. Even with a "No trespassing" sign on the front gate, there would seem to be little harm in knocking on the woman's door. You have virtually no other way to announce your presence. If the gate is locked and you jump the fence, however, you may be guilty of trespassing.

Surveillance Photography

If the palm reader leaves her curtains open and her shades up, she might be expected to know that someone might attempt to take a picture. If you attempt to record sound with a shotgun or parabolic mike, however, the judge might rule that the palm reader had a reasonable expectation to privacy in her private conversations, even though her windows were open.

Hostage Coverage

Case 1. In this instance, the police have chosen to misrepresent their identity. Provided that you hand over your camera, you have chosen only to lend the police a camera. If the man holding hostages calls your station to confirm that the individuals with your camera are station employees, not police, serious harm could result to the hostages, especially if the assignment desk or news director is uninformed of your decision.

Case 2. In the first instance, retreat. The man's life and his children's lives may hang in the balance. In the second instance, when police do rush the house, your decision to follow immediately behind the police involves your own safety. No story is worth your life.

Entrapment

You have asked a minor to break the law by purchasing liquor, a common example of breaking the law to expose a wrongdoing. This job may better be left to police. You can then record the purchase through the window with a long lens from a van parked across the street, because generally you can photograph anything that you can see from a public location. The tactic of walking, unannounced, into the liquor store with camera rolling is less ethical. Ambush journalism gives interview subjects no time to collect their thoughts or to respond to questions in a rational, thoughtful way.

Invasion of Privacy

Honor the family's wishes. Wait for another day and another time when you do have permission. If you are convinced your cause is right, state your case once again, gently.

Violence

Case 1. The violence is the most eloquent statement you have to communicate the essence of this story. To edit it out would be to portray the demonstration as far more benign than it was. Be cautious, however, to avoid showing activities that would violate ordinary sensibilities and good taste.

Case 2.   Some stations air such footage, others convert it to a still-frame graphic or substitute a still photograph obtained from a newspaper photographer. Some viewers will expect to see the actual footage; other viewers will be outraged if you show it. The judgment call is yours.

Protecting Confidential Sources

The first step could be for you to plead with your source to inform the police or FBI himself. Otherwise, you might notify the police anonymously, without naming your source or his group, although such action would violate your promise not to reveal confidential information. You might also wish to inform your source of your decision to call police. If you fail to tell police, your decision could result in property damage and injury or death to innocent persons.

Breaking and Entering

Stay outside. Call police. Cover the action if they decide to enter the premises.

Destroying Police Evidence

You are better off staying outside. Murder trials can be lost over allegations of destruction of evidence.

Televising Executions

If viewers are given sufficient warning and time to prepare for a tape-delayed broadcast, then they can choose to watch or tune away from the broadcast as they wish. Unsuspecting viewers, however, may still tune into the delayed broadcast. To broadcast the execution live might capitalize on the event more nearly for sensational or shock value, because an understanding of capital punishment and its deterrent value is far more complex than watching a person being put to death on live television.

Covering Suicide Attempts

Case 1.   Delay the woman by calling the station. Do what you can to help save her and her child. Human decency and compassion take precedence over this story.

Case 2.   Do not cover the story. If you do, you will be subject to this form of modified "hostage taking" for months to come. Anyone with a message could threaten suicide and expect you to come running.

Illegally Obtained Information

Keep your eyes where they belong. Curiosity might kill the cat in this case, especially if the D.A. has planted the folder for your benefit anyway. Even if the information was accurate, it would be illegally or at least unethically obtained.

Yielding Editorial Control of News Content

Air the footage, provided you tell viewers how it was obtained. You may want to do a follow-up story at a later time to show the potential consequences of moving hazardous materials through populated areas.

Cooperating with Police

Air the footage and interviews, provided you inform your audience how the footage was obtained.

Private Lives of Public Officials

If the official's situation affects his or her ability to conduct the office, report it. Otherwise, let the information remain private. If the competition is reporting information that you believe should be kept private, refrain from reporting it. Most members of your audience will respect your decision.

Misrepresentation

Case 1. Inform the city attorney of your identity when he first begins to take you into his confidence.

Case 2. The misrepresentation of a journalist's identity may lead viewers to discredit the honor and integrity of all journalists. Don't pose as the coroner's assistant.

NOTES

1. Mark Gillespie, "Public Remains Skeptical of News Media," a Gallup Organization Article, www.gallup.com/poll/releases/pr030530.asp, 30 May 2003.

2. Excerpted from a panel participation seminar, "Situation Ethics for the TV News Photographer," presented by Dr. Carl C. Monk, then dean of Washburn University School of Law (Topeka, KS), at the National Press Photographers 24th Annual Television News-Video Workshop, Norman, OK, 22 March 1984, and drawing on discussions among professional journalists in similar sessions held at the workshop from 1985 through 2003.

3. Frederick Shook, Dan Lattimore and Jim Redmond, *The Broadcast News Process*, 6th ed. (Englewood, CO: Morton Publishing Co., 2000).

4. Gene Goodwin, "The Ethics of Compassion," *The Quill* (November 1983), 38–40.

■ ■ ■ ■ ■

SHOOTING TELEVISION NEWS
The Basics

Photographers take pictures. Photojournalists tell stories with their cameras. In fact, the best photojournalists use the camera much as the writer uses a computer keyboard—to report observations and tell stories. In essence, the camera is a writing and reporting instrument, an extension not so much of the outer eye as of the inner, mind's eye. What you see and think and feel about people and events you often can share with other people through your camera.

Photography is among the most technical of the creative arts. To capture mood, action, and meaning properly and place emphasis where you want it demands that you be not only creatively adept but technically proficient. Accordingly, it is important not only that you know yourself, your shot, and your story, but also your equipment.

THE CAMERA

In some respects the electronic camera is similar to a film camera, but with an important difference (Figure A.1). The electronic camera features the charge-coupled device (CCD), a solid-state chip the size of a thumbnail that converts reflected light directly to electrical signals. The camera circuitry translates these impulses into a broadcast quality video signal that can be fed to a television monitor, recorded onto a hard drive or video-tape, or routed to live transmission equipment. Because of their reduced size and weight, solid state cameras are easy to transport and use under arduous field conditions.

The Camera Viewfinder

A black-and-white or color image of the scene also is reproduced in the camera viewfinder, itself a tiny television screen. The scene in the viewfinder is the same image as that recorded or beamed live to home viewers. After a story is shot, it can be played back through the camera viewfinder. In this manner, the photographer can "field check" the video and be certain the scenes were properly recorded.

Charge-Coupled Device Chip Cameras

Among the most important breakthroughs in camera portability is the **charge-coupled device** (CCD). The CCD is a solid-state chip the size of a thumbnail that converts reflected light directly to electrical signals.

FIGURE A.1 The television camera creates images by converting light rays to electrical video signals that can be fed to a video recorder, hard drive disk, or to live transmission equipment, in effect making the direct observation of history possible.

White Balance

The camera must be white-balanced each time it is first used on a story, and thereafter each time the camera photographs scenes illuminated by a different light source. White balance is the adjustment of camera circuitry to reproduce pure whites under the light source at hand. When the camera is properly white-balanced, there is said to be an absence of color "at white." The camera automatically adjusts white balance whenever the photographer points the camera at a white card or other white object in the scene and presses a button. Most cameras also offer a factory-preset white balance that can be activated by throwing a switch. While the factory setting produces acceptable color under ideal circumstances, it is primarily intended to help save the photographer valuable setup time when important shots would otherwise be missed on fast-breaking news events.

How Videotape Works

During recording, the tape moves past magnetic recording heads in the videocassette recorder (VCR) that create fields within the tape and align the particles in specific patterns. In addition to picture signals, the tape records sound and sync control information. The magnetic particles that are arranged in particular patterns during one recording are "scrambled" and rearranged into new patterns during subsequent recordings. For replay, the tape again passes a replay head and the previously aligned patterns disturb the field of the head to cause generation of electrical signals that result in picture and sound.

When handled according to the manufacturer's recommendations, videotape can be used repeatedly and stored for long periods without significant degradation in quality. Editing also is simple and economical. Unlike film, where segments must be cut and joined with cement, videotape is edited electronically. Unwanted information can be erased by demagnetizing so that tapes can be used repeatedly.

Videotape Formats

Over the years, videotape formats have included the Sony DVCAM, MiniDV Beta, Beta SP, and Digital Betacam; the Panasonic digital video (DVC and DVCPRO) and older to ancient M-II, D-3, and D-4 formats; three-quarter-inch, 4 mm, 8 mm, 19 mm, one-quarter-inch, one-inch, and two-inch videotape; Super VHS (S-VHS); Hi-Band 8 mm (Hi-8), and a number of other digital video formats from manufacturers such as Canon and JVC.

Of these options, digital video's affordable price and features have made it a clear favorite in today's newsgathering operations and with cable and corporate producers. Even the smallest, handheld digital video cameras produce broadcast-quality images and offer other features such as computer disk (CD) sound quality and shutter speeds from 1/5th sec. to 1/15,000th sec., a range useful for everything from low-light exposures to slow-motion and stop-action photography. Some of these miniature, lightweight cameras can shoot and store still photographs on a mini hard disk drive simultaneously while recording video (capturing still photos for on-screen graphics, for example). As an added bonus, many digital video cassettes are so small that a photographer can carry several hours of videotape in a coat pocket. Briefcase-sized digital laptop editors provide unparalleled ease of editing virtually anywhere a power supply is available. The web site at www.digitaljournalist.org provides periodic updates on digital technology, including advances in "digital video field acquisition," the process of recording video on cameras equipped with hard disk drives, memory sticks, and DVD recorders.

THE LENS

The lens gathers and focuses light and controls the amount of light that enters the camera. The lens is made of a series of convex and concave elements. Focus is controlled by moving one or more of these elements back and forth inside the lens housing by rotating an external focus ring. If, while a shot is being made, the ring is rotated to shift the focus point from one subject to another, the effect is called a **rack focus.** Gradually, sharp focus is shifted from an object in the foreground to a more distant object, or vice versa. Like most such techniques, the rack focus is least effective when it is done so abruptly or obviously that it calls attention to itself.

Macro Lenses

Lenses on television news cameras commonly allow macro-focusing, to reproduce larger-than-life images. This feature is especially convenient in order to magnify very small objects, or whenever the photojournalist must reproduce printed material on the television screen, such as a section of testimony or other printed material from a court document or newspaper (Figure A.2).

Exposure Control

Exposure is controlled either automatically or manually through rotation of a separate external control that increases or reduces the size of the lens **aperture,** a device inside the lens that operates somewhat like the iris in the human eye. Under bright light, the aperture can be closed down; in low light, the aperture can be opened up to allow more light to enter the camera.

The Zoom Lens

The lens of choice in television news photography is the variable focal length or **zoom lens** (Figure A.3). This lens provides continuously variable focal length settings from wide angle to telephoto. With its ability to provide various focal settings through such representative ranges as 12–120 mm or 25–250 mm, the zoom lens gives the photographer the equivalent of several focal length lenses in one. Because focal length is continuously variable, the photographer also can more precisely "crop" or compose scenes to eliminate undesirable elements within the frame.

Originally the zoom lens was invented to keep the picture from going to black as camera operators rotated their fixed-lens turrets during live studio broadcasts. The problem was especially acute in broadcasts that originated in studios with a single camera. Home audiences were subjected to momentary screen blackout every time the camera operator rotated the turret to rack up a different lens.

FIGURE A.2   Macro lenses permit the photojournalist to record larger-than-life images, a feature that is especially convenient for magnifying small objects.

FIGURE A.3   The zoom lens allows for infinitely variable composition throughout the full range of its focal length settings. Many photographers abuse this lens, however, by choosing to zoom indiscriminately.

How to Focus the Zoom Lens.   To focus the lens, zoom all the way in to a close-up on your subject. Focus the lens. Now zoom back out to the composition you want. Everything within the range of your zoom will be in focus. If you zoom in and are able to obtain a clean focus but then lose focus when you zoom back out, the lens may have a back focus problem that will require service.

Lens Focal Length

Lens **focal length** (Figure A.4) is determined by measuring the distance from the optical center or node of the lens to the film plane, in the case of film cameras, or the front surface of the target or CCD chip in television cameras. The **optical center** is the

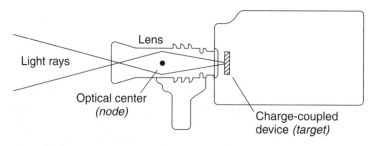

FIGURE A.4   Lens focal length is determined by measuring the distance from the optical center, or node, of the lens to the film plane or front surface of the CCD. The physical length of the lens housing is seldom an accurate expression of focal length.

point inside the lens at which light rays first bend as they are directed or brought to bear on the film plane or target during the focusing process. Seldom is the physical length of the lens housing an accurate measurement of the lens's focal length.

Focal length determines the image size of the subject and the angle of view. Each time the focal length is doubled, the image size of the subject is doubled. If the focal length is cut in half, so is image size. Whereas a normal lens might provide a 45-degree angle of view, a wide-angle lens might produce more than a 90-degree angle of view.

Lens Perspective

"Normal" lens perspective is equivalent to the human eye's view of the world. The sizes of objects in relation to one another at certain distances are approximately equal to how the human eye sees things.

From one format to another, manufacturers determine normal lens perspective for that format by measuring the diagonal size of the film negative or target. Thus, in many television news cameras, "normal lenses" are approximately 25 mm in focal length. For normal perspective, some video cameras require a lens setting of approximately 12 mm in focal length, while in the 35 mm still camera, normal perspective results from lenses of 45 mm to approximately 55 mm in focal length.

Wide-Angle Lenses. Lenses shorter than the focal length required to yield normal perspective are called **wide-angle lenses.** These lenses yield smaller image size and tend to emphasize subject matter in the foreground. Compared to normal and long lenses, wide-angle lenses also yield apparent greater depth of field, defined as the area of the scene that appears to be in sharp focus.

Long or Telephoto Lenses. Lenses or zoom lens settings greater than the focal length required to yield normal perspective are called **long** or **telephoto lenses.** Technically, all telephoto lenses are long lenses, although not all long lenses are telephoto lenses. Telephoto lenses qualify for the title because they are physically shorter than their focal length. Long lenses magnify image size and emphasize subject matter in the background. Most viewers are familiar with the tendency of long lenses to foreshorten distance, so that objects both far and near within the scene appear to be bunched up and shoved together, in an effect called *compression*. Long lenses also produce more shallow depth of field than normal and wide-angle lenses.

Lens Aperture (F/Stops)

Every camera requires an exact amount of light in order to produce perfect exposure. The amount of light required varies from one camera to the next depending on the type of film or CCD chip the camera uses. But from one application to another with a particular camera, the amount of light required to produce perfect exposure is always the same, regardless of whether the subject is photographed in the dark of night or on the brightest ski slope.

To control the amount of light entering the camera under varying light conditions, the lens is equipped with an adjustable **aperture.** Similar in function to the iris of the human eye, the aperture can be varied in size according to the prevailing light. The various aperture settings are expressed in **f/stops,** such as f/1.8, f/8, or f/22.

F/Stops Are Fractions

The f/stop number is a fraction, determined by comparing the effective diameter of the lens against its focal length. Because the f number is a fraction, the higher the f/stop number, the smaller the aperture size. Thus, f/1.2 is a larger aperture opening than f/22 (Figure A.5).

Each successive aperture either halves or doubles the amount of light entering the camera. At a setting of f/8 the lens admits only half the amount of light that it does when set to f/5.6. An aperture set to f/16 admits twice as much light as at f/22, while f/11 admits four times as much light as f/22. Thus, at the far end of the scale, f/1.2 admits 256 times more light than f/22.

As the aperture is made smaller, the photographer is said to "close down" or "stop down" the aperture. As the aperture size is made larger, the photographer is said to "open up" the aperture.

The most commonly encountered "whole" f/stop numbers are f/1.2, 2, 2.8, 4, 5.6, 8, 11, 16, and 22. For research, military, and related applications, some lenses are available with f/stop numbers that extend to 32, 45, and 64.

T/Stop

The f/stop is a theoretical value that assumes the lens is passing all the light available to it. A more accurate lens aperture setting is the **t/stop,** which takes into account the number of lens elements, lens coatings, and other light-absorbing properties of the lens elements and housing. If the lens is calibrated in t/stops, the letter *t* may appear on the lens housing next to the aperture numbers. Typically, the difference between the two values is about one half f/stop.

Aperture Size Influences Depth of Field

Aperture size also affects **depth of field** (DOF), defined as the area within a scene that appears to be in focus. The smaller the aperture, the greater the apparent DOF (Figure A.6). The larger the aperture, the more shallow the DOF.

Aperture size affects depth of field because of its effect on light rays entering the lens. Because the camera can focus on only one plane or point in space at a time, only

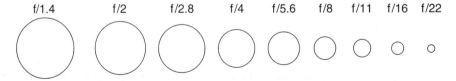

FIGURE A.5   F/stop numbers represent fractions. Hence, the larger the f number, the smaller the aperture.

FIGURE A.6 Depth of field is an expression of the area within a scene that appears to be in focus. The left example illustrates shallow depth of field; the right illustrates great depth of field.

objects at that one distance from the camera can be in true focus. To one degree or another, every object at any other distance is rendered out of focus.

Razor-crisp focus results from pinpoints of light that strike the film plane or target surface. If the light rays are out of focus, they register not as pinpoints of light but as circles of light called **circles of confusion.** If the circles of confusion are small enough, the subject may appear sharp enough to be in focus. If the circles of confusion are extraordinarily large, however, the object will be reproduced in fuzzy or soft focus. Small apertures produce smaller circles of confusion, and thus greater depth of field.

Other Factors That Affect Depth of Field

In addition to aperture size, depth of field also is determined by lens focal length and distance from subject. Wide-angle lenses produce greater apparent depth of field than long lenses, and depth of field increases as a lens is focused on objects further from the camera. Conversely, depth of field becomes more shallow as the lens is focused on objects that are progressively closer to the camera.

Focal length affects depth of field because of its influence on aperture size. Assuming all other factors remain equal, each time the lens housing is doubled in length, only half the original amount of light is passed. To compensate for the light loss, the aperture size must be doubled. Thus, if the effective diameter of a 12 mm lens at f/8 is 2 mm, the effective diameter of a 25 mm lens at f/8 must be approximately 4 mm. Doubling the focal length of the 25 mm lens to 50 mm would result in an effective diameter at f/8 of approximately 8 mm. Because aperture size controls the size of circles of confusion, out-of-focus objects within the scene are more obviously out of focus when photographed with the 50 mm or 25 mm lenses than with the 12 mm lens.

DEPTH OF FIELD

Most commonly, about one-third of the total range of depth of field occurs in front of the subject or focus point, and two-thirds behind the subject. Assume the lens is focused on a subject 45 feet from the camera, and that the total range of depth of field is 60 feet. In this example, the range of acceptable focus or depth of field would begin 20 feet in front of the subject (one-third of 60 feet) and extend to 40 feet behind the subject (two-thirds of 60 feet).

The near plane of acceptable focus would therefore begin at approximately 25 feet in front of the camera and extend to approximately 85 feet from the camera.

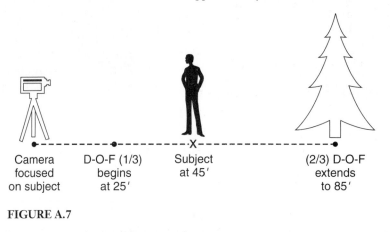

Camera	D-O-F (1/3)	Subject	(2/3) D-O-F
focused	begins	at 45'	extends
on subject	at 25'		to 85'

FIGURE A.7

A simple experiment helps illustrate how the camera's distance from the subject affects depth of field. Hold an object very close to your eye, then without changing focus become aware of the surroundings behind the object. If you maintain your focus on the object, the background will appear to be out of focus.

Now move the object further away from your eye and notice how depth of field increases. If you were to focus on the object several hundred feet away, the entire range of your view would appear to be in focus.

How to Obtain Maximum Depth of Field. Depth of field increases in a scene whenever the following conditions are met, whether separately or in combination. Thus, maximum depth of field results whenever all the conditions are met:

- small aperture setting (i.e., f/22)
- short focal length lens (wide angle)
- camera focused on objects far from it

How to Obtain Shallow Depth of Field. Shallow depth of field is desirable for artistic effect or when the photojournalist wishes to confine the viewer's attention to foreground subjects by throwing the background out of focus. Depth of field in a scene becomes more shallow when the following conditions are met, whether separately or in combination. The minimum depth of field results when all the conditions are met:

- large aperture setting (i.e., f/2.8 or smaller)
- long focal length lens (telephoto)
- camera focused on objects very near it

Even in bright light, larger aperture settings are possible if the photographer uses neutral density filters to reduce the amount of light entering the lens (see Chapter 5, The Magic of Light and Lighting).

Avoid Automatic Lens Settings

The television camera "sees" the scene in terms of the standard **gray scale** that is familiar to black-and-white photographers. At one end of the scale, represented by a value of 10, is pure white. At the other end of the scale, represented by a value of 0, is black. In between are the various shades of gray, ranging from light to very dark gray.

Objects within the scene are reproduced as various shades of white, gray, and black. The camera's color circuitry combines with the black-and-white picture to produce a color image. If you turn down the color on a television set, you can see the picture's underlying black and white image.

If a scene is made up mostly of white and black tones, it is reproduced as a high-**contrast** image. If the scene is made up mostly of objects that yield medium gray tones, it will be reproduced as a low-contrast image (Figure A.8). In determining exposure, the camera's automatic exposure circuitry samples all the white, black, and gray areas

FIGURE A.8 Variations between the brightest and darkest objects dictate the degree of contrast in a scene. Variations between bright and dark objects in low-contrast images (left) are far less pronounced than in high-contrast scenes (right).

in the scene, then calculates exposure based on an average of all the values represented. The camera is most easily fooled by high-contrast scenes such as when a person is photographed against a window, the sky, or a white wall. Images with such high-contrast ratios also typically sacrifice sharpness and subtle detail. The camera normally produces its most accurate exposure and fineness of detail when objects within the scene tend toward the middle of the gray scale.

Because the automatic circuitry adjusts constantly to changing light conditions, it also can produce an undesirable "bloom" or surge in exposure whenever moving objects within the scene pass in front of backgrounds with differing shades of contrast. Exposure surge would occur in the following shots if the camera is left on the automatic exposure setting:

- a child rides a tricycle past a white picket fence interspersed with dark, ornamental bushes
- a woman doing sit-ups moves into and out of the frame in front of a light-colored wall
- bright sunlight methodically appears and disappears in the gaps between freight cars as a train roars past a railroad crossing

In each instance, the automatic circuitry will struggle first to reduce exposure, then to increase exposure to accommodate the changing light intensities. To avoid surges in exposure, professional photographers first use the automatic meter in the camera to set proper exposure, then click it off while the shot is made. For even more precise exposure, the photographer can make additional adjustments with the manual exposure control.

BE CAREFUL WITH THAT CAMERA

Whenever you're in the field, always remember Peterson's Law: "Murphy was an optimist." If anything can go wrong in the world of television, it will. Leave your camera on the tripod, walk away for a moment, and be certain that fate will conspire, somehow, to tip it over: a wind gust, a puppy chasing cats, a clumsy passerby, whatever it takes to bring down that camera. Forget to lock down the tripod head, walk over to adjust the mike on your interviewee, and return to discover your $3,000 lens now dangles from a torqued camera body. It can happen.

SUMMARY

Today it is possible to photograph technically high quality images with little or no technical knowledge. Automatic focus, exposure, white balance, and simplified camera operation make this possible. But without an understanding of the basic processes involved in creating visual imagery, the photographer forfeits some supervision over content. Less achievable are the subtle distinctions in imagery that can be used to enhance the viewer's ability to experience the complex interrelations of nuance, mood, and meaning in stories.

The television field camera somewhat duplicates the function of the human eye. The camera converts light rays to electrical signals that can be transmitted to home viewers or recorded on videotape or hard drive for later broadcast. The camera lens gathers and focuses light, while the lens aperture or iris allows for precise exposure control. Lenses are available either in fixed focal lengths or, more commonly, as zoom lenses with continuously variable focal lengths. Changes in focal length allow the photographer to vary emphasis on subject matter by changing perspective and depth of field.

While entirely adequate stories can be shot with virtually no understanding of the camera, photojournalists who aspire to excellence soon discover that mastery without understanding is unlikely.

DISCUSSION

1. Define the term "white balance" and explain why it is important.

2. In general terms, explain how video signals from the camera are recorded onto videotape.

3. List and describe the primary functions of the camera lens.

4. List the distinguishing features of the zoom lens and discuss its strengths and weaknesses.

5. Explain how focal length affects lens perspective, image size, and depth of field.

6. Explain the relationship between lens aperture size and f/stop number.

7. Describe steps the photographer can take to achieve shallow depth of field and great depth of field.

8. Explain why duplicate copies of digital recordings show very little loss in quality.

EXERCISES

1. Practice handholding the camera until you can hold it rock steady.

2. Using a television field camera or home video camera, white-balance the camera for sunlight and, without further adjustment, record one scene under fluorescent light, a second scene indoors under artificial quartz lights, and a third scene outdoors under normal sunlight. Now repeat the process, but this time balance the camera for artificial quartz light. Play back the scenes and compare the camera's response to varying degrees of color temperature.

3. Study the aperture on a camera lens as you change f/stop settings. Notice the relationship between large aperture sizes and small f/stop numbers and vice versa.

4. Position a subject in front of a window or other source of strong illumination. Allow the camera metering system to determine proper exposure. Notice how the subject tends to silhouette unless supplementary light is added to the front of the subject.

5. Allow camera circuitry to determine the proper exposure in a scene, then purposefully underexpose and overexpose the scene by one half f/stop, next by one full f/stop, and finally by two full f/stops. Identify each stage of over- or underexposure by speaking

into the camera microphone as you record the shots on videotape, or else use a small slate in the scene on which you have written +½ stop, +1 stop, etc. Notice the effect of over- and underexposure on colors and contrasts within the scene.

6. Without changing camera position, shoot a wide-angle shot of a subject, then a telephoto shot of the same subject. Notice the effect of focal length setting on image size, depth of field, and emphasis on subject matter.

7. Shoot a subject in silhouette against a window, the sky, or other bright light source. Record the scene using the camera's automatic exposure meter. Next, switch the camera to manual exposure setting and record the scene two more times: first, so the subject is correctly exposed; second, so the background is correctly exposed. Play back the video and compare the three shots you have made, paying particular attention to variations in exposure, color reproduction, and fineness of detail between the respective scenes.

8. To become more familiar with the perspective produced at various lens focal settings, first shoot a series of shots with the camera in a fixed position. Make five individual shots, without zooming the lens during any individual shot, at the following or similar focal lengths: 15 mm, 30 mm, 50 mm, 75 mm, 100 mm. Now, set and keep the focal length at normal perspective for the camera you are using and make five more shots, this time beginning at least 100 feet from a subject and then physically moving the camera ten footsteps closer each time you make a shot. Compare the lack of real change in perspective when the camera is left in one position and the true change in perspective that results when you physically move the camera.

9. Focus the camera on a scene in which a number of highlights are visible. Purposefully but gradually throw the scene out of focus and notice how elements within the scene are reproduced as ever larger circles of confusion.

10. To become more familiar with the influences that affect depth of field, attach the camera to a tripod in a fixed location and shoot five shots of a subject at the following or similar focal lengths: 15 mm, 30 mm, 50 mm, 75 mm, 100 mm. Do not move the camera between shots. Next, set the lens on the widest focal length setting and make five more shots, this time physically moving the camera so that each shot is made approximately equidistant from the previous shot. Repeat the process, this time with the lens set on a long or telephoto length setting. Notice how depth of field decreases the closer the camera is to the subject and the longer the focal length setting becomes.

A REPORTING, WRITING, AND EDITING CHECKLIST

The reporting, writing, and editing checklist that follows is offered not only as a summary of the reporting process for television, but also as a catalyst for communication among all members of the reporting team. The checklist was developed as a product of ongoing interviews and correspondence with NBC News senior correspondent Bob Dotson.

STORY CHECKLIST

- *Always remember:* The reporter is not the story.
- *Story focus:* Is it present? Focus is the story stated in one sentence—what you want the audience to take away from the report. The focus should be stated during the story planning process as a complete sentence with subject, verb, and object. "Outside money is altering the city's architecture," "This cow has never taken an order in her life," "You can't murder a pumpkin," etc. Prove the focus visually. Very seldom will you state the focus verbally on air in any story.
- *Pictures:* Remember to write your pictures first, as you plan your story.
- *Beginning:* A strong lead, preferably visual, that instantly telegraphs the story to come.
- *Middle:* Main body of the story, usually no more than three to five main points, which you prove visually once you've identified them.
- *Ending:* A strong close that you can't top, something you build toward throughout the story. Ideally, the ending also is visual.
- *Writing:* Be hard on yourself as a writer. Say nothing in script your viewers would already know or that the visuals say more eloquently. Write loose.
- *Sequences:* Throughout the story, build your report around sequences—two or three shots of a guy buying basketball tickets; two or three shots of a husband and wife drinking coffee at a kitchen table, etc. Sequences demand matched action.
- *Moments of silence:* Stop writing occasionally and let two or three seconds or more of compelling action occur with natural sound, but without voice over. For a writer, nothing is more difficult to write than silence. For viewers, sometimes nothing is more eloquent.
- *Strong, natural sound:* To heighten realism, authenticity, believability; to heighten the viewer's sense of vicarious participation in the events you're showing. Some

reports merely let you watch what happened. The best reports let you experience what happened.

- *Storytelling through people:* People sell your story. Try to find strong central characters engaged in compelling action that is visual or picturesque.
- *Surprises:* Build in surprises to sustain viewer involvement. Surprises help viewers feel something about the story; surprises lure uninterested viewers to the screen. Surprises can be visual, nat sound, short bites, or poetic script. Always, surprises are little moments of drama.
- *Short sound bites:* Short bites prove the story you are showing. Don't use sound bites as substitutes for more effective storytelling.
- *The larger issue:* Most people will watch a story that tells them "Puppies are cute," but they may wonder subconsciously, "So what?" if that's all you tell them. Few viewers will forget your story if you address the larger issue: "Cute puppies carry more infectious diseases because they are more frequently handled at pet stores."
- *Making it memorable:* Can your viewers feel something about the story and its subjects? If feeling is present, the story will stick in viewer's minds.

APPLYING THE CHECKLIST

Applying the checklist to reporting assignments is a simple procedure—more nearly a way of thinking than of memorizing a list. In the following demonstration of how to apply the checklist, assume you are part of a reporter–photographer team assigned to prepare a report about people who eat on the run.

At this stage, you know the story assignment—eating on the run, a practice called "grazing"—and you begin to develop a "story mind set." As a journalist, you already know something about the story: You have observed people who graze, and as a journalist you probably eat meals on the run yourself; you also may have stored away other tidbits of information about your story subject from a variety of sources.

Even with all this information, you still have to ask yourself, "What's the story?" Remember, also, to ask other members of the reporting team what they think the story should be. Until you identify the story, you can't tell it to anyone else. At this point, research your subject so that you can begin to identify the real story.

Some of your research will occur as you cover the story, but ideally most of your background research will be finished before you leave the station. That way, you'll know well in advance whom you should interview, what pictures and sound you'll need, and what questions you should ask your sources.

State your story in a simple, declarative sentence that has a subject, verb, and object. This statement is your story focus. Perhaps your first story focus says, "Eating on the run affects physical health and the quality of our social interaction." You run the idea past the other members of the reporting team and all agree, the focus at this stage is too general.

If that's the case, try to restate your focus, realizing that as your understanding of the story changes, so will the pictures you need to tell the story:

- "America's garbage is America's portrait."
- "Our eating habits define personal values/self-image."

- "What we are is what we eat."
- "We are not only what we eat, but how we eat."
- "We are how we eat."

Finally, as you work through potential story lines, you settle on your final story focus: "Only we control what we put in our bodies and the rate at which we put it there." Now, from your research, identify the main points of the story. Too many main points will ruin the report, so try to keep the story to no more than three or four and remember to find visual proof for each. In this story, let's assume we've identified the following main points:

- Poor nutrition: "When we eat on the run, our predominant diet tends to consist of foods high in salt, sugar, caffeine, cholesterol, fat, and carbohydrates." Now, search for the visual proof that will communicate this main point. Perhaps you find a nutrition expert who can visually portray the amount of excess salt, caffeine, fat, and carbohydrates we consume over a year's time when we eat on the run.
- Isolation: "When we eat on the run, in isolation, we deprive ourselves of important social interactions." Again, ask what pictures will prove this point. Try to avoid the psychologist or other authority who merely tells you this information and instead seek visual proof for your message. Show people as they eat in isolation and interview them for their reactions and insights.
- Check your trash: "If you're concerned about your eating habits, check yourself with a look at your garbage." Even with a deadline to meet, you can no doubt find someone willing to sort through their own trash on camera as they recount the past week's meals.

Remember, also, to search for a visual lead that instantly communicates the story to come. In this story perhaps your opening shot is from a camera moving along the curbside, to show the remnants from meals consumed in cars. Voice over: "We are not only what we eat in America, we are also how we eat." Or perhaps your visual lead shows a jogger who runs into a fast food restaurant and right back out with a milk shake. Whatever the opening shot, be certain it instantly communicates the story to come. A word of caution: Remember never to unfairly stage or overstage a story just to get the visuals you need.

As soon as you arrive in the field, begin your search for a closing shot—a visual close you build toward throughout the entire piece, something so strong it's obvious the story is done. Because the primary message is "Only we control what we put in our mouths, and the rate at which we put it there," a strong closing shot might be of an overweight man who sips club soda as he says, "I still have twenty pounds to lose. But you know, it's easy to lose weight when the doctor says you can either lose weight and live until you're seventy, or you can remain overweight, live maybe twenty more years—and be sick." Once you have such a closing shot on tape, you can build every component of the report toward that final moment.

USING THE INTERNET AS A REPORTING TOOL

Like the world's great cities, the **Internet** represents an expression of the collective human mind. Virtually everything the human being can do, think, or imagine finds representation. Some sites scream with obscenity. Others waste the reader's time with their shallowness and pointlessness. The best are invaluable. With only a few mouse clicks or verbal commands, they give the journalist unparalleled access to a mother lode of information about almost every topic imaginable. Background information, maps, names, addresses, telephone numbers, you name it and you'll find it on the Internet. Radio and television stations also stream digital audio and video, including live broadcasts and 24-hour access to archived news programs.

Anyone with a computer, Internet access, and an Internet service provider can access **search engines** that quickly winnow through thousands, sometimes millions, of sites to find vital information. A few of the most well-known search engines follow. Some search only the "net"; some activate ten or more search engines to locate information and display their findings.

Once the main page opens on any of the following sites, list one or more words or a phrase and click the "submit" or "find" button. In moments the search engine will return a list of possible resources.

MULTI-ENGINE SEARCH TOOLS

AltaVista:	www.altavista.com
Excite:	www.excite.com
Google:	www.google.com
HotBot:	www.hotbot.com
Infoseek:	www.infoseek.com
Lycos:	www.lycos.com
Magellan:	www.mckinley.com
MetaCrawler:	www.metacrawler.com
Yahoo:	www.yahoo.com

Once again, while extremely powerful, the above sites represent only a few of the Internet search engines available on the **World Wide Web.** Perhaps you use other engines that you find even more effective.

INTERNET SITES OF INTEREST TO JOURNALISTS

Also of interest to professional journalists are the following sites. Again, they represent only a starting point. Undoubtedly, you can add to the list and will find other valuable sites as you surf the 'net.

FACSNET

www.facsnet.org
An excellent research site for reporters. The following news organizations helped launch FACSNET: A. H. Belo Corp., *Chicago Tribune*, CNN, Cox Newspapers, *The Dallas Morning News*, *The Detroit News*, Gannett Co., Hearst Newspapers, *Los Angeles Times*, Media General, NBC, Phoenix Newspapers, E. W. Scripps Company.

Niles On Line

www.robertniles.com
Another excellent site for reporter research.

Radio-Television News Directors Association

www.rtnda.org

National Press Photographers Association

www.nppa.org

National Association of Broadcasters

www.nab.org

Poynter Institute

www.poynter.org
An organization for the continuing education of professional journalists.

The Associated Press

www.ap.org
A premiere site for news stories and updates.

ABC News

www.abcnews.com

CBS News

www.cbsnews.com

CNN

www.cnn.com

NBC/MSNBC

www.nbcnews.com

FOX Television

www.foxnews.com

ENG Safety

www.engsafety.com

Jobs in Television

www.tvjobs.com
Includes entry-level jobs and U.S. television markets, listed alphabetically and by market size.

The Rundown

www.tvrundown.com
Since 1981, The Rundown has reported weekly on local television news, programming, and community service projects. Top executives and newspeople share their insights and lessons learned. Easily the largest record of hometown television's activities.

Digital Journalist

www.digitaljournalist.org
An excellent site for staying abreast of changes in digital technology. Focuses both on changes in still and television digital photography and editing.

NewsBlues

www.newsblues.com
A good source for links to other broadcast sites, as well as the lowdown on what it's like to work at dozens of stations across the country.

Ken Linder Agency (KLA)

www.kenlindner.com
A talent agency site that features information about the people, services, and philosophy of KLA and provides valuable insights and resources for broadcast talent.

Don Fitzpatrick's Job "Pipeline" (fee-based)

www.tvspy.com

Don Fitzpatrick's "Shoptalk"

www.shoptalk.com
A not-to-be missed daily summary and discussion of issues, career moves, jobs, and points of view from news managers and broadcast news practioners.

U.S. Local TV Stations on WWW

www.newsdirectory.com/tv
www.100000watts.com/listings.html

A WORD OF CAUTION

Every Internet site poses a risk to the journalist. Who originated the information? Is it factual? Will you risk legal exposure by quoting the information? Can you independently verify the information? Experience suggests that you verify all information you find on the Internet. Find at least one and preferably two other sources to verify Internet information.

Perhaps you need information about a new law that affects all veterans. Using search engines, you find a site with apparently valid information about the story. The site says any veteran who has not registered at a Veterans Affairs' office or hospital since October 1, 1996 would have lost all medical benefits for life as of October 1, 1998. If you used that information, however, your story would be grossly inaccurate. The law required only that Veterans Affairs establish an *enrollment system* by October 1, 1998. Veterans can apply for enrollment anytime, and all veterans who received health-care services after October 1, 1996 are automatically enrolled.*

Obviously, many sites represent the originator's point of view, whether the originator be a politician, an auto maker, a fund-raising organization, or a special interest group. While quick access to the originator's point of view is valuable, that point of view is just like any other source: it rarely will reflect journalistic balance in and of itself. Other sites, including those operated by major media outlets such as the *New York Times*, ABC News, CNN, and others, are as accurate and carefully verified as their print and on-air versions. Yet even they sometimes are prone to error, so whatever the source, it pays to verify information you find on the Internet.

Denver Post, 25 September 1998, 34E.

Aerial Shot. Shot taken from a camera mounted in an airplane, helicopter, or similar conveyance. (The Visual Grammar of Motion Picture Photography)

Analog. The video output of nondigital cameras and tape decks that convert or store light rays to electrical signals rather than 1's and 0's. A quality loss occurs with every generation. (The Visual Grammar of Motion Picture Photography)

Anchor Debrief. The question-and-answer period between an anchor and on-set reporter immediately after the reporter's story has aired. (The Role of Talent Performance in Field Reporting)

Aperture. An adjustable iris inside the camera lens that can be regulated to control the amount of light entering the camera. (Shooting Television News: The Basics)

Apparent Authority. The authority of an individual that can be reasonably assumed to be sufficient for a reporter to enter someone's premises or other property, as in the case of permission from a police officer to enter an apartment building in the absence of the building's owner. (Law and the Broadcast Journalist)

Aspect Ratio. The ratio of width to height in a television image. (The Visual Grammar of Motion Picture Photography)

Axis Line. An imaginary straight line projected from the tip of the camera lens through the center of the subject and beyond. If the photographer shoots on both sides of the axis line, false reverses in the action may result. (The Visual Grammar of Motion Picture Photography)

Backlight. A light placed opposite the key and shined down on the subject from behind. Also called a "rim light." (The Magic of Light and Lighting)

Barndoors. The hinged metal doors used on light heads to block or direct light. (The Magic of Light and Lighting)

Bidirectional. A microphone pickup pattern in which sound is picked up in front and back, but not to the sides of the microphone. (The Sound Track)

Blue Eye. A live television report that consists solely of a reporter talking on camera from a remote location, without supporting video or prerecorded interviews. See also "Naked Live" and "Thumb Sucker." (Live Shots and Remotes)

BOPSA. A term used to describe boring scenes normally shot at meetings and luncheons that show a "bunch of people sitting around."

Bounce Light. Light is reflected off a surface to make it appear more soft and natural. (The Magic of Light and Lighting)

Broadlighting. The lighting pattern that results when the key light illuminates the side of the subject's face closest to camera. (The Magic of Light and Lighting)

Butterfly Light. A variation of top lighting in which the main light is placed high and slightly in front of the subject, resulting in a butterfly-shaped shadow beneath the subject's nose. Also called "glamour lighting." (The Magic of Light and Lighting)

CG. Character generator, a computer device that electronically produces words to be superimposed over a live or recorded image. (Live Shots and Remotes)

Charge-Coupled Device (CCD). A solid-state chip that converts reflected light directly to electrical signals. (Shooting Television News: The Basics)

Circles of Confusion. Light rays that register as overlapping circles of light on the film plane or target surface, rather than as pinpoints of light that result in crisp focus. (Shooting Television News: The Basics)

Close. The closing shot of the story; the ending toward which the rest of the story builds. (Live Shots and Remotes, Television Script Formats, Writing the Package)

Close-Up (CU). A shot that fills the screen with the subject or with only a portion of the subject, as for example the face of a person or the full screen shot of a wrist watch. (Telling the Visual Story, The Visual Grammar of Motion Picture Photography)

Cold Cut. A cut in which an outgoing shot and its accompanying sound end simultaneously, only to be replaced at the splice line by new picture with new sound. The effect can destroy a story's otherwise smooth, fluid pace. (Video Editing: The Invisible Art)

Color Temperature. An expression of the proportion of red to blue light that the light source radiates. As color temperature increases, the light becomes progressively more bluish. (The Magic of Light and Lighting)

Combination Shot. Camera follows action until a new moving subject enters frame, then picks up the new subject and follows it. (The Visual Grammar of Motion Picture Photography)

Command Post. A temporary headquarters established at the scene of emergencies to control the flow of information, and to help reporters and photographers obtain access to the scene. (Live Shots and Remotes)

Commitment. A declarative sentence that identifies the story to be told. The journalistic equivalent of the terms *theme, storyline, premise,* or *point of view* as commonly used in literature and theatre. See also "Focus." (Writing the Package, Telling the Visual Story, How to Improve Your Storytelling Ability)

Composition. The placement and emphasis of visual elements on the screen. (The Visual Grammar of Motion Picture Photography, Video Editing: The Invisible Art)

Contrast. The proportion of white tones in a scene in relationship to black or gray tones. High contrast results when objects in a scene are white and black, with few intermediate gray tones. Low contrast results when objects in scenes are white on white, black on black, or mostly medium gray. (Shooting Television News: The Basics)

Contrast Ratio. The difference between the most brightly illuminated areas of a subject and the areas of least exposure. (The Magic of Light and Lighting)

Cookies. Opaque panels with cutouts that create patterns of light and shadow on backgrounds. See "Flags." (The Magic of Light and Lighting)

Crossroll. Prerecorded video or interviews that roll on air following the reporter's live, on-camera introduction in a remote field report. (Live Shots and Remotes)

Cut. The point in edited video at which audience attention is transferred instantly from one image to the next. See "Edit Point." (Video Editing: The Invisible Art)

Cutaway. A shot of some part of the peripheral action, such as a clock on the wall or football fans in a stadium, that can be used to divert the viewer's eye momentarily from the main action. Commonly used as an editorial device to help eliminate jump cuts and to condense time. See "Motivated Cutaway." (The Visual Grammar of Motion Picture Photography, Video Editing: The Invisible Art)

Cut-In Shot. A shot such as a close-up or insert that emphasizes particular elements of the action in a master shot. (The Visual Grammar of Motion Picture Photography)

Cutting at Rest. Editing together scenes of matched action at points in which the action has momentarily stopped. (Video Editing: The Invisible Art)

Cutting on Action. Cutting out of a scene as the action progresses and continuing the action without interruption at the start of the incoming scene. (Video Editing: The Invisible Art)

Decibel (dB). A measure of sound intensity that corresponds roughly to the minimum change in sound level that the human ear can detect. (The Sound Track)

Defamation. Any statement that damages a person's name, reputation, or character. (Law and the Broadcast Journalist)

Demonstration Standup. The reporter addresses the field camera while engaging in an activity that helps visually prove and reinforce the story being reported. (The Role of Talent Performance in Field Reporting)

Depth of Field (DOF). The range of acceptable focus in a scene. Normally, about one-third of the total range of depth of field occurs in front of the subject or focus point, and two-thirds behind the subject. (Shooting Television News: The Basics)

Digital. Information is recorded on videotape, disk drive, computer, or other medium as a series of 1's and 0's. No quality loss occurs during duplication. (The Visual Grammar of Motion Picture Photography)

Digitize. The process of transferring pictures from tape to disk, where they reside in final form as digital data. (Video Editing: The Invisible Art)

Dissolve. A scene optically fades to black on top of another scene, which optically fades from black to full exposure. The effect is a melting of one scene into the next. (The Visual Grammar of Motion Picture Photography, Video Editing: The Invisible Art)

Distancing. The feeling that a news happening is remote or even unreal, which can overcome photographers as they watch events unfold in the camera viewfinder. (Field Techniques of Shooting Television News)

Distortion. Any signal that unintentionally sounds or appears different on output from a transmission or recording device than it did on input. (The Sound Track)

Dolly Shot. A shot made from a camera mounted on a wheeled conveyance that is moved either toward the subject or away from it. See "Tracking Shot." (The Visual Grammar of Motion Picture Photography)

Double-System Film Editing. A process in which film scenes and multiple sound tracks are manipulated independently of one another, in full synchronization. (Video Editing: The Invisible Art)

Dropouts. Temporary interruptions in transmitted or recorded sound or picture. (The Sound Track)

Dynamic Microphone.   A rugged, handheld microphone often used in news applications. (The Sound Track)

Editing.   The editing of video and its attendant sound is the "conscious and deliberate guidance of viewer thoughts and associations." The editor strives both to create illusion and to reconstruct reality, as well as to guide viewers' emotional responses. (Telling the Visual Story, Video Editing: The Invisible Art)

Editing in the Camera.   The practice of shooting sequences and overlapping action in generally the same order in which they are to be aired. (Field Techniques of Shooting Television News, Live Shots and Remotes)

Edit Point.   The point at which one shot is surrendered and a new shot begins. See "Cut." (Video Editing: The Invisible Art)

ENG.   Electronic news gathering. (Preface, Video Editing: The Invisible Art)

Establishing Shot.   Used to introduce viewers to the story's locale or to the story itself. (The Visual Grammar of Motion Picture Photography)

Ethics.   A philosophy of what is right and acceptable as it governs the rules of living and conduct that impact on professional deportment. (Journalistic Ethics)

Exterior Shot.   A shot made out-of-doors. (The Visual Grammar of Motion Picture Photography)

Eyewash.   Pictures whose meaning has little to do with the main point of the story being reported. See "Wallpaper Video" and "Generic Video." (Introduction)

Fade.   The scene fades to black (fade-out) or fades from black to full exposure (fade-in). (Video Editing: The Invisible Art)

False Reverse.   A subject moving in one screen direction is seen in the next shot to be moving in the opposite direction. (The Visual Grammar of Motion Picture Photography, Field Techniques of Shooting Television News, Video Editing: The Invisible Art)

Fast Lenses.   Lenses useful in low light situations because of their large maximum aperture sizes, generally in the range of f/1.2 or f/1.4. (Shooting Television News: The Basics)

Feather.   A technique used in zooming and panning shots, in which the artificial camera movement begins almost imperceptibly and builds to the intended speed, then slows and again ends almost imperceptibly. The technique reduces audience distraction by eliminating the abrupt and obvious beginning and ending of artificial camera movement. (The Visual Grammar of Motion Picture Photography)

Fill Light.   A secondary light source set to produce illumination approximately one-fourth to one-half as intense as the key light. (The Magic of Light and Lighting)

Filmic Time.   The representation of time in motion picture media as an elastic commodity. In television and film, time can be compressed or expanded far beyond the constraints of real time, which is inelastic. (Video Editing: The Invisible Art)

Filter.   A colored glass or optical gel used in photography to control exposure, contrast, or color temperature. (The Magic of Light and Lighting)

Filter Factor.   A measure of the amount of light that is lost when a filter is used in photography. Each factor of 2 cuts the original amount of light in half. (The Magic of Light and Lighting)

Flags.   Opaque panels used to block light from certain areas. See "Cookies." (The Magic of Light and Lighting)

Flash Cut.   Brief fragments of shots are cut to exact rhythm against a musical beat or sound. (Video Editing: The Invisible Art)

Flat Light.   A flat, uninteresting light with little sense of depth or modeling which results when the primary light is mounted on the camera or very near it. (The Magic of Light and Lighting)

Focal Length.   The designation of a camera lens and its angle of view as determined by measuring the distance from the optical center of the lens to the front surface of the CCD chip in television cameras. (Shooting Television News: The Basics)

Focus (of the story).   A simple, vivid, declarative sentence expressing the heart, the soul, of the story as it will be on air. See "Commitment." (Writing the Package, Telling the Visual Story)

F/Stop.   An aperture setting expressed as a fraction. (Shooting Television News: The Basics)

Future File.   A collection of story ideas, notes, and news releases about upcoming events. (The Assignment Editor and Producer: Architects of the Newscast)

Generic Video.   Visuals from file video or similar source originally shot for one purpose, then later used to haphazardly "illustrate" a script. Often the pictures are inappropriate to the message being communicated. (Telling the Visual Story, Journalistic Ethics)

Gray Scale.   A printed scale of contrast values ranging from black, through the various shades of gray, to pure white. (Shooting Television News: The Basics)

Great Depth of Field.   The term used when a scene appears to be in focus from quite near the camera to and including the background. See "Maximum Depth of Field" and "Shallow Depth of Field." (Shooting Television News: The Basics)

Gyro-Lens. A lens that electronically compensates for unintentional camera motion and vibration to produce a smoother, steadier shot. The lens is especially useful to smooth out aerial shots and handheld shots made on long focal length settings. (Shooting Television News: The Basics)

Hardware. The equipment and accessories needed for nonlinear editing. Everything from computers, monitors, hard disk drives, microphones, and audio speakers to amplifiers, cables, and keyboards. (Video Editing: The Invisible Art)

Hatchet Light. Side light that appears to "split" the subject's face in half. (The Magic of Light and Lighting)

Head-On Shot. Action in the shot moves directly toward camera. (The Visual Grammar of Motion Picture Photography, Video Editing: The Invisible Art)

Heat. The emotional or intellectual intensity often present in sound bites that are spontaneous and believable. (Field Techniques of Shooting Television News)

Hertz. A unit of frequency expressed as one cycle per second. See "Kilohertz." (The Sound Track)

HDTV. High Definition Television, a digital transmission system that allows up to 1,080 horizontal lines of video information on the screen and 1,920 on the vertical, with roughly three times more resolution than standard U.S. televisions can provide. Screen sizes can exceed five feet in width, with an aspect ratio similar to theatrical movie screens. (The Visual Grammar of Motion Picture Photography)

High-Angle Shot. A shot taken with the camera high and looking down at the subject. High angles tend to diminish the subject and give viewers a sense of superiority. (The Visual Grammar of Motion Picture Photography)

Highlights. Vignettes of the most noteworthy happenings in sports or news events. (Sports Reporting and Photography)

High-Pass Filter. An audio filter that diminishes the low frequencies where most wind and some equipment noises originate. (The Sound Track)

Illustrative Video. Separate shots of video keyed to each sentence or paragraph of script, with little regard for continuity in subject matter or consecutiveness from one shot to the next. (How to Improve Your Storytelling Ability)

Impedance. A characteristic of microphones similar to electrical resistance. (The Sound Track)

Insert Shot. Close-up, essential detail about some part of the main action. (The Visual Grammar of Motion Picture Photography, Video Editing: The Invisible Art)

Internet. A global network of cables and computers encompassing thousands of smaller regional networks scattered throughout the world. See also "World Wide Web (WWW)," which provides the means for worldwide retrieval of information via computer. (Law and the Broadcast Journalist, Appendix B)

Interior Shot. A shot made inside a building or other interior location. (The Visual Grammar of Motion Picture Photography)

Invasion of Privacy. Any act of intrusion, including trespass and publication of embarrassing facts, even if true, that violates an individual's reasonable expectation to privacy. (Law and the Broadcast Journalist)

Inverse-Square Law of Light. The law of physics that states that at twice the distance from a subject, artificial lights provide only one-fourth their original level of illumination. (The Magic of Light and Lighting)

Iris. An adjustable aperture inside the camera lens that can be regulated to control the amount of light entering the camera. (Shooting Television News: The Basics)

Jump Cut. An action that is seen to jump unnaturally into a new position on the screen. (The Visual Grammar of Motion Picture Photography, Video Editing: The Invisible Art)

Key. Words or graphics electronically inserted into the video scene. (Live Shots and Remotes)

Key Light. The primary or dominant light that illuminates a subject. (The Magic of Light and Lighting)

Kilohertz. A unit of frequency equal to 1,000 cycles per second (kHz). See "Hertz." (The Sound Track)

Lavaliere Microphone. A miniature microphone that can be clipped to or hidden beneath the speaker's clothing. (The Sound Track, Live Shots and Remotes)

Law. The rules and principles of conduct enacted through legislation, and enforced by local, state, and federal authority, that dictate how the affairs of a community or society are to be conducted. (Law and the Broadcast Journalist)

Lead. The first shot in a news package. Its purpose is to telegraph the story to come instantly. (Telling the Visual Story)

Lead-In. The anchor copy that introduces the story and sets up the video package or prerecorded audio report in radio and television newscasts. To best serve audience understanding, the lead-in should instantly reveal the story rather than act merely as the introduction to a package still to come. The term "lead-in" also can refer to the sentence of copy that leads into a sound bite in a radio or television report. (Writing the Package)

Libel.   The use of factual information, as opposed to opinion, that holds someone in hatred or contempt, subjects the person to ridicule, or otherwise lowers one's esteem for the individual. (Law and the Broadcast Journalist)

Limited Invitation.   A principle that holds that even in public places, such as restaurants and supermarkets, photography may be prohibited and the reporter's conduct limited to the primary activities of the business in question—in this example, eating or shopping. (Law and the Broadcast Journalist)

Linear Editing.   The process by which images are recorded, one after another, on videotape. No change in length is possible without re-editing everything following the change. (Video Editing: The Invisible Art)

Long Shot (LS).   A full view of a subject. (Telling the Visual Story, The Visual Grammar of Motion Picture Photography)

Low-Angle Shot.   A shot taken with the camera low and looking up at the subject. This shot tends to make the subject more dominant and to reduce the viewer's sense of control or superiority. (The Visual Grammar of Motion Picture Photography)

Macro-Focusing.   An adjusting lever permits the front lens element to be extended beyond the limit for normal focus in order to produce larger-than-life images. (Shooting Television News: The Basics)

Master Shot.   A single camera is used to record a continuous take of the entire event from one location and generally at one focal length lens setting. (The Visual Grammar of Motion Picture Photography)

Matched Action.   The action of a subject in an edited sequence appears to flow smoothly and without interruption from one shot to the next. See "Overlapping Action." (Telling the Visual Story, The Visual Grammar of Motion Picture Photography, Video Editing: The Invisible Art)

Maximum Depth of Field.   The maximum or deepest range of depth of field, or what appears to be in focus in a scene, available in a given shot at a particular focus setting, focal length, and aperture setting. See also "Great Depth of Field" and "Shallow Depth of Field." (Shooting Television News: The Basics)

Medium Shot (MS).   Brings subject matter closer to the viewer than a long shot and begins to isolate it from the overall environment. (Telling the Visual Story, The Visual Grammar of Motion Picture Photography, Live Shots and Remotes)

Mike Flags.   A small, four-sided box imprinted with the station logo and attached to handheld microphones. (The Sound Track)

Motivated Cutaway.   A cutaway that contributes desirable or essential new information to the story. (The Visual Grammar of Motion Picture Photography)

Moving Shot.   The camera swivels on a tripod or other fixed base to follow action. Different from a pan because the photographer's motivation is to follow action, rather than to show a static object in panorama. (The Visual Grammar of Motion Picture Photography)

Multidimensional Reporting.   An attempt to heighten the viewer's sense of experience by addressing as many of the five senses as possible in a report, and by allowing viewers to see the reporter think, interpret, and react to the story. (The Role of Talent Performance in Field Reporting)

Naked Live.   A live television report that consists solely of a reporter talking on camera from a remote location, without supporting video or prerecorded interviews. See also "Blue Eye" and "Thumb Sucker." (Live Shots and Remotes)

Nats.   Natural (nat) sounds from an environment which help communicate a sense of experience and often serve to heighten the listeners' or viewers' sense of realism. See also "Natural (nat) Sound." (Live Shots and Remotes)

Natural (Nat) Sound.   Natural sounds from an environment that often serve to heighten the viewer's sense of realism. (Telling the Visual Story, The Sound Track, Live Shots and Remotes)

Negative-Action Shot.   Action in the shot moves away from camera. (The Visual Grammar of Motion Picture Photography, Video Editing: The Invisible Art)

Nets.   Panels or other devices used in artificial lighting to enrich or subdue particular areas of illumination within the scene. (The Magic of Light and Lighting)

Networking.   The ability to tie multiple computers together so they can share information and communicate with one other. (Nonlinear Video Editing)

Node.   The optical center of a lens. (Shooting Television News: The Basics)

Nonlinear Editing.   A computerized editing process that allows digitally stored images and sounds to be moved about, shortened, and even lengthened independently of one another, something in the manner of a word processor with pictures. Anytime an element is added or deleted, the system automatically reconfigures everything before and after the change so as to maintain synchronization. (Video Editing: The Invisible Art)

NPPA.   National Press Photographers Association. (Preface, Ethics)

Objective Camera. Action is portrayed as an observer on the sidelines would see it. See "Subjective Camera." (The Visual Grammar of Motion Picture Photography)

Ohm. A measure of electrical resistance. (The Sound Track)

Omnidirectional. A microphone pickup pattern in which sound is picked up from all directions. (The Sound Track)

One-Person Band. Any person who shoots, writes, reports, and edits his or her own news stories. (Field Techniques of Shooting Television News)

Open Shade. The quality of shade produced when an outdoor environment is protected from direct sunlight, but with nothing above the subject to obstruct secondary light from the sky itself. (The Magic of Light and Lighting)

Optical Center. The point inside the lens at which light rays first bend as they are brought to bear on the target during the focusing process. (Shooting Television News: The Basics)

Overlapping Action. Action that is contained in one shot to be edited also is present in the shot to which it will be joined. See "Matched Action." (The Visual Grammar of Motion Picture Photography, Video Editing: The Invisible Art)

Package. An edited, self-contained videotape report of a news event or feature, complete with pictures, sound bites, voice-over narration, and natural sounds. (Telling the Visual Story, Writing the Package)

Pack Journalism. A high concentration of journalists from competing news organizations jammed into an area, each concerned primarily with his or her own interests. (The Magic of Light and Lighting)

Pan. The camera swivels on a tripod to show an overall scene in a single shot, or the handheld camera is moved in similar fashion. See "Moving Shot." (The Visual Grammar of Motion Picture Photography)

Parallel Cutting. Intercutting between separate but developing actions. (Video Editing: The Invisible Art)

Perspective. The apparent sizes of photographed objects in relationship to one another as they appear at certain distances, in comparison with how the human eye would view the same scene from the same distance. (Shooting Television News: The Basics)

Phoner. A telephone interview either recorded or broadcast live as part of a radio or television report. (Live Shots and Remotes)

Photojournalist. An individual who uses or relies on the camera not merely to take pictures, but to tell stories. (Telling the Visual Story)

PIO. Public Information Officer. A police, fire, sheriff's, or similar agency official who coordinates news coverage and access to news events, provides information, and helps arrange access to official sources during emergencies. (Live Shots and Remotes)

Pickup Shot. Any shot, such as a close-up or insert shot, reaction shot, point of view, or even a new camera angle, that emphasizes particular elements of action in the master shot. See "Cut-In Shot." (The Visual Grammar of Motion Picture Photography)

Point of View (POV) Shot. The view as seen through the subject's eyes. (The Visual Grammar of Motion Picture Photography, Video Editing: The Invisible Art)

Pool Coverage. An effort to minimize distraction by which information or television signals generated by one news agency are made available to all interested stations. (Law and the Broadcast Journalist)

Pop Cut. The visual "pop" or jump created when the zoom lens is used to shoot a long shot of a subject from a distance, followed immediately by a cut to a close-up from the same camera taken without having moved the camera off the original axis line. (Video Editing: The Invisible Art, Field Techniques of Shooting Television News)

Public Information Officer (PIO). A police, fire, sheriff's, or similar agency official who coordinates news coverage and access to news events, provides information, and helps arrange access to official sources during emergencies. (Live Shots and Remotes)

Rack Focus. Rotating the lens focus ring to shift the focus point from one subject to another while a shot is being recorded. (Shooting Television News: The Basics)

Rambo Video. Video recorded by a photographer who shoots everything in sight with little regard to story line or subject matter. (Video Editing: The Invisible Art)

Reaction Shot. A shot that shows a subject's reaction to an action in the previous shot. (The Visual Grammar of Motion Picture Photography, Video Editing: The Invisible Art)

Reestablishing Shot. A shot similar to the original establishing shot of an overall scene. Used to reintroduce locale or to allow the introduction of new action. (The Visual Grammar of Motion Picture Photography)

Remote. A news report originating live from a remote field location using a telephone, portable radio transmitter, microwave relay facility, or satellite truck. (Live Shots and Remotes)

Reportorial Editing. The process of previsualizing the story, including the pictures, sounds, words, and other production elements that will be needed to give the story logical structure and continuity; a form of mind's-eye storyboard. (Telling the Visual Story)

Reveal Shot. See "Transition Shot." (The Visual Grammar of Motion Picture Photography)

Reverse-Angle Shot. A shot made by moving the camera so that it shoots back along the axis line as originally established in the first shot. (The Visual Grammar of Motion Picture Photography)

RF. Radio frequency, the means through which audio and some video signals are transmitted. (The Sound Track)

Room Tone. The ambient sound peculiar to each separate environment that is inserted during editing to prevent sound dropouts. (The Sound Track)

RTNDA. Radio-Television News Directors Association. (Appendix B)

Rule of Thirds. An approach to photographic composition in which the viewfinder is mentally divided into thirds both horizontally and vertically. Subjects are placed at points within the viewfinder where the lines can be imagined to intersect. (The Visual Grammar of Motion Picture Photography)

Scanner. A radio receiver that constantly monitors crosstalk on police, fire, aviation, Coast Guard, military, and similar noncommercial broadcast frequencies. Scanners help alert journalists to breaking news. (Live Shots and Remotes)

Screen Space. The space that surrounds subjects in the frame, including headroom, gaps between people, and the space into which subjects move. Improper use of screen space results in visual imbalance. (The Visual Grammar of Motion Picture Photography)

Sequence. A series of related shots of an activity in which continuing action flows smoothly from one shot to the next to create the illusion of an uninterrupted event. (Telling the Visual Story, The Visual Grammar of Motion Picture Photography)

Sequential Video. Video that produces a continuous, uninterrupted flow of action that tells a story and communicates a sense of experience. (How to Improve Your Storytelling Ability)

Shallow Depth of Field. Only a narrow area of depth within the scene appears to be in focus, as when a foreground object is reproduced in razor-crisp focus but the background is blurred. (Shooting Television News: The Basics)

Shield Law. A law that protects journalists from having to disclose the identities of confidential sources. (Law and the Broadcast Journalist)

Shooting Ratio. The ratio of footage recorded in the field to that which is used in the finished story. (Field Techniques of Shooting Television News)

Short Lighting. The lighting pattern that results when the fill light shines on the side of the subject's face closest to camera. (The Magic of Light and Lighting)

Shot. The single, continuous take of material that is recorded each time the camera is turned on until it is turned off. (The Visual Grammar of Motion Picture Photography)

Shotgun Microphone. A long, cylindrical microphone with a pickup pattern similar to a telephoto lens that picks up sound from as far away as thirty feet or more. (The Sound Track)

Slander. The defamation of a person made orally, as opposed to in writing. Generally, a broadcast organization would not be charged with slander, but rather with libel (i.e., written defamation) especially whenever the broadcast originates from a written script or notes. (Law and the Broadcast Journalist)

Slow Lenses. Lenses restricted for reasons of manufacturing economy to maximum aperture sizes in the range of f/3.5 or f/4. Such lenses are less suitable in low light situations. (Shooting Television News: The Basics)

Snap Zoom. A shot in which the photographer snaps the zoom lever, instantly zooming in or out to a different composition of an action. When the few frames of the snap zoom are eliminated during editing, two separate shots result. (The Visual Grammar of Motion Picture Photography)

SNG. Satellite news gathering.

Soft Focus. A scene, or an area within the scene, appears to be out of focus. (Shooting Television News: The Basics)

Software. Any list of instructions written for a computer that allows it to perform specific tasks. (Video Editing: The Invisible Art)

SOT. Sound on tape, a standard reference to a sound bite. (Television Script Formats)

Sound Bite. A short excerpt from an interview, public statement, or spontaneous comment that normally is aired as part of a broadcast news story. (Telling the Visual Story)

Specular Light. The effect created when direct light rays throw strong highlights and distinct shadows. (The Magic of Light and Lighting)

Split-Focus Presentation. The practice of a reporter dividing attention between the anchor and the audience (via camera) during on-set interaction with the anchor. (The Role of Talent Performance in Field Reporting)

Spot News. Hard news events, such as fires, explosions, airline crashes, hurricanes, and tornadoes, that break suddenly and without warning. A hallmark of many spot news events is their unpredictability. (Telling the Visual Story, How to Improve Your Storytelling Ability, Live Shots and Remotes, Writing the Package)

Staging. The practice of asking people to do on camera what they normally don't do in real life, or directing people to engage in activities that are out of character. (The Visual Grammar of Motion Picture Photography, Field Techniques of Shooting Television News)

Standup. A reporter in the field delivers one or more sentences of dialogue while appearing on camera. (Telling the Visual Story, The Role of Talent Performance in Field Reporting, Writing the Package, Live Shots and Remotes)

Storyboard. A drawing, still photograph, or the reproduction of a single frame of video that represents one scene or sequence in a video story. Similar to cartoon panels, storyboards can be hand-drawn, computer-generated, or reproduced as photographs from still slides or film. (Telling the Visual Story, Writing the Package)

Subjective Camera. Action is portrayed as the subject would see it. See "Point of View Shot." (The Visual Grammar of Motion Picture Photography)

Subpoena. A court order to produce documents or other information, including on-air tape, a reporter's notes, or perhaps even the names of sources. (Law and the Broadcast Journalist)

Talking Head. Any interview or sound bite; often, a tedious or boring interview or sound bite. (The Broadcast Interview: Shooting the Quotation Marks, How to Improve Your Storytelling Ability)

Throw. To pitch or offer reporting opportunities to news sources, as during a conversation; or, the distance that rays from artificial light sources penetrate the environment to be photographed. (The Broadcast Interview: Shooting the Quotation Marks, The Magic of Light and Lighting)

Thumb Sucker. A live television report that consists solely of a reporter talking on camera from a remote location, without supporting video or prerecorded interviews. See also "Blue Eye" and "Naked Live." (Live Shots and Remotes)

Tilt Shot. The vertical equivalent of a pan shot in which the camera tilts up or down to reveal new action or subject matter. (The Visual Grammar of Motion Picture Photography)

Toss. The introduction and hand-off from studio anchor to a reporter live in the field. When the report ends, the reporter hands off or "tosses" back to the studio anchor. (Live Shots and Remotes)

Tracking Shot. Camera is moved physically through space to keep moving subjects in frame. Sometimes referred to as a "dolly shot." (The Visual Grammar of Motion Picture Photography)

Transition Shot. A shot that transfers the viewer's attention from the end of one sequence to the start of another (a close shot of a ship's whistle serves as the transition shot from scenes at a fish market along the wharf to shots of canning operations aboard a fishing ship, for example). Also called a "reveal shot." (The Visual Grammar of Motion Picture Photography, Video Editing: The Invisible Art)

Trespass. The illegal entry onto another's land, property, or premises. Also, the unlawful injury to a person, or to a person's rights or property. (Law and the Broadcast Journalist)

Trucking Shot. Camera moves through space past fixed objects. (The Visual Grammar of Motion Picture Photography)

T/Stop. A lens aperture setting somewhat equivalent to an f/stop, but which takes into account the various light-absorbing properties of the lens. (Shooting Television News: The Basics)

Two Shot. A shot that shows two people in the frame. (The Visual Grammar of Motion Picture Photography)

TV Cutoff. The phenomenon by which home television receivers, whether because of their design or faulty adjustment, clip off the edges of the transmitted video image. (The Visual Grammar of Motion Picture Photography)

Umbrella Lighting. A soft, indirect form of light created by shining artificial light into a metallic-colored, heat-resistant umbrella. (The Magic of Light and Lighting)

Unidirectional. A microphone pickup pattern in which only sound in front of the mike is picked up. (The Sound Track)

VCR. Videocassette recorder. (Shooting Television News: The Basics)

Visual Essayist. A photojournalist, whether photographer or reporter, who incorporates all the writing instruments of television—words, camera, microphone, and edit console—to tell compelling visual stories. (Preface)

Visual Grammar. The rules that govern the visual reconstruction of events, including the raw material shot and recorded in the field and the process of editing the material for broadcast. (The Visual Grammar of Motion Picture Photography)

VO. Voice-over narration. The reporter's voice can be heard "over" the pictures on the screen. (Telling the Visual Story, Video Editing: The Invisible Art, Writing the Package)

Voice Over (VO). Voice-over narration. The reporter's voice can be heard "over" the pictures on the screen. (Telling the Visual Story, Video Editing: The Invisible Art, Writing the Package)

Voicer. A live radio report that features only the reporter's voice, without interviews or other sound. (Live Shots and Remotes)

Wallpaper Video. Pictures with little meaning but whose subject matter is close enough to illustrate the reporter's script. See "Eyewash" and "Generic Video." (Introduction)

White Balance. The adjustment of camera circuitry to reproduce pure whites under the light source at hand; the absence of color "at white." (Shooting Television News: The Basics)

White Light. The quality that occurs when a subject is natural, unaffected, and emotionally transparent while on camera. (Field Techniques of Shooting Television News)

White Space. Pauses in voice-over narration that allow compelling pictures and sounds to involve the viewer more directly in the story. (Telling the Visual Story, Video Editing: The Invisible Art)

Wild Sound. Natural sounds from an environment that help communicate a sense of experience and often serve to heighten the listener's or viewer's sense of realism. (Telling the Visual Story)

Windscreen. A foam or metallic mesh microphone shield that reduces wind noise. (The Sound Track)

Wipe. An optical effect in which one shot appears to be shoved off the screen by an incoming shot. (The Visual Grammar of Motion Picture Photography, Video Editing: The Invisible Art)

Wrap. A live radio or television report in which the reporter's live intro and close "wraps around" a prerecorded interview or package: live intro/package or recorded interview/live close. (Live Shots and Remotes)

World Wide Web (WWW). An information system that gives users on computer networks access to a large universe of documents and variety of media. See also "Internet," which refers to the global network of cables and computers that allow access to the WWW. (Law and the Broadcast Journalist, Appendix B)

Zoom. A shot produced from a fixed location with a continuously variable focal-length lens. When the lens is said to "zoom in," the subject appears to grow larger and move closer to the screen. When the lens is said to "zoom out," the subject appears to grow smaller and move away from the screen. (The Visual Grammar of Motion Picture Photography, Field Techniques of Shooting Television News)

Zoom Lens. A lens that provides for continuously variable focal length settings from wide angle to telephoto, such as 12–120mm or 25–250mm. (Shooting Television News: The Basics)

INDEX

CREDITS

Chapter 1, pp. 19–23, "A Blueprint for Shooting Spot News" by John DeTarsio. Used by permission.

Chapter 2, pp. 50, 52, "Composing for HDTV" by Kirk Bloom. Used by permission.

Chapter 8, "Television Script Formats" by Luan Akin. Used by permission.

Chapter 12, "Live Shots and Remotes" by Luan Akin. Used by permission.

Chapter 14, "Sports Photography and Reporting" by Bob Burke and Marcia Neville. Used by permission.

Photograph on page 18 by Vicki Hestermann, © 1994. Printed by permission.

All other photographs are the original work of Ernie Leyba. Copyright © 1995, 1999, and 2004. Printed by permission of the author and Ernie Leyba.